# Social Science and the Christian Scriptures

# Social Science and the Christian Scriptures

Sociological Introductions and New Translation,

Volume 3

Anthony J. Blasi

WIPF & STOCK · Eugene, Oregon

SOCIAL SCIENCE AND THE CHRISTIAN SCRIPTURES
Sociological Introductions and New Translation, Volume 3

Copyright © 2017 Anthony J. Blasi. All rights reserved. Except for brief quotations in critical publications or reviews, no part of this book may be reproduced in any manner without prior written permission from the publisher. Write: Permissions, Wipf and Stock Publishers, 199 W. 8th Ave., Suite 3, Eugene, OR 97401.

Wipf & Stock
An Imprint of Wipf and Stock Publishers
199 W. 8th Ave., Suite 3
Eugene, OR 97401

www.wipfandstock.com

PAPERBACK ISBN: 978-1-5326-1512-2
HARDCOVER ISBN: 978-1-5326-1514-6
EBOOK ISBN: 978-1-5326-1513-9

Manufactured in the U.S.A. APRIL 5, 2017

Scripture quotations from the Old Testament or Hebrew Scriptures and New Testament cases that take up translation per se are from the Revised Standard Version of the Bible, © 1946, 1952, and 1971 National Council of Churches of Christ in the United States of America. Used by permission. All rights reserved worldwide. Nrsbibles.org/index.php/licensing/

# Contents

## Volume 3

*Preface* | ix

Chapter 17    Pseudepigraphic Letter of James | 1

    Introduction
        The Poor
        Illness
    English Translation
        Pseudepigraphic Letter of James

Chapter 18    Revelation from Jesus, Messiah | 14

    Introduction
        Literary Apocalyptic
        Sect Theory
    English Translation
        Revelation of Jesus the Messiah

Chapter 19    The Johannine Letters | 55

    Introduction
        The Sociology of Converging and Diverging Tendencies
    English Translations
        1. Second Johannine Letter
        2. First Johannine Letter
        3. Third Johannine Letter

Chapter 20    First Pseudepigraphic Letter of Peter | 67

    Introduction
        The Early Christian Movement: Not Quite an Entrenched Sect

　　　　Levels of Inclusiveness
　　　　Trans-Local Organization
　　　　Household Code
　　English Translation
　　　　First Pseudepigraphic Letter of Peter

Chapter 21　　The Pastoral Epistles | 81

　　Introduction
　　　　The Sociology of Degradation Ceremonies
　　　　The Greater Oikos
　　English Translations
　　　　First Letter to Timothy
　　　　Second Letter to Timothy
　　　　Letter to Titus

Chapter 22　　Pseudepigraphic Letter to the Thessalonians:
　　　　　　　(Second Thessalonians) | 100

　　Introduction
　　　　Populism
　　English Translation
　　　　Pseudepigraphic Letter to the Thessalonians

Chapter 23　　The Johannine Gospel | 109

　　Introduction
　　　　Date of Final, Published Edition
　　　　Author/Source
　　　　Composition of the Text
　　　　Particular Features
　　　　The Sociology of Religion and Migration
　　　　Sociology of Calendars
　　　　The Sociology of Saints
　　　　Church Mergers
　　Translation
　　　　The Johannine Gospel

Chapter 24　　Fragment on the Woman Accused of Adultery (John 7:53—8:11) | 176

　　Introduction
　　　　An Approach from the Sociology of Law
　　English Translation
　　　　Fragment on the Woman Accused of Adultery

Chapter 25      The Pseudepigraphic Letter of Jude | 180

     Introduction
         The Sociology of Doctrinal Orthodoxy
             Boundary Maintenance
     English Translation
         Pseudonymous Letter of Jude

Chapter 26      Second Pseudepigraphic Letter of Peter | 192

     Introduction
         The Sociology of Written Communication
     English Translation
         Second Pseudonymous Letter of Peter

*References* | 201

# Preface

VOLUMES 1 AND 2 covered the canonical Christian literature from the time of Paul of Tarsus up to about the year 90 CE. The present volume begins with the literature from after that time and concludes with the latest canonical book, the Second Pseudepigraphic Letter of Peter, which dates from about some point in time after 110 CE.

*Chapter 17*

# Pseudepigraphic Letter of James

## Introduction

THE NAMED AUTHOR OF the *Letter of James* in Christian Bibles is Jacob, usually rendered with another English equivalent name, James. James was and is a common name, and a number of people with that name are mentioned in the New Testament. The most prominent James in the early Christian movement was James the Brother, a leader of the Jerusalem church. Consequently, it is generally assumed that he is the intended James, since no further identifiers appear in the letter.[1] There appears to be no solid consensus, however, over whether James the Brother actually wrote the "letter." In fact it is only perfunctorily presented as a letter; as with a number of other early Christian works, it is actually an essay presented as a letter. A number of recent commentators argue that James the Brother, who was executed in 62 in Jerusalem and whom Paul, Luke, and Josephus[2] mention as a leader of a Jerusalem Christian church, wrote it; however, I find the opposite view persuasive.[3] Bo Reicke argues that James the Brother did not write it:

> . . . (N)owhere in the epistle is there any indication of a strong concern for Jerusalem and Judaism. The message is directed toward converts who have joined Christian congregations in the dispersion, that is, the Roman empire. Not problems of the Jerusalem church but persecution by heathens, relations with secular powers, and other problems of the church in the Greco-Roman world are treated by the author.[4]

After a hiatus following the terrible persecution under Nero, persecution of the church in the Roman Empire resumed toward the close of the reign of Domitian (81–96 CE), as Reicke points out.[5] Moreover, when the *Letter of James* sides with the poor against the

---

1. Reicke, *Epistles of James, Peter, and Jude*, 3; L. Johnson, *Letter of James*, 93; Hartin, *James*, 16.
2. Gal 2:9 and 12; Acts 15:13; Josephus, *Antiquities* 20:200.
3. L. Johnson, *Letter of James*, 121; Baukham, *James*, 17; Hartin, *James*, 24.
4. Reicke, *Epistles of James, Peter, and Jude*, 4.
5. Ibid, 5.

rich, it was not a mere matter of wealth but imperial politics. The wealthy were conspiring against Emperor Domitian during his reign, and James explicitly warns against giving special recognition to people who wore gold rings—a prerogative of senatorial or equestrian ranked notables.[6] It would be hard to imagine, as the letter proposes, someone of senatorial or equestrian rank visiting a Christian assembly during Nero's reign or in Jerusalem, but it could well occur later anywhere in the Empire (except Jerusalem, which had been destroyed) when deviating from Emperor Domitian's policies was much in fashion. Significantly, the ancient Christians doubted that James the Brother wrote the letter. Eusebius, after recounting the history of James, proceeds to say, "Such is the story of James, whose is said to be the first of the Epistles called Catholic. It is to be observed that its authenticity is denied, since few of the ancients quote it. . . ."[7]

In referring to James the Brother as prominent, it is useful to consider how his prominence came about. He was prominent in Jerusalem, which is how Josephus knew of him. He participated in the discussion about whether gentile converts to Christianity should be required to be circumcised, which is why Paul and Luke mention him. However, it is in *Galatians*, a letter that does not seem to have been widely circulated at the time of Luke's writing,[8] that Paul mentions James. There is no reason to believe that James the Brother was a known personage outside of Jerusalem prior to Josephus and Luke writing about him. If James were to send an encyclical to the Christians in the Roman Empire, he would have had to identify himself more completely or associate himself at the opening of the letter with the community of Christian Brothers in Jerusalem; the author does neither. All this suggests that the author of the letter wrote under the pseudonym *James* after Luke's *Acts of the Apostles* made James the Brother a known personage in the broader Christian community.[9]

Luke Timothy Johnson makes a careful analysis of the language and rhetorical nature of the letter. The language is modeled on the Greek of the Septuagint, a fact which is responsible for the "semitisms" in its text.[10] The general character of the prose is hortatory, with imperatives followed by explanatory participial constructions.[11] There are frequent alliterations. While some commentators had proposed that the letter was a non-Christian Jewish tract adapted by a Christian, Johnson points to a number of typically Christian usages throughout: references to Jesus the Messiah, references to Jesus as Lord, the author as slave or servant, the office of teacher, kinship language for the community, references to faith and salvation, the centrality of loving

---

6. Ibid., 6; see James 2:4.

7. Eusebius, *Ecclesiastical History*, 2:23:23.

8. See Blasi, *Making Charisma*, 67, for evidence that Luke did not know of *Galatians*.

9. For this reason, as well as the development of a Christian linguistic community described immediately below, I cannot accept the proposal in *Das neue Testament*, 73, that the letter dates from about 50 CE.

10. L. Johnson, *Letter of James*, 7; see Thurén, "Risky Rhetoric," 263.

11. L. Johnson, *Letter of James*, 8.

neighbor as oneself, kingdom of God bestowed on heirs, and allusions to the Jesus sayings.[12] While Johnson believes James the Brother, who died in 62, wrote the letter, it seems more likely to me that quite some time had to pass for such characteristically Christian language to solidify; one would expect several such features to turn up in a very early Christian work by one author such as Paul, but not in the works of two different early authors such as Paul and another, contemporaneous author. It takes time for a characteristic discourse to migrate from one author to another.

In making allusions to the Jesus sayings, *James* does not quote them or explicitly cite them and does not use them to support an argument. Rather, phrases from the sayings simply turn up in the text of the letter. The author uses the sayings as a "resource for mimesis and paraphrase."[13] The sayings may well have originated for the most part in rural Palestine; John Kloppenborg proposes that the "Q" formulation of them was similarly Palestinian. As explained in the chapter on the *Gospel of Matthew*, I cannot conclude one way or the other about the place of origin of "Q," but in the case of the allusions to the sayings as formulated in the *Letter of James* Kloppenborg is well justified in pointing out that they are concerned not with subsistence and social pressure but with concerns of the educated or semi-educated in the urban Diaspora with concerns over the proper subjective disposition toward everyday life.[14] The letter's author is concerned with disposing souls for a proper community life.

A sociologically important feature of the letter is its seeming addressees. The author addresses, nominally, the twelve tribes of Israel in the Diaspora, but that is a mythic reference to a broader covenant people; the restoration of such an Israel would be an eschatological event.[15] The actual addressees seem to be a number of churches, an ecclesiastical community. It is not a question of a household; there is no mention of household codes, domestic life, or sexual mores. As Luke Timothy Johnson phrases it, the letter addresses an *ekklesia*, an intentional community. Moreover, there is no resort to authority; indeed James is egalitarian.[16] This reveals what James's community was not, but there are very few facts that give us an idea of what that community was. We can only discern that the readers gathered in assemblies for decision-making (2:1–4) and prayer (5:13–16), that they had leaders called teachers and elders (3:1, 5:14), and that they were experiencing persecution at the hands of "the rich" (2:6, 4:13—5:6).[17] From the viewpoint of the author, socio-economic disequilibrium among the believers had become the seed-bed for internal discrimination and the currying of favor from wealthy and powerful patrons from outside the community; the poor were dishonored, neglected, exploited, and oppressed by the

12. Ibid., 48.
13. Kloppenborg, "James 1:2–15," 38.
14. Ibid.
15. Jackson-McCabe, "Messiah Jesus," 713–14.
16. L. Johnson, *Letter of James*, 81–82.
17. Ibid., 91.

wealthy. The latter defrauded laborers, stockpiled harvests, and killed the righteous. Not only were individuals victimized in the process, but social cohesion suffered, with brother speaking evil and passing judgment upon brother, which created an instability of commitment, duplicity in speech, an inconsistency between words and action, and even apostasy and defection from the community.[18] The situation reflected a crisis of wholeness, expressed in terms of a common, even cosmic, holiness and purity on the one hand and pollution on the other.[19] While one could reasonably relate such a viewpoint on the part of the author to the anthropological theory of natural symbols of Mary Douglas,[20] that is more a typological scheme than an explanatory one. I will return to the concept of communal wholeness below in the discussion of healing.

## The Poor

The *Letter of James* makes two points about the poor. The first point is that one should not make distinctions between the rich and powerful on the one hand (someone in fine clothing and wearing a gold ring) and a poor person on the other (someone in shabby clothing). The second point is that one should give the poor what they need for the body.[21] These pertain to two different facets of the social situation in which "the poor" come to be defined as such. The classic sociological theorist Georg Simmel characterizes the social situation of the poor person in terms of a dialectic of rights and duties.[22] The right of the needy is the basis of all poor relief. Recognition of such a right neutralizes the dejection, the shame, and the degradation that is inherent in receiving charity. If one were to be charitable to a poor person in the sense of providing material goods but not recognizing the recipient's right to such, one would be doing social damage, so to speak. For a poor person would only be a biological phenomenon of hunger and cold, for example, if not a full member in a social setting where there are non-poor people; it is in such a setting that the biological phenomenon becomes a social one, according the individual the status of a poor person. And it is from that status that the poor person has a claim on the help that can be provided by a non-poor person. "The poor person whose situation seems to be an injustice of the world order and who demands a remedy from, so to speak, the whole of existence, will easily make every individual who is found better situated by chance answerable to this demand out of solidarity."[23] From this perspective, social solidarity stands at the basis of generosity toward a poor person.

The second point, that one should meet the needs of the poor, derives from the duty of the giver that corresponds to the right of the recipient. If one simply verbalizes

18. Elliott, "Epistle of James," 75, with numerous citations to the text of the letter.
19. Ibid., 77; Jackson-McCabe, "Messiah Jesus," 707.
20. Douglas, *Natural Symbols*.
21. Jas 2:2, 2:16.
22. Simmel, *Sociology*, 409–42.
23. Ibid., 411.

solidarity with a poor person ("Go in peace, be warmed and filled")[24] but does not honor the poor person's right, the solidarity is not actual, but rather a mere social grace—somewhat on the order of being polite toward somebody that one hates. Thus there should be actual generosity, as the letter's author would have it, along with a solidarity that allows for no distinctions among persons. Again, however, it is important that the recipient be accepted as a person having rights. Simmel warns against "Christian" alms-giving that is nothing but a form of asceticism "that improves the otherworldly fate of the giver."[25]

But the letter's author does not stop with what Simmel describes as a solidarity that underlies the rights of the poor and duties toward the poor. The letter is a public communication, not spiritual counsel for an individual. The author is raising consciousness. Showing partiality in favor of the rich and powerful on the one hand and against the poor on the other would be recognized, if the author's wishes were satisfied, as a social problem. As the famous sociologist Herbert Blumer argued, a social problem does not consist merely of external conditions but also of widely-shared recognitions of them as problems: Social problems "are fundamentally products of a process of collective definition instead of existing independently as a set of objective social arrangements with an intrinsic makeup."[26] This is because widely shared definitions of situations as social problems are necessary in what might be called their natural histories. Blumer identified five typical stages in the process of collectively defining social problems: 1) Emergence of a social problem, 2) Legitimation of the problem as a problem, 3) Mobilization of actions with respect to the problem, 4) The formulation of an official plan of action, and 5) The transformation of the official plan in its empirical implementation.[27] The *Letter of James* appears to be legitimizing the treatment of the poor as a social problem. The later stages of such social problem "careers" would lead sociologists to study claims and rhetoric attached to the claims, who the claims-makers are, the role of communications, public reactions to claims, policy-making in response to social problems, people who work on social problems, and policy evaluations.[28]

## Illness

James 5:14 asks whether any people among those who read the letter or have it read to them are sick.

> Let them call for the presbyters of the church, and they should pray over them, anointing them with oil in the name of the Lord. Both the prayer of faith will save the sick, and the Lord will raise them; and if they have committed sins,

---

24. Jas 2:16.
25. Simmel, *Sociology*, 412.
26. Blumer, "Social Problems," 298.
27. Ibid., 301.
28. Best, "Social Problems."

it will be forgiven them. So confess sins to one another, and pray over one another for you to be healed.[29]

One might infer an etiology that explains sickness in terms of sin from this passage, though a closer reading suggests that the calling of the elders and the saying of prayers has more to do with salvation than physical illness. The point of the present discussion, however, is not theological but sociological. So however the letter's author understands sickness and its etiology, our question is, Why do sickness and sin appear in the same passage, along with healing? It should be noted that the passage does not speak of miracles. The concern is not with miraculous cures but what should be done in the face of illness.

Sociologically speaking, illness "is a state of disturbance in the 'normal' functioning of the total human individual. . . ."[30] Obviously, the biological organism is involved in the disruption, but the disruption goes beyond the biological. Illness involves personal and social adjustments; hence illness needs to be identified as both a biological and a social phenomenon. The famous Harvard sociologist Talcott Parsons wrote of the sick role: It involved an exemption from normal social role responsibilities, an expectation that assuming the role be unavoidable and that the sick individual desires to get well, and in the modern era it includes an expectation that the sick person seek technically competent help from medical professionals.[31] What is most relevant in the present context is the exemption from performing normal role responsibilities. That disrupts the community. When one person substitutes for the sick and meets responsibilities that are usually met by the sick person, the outcome may be a greater bonding of community or family members together, but the previous social order must change, at least temporarily. If the sickness is sufficiently serious to raise the specter of death, the change in the social order promises to be more permanent. As is well known, emotional problems accompany all this: frustration of the expectations of one's normal life pattern, frustration at being cut off from normal spheres of activity and enjoyments, disrupted social relationships, and possibly alterations of future prospects.[32] It is because of these dimensions of illness that James would have one seek community support by sending for the elders and praying. Similarly, in her study of ritual healing, Meredith McGuire distinguishes between disease (a biological disorder) and illness (the way the ill person experiences the disorder). The ritual healing she studied had more to do with illness than disease. "Healing is typically part of a larger system of beliefs and practices that deals with issues such as moral responsibility, social status, and family or community cohesion."[33] In particular, healing may address the threat of illness upsetting order.[34]

29. Jas 5:14b–16a.
30. Parsons, *Social System*, 431.
31. Ibid., 436–39.
32. Ibid., 443.
33. McGuire, *Ritual Healing*, 6.
34. McGuire, *Pentecostal Catholics*, 125.

If one considers sin, it too disrupts the social order. It either involves a symbolic violation, such as having a strange god, that leads family and community members to doubt the sinner's loyalty and identification with the group, or it victimizes someone in the family or community. Sin creates disorder in the family and community; it breaks bonds of trust. As with illness, it may ultimately strengthen the social bonds through a process of forgiveness and reconciliation, but it is a problem precisely because it accomplishes the very same untoward effects that illness can bring about. At the level of experience, there is an analogy between sin and sickness, iniquity and illness. While a disease may run its course, its effects that are similar to and merged into the persisting effects of one's sins. The actual wording of the passage in the *Letter of James* suggests that the author sensed all this in some way, though probably not cognitively.

To account scientifically for a non-cognitive social awareness on the part of the members of a community or society, it helps again to take the sociological approach of the Russian French scholar Georges Gurvitch. Gurvitch would have the researcher place a given phenomenon—in the present instance verse 14 of the fifth chapter of the *Letter of James*—in its total context, i.e. in the context of every other social phenomenon that is relevant to it. He called the resultant constellation the "total social phenomenon." Every total social phenomenon can be approached from the perspective of "depth"; some facets are close to the observable level that we can perceive through the five senses while other facets may be *occasioned* in our consciousness through the five senses but not directly perceived. One may hear the opening notes of Schubert's C Major Symphony played on a horn, but the total social phenomenon includes the occupational structure of the modern symphony orchestra, the traditions of performance, the audience expectations of Schubert's own time, aesthetic values in general, one's own memory of first "really" hearing the work, and so forth. In the case of James 5:14, we have what Gurvitch called a *social symbol*. "We understand by social symbols signs that express only partially the contents signified and serve to mediate between the contents and the collective and individual actors who formulate them and to which they are addressed...."[35] It is significant that social symbols express only partially. We can only infer the collective attitudes that are related to James 5:14. We have very limited historical information about the texture of the sick role, the role of one praying, and the role of elders in the community presupposed by the author of the letter. We are not really familiar with the relevant flow of everyday life. We must infer the relevant collective ideas and values from the rest of the letter. This is precisely what I attempted to do in the previous paragraphs concerning illness and sin. The point of sociology is to proceed from understanding a text (in this case, a literary text) to interpreting it by establishing a text/context dialectic.

---

35. Gurvitch, "Sociologie en profondeur," 164–65, my translation.

# English Translation

## Pseudepigraphic Letter of James

1 ¹James, slave of God and of the Reverend Jesus, Messiah, to the twelve tribes who are in the diaspora. Greetings.

²My brothers and sisters, consider it all a joy when you encounter various trials, ³knowing that the test of your faith brings about endurance. ⁴Let endurance have complete effect, so that you would be complete and intact, lacking in nothing. ⁵But if any of you lack wisdom, ask for it from God, Who gives to all generously and unbegrudgingly, and it will be given.³⁶ ⁶But one should ask in faith, not doubting, for one who doubts resembles the billows of the sea, blown and tossed; ⁷for such a person, ⁸a double-minded man,³⁷ unstable in all his ways, ⁷should not expect to receive anything from the Lord.

⁹But the brother or sister who is poor should boast in exultation, ¹⁰and the rich be in humiliation, because the latter will pass by as would a flower of the field. ¹¹For the sun with its heat rises and parches the field, and the flower in it withers and the beauty of its appearance falls; so also will the rich person disappear in due course.

¹²Blessed is the man who endures a test, because having been tried he will receive the crown of life that was promised to those who love the Lord.³⁸ ¹³Let no one who has been tested say, "I am tested by God"; for God is not tested by evil and does not Himself test anyone.³⁹ ¹⁴But each person is tested by one's own desire, being taken in tow and enticed. ¹⁵Then desire, taking hold, gives birth to sin, and sin, coming to fruition, brings about death.

¹⁶Do not be deceived, my beloved brothers and sisters. ¹⁷Every good act of giving and every perfect gift is from above, coming down from the Father of the heavenly lights,⁴⁰ from Whom there is no change of course or shadow of relocation.⁴¹ ¹⁸Making a decision, He brought us into being by the word of truth, for us to be a first fruit of His creatures.

---

36. Literally: "Let him ask for it from God ... and it will be given him." Kloppenborg, "James 1:2–15," associates this verse with the Q saying found in Luke 11:9: "And I say to you, *ask, and it will be given to you; seek, and you will find; knock and it will be opened to you*" (italics indicating a Matthean parallel).

37. Sometimes James uses *Anthropos*, which means human, and one must use circumlocutions to avoid the pronoun problem in English—e.g., *such* or *one* rather than *he*. But here and occasionally elsewhere James uses *aner*, a man or husband.

38. "The Lord": literally, "him." Kloppenborg, "James 1:2–15," sees this as an allusion to the Q saying found in Luke 6:22: "*Blessed are you when people hate you and* when they excommunicate and insult you and spurn your name as evil *because of* the son of humanity"

39. The author of the letter rejects the suggestion that illness comes directly from God, a point that should be recalled below at 5:14—Albl, "'Are Any among You Sick?'" 134.

40. "Father of lights": Morning prayer in Jewish worship included praising God for the provision of light—Verseput, "James 1:17." Some would take such parallels with Jewish liturgical practice to argue that the author wrote from a Jewish context.

41. To grasp the author's image, it needs to be noted that the "Do not be deceived" of the previous

¹⁹Know this, my beloved brothers and sisters, and let every person be quick to listen, slow to speak, slow to anger. ²⁰For a man's anger does not produce the justice of God. ²¹So ridding yourselves of all sordidness and excess of evil, accept in humility the implanted word that is able to save your souls.[42]

²²And become doers of the word and not only self-deceiving hearers. ²³For if anyone is a hearer of the word and not a doer, such resembles a man looking at his natural face in a mirror; ²⁴for he looks at himself and has gone away and right away forgets what he was like. ²⁵But one who looks into a law that has attained its purpose, the law of freedom, and who stays with it, becoming not a forgetful hearer but a doer of a work, that person will be blessed in the doing.

²⁶If any deem themselves religious, not bridling their tongues but rather deceiving their hearts, their religion is useless.[43] ²⁷Religion pure and undefiled before God and Father is this: looking after orphans and widows in their difficulty, keeping oneself unblemished from the world.

2 ¹My brothers and sisters, do not hold the faith of our Lord Jesus, Messiah, as a faith in reputation,[44] by showing partiality.[45] ²For if a man with a gold ring on a finger enters into your synagogue[46] in radiant clothing, and a poor man also enters in filthy clothes, ³and you gaze upon the one wearing the radiant clothing and say, "Sit here in a good place," and you say to the poor man, "Stand there," or "Sit on my footstool," ⁴did you not make distinctions among yourselves and become judges having evil opinions?

⁵Listen, my beloved brothers and sisters, did God not chosen the poor in the world to be rich in faith and heirs of the kingdom that He promised to

---

verse uses the verb *planaō*, from which our word *planet* derives. The Father of the heavenly lights (literally, Father of the lights), keeps the sun, moon, and stars in their unchanging courses rather than allowing them to change course and wander into various constellations in the manner of the planets.

42. James emphasizes a law that correlates with an implanted *logos* that is able to save souls; the implanted *logos* is able to save if one becomes the doer of the *logos*, with works, for which one will be blessed—Jackson-McCabe, "Messiah Jesus," 710.

43. The pronouns are in the singular in the Greek.

44. "As a faith in reputation," τῆς δόξης: This is usually translated as "of glory" and made dependent on "Messiah"; hence "Messiah of glory." The string of possessives seems awkward and has generated theories of Christian interpolations into a preexisting Jewish text (noted by L. Johnson, *Letter of James*, 220, and Hartin, *James*, 117). However, according to Johnson, *Letter of James*, 220–21, "Erasmus made the fascinating suggestion (followed by Calvin and Michaelis) that *doxa* should be taken in the sense of 'opinion,' which would connect directly to 'acts of favoritism.'" I am following Erasmus here, translating τῆς δόξης as *reputation* and taking it to be dependent on *faith*; to do that in English requires "as a faith" to resume the thought. Note also that while the other genitives are subjective, this one, as I translate it, is objective—"faith in" as opposed to "faith of."

45. "By showing partiality": This is a prepositional phrase, ἐν προσωπολημψίαις, a literal translation of which would be "by face-acceptance." Hartin, *James*, 117, and L. Johnson, *Letter of James*, 221, note that the noun and a verb with the same stem in 2.9 do not appear in secular Greek but resemble a Septuagint expression.

46. The synagogue or assembly need not be a liturgical setting, but could be a judicial one—Ward, "Partiality."

those who love Him? But you dishonored the poor person. Do not the rich oppress you, and do they not drag you into courts? ⁷Do they not blaspheme the good name that was invoked over you? ⁸If you actually fulfil the royal law according to scripture, "You shall love your neighbor as yourself,"[47] you do well; ⁹but if you show partiality, you commit a sin, convicted by the law as transgressors. ¹⁰For whoever keeps the whole law but stumbles over one thing becomes guilty of everything. ¹¹For the one saying, "You shall not commit adultery,"[48] also said, "Do not murder."[49] But if you do not commit adultery but do murder, you have become a transgressor of the law. ¹²So speak and act as people about to be judged by the law of freedom. ¹³For judgment is without mercy for those who did not act with mercy; mercy triumphs over judgment.

¹⁴What good is it, my brothers and sisters, if some say they have faith, but have no works? Can faith save them?[50] ¹⁵If a brother or sister is present naked and in want of food for the day, ¹⁶and one of you says to them, "Go in peace, be warm and well fed," but do not give them what is necessary for the body, what good is that? ¹⁷So too faith, if it does not have works, is dead by itself.

¹⁸"But," someone will say, "you have faith and I have works." Show me your faith without works, and I will show you my faith from the works. ¹⁹Do you believe that God is one?[51] You do well; the demons also believe, and they shudder. ²⁰Do you wish to know, O empty human, that faith without works is idle? ²¹Was not our father Abraham justified by works after bringing his son Isaac to the altar? ²²You see that faith cooperated with his works and that faith was fulfilled by works, ²³and the scripture was fulfilled which says, "And Abraham was trusting God, and it was reckoned to him as justification,"[52] and he was called a friend of God. ²⁴You see that a person is justified by works and not by faith alone. ²⁵And likewise, was not Rahab the prostitute also justified by works, welcoming the messengers and sending them out by another road? ²⁶For as the body without a spirit is dead, so also faith without works is dead.

3 ¹Let many not be teachers, my brothers and sisters; you know that we[53] will receive a more severe verdict, ²for we all often stumble. If someone does not

---

47. Lev 19:18, following the Septuagint. The fact that the author relies on the Septuagint rather than making ad hoc translations from the Hebrew argues against the author being a Judean writing in Jerusalem.

48. Exod 20:14, following Septuagint Exod 20:13.

49. Exod 20:13, following Septuagint Exod 20:15.

50. In Greek, the verse is in the singular; I adopt the plural here to avoid the English pronoun problem.

51. Verseput, "James 1:17," observes that the phrase "God is one" parallels the first line of the Shema: "Hear, O Israel! The Lord is our God, the Lord is one!" He infers from this that the community of the author still considered itself a part of Jewish culture. The point that faith alone is insufficient is consistent with the Jewish prophetic tradition.

52. Gen 15:6, following the Septuagint, with the exception of the initial "and," which is δὲ in James and καὶ in the Septuagint Genesis.

53. Here the author self-identifies as a teacher—Hartin, *James*, 173; Reicke, *Epistles of James, Peter, and Jude*, 36, translates as "we [teachers] will receive".

stumble by word, he is a perfect man, able to bridle even the whole body. ³But if we put bridles into the mouths of horses so that they obey us, we also guide their whole bodies. ⁴And look at the ships, great as they are and driven by strong winds, are guided by a very small rudder where the desire of the one steering wishes. ⁵So also the tongue is a small member yet boasts of great things.

What size a fire kindles so great a forest! ⁶And the tongue is a fire, a world of injustice. The tongue is placed among our members, defiling the whole body and setting the cycle of existence aflame and set aflame under Gehenna. ⁷For all species of animals as well as birds, reptiles, as well as sea creatures are subdued and have been subdued to the human species; ⁸but no human can subdue the tongue—a restless evil, full of death-dealing poison. ⁹We bless the Lord and Father with it, and we curse people, who are made in the likeness of God, with it. ¹⁰Blessing and curse come out from the same mouth. It ought not be so, my brothers and sisters. ¹¹Does the spring pour forth sweet and bitter water from the same opening? ¹²My brothers and sisters, can a fig tree bear olives or a grapevine figs? Nor does a salty spring spout sweet water.

¹³Who are wise and knowledgeable among you?[54] Let them demonstrate their works from the good way of life with the gentleness of wisdom. ¹⁴But if you have bitter jealousy and ambition in your heart, do not boast and do not tell lies against the truth. ¹⁵This is not the wisdom that comes down from above, but earthly, physical, demonic; ¹⁶for where there is jealousy and ambition, there is unruliness and every evil deed. ¹⁷But the wisdom from above is first pure, then peaceful, gentle, obedient, filled with mercy and good fruits, impartial, sincere; ¹⁸and the fruit of justice is sown in peace by those who make peace.

4 ¹From where come wars and from where come strife among you? Is it not from your desires that are at war in your members? ²You hanker after something, and do not have it; you murder. And you are envious, and you cannot acquire; you kill and go to war. You do not have because you do not ask: ³You ask and do not receive because you ask evilly in order to spend on your desires. ⁴Adulteresses,[55] do you not know that friendship of the world is enmity of God? Whoever wishes, then, to be a friend of the world becomes an enemy of God. ⁵Or do you suppose there is some scripture that vainly says, "He made the spirit that dwells in us yearn with envy"?[56] ⁶But He gave a greater gift; so it says, "God resists arrogance, but to the lowly He gives a gift."[57] So be obedient to God; but

---

54. L. Johnson, "James 3:12—4:10," sees 3:13—4:10 as a rhetorical unit having envy as its theme. "Who are . . .": In Greek the verse is in the singular.

55. The original, adulteress, is clearly in the feminine. This is because it derives from Prov 30:20, where the focus is on the adulteress's remorselessness—Schmitt, "You Adulteresses!" 336.

56. There are numerous difficulties in translating and interpreting this question, beginning with text critical issues, how to punctuate, and how to interpret—Hartin, *James*, 199–200. I take "do you suppose" as an ironic introduction to something contrary to fact. In fact, there is no such passage in the known scriptures.

57. Prov 3:34, following the wording of the Septuagint, save using "God" (Ὁ θεὸς) rather than "Lord" (κύριος).

resist the devil and he will flee from you. ⁸Draw near to God and He will drew near to you. Clean your hands, sinners, and purify hearts, you double-minded. ⁹Be sorrowful, mourn, and weep; let your laughter be turned into mourning and joy into gloom. ¹⁰Be humble before the Lord, and He will exalt you.

¹¹Do not speak evil of one another, brothers and sisters: One speaking evil or judging one's brother or sister speaks evil of and judges the law, but if you judge the law, you are not a doer of the law but a judge. ¹²There is one Legislator and Judge, Who is able to save and destroy; but who are you who is judging the neighbor?

¹³Come now, you who are saying, "Today or tomorrow we will go into such or such a city and spend a year there and buy and sell and make a profit." ¹⁴You are the kind of people who do not know about how things or your life will be like tomorrow. For you are a mist that appears a little while and then disappears. ¹⁵Instead you are to say, "If the Lord wishes, we will both live and do this or that." ¹⁶But now you boast in your arrogance; every such boast is evil. ¹⁷So, for one knowing the good thing to do and does not do it, it is a sin.

5 ¹Come now, you rich, weep, wailing over troubles coming upon you.[58] ²Your wealth has decayed and your garments become moth-eaten; ³your gold and silver has corroded,[59] and their poisonous rust[60] will be in witness to you and eat your fleshy places like fire.[61] You stored up treasure in the last days. ⁴Look: the wage of the workers who mowed your fields, which were withheld by you, cry out, and the cries of the harvesters have entered into the ears of the Lord of hosts. ⁵You led a soft life on the earth and lived in delicacy;[62] you fattened your hearts on a day of slaughter. ⁶You condemned, you murdered the just one. He does not resist you.[63]

---

58. Batten, "Characterization of the Rich," 53, argues that public weeping and wailing was gendered behavior and that the author is feminizing the rich in this passage.

59. The Greek has the anomaly of two nouns and a singular verb.

60. "Poisonous rust," ἰός: The word translates as either *poison* or *rust*.

61. Eating the flesh of the rich implies that they were wearing gold and silver jewelry; Batten, "Characterization of the Rich," 54, points out that this too was gendered behavior in Roman antiquity, so that the author is again depicting the rich as effeminate. "Fleshy places" is "flesh" in the plural, σάρκας; ibid., 55, suggests the author is depicting the rich as soft and flabby.

62. "Soft life," "delicacy": ibid., sees feminization here too.

63. Because of a similarity in vocabulary with the Septuagint, L. Johnson, *Letter of James*, 304, and Hartin, *James*, 230, see this as an allusion to Wis 2:10–20: "Let us oppress the righteous poor man; let us not spare the widow nor regard the gray hairs of the aged. But let our might be our law of right, for what is weak proves itself to be useless. Let us lie in wait for the righteous man, because he is inconvenient to us and opposes our actions; he reproaches us for sins against the law, and accuses of sins against our training. He professes to have knowledge of God and calls himself a child of the Lord. He became to us a reproof of our thoughts; the very sight of him is a burden to us, because his manner of life is unlike that of others, and his ways are strange. We are considered by him as something base, and he avoids our ways as unclean; he calls the last end of the righteous happy, and boasts that God is his father. Let us see if his words are true, and let us test what will happen at the end of his life; for if the righteous man is God's son, he will help him, and will deliver him from the hand of his adversaries. Let us test him with insult and torture, that we may find out how gentle he is, and make trial of his forbearance. Let us condemn him to

⁷Have patience, then, brothers and sisters, until the coming of the Lord. Look, the farmer waits for the precious fruit of the earth, being patient over it until it receives the early and late rains. ⁸You should be patient too. Stand firm,[64] for the coming of the Lord is near. ⁹Do not complain about one another, brothers and sisters, so that you will not be judged. Look, the judge is standing at the doors. ¹⁰Brothers and sisters, take the prophets, who spoke in the name of the Lord, as a model of sufferings and patience. ¹¹See, we consider those who endure blessed: You heard of the patience of Job, and you know the outcome of the Lord, for the Lord is compassionate and merciful.

¹²Before all people,[65] my brothers and sisters, do not take oaths, either by heaven or earth, or any other oath; but let your "Yes" be yes and "No" be no, so that you will not fall under judgment.

¹³Are any of you suffering hardship? Let them pray. Are any happy? Let them sing praise.[66] ¹⁴Are any among you ill? Let them call for the presbyters of the church, and they should pray over them, anointing them with oil in the name of the Lord.[67] ¹⁵Both the prayer of faith will save the sick, and the Lord will raise them; and if they have committed sins, it will be forgiven them. ¹⁶So confess sins to one another, and pray over one another for you to be healed. The petition of the just is very powerful when at work.[68] ¹⁷Elijah was a man with the same nature as us, and he prayed with a prayer that it not rain, and it did not rain on the earth for three years and six months; ¹⁸and he prayed again, and the sky gave rain and the earth sprouted its fruit.

¹⁹My brothers and sisters, if any among you are misled from the truth and someone brings them back,[69] ²⁰let it be known that those who bring sinners back from their way of error will save their souls from death and cover a multitude of sins.

---

a shameful death, for, according to what he says, he will be protected" (RSV).

64. Literally: "Strengthen your hearts."

65. Literally, "before all." Hartin, *James*, 258, interprets the expression quite differently, as "finally," holding that the expression marks the end of a letter. The problem with that view is that there is more to come before the end of the letter. L. Johnson, *Letter of James*, 326–27, takes it to mean "most importantly," arguing that the verse is linked to the preceding by continuing a discussion of the use of speech. Again, there is a problem: why would taking an oath be a more serious matter than speaking ill of one another?

66. This section is in the singular in Greek, creating the gendered pronoun problem in English.

67. Albl notes that James's description of the sick person calling for the elders implies a separation between the sick person and the rest of the community. Sin, associated with illness (5:16) manifests itself in division among community members. Both the gathering of the elders as representatives of the community and the mutual prayer and forgiveness of sin among all community members serve to restore the unity of the corporate body. Oil was thought in antiquity to have healing power, but it was also used to mark people as sacred. Albl, "'Are Any among You Sick?'" 137.

68. "When at work," ἐνεργουμένη. Translators have rendered this term a number of ways; see Hartin, *James*, 270–71.

69. Again, this section is in the singular in Greek, creating the gendered pronoun problem in English.

*Chapter 18*

# Revelation from Jesus, Messiah

## Introduction

THE BOOK, USUALLY TITLED "Revelation of John" and appearing at the end of modern New Testaments, actually bears the title "Revelation from Jesus, Messiah." It has two major sections: a set of letters to Christian assemblies in the western region of what is now modern Turkey, and the other is a series of apocalyptic images. The first part mentions a few people and a faction who are not known about from any other source, and it alludes to issues that were likely recognizable to the author's contemporaries but are opaque for the modern reader. The second part employs arcane allusions to the Hebrew scriptures and to legends that were current in the first century CE, and it takes the form of literary apocalyptic, a genre that in some ways resembles modern science fiction as well as the insider knowledge world of the Star Trek series. Beginning in the nineteenth century, some readers have had no problem accepting the book as an extended oracle of predictions; one wonders whether a millennium from now some people would view Star Trek videos that way. The author, named *John*, seems to have had something quite different on his mind. As will be seen below, he was writing about the situation of Christian churches in his day.

The author himself says his name is *John*;[1] he is an otherwise unknown prophet of the Roman Province of Asia. He is not the author of the Fourth Gospel or one of the sons of Zebedee, and it would be gratuitous to identify him with the author of the three letters of John. He knows the Hebrew scriptures well enough to create parallels that stand the scriptural stories on their head.[2] Where John was while he was writing is not clear, but he says he was on the Island of Patmos when he heard a voice that instructed him to write the letters to the seven churches. Patmos is located off the southwestern coast of modern Turkey. The seven churches were on or just inland from the central western coast of modern Turkey, in the Roman province of Asia.

---

1. Rev 1:1.
2. W. Harrington, *Revelation* 6, 8–9.

There is quite some discussion in the scholarly literature over when John wrote. According to Wilfred Harrington, Irenaeus of Lyons, writing between 175 and 185 CE, says John wrote *Revelation* during the reign of Emperor Domitian (81–96 CE).[3] How did Irenaeus know this? Was he right? We need to analyze the text of *Revelation* ourselves. Chapter 13 introduces two beasts, one rising out of the sea, having ten horns and seven heads, and the other rising out of the earth, having two horns like a lamb and speaking like a dragon. The second beast "acts with all the authority of the first beast in its presence. And it makes the earth and all dwelling on it worship the first beast, whose mortal wound was cured."[4] Confusion can arise as to which beast had a mortal wound that had healed. There is a succession of clauses in Chapter 13, each beginning with *and*, and whether one treats them in English translation as separate sentences or as one in English matters. In the Greek, these various clauses, stretching from 13:11 to 13:17, form a unit, with 13:18 as a conclusion. I would maintain that the continuing subject at verse 11 is the beast that rose out of the earth. So I translate 13:12 that way, suggestive of two beasts. Why two beasts? Why will one not do? It was because there was the formal Roman Empire, led by the Senate, and then the Principate of the emperors, which exercised authority in the presence of the Senate. Now this second beast "has a number," which is 666,[5] which most interpreters take to identify Nero on the basis of the letters that were used to make up 666 in the Hebrew numbering system with the Hebrew transliteration of the Greek. So the concluding verse of the section points to Emperor Nero as a beast exercising authority in the presence of another beast, the formal Roman state.

The Roman emperors made the earth and its inhabitants worship Rome, according to 13:12. In fact, in the ancient province of Asia there were temples dedicated to Roma as a goddess. Chapter 17 provides an insulting depiction of that goddess:

> . . . And I saw a woman sitting on a red beast, it being full of names of blasphemy and having seven heads and ten horns. And the woman was clothed in purple and red, and adorned with purple, precious gems, and pearls, and she was holding a golden cup in her hand full of abominations and the unclean things of her harlotry, and on her forehead had been written a name, with hidden meaning, "Babylon the great, mother of harlots and of the abominations of the earth." And I saw the woman drunken from the blood of the saints and from the blood of the martyrs of Jesus.[6]

Purple and scarlet would be imperial and military colors. Babylon was the empire that destroyed Jerusalem, and after the destruction of Jerusalem in 70 CE it was common

---

3. Ibid., 9.
4. Rev 13:1; 13:11; 13:12.
5. Rev 13:18.
6. Rev 17:3b–6a.

usage in Jewish circles to refer to Rome as the second Babylon.[7] If the point was lost on the part of the reader/hearer, verse 9 identifies the seven heads as the seven mountains on which the woman is seated, and they are also seven kings: "Five have fallen, one is, another is not yet come...."[8] We need one more piece of information to decode the imagery: Numerous legends, especially in the Roman province of Asia, held that Nero had not really committed suicide but had escaped to Parthia and was to return with an army. There were even pretenders who claimed to be Nero.[9] Scholars who set about counting emperors (kings) often begin with Julius Caesar or Octavian, coming to Nero at the end of the sequence.[10] But, as Alan J.P. Garrow notes, John has Nero in mind as one whose head bore a mortal wound that healed.[11] If one counts from Nero, the sequence is Nero, Galba, Otho, Vitellius, Vespasian, Titus; and the one to come would be Domitian. Garrow dates *Revelation* to the reign of Titus (79–81), but as I understand the sequence, John was writing at the time of the one who was to come, Domitian, because the vision John reports had come to him in the *past*. So we, and perhaps Irenaeus, can arrive at the reign of Domitian (81–96 CE) on the basis of the text.[12]

Reasonably assured that John's writing reflected the late first century context of the Roman province of Asia, we can concentrate on what he had to say about that world. John rejected the first century Roman world as evil. "He perceives a radical incompatibility between that Roman world and the gospel message."[13] John did not offer downtrodden Christians comfort with an other-worldly orientation, as has sometimes been thought, but took on the power structure of his day with a critique in the form of apocalyptic.[14] He saw the indifference of the rich and powerful toward the needy as something that will be condemned.[15] John's hostility to Rome used to be explained in terms of a persecution undertaken by Domitian, but there does not

---

7. A. Collins, "Dating the Apocalypse," 35; W. Harrington, *Revelation*, 9.

8. Rev 17:10.

9. Garrow, *Revelation*, 86; W. Harrington, *Revelation*, 5, noting the legends were presupposed in the *Sibyline Oracles*.

10. Kooten, "Year of the Four Emperors," is a relatively recent example.

11. Garrow, *Revelation*, 79–81.

12. Ulrichsen, "Die sieben Häupter," would begin counting emperors with Caligula because he was the first to come into conflict with the Jews by demanding an emperor cult; the arithmetic works if one leaves out three emperors with short reigns—Galba, Otho, and Vitellius. John's imagery also has ten horns, and this time by including those three short-term emperors, Ulrichsen, again beginning with Caligula, can use the emperor count to explain the ten horns in the imagery. Some would take the vision of measuring the Temple in Rev 11:1–2 as evidence that the Temple was still standing, and hence the work would have been written before 70; A. Collins, "Dating the Apocalypse," 37, refutes this by observing that John refers to Jerusalem as a holy city, something he would not have written of the earthly Jerusalem, given his hostility to non-Christian Jews; she also points out that in Rev 21 John explicitly says there is no temple in the New Jerusalem.

13. W. Harrington, *Revelation*, xiv.

14. deSilva, "Revelation to John," 376.

15. See Rev. 6:5–6.

seem to have been any such program of official persecution. Domitian appears as a megalomaniacal tyrant in works written soon after his reign, but contemporary scholars see that as a caricature created for political purposes; in reality, according to recent depictions, he was a balanced and competent administrator. The imperial cult was not of his making but was well entrenched by his day.[16] John's hostility to Rome was based on more permanent aspects of the Empire—a system of power relations infused with idolatrous honorifics. The Romans co-opted local elites by appointing them to prestigious priesthood positions in the cults of the goddess Roma and the deified emperors; the imperial cult substituted a voluntary respect for the authority of the emperor for coercion by the Roman army.[17] John would have Christians dissociate themselves from that system; he opposed not only the imperial idolatry but the very governance that the emperors exercised.[18]

For Christians to dissociate themselves from the imperial cult required everyday sacrifice. People who worked in trades were expected to participate in the cult of the patron deity of their guild as well as that of the emperor. The cultic rituals were followed by a meal wherein a collective identity was established, and the food served had been idolatrously dedicated. Christians would be tempted to at least witness the rituals and partake of the meal, albeit while privately maintaining that the deities were not real or at least not really divine. John would have them resist any such accommodation.[19] Jews enjoyed a legal concession not to participate in the official cultus, and while they were not forbidden to engage in the trades because of their aversion to idolatry they did incur resentment from some of the public for their abstention. When the synagogues would not recognize the Christians as genuinely Jewish, abstention on the part of the Christians could result in both commercial and social exclusion.[20] Consequently, *Revelation* reveals a continuing tension between the Christians and the synagogues as well as between John and the imperial system.

## Literary Apocalyptic

*Revelation* is an example of literary apocalyptic. In both major parts of the book—the letters to the seven churches and the section of dramatic imagery—the author depicts himself as a recipient of visions and as a visitor to a heavenly world. Especially in the second part, the visions traverse temporal and spatial worlds to arrive, ultimately, at a heavenly haven for the saved. These depictions conform to the requirements of the apocalyptic genre, a "genre of revelatory literature with a narrative framework in which a revelation is mediated by an otherworldly being to a human recipient disclosing

---

16. W. Harrington, *Revelation*, 9–10.
17. deSilva, "Revelation to John," 379.
18. A. Collins, "Vilification and Self-definition," 315.
19. deSilva, "Revelation to John," 381–82.
20. Ibid., 383.

a transcendent reality which is both temporal, insofar as it envisages eschatological salvation, and spatial insofar as it involves another, supernatural world."[21] Most apocalyptic works came out of the Jewish literary world; Wilfrid J. Harrington mentions 1 *Enoch*, which reflected events before and after the Maccabean Revolt, 167–164 BCE, and featured the legend of fallen angels and "woes" expressed in terms of a final judgment; *Daniel* 7–12, dating from 165 BCE; *Ezra* (also known as 2 *Esdras*), which was written after 70 CE, a Jewish anti-Roman work in Aramaic with a Christian Greek introduction; 2 *Baruch*, an anti-Roman work from about the same time as *Revelation*; the *Apocalypse of Abraham*, which addresses the problem of idolatry in the world, and the early sections of the *Sibyline Oracles*.[22] One should not assume that a work of apocalyptic, by virtue of the fact of being apocalyptic, reflects any particular social situation—a conquest of a higher civilization by a less literate one, the presence of a downtrodden stratum, or whatever.

Apocalyptic could be much more rhetorically effective in spoken form than when read silently. Since the ancients did not have the printing press or high levels of literacy, literature was recited and performed. A performer had a text to work from that lacked spaces between words, capital and lower case lettering, and punctuation. To make a passable performance at all required considerable skill. When reciting apocalyptic, voicing the text would be particularly important. Consequently, what may not be a particularly engaging read in the modern experience of reading would be a spectacular rendition in antiquity. The purpose of the text would be to have an effect, not to drop calendric clues for use in marking off progress to the end times. A modern parallel in the arts would be the Prologue to Boito's opera *Mefistofele*, or perhaps the "Dies Irae" from Verdi's *Requiem*.

## Sect Theory

John's stance is a *sectarian* one, one that is in high tension with the wider society and would have strong boundaries between the elect and the wider society. The term *sect* has had many meanings over time, and we need to review its history to distinguish among them. Max Weber first used the term as a sociological term of art to refer to the opposite of a *church*.

> In formulating the concept of a hierocratic organization, it is not possible to use the character of the religious benefits it offers, whether worldly or otherworldly, material or spiritual, as the decisive criterion. What is important is rather the fact that its control over these values can form the basis of a system of spiritual domination over human beings. What is most characteristic of the church . . . is the fact that it is a rational, compulsory association with

---

21. J. Collins, *Apocalyptic Imagination*, 4.
22. W. Harrington, *Revelation*, 2, 4, 5.

> continuous operation and that it claims a monopolistic authority.... It is its character as a compulsory association, particularly the fact that one becomes a member of the church by birth, which distinguishes the church from a "sect." It is characteristic of the latter that it is a voluntary association and admits only persons with specific religious qualifications.[23]

In his travels in the United States, Weber observed that membership in sects, as opposed to churches, was tantamount to "a certificate of moral qualification and especially of business morals for the individual."[24] For Weber, "it is not the ethical *doctrine* of a religion, but that form of ethical conduct upon which *premiums* are placed" that mattered.[25] The theologian Ernst Troeltsch shifted Weber's ideal types of religious organization to types of religious behavior, resulting in three types: church, sect, and mysticism (Christiano, Swatos, and Kivisto.)[26] For Troeltsch, the difference between church and sect was not how one became a member but accommodation, compromise with the world. The American theologian H. Richard Niebuhr applied the church/sect distinction to religions in the United States, using church and sect as poles of a continuum; Niebuhr analyzed the dynamic process of groups moving along this continuum.[27] Consequently, it has not always been clear what sociologists of religion have meant by *church* and *sect*, and the related terms *denomination* and *cult*. A 1971 essay by Benton Johnson has been most influential in the development of church/sect theory; for him *church* is a polar type of acceptance of the social environment, whereas *sect* is the polar type of its rejection.[28] The term *church*, used as a polar type of environment acceptance, implies an established status, where the hierocratic organization is identical with the organized aspects of the society in general—especially the state. The first century imperial cult would be a church in that sense of the term. In the modern world, we are more familiar with church-like organizations, *denominations*, which accept the social environment, as opposed to sects that do not accept it.

Of course, to not accept an environment implies some minimal identification with it. Just as one does not hate a complete stranger, one does not distance oneself from an environment that one does not share to some extent. A sect-like stance can thus have some root within the setting it rejects. The environment of such a setting as Ephesus, for example, included not only the dominant Roman governance and the co-opted local commercial and political elites, but also indigenous elements of resistance that the Christian stance of John may well have grafted onto.

---

23. Weber, *Economy and Society*, 56.
24. Weber, "Protestant Sects," 305.
25. Ibid., 321.
26. Christiano, et al., *Sociology of Religion*, 88–89.
27. Niebuhr, *Social Sources of Denominationalism*.
28. B. Johnson, "Church and Sect Revisited."

> When Rome assumed power in 133 BC under the terms of the bequest of Attalus III, the wealthy seaport was open to exploitation by ruthless officials. The hatred for Rome was seen in the response of the Ephesians to Mithridates' command for a massacre of Romans in the province of Asia in 88 BC. Not even the suppliants at the asylum of Artemis[29] were spared.[30]

It was almost 180 years since Mithridates' command, but it would be naïve to believe that the Roman Empire and those co-opted by it became any more benign to the earlier exploited population and its descendants.

The meaning of terms of art can be adapted as needed. The discussion of church and sect in the literature has provided us with a vocabulary. As applied to the world of John the author of *Revelation*, the imperial cult is a church, the various trade and civic cults are denominations, and John would have the Christian movement be a sect. The Christians whom he criticized for becoming too accommodative toward the civic environment would be sect members who had a denominationalizing propensity. A sociological analysis, of course, needs to go beyond vocabulary. An explanatory approach to the Christian communities to whom *Revelation* was directed may well be found in the organizational dynamics of those communities themselves, not endeavors on the part of the Roman state to persecute them. John would bolster the boundary between the Christian community and the Roman world to resolve dilemmas within the former.

A classic essay by Thomas F. O'Dea speaks of dilemmas that arise in the very process of organizing, or institutionalizing, religion. There is the dilemma of mixed motivation: "With the emergence of a stable institutional matrix, there arises a structure of offices—of statuses and roles—capable of eliciting" a kind of motivation "involving needs for prestige, expression of teaching and leadership abilities, drives for power, aesthetic needs, and the quite prosaic wish for the security of a respectable position in the professional structure of the society."[31] There is the dilemma of administrative order: A bureaucracy develops that self-complicates itself, producing an unwieldy organization with blocks and breakdown in communication, overlapping of spheres of competence, and ambiguous definitions of authority and related functions."[32] O'Dea goes on to speak of a dilemma of delimitation—substitutions of letter for spirit—and a dilemma of power—conversion versus coercion—and a symbol dilemma—objectivation versus alienation. John's *Revelation* appears to address principally the problem of mixed motivation, with the other dilemmas at best incidentally correlated with that problem. Those who aspire to Christian leadership as an occasion of general civic respectability may also be tempted to maintain structures at the expense of commu-

---

29. The shrine of Artemis near Ephesus and the land associated with it had been and would be otherwise universally respected as a refuge—Hemer, *Letters to the Seven Churches*, 48–50.

30. Ibid., 36.

31. O'Dea, "Five Dilemmas," 33.

32. Ibid., 35.

nication and organizational simplicity, to be satisfied with the letter rather than worry over the spirit, to exert pressure rather than elicit commitment through persuasion, to go through alien motions.

# English Translation

## Revelation of Jesus the Messiah

1 [1]A revelation of Jesus the Messiah, which God gave him to show his servants what must soon come to be, and he made it known sending it through his messenger to his servant John, [2]who testified to what he saw, to God's speaking, and to the testimony of Jesus the Messiah. [3]Blessed is one who reads aloud and those hearing the words of the prophecy and treasuring what is written in it, for the time is near.

[4]John, to the seven churches that are in Asia: grace to you and peace from the One Who is, Who was, and Who is coming, and from the seven spirits that are before his throne,[33] [5]and from Jesus the Messiah, the faithful witness, the first born of the dead and ruler of the kings of the earth.

To him who loves us and frees us from our sins with his blood—[6]and he made us a kingdom, priests of his God and Father—to him be the glory and the power forever and ever. Amen.

[7]Behold, he is coming with the clouds,[34]

And every eye will see him,

Even those who pierced him.[35]

And all the tribes of the earth will mourn over him. Yes. Amen.

[8]"I am," says the Lord God, "the Alpha and the Omega that is, was, and will come: the Almighty."[36]

[9]I, your brother John and sharer in the tribulation, kingdom, and endurance in Jesus, was on the island called Patmos for the sake of God's saying and the testimony of Jesus.[37] [10]I was in the spirit on the Lord's Day, and I heard

---

33. The image of the seven lamps, corresponding to the seven spirits, seems to be inspired by Zech 4:2 and 4:10; it reappears several times in Rev.

34. An allusion to Dan 7:13, which serves to inform the reader and hearers that what follows is a work in the apocalyptic genre.

35. Allusion to Zech 12:10. Matt 24:30 also alluded to Dan 7:13 and Zech 12:10 together.

36. "The Almighty," ὁ παντοκράτωρ: W. Harrington, *Revelation*, 47, notes that this is the regular Septuagint rendering of "Yahweh Sabaoth," "Lord of hosts," John's favorite title for God.

37. Patmos is a small island among the group of Sporades off the southwest coast of Asia Minor. Nothing in the pedestrian statement of his being there suggests a judicial banishment from the mainland—ibid., 50.

a loud voice behind me, like a trumpet,[38] [11]saying, "Write what you see on a scroll and send it to the seven churches: to Ephesus, Smyrna, Pergamum, Thyatira, Sardis, Philadelphia, and Laodicea."[39]

[12]And I turned to see whose voice was speaking behind me, and turning I saw seven golden lamps,[40] [13]and in the middle of the lamps was one like a son of humanity,[41] dressed to the feet and a golden belt girt about up towards the breasts;[42] [14]and his head and hair were white as white wool, as snow,[43] and his eyes aflame like fire,[44] [15]and his feet were like brilliant metal[45] as in a kiln of things made to glow, and his voice like the roar of many waters,[46] [16]and he had seven stars in his right hand, and coming out from his mouth a sharp two-edged sword,[47] and his countenance was as the sun shines during its strength.

[17]And when I saw him, I fell as dead before his feet; and he placed his right hand upon me, saying, "Fear not. I am the first and the last,[48] [18]and the living one; I also became dead, and behold I am living for ever and ever, and I hold the keys of death and hell. [19]So write what you see, the things that are, and the things about to come to be after them.[49] [20]The mystery of the seven stars which you see in my right hand, and the seven lamps of gold: The seven stars are messengers of the seven churches, and the seven lamps are the seven churches.[50]

---

38. "Trumpet," σάλπιγγος; see Exod 19:16 and 19 in the Septuagint, where a σάλπιγγος is part of a theophany on Mount Sinai. Technically, the instrument is a shofar, a horn made from a ram's horn; the shofar is of symbolic significance in Jewish ceremonial to this day.

39. "The seven Churches are not listed haphazardly but in order: they were linked by a circular road that from Ephesus, went north to Smyrna and Pergamum and then swung southwards to take in the others. A messenger could carry the scroll to each of the Churches in turn . . . "—W. Harrington, *Revelation*, 50–51.

40. Zech 4:4 has a vision of seven lamps on a gold lampstand.

41. Dan 7:13.

42. "Breasts," μαστοῖς, on one like a male: According to Rainbow, "Male μαστοί," the anatomical anomaly is based on the Septuagint translation of the *Song of Songs*, where the Greek for *breasts* rather than *love* appears at Song 1:2; 1:4; 4:10 (twice), and 7:13 (12 in the Septuagint), and possibly 6:11. Thus, the Septuagint Song at 1:2a has the female referring to the male breasts of her beloved. Incidentally, this allusion in *Revelation* is an early example of an allegorical reading of Song—Friesen, "Myth and Symbolic Resistance."

43. Dan 7:9.

44. Dan 10:6.

45. "Brilliant metal," χαλκολιβάνῳ: An alloy of copper with metallic zinc made in Thyatira; it was a finer and purer brass than what was used in coinage—Hemer, *Letters to the Seven Churches*, 111–17.

46. "Many waters": Ezek 43:2.

47. "Sharp sword" alludes to Isa 49:2.

48. Isa 44:6 and 48:12.

49. "Verse 19 in effect divides the whole into three sections: the foregoing vision of ch. 1, the 'things which are' in chs. 2–3, and the 'things which shall be' in chs. 4–22"—Hemer, *Letters to the Seven Churches*, 31.

50. "Messengers," ἄγγελοι: Hemer, *Letters to the Seven Churches*, 32–34, reviews five different understandings of *angeloi* here. 1) They are heavenly guardians. One would have to ask why John,

2 ¹Write to the messenger of the church in Ephesus:⁵¹ Thus says the one holding the seven stars in his right hand, who walks in the midst of the seven lamps of gold: ²I know your works, travail, and your endurance, though you cannot endure evil people; and you tested those calling themselves apostles and were not, and you discovered them to be false; ³and you have endurance and bore up on account of my name and have not grown weary. ⁴But I hold against you that you have abandoned your first love. ⁵Keep in mind, then, where you have fallen from, and repent and do the works you did at first; otherwise I am coming to you and I will take your lamp from its place if you do not repent. ⁶But you do have this, that you hate the works of the Nicolaitans,⁵² which I also hate. ⁷Let the one having ears hear what the spirit is saying to the churches. To the victor I will grant it to eat from the tree of life, which is in God's garden.⁵³

⁸And write to the messenger of the church that is in Smyrna:⁵⁴ Thus says the first and the last,⁵⁵ who became dead and lived: ⁹I know your afflictions and poverty, but you are rich, and I know of the vilification by those who say they are Jews but are not, but rather are a synagogue of Satan.⁵⁶ ¹⁰Do not fear what you are about to suffer. Behold, the devil is about to cast some of you into

---

a human, would be instructed to write to heavenly guardians. 2) They are the bishops. There is no precedent for such a usage in Christian literature. 3) They are personifications of the churches. One must ask why they would be symbolized with stars and lamps. 4) They are human messengers who would carry the letters to their churches. In that case, the symbolizing of them with stars seems odd and extravagant. 5) This is a deliberate ambiguity. The third proposal seems most probable to me.

51. Concerning Ephesus, see the note on Acts 18:19.

52. John will refer to the Nicolaitans again (2:15 and 2:20–23); they seem to be lax, from John's perspective, concerning involvement in civic idolatry and the banquets associated with it.

53. "Garden," παραδείσῳ, "Paradise." The tree of life is a double allusion to Gen 2:9 and to the cross. The term for "tree" is not δένδρον, which normally refers to a live tree, but ξύλον, normally translated as "wood" or as a reference to a cross or pillory. Ξύλον is used, surprisingly, in Septuagint Gen 2:9 to refer to the tree in the Garden of Eden.

54. Strabo, *Geography* 14:1:37 says "a part of it (Smyrna) is on a mountain and walled, but the greater part of it is in the plain near the harbor and near the Metröum (temple of Cybele) and near the gymnasium. The division into streets is exceptionally good in straight lines as far as possible; and the streets are paved with stone; and there are large quadrangular porticos, with both lower and upper stories. There is also a library; and the Homereium, a quadrangular portico containing a shrine and wooden statue of Homer; for the Smyrnaeans also lay special claim to the poet; and indeed a bronze coin of theirs is called Homerium. The River Meles flows near the walls; and, in addition to the rest of the city's equipment there is also a harbor that can be closed. But there is one error, not a small one, in the work of the engineers, that when they paved the streets they did not give them underground drainage; instead, filth covers the surface, and particularly during rains, when the cast-off filth is discharged upon the streets."

55. Isa 44:6b: "I am the first and I am the last; beside me there is no god." See also Isa 48:12.

56. This is probably a reference to a local Jewish synagogue rather than a Judaising Christian one. The vilification may refer to synagogue members denouncing Christians in court. Heber, *Letters to the Seven Churches*, 67, notes the shift from Σατανᾶ to διάβολος, "adversary" to "slanderer." John uses the rhetorical stratagem of identifying the Christians as the genuine Jews—A. Collins, "Vilification and Self-definition," 313–14.

prison so that you will be tested, and you will have tribulation ten days.[57] Be faithful up to the point of death, and I will give you the crown of life. [11]Let one who has ears hear what the spirit is saying to the churches. The victor will not be wronged by a second death.

[12]And write to the messenger of the church that is in Pergamum:[58] Thus says the one having the sharp two-edged sword: [13]I know where you live, where the throne of Satan is.[59] You are both holding fast to my name and did not deny my faith even in the days of Antipas my faithful witness, who was killed in your city, where Satan dwells. [14]But I have something minor against you, that you have there those who support the teaching of Balaam, who taught Balak to set up a stumbling stone before the sons of Israel: to eat meat offered to idols and to commit adultery.[60] [15]And thus you likewise have those supporting the teaching of the Nicolaitans. [16]Repent, then.[61] Otherwise, I will come upon you suddenly, and I will make war on them with the sword of my mouth. [17]You having ears, hear what the spirit is saying to the churches. I will give to the victor the manna that has been hidden,[62] and I will give the victor a white stone,[63] and upon the stone a new written name[64] that no one will know except the one receiving it.

---

57. Hemer, *Letters to the Seven Churches*, 69, interpreting an inscription in Smyrna, suggests the imprisonment would be holding someone for ten days before execution or being thrown into the arena to be killed by gladiators or beasts.

58. According to Strabo, *Geography* 13:4:3, Pergamum was known in his day (a century and a half before John) for a rhetorician, Apollodorus, who led a sect of Apollodorians, which Strabo could not describe because of "numerous philosophies" that prevailed. Apollodorus was a teacher of Caesar Augustus and the sophist historian and speech-writer Dionysius Atticus. Strabo also mentions a sect that followed one Theodorus.

59. Satan's throne in Pergamum: Pergamum Christians experienced hostility; Antipas was martyred there. The throne of Satan may refer to the place of the killing—Friesen, "Satan's Throne," but Hemer, *Letters to the Seven Churches*, 87, notes that Pergamum was a center of the emperor cult.

60. The leaders whom John criticizes as morally deficient are "Nicolaitans"; they "seem to stand behind Jezebel"—deSilva, "Revelation to John," 384. John says they hold to the teaching of Balaam; Balaam refers to the apostasy of Israel at Peor (Num 25:1–3); they bowed down to the gods of the Moabites, ate their sacrifices, and "began to play the harlot with the daughters of Moab." Jezebel materially supported the prophets of Baal in Israel—ibid., 384–85. "Commit adultery": This can mean engaging in idolatry.

61. This is evidently directed at the Nicolaitans, who would be the antecedents of "them" later on in the verse—W. Harrington, *Revelation*, 62.

62. Manna that has been hidden: "Reference to a Jewish apocalyptic tradition (see 2 Baruch 29:8) according to which the manna will reappear as food of the messianic kingdom . . ."—ibid. Hemer, *Letters to the Seven Churches*, 92, sees a contrast of meat offered to idols and manna.

63. Arndt and Gingrich, *Greek-English Lexicon*, 892, article on ψῆφος, define the word as *pebble*: "used in voting, in juries and elsewh., a black one for conviction, a white one for acquittal . . ."; surprisingly, they go on to suggest that the use in Rev 2:17a is evidently as a wonderworking amulet stone. Given the connection of a divine judgment with reference to the future, the first meaning would be the more obvious fit. Hemer, *Letters to the Seven Churches*, 102–03, reviews suggestions concerning the "new name" written on the white stone.

64. New name: "The nations shall see your vindication, and all the kings your glory; and you shall

¹⁸And write to the messenger of the church of Thyatira:⁶⁵ Thus says the son of God, who has eyes like fiery flames and feet like brilliant metal.⁶⁶ ¹⁹I know your efforts and the love, faith, service, and your endurance; and your latest works are better than the earlier ones. ²⁰But I have against you that you allow the woman Jezebel, who calls herself a prophetess, and she teaches and misleads my servants to commit adultery and eat meet offered to idols.⁶⁷ ²¹And I gave her time to repent, and she does not want to turn back from her adultery. ²²Behold, I will throw her onto a sickbed and those committing adultery with her into great affliction if they will not turn away from her works; ²³and I will kill her children with pestilence; and all the churches will know that I am the one who searches minds and hearts, and I will accord to each of you according to your works. ²⁴But I say to you others among the Thyratirans who do not hold to that teaching, who did not learn the deep things of Satan, as they say, I will put not any other burden on you; ²⁵only hold fast to what you have until I come. ²⁶And the victor and the one keeping my works until the end, I will give to that one authority over the nations—²⁷and he will smash them with an iron rod, as the potter's vessel is shattered⁶⁸—²⁸as I also have received from my Father, and I will give the morning star to that one.⁶⁹ ²⁹Let him having ears hear what the spirit is saying to the churches.

3 ¹And write to the messenger of the church in Sardis:⁷⁰ Thus says the one having the seven spirits of God and the seven stars: I know of your works, that you have a name that is of life though you are dead. ²Become vigilant, and strengthen the rest who are at the point of death, for I have not found your works completed before my God. ³Be mindful, then, how you received and

---

be called by a new name which the mouth of the Lord will give"—Isa 62:2 RSV; see W. Harrington, *Revelation*, 62.

65. Strabo, *Geography* 13:4:4, says Thyatira was "a settlement of the Macedonians, which by some is called the farthermost city of the Mysians." Lydia, Paul's host in Philippi, was from Thyatira. The city had inhabitants of multiple ethnicities and syncretistic religion—Hemer, *Letters to the Seven Churches*, 110–11. Occupational associations, which the Romans discouraged elsewhere, were essential to civic life in Thyatira—ibid., 108.

66. "Brilliant metal," χαλκολιβάνῳ: See the note at 1:15.

67. "Commit adultery" here may mean to engage in idolatry. "Jezebel" in Num 25 also encouraged syncretism—ibid., 120. Social participation in syncretistic rites would have been normal in a city dominated by trade associations.

68. Allusion to Ps 2:9, based on the Septuagint translation. The Septuagint, and this verse, use ποιμανεῖ to mean shatter, even though the usual meaning of the term is to shepherd—W. Harrington, *Revelation*, 65. Since verse 28 logically goes with verse 26, Harrington relocates it before verse 27 in his translation—ibid., 64; the RSV simply leaves the incongruity in place. Here I have used dashes, marking off verse 27 as a digression.

69. At 22:16, below, John identifies the Messiah as the morning star.

70. People in Sardis had reason to be well-disposed to the Caesars because Tiberius restored the city after a major earthquake—Strabo, *Geography*, 12:8:18. In Roman times, Sardis was a commercial city with a shrine to the goddess Cybele and a prominent Jewish community—W. Harrington, *Revelation*, 68. The Jewish community is mentioned by the prophet Obad 20: "the exiles of Jerusalem who are in Sepharad," a rendering of Sardis—Hemer, *Letters to the Seven Churches*, 141.

heard; both keep it and repent. If, then, you are not vigilant, I will come like a thief, and you will not know at what hour I will come upon you.⁷¹ ⁴However, you have a few names in Sardis who did not defile their garments, and they will walk with me in white, since they are worthy. ⁵The victor will be clothed thusly in white garments, and I shall not erase the name of that one from the book of life,⁷² and I will acknowledge the name of that one before my Father and before His messengers. ⁶Let one who has ears hear what the spirit is saying to the churches.

⁷And write to the messenger of the church that is in Philadelphia:⁷³ Thus says the holy one, the true one:

> The one having the key of David,
> The one opening and no one locks,
>    And locking and no one opens.⁷⁴

⁸I know your works—behold, I have set before you a door that has been opened, which no one can close—though you have little strength you kept my word and did not despise my name. ⁹Behold, I am putting those from the synagogue of Satan⁷⁵ who say of themselves they are Jews and are not but lie—behold I will make them be at and bow down before your feet,⁷⁶ and they will know that I love you.⁷⁷ ¹⁰Because you kept my word of endurance, I will also keep you from the hour of the test which is about to come upon the whole world to test those dwelling on the earth. ¹¹I am coming soon; hold onto what you have, so that no one would take your crown.⁷⁸ ¹²The victor I will make a pillar⁷⁹ in the sanctuary of my God, and I will never go out from it, and I will

---

71. Sardis had a history of being conquered in war because of insufficient vigilance, a fact commonly cited in antiquity—Hemer, *Letters to the Seven Churches*, 144.

72. "Book of life": a similar expression is in Ps 69:28. A register of citizens was common in cities—ibid., 148.

73. According to Strabo, *Geography,* 13:4:10, Philadelphia was "ever subject to earthquakes. Incessantly the walls of the houses are cracked, different parts of the city being thus affected at different times. For this reason but few people live in the city, and most of them spend their lives as farmers in the country, since they have a fertile soil. Yet one may be surprised at the few, that they are so fond of the place when their dwellings are so insecure...."

74. Isa 22:22, not using the Septuagint text; in Isaiah, the Lord is replacing an unworthy steward with Eliakim.

75. See the note at 2:9.

76. Isa 60:14: "The sons of those who oppressed you shall come bending low to you; and all who despised you shall bow down at your feet ..." (RSV).

77. See Isa 43:4.

78. An athlete's crown of victory—apt since many coins of Philadelphia refer to games and festivals—Hemer, *Letters to the Seven Cities*, 165.

79. The pillar was a biblical symbol of the stability of a king's governance, used in coronation ceremonies; see 2 Kgs 11—Wilkinson, "ΣΤΥΛΟΣ of Revelation." Stability would be a significant issue in Philadelphia, given the seismic situation described by Strabo. The verse goes on to mention not having

write the name of my God on it and the name of the city of my God, New Jerusalem,[80] which is coming down from heaven from my God, and I will write my new name on it. [13]Let one who has ears hear what the spirit is saying to the churches.

[14]And write to the messenger of the church which is in Laodicea:[81] Thus says the Amen,[82] the faithful and truthful witness, the beginning of God's creation: [15]I know your works, that you are neither cold nor hot. Would that you were cold *or* hot! [16]Thus, because you are lukewarm and neither hot nor cold, I am about to spit you out of my mouth.[83] [17]Because you are saying, "I am rich and I have become rich and I have need of nothing,"[84] and you do not know that you are wretched, pitiable, poor, blind, and naked, [18]I am advising you to buy from me gold purified by fire so that you may be rich, white garments so that one would clothe you lest the shame of your nakedness be shown, and ointment to rub into your eyes so that you may see.[85] [19]Whomever I love I discipline and train;[86] be eager, then, and repent. [20]Behold, I am standing outside the door and I am knocking; whoever heeds my voice and opens the door, I will also come in to them and dine with them and they with me.[87] [21]I will grant

---

to go outside, which is what people did in Philadelphia, given the frequent earthquakes—Hemer, *Letters to the Seven Churches*, 157.

80. Analogously, Philadelphia was renamed "Neocaesarea," after Tiberius gave assistance in rebuilding the city after an earthquake, but the name did not stick—ibid., 157, probably because Emperor Claudius decreed that grape production, which fit the volcanic soil of the area, be halved and replaced by corn production, needed by the army. The economic consequence for Philadelphia was disastrous. For the naming of the city of God, ibid., 160, cites Isa 62:2.

81. Laodicea was "a city most beautifully built," having a good harbor and a territory with good crops and abounding with wine—Strabo, *Geography* 16:2:9. People there had reason to be well-disposed to the Caesars because Tiberius restored the city after a major earthquake—ibid., 12:8:18. It was "a major commercial city. It was a banking center, a manufacturer of clothing and carpets of the native glossy-black wool, and the seat of a medical school noted for 'Phrygian powder' used in the making of eye salve"—W. Harrington, *Revelation*, 74–75. It was a rich city and, after another disastrous earthquake in 60 CE, recovered without the aid of an imperial grant—ibid., 75. Hemer, *Letters to the Seven Churches*, 196–99, discusses the circumstantial evidence on eye treatments in Laodicea.

82. Isa 65:16 speaks of the God of the Amen in the Hebrew, translated in RSV as "the God of truth"—W. Harrington, *Revelation*, 73.

83. The water in Colossae was cold, and that in Hierapolis was hot; but that in Laodicea came by way of an aqueduct and was not particularly good. The problem was not necessarily the temperature of the water but its nauseous mineral content—Hemer, *Letters to the Seven Churches*, 187–91.

84. Some see this as an allusion to Hos 12:8—ibid., 184. Laodicea had become a banking center and even rejected help from Rome after a major earthquake, rebuilding itself as a matter of pride—ibid., 191–96.

85. This seems to be alluding to Laodicea as a banking center, ophthalmology school, and manufacturer of black wool.

86. Some see this as an allusion to Prov 3:12—ibid., 184.

87. The Greek has *whoever*, *them*, and *they* in the masculine singular. Some see this verse as an allusion to Canticles 5:2—ibid., 184. As a city located at a crossroads often visited by Roman officials who imposed themselves on the local elite and quartered their troops in private residences, the Christian Messiah calling at the door is a contrasting image—ibid., 204–05.

that the victor will sit with me on my throne, as I myself was victorious and sat with my Father on His throne. ²²Let the one having ears hear what the spirit is saying to the churches.

4 ¹After these, I looked, and behold there was an opened door in heaven, and the first voice I heard was like a trumpet[88] speaking with me, saying, "Come up here, and I will show you what should come to be after these." ²I was straightway in the spirit; and behold, there was a throne there in heaven, and one seated on the throne, ³and the one seated was like jasper and ruby stone in appearance, and a radiance around the throne was likewise emerald in appearance. ⁴And there were twenty-four thrones around the throne, and on the thrones were seated twenty-four presbyters enrobed in white garments,[89] and there were gold crowns on their heads. ⁵And out of the throne came lightning, sounds, and thunder; and seven flaming lamps[90] lit before the throne, which are the seven spirits of God, ⁶and before the throne like a glass sea similar to ice.[91]

And in front of the throne and around the throne,[92] there were four live beings replete with eyes, front and back; ⁷and the first live being was like a lion, and the second live being was like a young ox, and the third live being had a human-like face, and the fourth live being was like a flying eagle.[93] ⁸And the four live beings, each of them having six wings,[94] were replete with eyes all over and inside. And not having days and nights they do not cease saying,

Holy, holy, holy Lord, the God almighty,[95]
Who was and Who is and Who is coming.

⁹And when the live beings give glory, honor, and thanksgiving to the One sitting on the throne, Who is living forever and ever, ¹⁰the twenty-four presbyters fall down before the One sitting on the throne and worship the One living for ever and ever, and they lay their crowns down before the throne, saying,

---

88. Trumpet: see the note at 1:15.

89. W. Harrington, *Revelation*, 79, suggests the number twenty-four reflects that number of divisions of Aaronic priests in 1 Chr 24:1–18. In any case, the image is intended to represent a Christian organization of churches.

90. "Seven lamps"—Zech 4:2: "I see, and behold, a lampstand all of gold, with a bowl on the top of it, and seven lamps on it, with seven lips on each of the lamps which are on the top of it" RSV.

91. "Ice," κρυστάλλῳ, could also mean "crystal."

92. "In front of": literally, "in the center." The image is based on the Greek theatre. "In between," ἐν μέσῳ, refers to the space between center stage, where the throne is pictured to be, and the audience. The elders would be in the front row. The live beings were also "around the throne," in a semi-circle before the throne—Brewer, "Revelation 4:6."

93. Based on Ezek 1:10, but not reproducing the image exactly.

94. Isa 6:2–3: "Above him stood the seraphim; each had six wings: with two he covered his face, and with two he covered his feet and with two he flew. And one called to another and said: 'Holy, holy, holy is the Lord of hosts; the whole earth is full of his glory'" (RSV).

95. "Lord, the God almighty": This duplicates the Septuagint text of Amos 3:13.

> Worthy are you, our Lord and God,
>
> to receive glory, honor, and power,
>
> because You created all,
>
> and they were and were created through Your will.

5 ¹And I saw in the right hand of the one sitting on the throne a scroll, written upon front and back,[96] sealed with seven seals.[97] ²And I saw a powerful messenger calling out in a loud voice, "Who is worthy to open the scroll and break its seals?" ³And no one in heaven, on the earth, or under the earth was able to open the scroll or look into it. ⁴And I wept much because no one was found worthy to open the scroll or look into it. ⁵And one of the presbyters says to me, "Do not weep: behold, the lion who is from the tribe of Judah,[98] the root of David, was conquering to open the scroll and its seven seals."

⁶And I saw between the throne and four live beings and the presbyters a lamb standing as one that had been slaughtered, having seven horns[99] and seven eyes, which are the seven spirits of God sent out to all the earth. ⁷And he went and takes it from the right hand of the one sitting on the throne. ⁸And when he was taking the scroll, the four live beings and the twenty-four presbyters fell before the lamb, each having a lyre and golden bowls full of incense, which are the prayers of the saints. ⁹And they sang a new song:[100]

> You are worthy to take the scroll
>
> And break open its seals
>
> Because you were slain and purchased for God by your blood
>
> Persons from every tribe, tongue, people, and nation,[101]
>
> ¹⁰And made them a kingdom and priests for our God,
>
> And they shall rule over the earth.

¹¹And I saw, and I heard the voice of many messengers around the throne and of the live beings and of the presbyters, and their number was myriads of myriads and thousands of thousands, ¹²saying in a loud voice: "Worthy is the lamb who was slain, to receive the power, richness, wisdom, strength, honor, glory, and blessing." ¹³And I heard every creature which is in heaven, on the

---

96. See Ezek 2:10, where there is a scroll with writing front and back.

97. A Roman prescription required wills to be sealed with seven seals—W. Harrington, *Revelation*, 84.

98. Gen 49:9 refers to Judah, one of the twelve sons of Jacob, as a lion's whelp.

99. A horn is symbolic of power—W. Harrington, *Revelation*, 84.

100. There are many references to singing a new song in the Hebrew Bible; the Greek terminology is close to Septuagint Ps 143:9, in most modern Bibles Ps 144:9.

101. This stands in contrast to the mission in Ezekiel's vision, which is directed only to the house of Israel—Ezek 2:3; 3:1; 3:4; see W. Harrington, *Revelation*, 86.

earth, under the earth, and on the sea, and all that were among them saying, "To the one seated on the throne and to the lamb be blessing, honor, glory, and power forever and ever." ¹⁴And the four live beings were saying, "Amen"; and the presbyters fell down and worshipped.

6 ¹And I looked when the lamb was breaking open one of the seven seals and I heard one of the four live beings speaking like thunder: "Come." ²And I looked, and behold, there was a white horse,[102] and there was one seated on it holding a bow,[103] and a crown was given him, and the victor went out so that he too would be victorious.

³And when he was breaking open the second seal, I heard the second live being saying, "Come." ⁴And another, red horse went out, and the one seated on it was granted to take peace away from the earth so that people would even slaughter one another, and a huge sword was given to him.

⁵And when he was breaking open the third seal, I heard the third live being saying, "Come." And I looked, and behold, there was a black horse, and there was one sitting upon it holding a pair of scales in his hand. ⁶And I heard what sounded like a voice in the midst of the four live beings saying, "A quart[104] of wheat for a denarius,[105] and three quarts of barley for a denarius; and do not interfere with the oil and the wine."[106]

⁷And when he was breaking open the fourth seal, I heard the voice of the fourth live being saying, "Come." ⁸And I looked, and behold there was a yellowish green horse, and the one seated over it, whose name was pestilence,[107] and Hades followed with him; and authority over a fourth of the earth was given to them, to kill by sword, famine, pestilence, and by the beasts of the earth.[108]

---

102. The vision of horses of various colors resembles Zech 1:8–11, where a man is on a red horse accompanied by other horses (and presumably riders) is "sent to patrol the earth": "We have patrolled the earth, and behold all the earth remains at rest"—1:10 and 11 RSV.

103. According to W. Harrington, *Revelation*, 89, "mention of the bow points to the Parthians, the only mounted archers of the first century CE The Parthians, along the eastern frontier of the Empire, were the great contemporary threat to Rome. . . . "

104. "Quart," translates Χοῖνιξ, a dry measure, about equivalent to a quart; a *choenix* of grain was a daily ration for one person—Arndt and Gingrich, *Greek-English Lexicon*, 883, article on χοῖνιξ.

105. A denarius was one full day's pay—ibid., 179, article on δηνάριον.

106. "The conditions suggest famine, but not total famine (v. 8). It is possible that v. 6 may refer to a 92 C.E. edict of Domitian requiring half of the vineyards in the provinces to be cut down in favor of grain-growing"—W. Harrington, *Revelation*, 90. Harrington's is the usual interpretation of this enigmatic passage. Vanni maintains that explaining an apocalyptic passage in terms of specific historical events misses the broader implications inherent in that literary genre. The black horse would be a demonic force invading the world—Vanni, "Il terzo 'sigillo,'" 703. The balance the rider holds represents justice and injustice—ibid., 704. The rider of the black horse expresses an unmoved capriciousness of injustice, fixing the price of necessities at levels difficult for the poor to pay, even while not impeding the supply of wine and oil, consumables of the more prosperous—ibid., 711.

107. "Pestilence," θάνατος, could also be read as "death."

108. Ezek 14:21: "For thus says the Lord God: How much more when I send upon Jerusalem my four sore acts of judgment, sword, famine, evil beasts, and pestilence, to cut off from it man and beast!" RSV, cited by W. Harrington, *Revelation*, 90.

⁹And when he was breaking open the fifth seal, I saw under the altar the souls of those slaughtered on account of the word of God and on account of the witness that they were maintaining. ¹⁰And they were crying out in a loud voice, "How long, O holy and true Master, before You judge and avenge our blood on those who dwell on the earth?" ¹¹And a white robe was given to each of them, and they were told to rest for a short time more, until the complement[109] would be completed of their fellow servants and their brothers and sisters who were about to be killed as they were.

¹²And I looked when he was opening the sixth seal, and there was a great earthquake, and the sun became as black as sackcloth made of black goat hair, and the full moon became like blood, ¹³and the stars of the sky fell to earth as a fig tree drops its summer figs when shaken by a gust of wind, ¹⁴and the sky was separated like a scroll rolled apart, and every mountain and island was moved from their places. ¹⁵And the kings of the earth, courtiers, military commanders, plutocrats, strongmen, every slave, and every free person hid themselves in caves and rocks of every region; ¹⁶they say to the mountains and rocks, "Fall on us and hide us from the face of the one sitting on the throne and from the wrath of the lamb, ¹⁷for the great day of their wrath came, and who can stand?

7 ¹After this I saw four messengers standing on the four corners of the earth, restraining the four winds of the earth,[110] so that wind would not blow on the earth, sea, or any tree. ²And I saw another messenger ascending from the sunrise, holding the seal of the living God, and he cried out with a loud voice to the four messengers to whom it was granted to damage the land and sea, ³"Do not damage the land, sea, or trees until we seal the servants of our God on their foreheads.[111] ⁴And I heard the number of those to be sealed, one hundred forty-four thousand, sealed from all the tribes of the sons of Israel: ⁵Twelve thousand sealed from the tribe of Judah, twelve thousand from the tribe of Reuben, twelve thousand from the tribe of Gad, ⁶twelve thousand from the tribe of Asher, twelve thousand from the tribe of Naphtali, twelve thousand from the tribe of Manasseh, ⁷twelve thousand from the tribe of Simeon, twelve thousand from the tribe of Levi, twelve thousand from the tribe of Issachar, ⁸twelve thousand from the tribe of Zabulon, twelve thousand from the tribe of Joseph, twelve thousand sealed from the tribe of Benjamin.[112]

---

109. "Complement": This is supplied to give the clause a subject, which is required in English.

110. "In Jewish tradition the winds that blew from the four angles or corners of an earth square in shape (as distinct from the winds that blew from the sides) were harmful"—W. Harrington, *Revelation*, 9.

111. Ezek 9:4: "And the Lord said to him, 'Go through the city, through Jerusalem, and put a mark upon the foreheads of the men who sigh and groan over all the abominations that are committed in it'" (RSV). In the Septuagint Greek "mark" is σημεῖον, "sign," rather than "seal." Ford, *Revelation*, 116–17, describes the practice in antiquity of branding or tattooing slaves, members of a military, and initiates into a cult.

112. The list of tribes is unique insofar as Levi, which was absorbed into the priesthood, with Joseph being divided into Ephraim and Manasseh to make the total twelve, is included along with the two substituting for Joseph. To make the total come to twelve, Dan is dropped—W. Harrington,

⁹After these things, I looked, and behold there was a great crowd that no one can number, from all nations, tribes, peoples, and languages, standing before the throne and before the lamb, dressed in white robes, and palm branches in their hands. ¹⁰And they called out with a loud voice, "Safety is in our God Who is seated on the throne, and in the lamb."[113] ¹¹And all the messengers stood around the throne, presbyters, and four live beings, and they fell on their faces before the throne and worshipped God, ¹²saying: "Amen! Praise, glory, wisdom, thanksgiving, honor, power, and strength are our God's forever and ever. Amen."

¹³And one of the presbyters responded to me, asking, "Who are those dressed in white robes and where did they come from?" ¹⁴And I said to him, "My lord, you know." And he said to me, "These are those coming from the great tribulation, and they washed their robes and whitened them in the blood of the lamb."

¹⁵For that reason they are before the throne of God,

    And they adore Him day and night in His temple,

    And the One seated on the throne shall dwell over them.[114]

¹⁶They shall not hunger any more or thirst any more,

    Nor will the sun beat down upon them,

    Nor any heat,

¹⁷Because the lamb that is at the center of the throne will shepherd them,

    And he will guide them to the spring of the waters of life;[115]

And God will wipe away every tear from their eyes.[116]

8 ¹And when he was opening the seventh seal, there was a quiet in heaven for about a half hour.[117] ²And I saw the seven messengers who stood before God, and they were given seven trumpets.[118]

---

*Revelation*, 98. "Perhaps Dan is omitted because of the tradition that the Antichrist would come from this tribe, as suggested in Irenaeus and Hippolytus. Both quote Jer 8:16 . . . and Hippolytus cites Deut 33:22 and Gen 49:17. . . . Nevertheless, the reason for omission from our list may be simply the idolatry of Dan as recorded in Judg 18:30 and 1 Kings 12:29"—Ford, *Revelation*, 118. W. Harrington, *Revelation*, 99, observes that there is no "rapture" for the elect in this vision.

113. "Safety," σωτηρία, also means "salvation," and the construction is literally "belongs to"; however both meanings are awkward in English. Some translations have "victory" belonging to God and the lamb.

114. "Over them"; this has the connotation of protecting them; see the RSV translation, and Ford, *Revelation*, 119.

115. Isa 49:10, "they shall not hunger or thirst, neither scorching wind nor sun shall smite them, for he who has pity on them will lead them, and by springs of water will guide them" (RSV).

116. Isa 25:8: ". . . and the Lord God will wipe away tears from all faces . . ." (RSV). Friesen, "Myth and Symbolic Resistance," notes that these verses are a paradoxical pastiche of salvation oracles.

117. Corresponding to the seventh day of creation, there would be rest, but it was not to last.

118. "Trumpets": i.e., ceremonial ram's horn trumpets, shofars.

³And another messenger came and stood at the altar holding a golden censer; much incense was given him so that he would give it for the prayers of all the saints at the golden altar which was before the throne. ⁴And the smoke from the incense wafted up with the prayers of the saints at the hand of the messenger before God. ⁵And the messenger had taken the censer, and he filled it with the fire of the altar and hurled it down onto the earth; and there were thunder, voices, lightning, and an earthquake.

⁶And the seven angels who had the seven trumpets readied them for sounding.

⁷And the first sounded a trumpet; and there were hail and fire mixed with blood, and that was cast upon the earth; and a third of the earth burned, and a third of the trees burned, and all the green grass burned.[119]

⁸And the second messenger sounded a trumpet; and something like a great burning mountain of fire was cast into the sea; and a third of the sea became blood, ⁹and a third of the live creatures that were in the sea died, and a third of the ships were destroyed.

¹⁰And a third messenger sounded a trumpet; and a great star fell from the sky, burning like a torch, and it fell on a third of the rivers and upon the springs of water. ¹¹And the name of the star was Wormwood.[120] And a third of the waters turned into wormwood, and many of the humans died from the water, because they were made bitter.

¹²And the fourth messenger sounded a trumpet; and a third of the sun was struck, a third of the moon, and a third of the stars, so that a third of them darkened, and the day did not show a third of itself, and similarly the night.

¹³And I looked, and I heard one vulture[121] as it flew in mid-sky, saying in a loud voice, "Woe, woe, woe on those dwelling upon the earth, because of the remaining trumpet sounds of the three messengers who are about to sound them.

9 ¹And the fifth messenger sounded a trumpet; and I saw a star fallen from heaven onto the earth, and the key to the shaft to the underworld was given him. ²And he opened the shaft to the underworld, and smoke rose up from the shaft like smoke from a great furnace, and the sun and the air were darkened by the smoke from the shaft. ³And locusts came out of the smoke onto the earth, and authority was given to them as the scorpions of the earth having authority. ⁴And it was said to them that they should not harm the grass of the earth or anything green or any tree, but rather the humans who did not have the forehead seal of God. ⁵And it was granted to them not to kill them, but to torture them for five months; and their torture was like the torture of a

---

119. W. Harrington, *Revelation*, 107, points out that the seven trumpets and their attendant disasters are modeled on the seven plagues of Egypt in Exod 7–10. A second set of such correspondences will occur in chapter 16.

120. Wormwood (Artemisia absinthiaca) has a bitter taste—W. Harrington, *Revelation*, 106.

121. "Vulture," ἀετοῦ, can also mean "eagle." The Roman military used the eagle as its symbol or standard.

scorpion when it stings a human. ⁶And in those days people will seek death and not find it, and they will long to die and death will flee from them.

⁷And the form of the locusts was like horses prepared for war, and on their heads gold-like crowns, and their faces were like the faces of humans, ⁸and they had hair like the hair of women,¹²² and their teeth were like those of lions. ⁹And they had chests like iron chests,¹²³ and the sound of their wings were like the sound of many chariot horses galloping into combat. ¹⁰And they have tails and stings like scorpions, and on their tails was their power to injure humans for five months. ¹¹They have the messenger of the underworld over them as emperor;¹²⁴ his Hebrew name is Abaddon and in Greek he has the name Apollyon.¹²⁵

¹²The first woe has passed. Behold two more woes are coming after it.

¹³And the sixth messenger sounded the trumpet: and I heard one voice from the four horns¹²⁶ of the golden altar that is before God, ¹⁴saying to the sixth messenger who had the trumpet, "Release the four messengers who have been bound at the great river Euphrates."¹²⁷ ¹⁵And the four messengers who had been prepared for the hour, day, month, and year were loosed so that they would kill a third of the humans. ¹⁶And the number of the cavalrymen was twice ten thousand times ten thousand: I heard their number. ¹⁷And in the same way I saw the horses on the mountain and those seated on them, wearing fiery red, dark blue, and sulfur-colored breastplates; and the horses' heads were like the heads of lions, and fire, smoke, and sulfur came out of their mouths. ¹⁸By these three plagues a third of the humans were destroyed, by the fire, smoke, and sulfur coming out of their mouths. ¹⁹For the power of the horses is in their mouths and on their tails; for their tails were like snakes, having heads and doing harm with them.

²⁰And the rest of the humans, who were not killed by these plagues but did not turn away from the works of their hands so that they would not be worshipping demons and gold, silver, brass, stone, and wooden idols, which cannot see, hear, or walk, ²¹and they did not turn away from their murders, their magic potions, their fornication, or their thievery.

---

122. W. Harrington, *Revelation*, 110, suggests that John may have had the long-haired Parthians in mind.

123. "Chests," θώρακας, could also mean "breastplates," but iron breastplates would not have been all that striking.

124. Or "king."

125. The Hebrew means "destruction" or the region of the dead; the Greek means "the destroyer." "There may be an intentional pun, if Domitian had affected the divine name Apollo"—W. Harrington, *Revelation*, 110.

126. "Horns": the raised corners of the altar—ibid., 112. Ford, *Revelation*, 145, points out that horns of the altar in the Temple in Jerusalem served as an asylum for criminals, but that in this verse "the voice releasing hostile forces comes from the very place where one would look for reconciliation and asylum."

127. W. Harrington, *Revelation*, 112, identifies the bound messengers, or angels, as an allusion to the myth of fallen angels. He notes that the Euphrates River marked the eastern frontier of the Roman Empire, and that the Romans had a paranoia over a Parthian threat from beyond the river.

10 ¹And I saw another powerful messenger descending from heaven, enveloped in a cloud, and a radiance was over his head, and his face was like the sun, and his feet were like fiery pillars, ²and he had in his hand a small book that was opened. And he placed his right foot on the sea, but his left on the land, ³and he cried out with a great voice the way a lion roars. And when he cried out, the seven thunders spoke in their own voices.[128] ⁴And when the seven thunders spoke, I was about to write. And I heard a voice from heaven saying, "Seal up what the seven thunders said, and do not write it."[129] ⁵And the messenger whom I saw standing on the sea and on the land raised his right hand to heaven ⁶and swore by the One Who lives forever and ever,[130] Who was creating heaven and what was in it and the earth and what was on it and the sea and what was in it, that time would no longer be, ⁷however,[131] in the days of the voice of the seventh messenger, when he would be about to sound the trumpet and the mystery of God would be accomplished, as he announced the good news to his servants the prophets.

⁸And the voice that I heard spoke with me from heaven again and was saying, "Get up and take the small scroll that is opened in the hand of the messenger who is standing on the sea and on the land. ⁹And I approached the messenger telling him to give the small scroll to me. And he says to me, "Take and eat it, and it will make your stomach sour, but in your mouth it will be as sweet as honey." ¹⁰And I took the small scroll from the hand of the messenger and ate it, and it was as sweet as honey in my mouth; and when I ate it, my stomach was made sour. ¹¹They say to me, "You must prophesy again to peoples nations, tongues, and many kingdoms."[132]

11 ¹And a reed like a staff was given to me, as it was said, "Rise and measure the sanctuary of God and the altar and those who are worshipping in it.[133] ²And exclude the courtyard that is outside the sanctuary and do not measure it, because it is given to the nations, and they shall tread upon the holy city

---

128. The voice of God—ibid., 115.

129. Dan 12:9: "He said, 'Go your way, Daniel, for the words are shut up and sealed until the time of the end'" (RSV).

130. Dan 12:7: "The man clothed in linen, who was above the waters of the stream, raised his right hand and his left hand toward heaven; and I heard him swear by him who lives for ever . . ." (RSV).

131. W. Harrington, *Revelation*, 117, points to the contrast with Dan 12:7: " . . . that it would be for a time, two times, and half a time . . . " (RSV).

132. Ezek 3:1–6a: "And he said to me, 'Son of man, eat what is offered to you; eat this scroll, and go, speak to the house of Israel.' So I opened my mouth, and he gave me the scroll to eat. And he said to me, 'Son of man, eat this scroll that I give you and fill your stomach with it.' Then I ate it; and it was in my mouth sweet as honey. And he said to me, 'Son of man, go, get you to the house of Israel, and you are not sent to a people of foreign speech and a hard language, but to the house of Israel—not to many peoples of foreign speech and a hard language, whose words you cannot understand" (RSV). The verse in *Revelation* stands in contrast to this last provision.

133. Ezek 40:3—48:35 similarly has a vision in which the visionary is given a measuring rod to measure dimensions in the Temple. In Zech 2.2, in a similar vision, a messenger or angel is going to take the measurements.

forty-two months."[134] ³And I will grant my two witnesses[135] power, and they will prophesy for the one thousand two hundred and sixty days, dressed in sackcloth. ⁴They are the two olive trees[136] and the two lamps that are standing before the Lord of the earth. ⁵And if anyone wishes to harm them, fire will come out from their mouth and consume their enemies. And if anyone should wish to harm them, so shall it be necessary to destroy such a person. ⁶They have the authority to shut heaven, so that the rain will not fall during the days of their prophecy,[137] and they have authority to turn the waters into blood and to strike the earth with every plague as often as they wish.[138] ⁷And when they complete their prophecy, the beast that came up from the underworld will make war with them, defeat them, and kill them. ⁸And their corpse will be on the wide roads of the great city, which is called allegorically "Sodom" and "Egypt," where also their Lord was crucified.[139] ⁹And people from the populaces, tribes, tongues, and nations see their corpse three and a half days, and they do not permit their corpses to be placed in a tomb. ¹⁰And those dwelling on the earth rejoice over them, make merry, and will send gifts to one another, because these two prophets tormented those dwelling upon the earth. ¹¹And after the three and a half days the breath of life from God entered them, and they stood up on their feet,[140] and a great fear fell upon those watching them. ¹²And they heard a great voice from heaven saying to them, "Come up here." And they went up into heaven in a cloud, and their enemies watched them. ¹³And at that hour there was a great earthquake, and a tenth of the city fell, and seven thousand were killed individually in the earthquake, and the rest became terrified and gave glory to the God of heaven.

¹⁴The second woe passed; behold, the third woe is coming quickly.

¹⁵And the seventh messenger sounded the trumpet; and there were loud voices in heaven saying, "The kingdom of the world became our Lord's and his Messiah's, and he will rule for ever and ever." ¹⁶And the twenty-four presbyters

---

134. Forty-two months: such temporal limits are set against the Roman mythology of an eternal empire; John uses a similar stratagem at 12:6 and 13:5—Friesen, "Myth and Symbolic Resistance." W. Harrington, *Revelation*, 119, sees the 42 months as "nothing else than the 'time, two times and half a time' of Dan 7:25, that is, three and a half years, the approximate duration of the persecution of Antiochus IV, and hence a symbol of a time of trial...."

135. The two witnesses are Elijah and Moses, who in apocalyptic imagery were to usher in the eschatological age—W. Harrington, *Revelation*, 121.

136. Zech 4:3 has two olive trees in a vision; in 4.14 they are identified as "the two anointed who stand by the Lord of the whole earth" (RSV). Ford, *Revelation*, 171, observes that the phrase "stand before the Lord" is something often said of prophets.

137. Allusion to Elijah: 1 Kgs 17:1—W. Harrington, *Revelation*, 121.

138. W. Harrington, *Revelation*, 121, identifies this as an allusion to Moses in Egypt: Exod 7:14–25.

139. See Isa 1:8–10, where Jerusalem (daughter of Zion) is said to have been like Sodom. The "great city" is obviously Rome, and the place where the Lord was crucified is obviously Jerusalem. John is seemingly making the two cities morally equivalent.

140. Ezek 37:10: "So I prophesied as he commanded me, and the breath came into them, and they lived, and stood upon their feet..." (RSV).

who are seated on their thrones before God fell on their faces and worshiped God, ¹⁷saying:

> We give thanks to you, Lord God almighty,
>   Who is and Who was,
> Because You have accepted Your great power,
>   And You will rule;
> ¹⁸And the nations raged,
>   And Your anger came, as well as the time for the dead to be judged,
> And the reward to be given to Your servants the prophets
>   And to Your saints and those who fear Your name,
> Small and great (to be judged),
>   And for those destroying the earth to be destroyed.

¹⁹And in heaven the sanctuary of God opened, and the ark of his covenant[141] appeared in His sanctuary; and there was lightning, voices, thunder, an earthquake, and a great hail.

12 ¹And a great sign appeared in heaven, a woman[142] robed in sun and the moon under her feet, and on her head a crown of twelve stars, ²and she was having a child, and she cries out having birth-pains and in labor.[143] ³And another sign appeared in heaven, and behold there was a great fiery-red dragon,[144] having seven heads and ten horns, and seven crowns on its heads, ⁴and its tail swept away a third of the stars of heaven and cast them onto the earth.[145] And the dragon stood before the woman who was about to give birth, so that when she gives birth to her child it would devour it.[146] ⁵And she gave birth to a son, a male, who was about to shepherd all the nations with an iron rod; and her child was snatched up to God and to His throne. ⁶And the

---

141. The Ark of the Covenant disappeared centuries beforehand; it does not appear in Ezekiel's Temple—Ford, *Revelation*, 172; hence this is a reappearance.

142. "The woman is surely the bride, the heavenly Jerusalem (19:7–8; 21:9–10), antithesis of the harlot (Rome) (17:14; 18:16)"—W. Harrington, *Revelation*, 128. Harrington goes on to note that a mother goddess, queen of heaven, was worshiped in the cities of Asia and that John may be presenting this image by way of contrast.

143. The passage reflects the curse in Gen 3:15–20 concerning pain in childbirth—Minear, "Far as the Curse is Found."

144. John is using Leviathan imagery—Friesen, "Myth and Symbolic Resistance."

145. W. Harrington, *Revelation*, 128, notes a parallel with Dan 8:10, which refers to Antiochus IV as a little horn that "grew great, even to the host of heaven; and some of the host of the stars it cast down to the ground, and trampled upon them" (RSV).

146. The passage reflects the curse in Gen 3:15–20 concerning enmity between the woman's seed and the serpent's. The "birth" is not the Nativity of Christ but the Crucifixion—Minear, "Far as the Curse is Found."

woman fled into the wilderness,[147] where she had a place prepared by God so that they would sustain her twelve hundred and sixty days.

⁷And there was a war in heaven, Michael[148] and his messengers fighting against the dragon. And the dragon and his messengers were fighting ⁸and were not strong enough, nor was room for them found in heaven any more. ⁹And the great dragon was cast out, the ancient serpent called Devil and Satan, who misleads the whole world—he was cast out into the world, and his messengers with him were cast out. ¹⁰And I heard a loud voice in heaven saying:

> Just now has salvation and power come about,
> > The kingdom of our God,
> > And the authority of our Messiah,
> Because the accuser of our brothers and sisters is driven out,
> > Who accused them before our God day and night.
>
> ¹¹And they were victorious over him with the blood of the lamb,
> > And with the word of their testimony,
> > And they did not love their life at the time of death.
>
> ¹²Therefore rejoice, you heavens,
> > And you pitching dwelling in them;
> Woe to you earth and sea,
> > Because the devil is cast upon you,
> Having great anger,
> > Knowing that he has little time.

¹³And when the dragon saw that he had been cast upon the earth, he pursued the woman who gave birth to the male child. ¹⁴And the two wings of the great eagle[149] were given to the woman, so that she would fly to the wilderness, to her place, where she is being nourished for a time and times and half a time,[150] away from the face of the serpent. ¹⁵And the serpent spewed water

---

147. The destination of the woman parallels Mic 4:10, only to contrast its final words: "Writhe and groan, O daughter of Zion, like a woman in travail; for now you shall go forth from the city and dwell in the open country; you shall go to Babylon" (RSV).

148. Dan 11:21: "There is none who contends by my side against these except Michael, your prince" (RSV). Dan 12:1–2: "At that time shall arise Michael, the great prince who has charge of your people. And there shall be a time of trouble, such as never has been since there was a nation till that time; but at that time your people shall be delivered, every one whose name shall be found written in the book. And many of those who sleep in the dust of the earth shall awake, some to everlasting life, and some to shame and everlasting contempt" (RSV).

149. W. Harrington, *Revelation*, 135, cites Isa 40:31: "But they who wait for the Lord shall renew their strength, they shall mount up with wings like eagles . . ." (RSV), as well as Exod 19:4 and Deut 32:11.

150. Allusion to Dan 7:25, where it says a king who speaks words against the Most High and wears out the saints will subdue other kings for a time, two times, and half a time. Similar phraseology appears in Dan 12:7.

like a river from its mouth after the woman so that she would be swept away. ¹⁶And the earth came to the aid of the woman, and the earth opened its mouth and swallowed the river that the dragon spewed out of its mouth.[151] ¹⁷And the dragon was angry with the woman and left to make war against the rest of her offspring, which were keeping the commandments of God and keeping the witness of Jesus. ¹⁸And he stood at the shore of the sea.

13 ¹And I saw a beast coming up from the sea, having ten horns[152] and seven heads, and its horns ten crowns, and on its heads names of blasphemy.[153] ²And the beast that I saw was like a leopard, and its feet like a bear's, and its mouth like a lion's mouth.[154] And the dragon gave it its power, its throne, and great authority.[155] ³And one of its heads looks like it is mortally wounded, and its mortal wound healed.[156] And the whole earth was amazed by the beast, ⁴and they worshiped the dragon that gave authority to the beast, and they worshiped the beast, saying, "Who is like the beast?" and "Who can make war against it?"[157]

⁵And its mouth was allowed to speak great things[158] and blasphemies, and authority was given to it to act for forty-two months. ⁶And it opened its mouth in blasphemies against God,[159] to blaspheme His name and His dwelling, those dwelling in heaven.[160] ⁷And it was allowed to make war against the saints[161] and be victorious over them, and it was given authority over every tribe, people, tongue, and nation. ⁸And all those dwelling on the earth,[162]

---

151. These verses reverse the serpent's deceptive speech in Gen 3:1–5 and the curse on Cain, making the earth a haven rather than a place to wander aimlessly—Gen 4:10–22. See Minear, "Far as the Curse is Found."

152. The fourth, most terrible, beast described in Dan 7:7 had ten horns.

153. Each head is obviously an emperor making a claim to divinity. In the Introduction above, I have discussed the seven heads in terms of assigning an approximate date of composition to *Revelation*. John wanted seven heads, and hence found it convenient to begin counting from Nero rather than Julius Caesar or Caesar Augustus, to correspond to the total number of heads of the four beasts in Dan 7; the blasphemous names correspond to the arrogant speech of the fourth beast in Dan 7:8, 11, 20—Friesen, "Myth and Symbolic Resistance." In the verses that follow, John will be making numerous allusions to the seventh chapter of Daniel.

154. The first three beasts described in Dan 7:4–6 looked like, respectively, a lion, a bear, and a leopard.

155. This would be the Roman state, led by the Senate, turning the real power over to the imperial household of the Caesars.

156. This would be Nero, rumored to have survived and threatening to invade with a Parthian army. W. Harrington, *Revelation*, 138, sees this also as a parody of the lamb that was slain (Rev 5:6).

157. John agreed with Roman mythology of an empire based on military victory, but he made the monster a source of danger rather than a Pax Romana—Friesen, "Myth and Symbolic Resistance."

158. Dan 7:8: "... a mouth speaking great things" (RSV).

159. Dan 7:25 refers to words against the Most High.

160. The saints in heaven composed the Temple of the Lord.

161. Dan 7:21 refers to making war with the saints and prevailing over them.

162. Ford, *Revelation*, 212, points to the contrast between those who dwell in heaven in verse 6 and those who dwell on the earth in verse 8.

whose name was not written in the book of life of the lamb slain from the foundation of the world, will worship it.

⁹If anyone has ears, listen.

¹⁰If anyone is to go into captivity, that one goes into captivity.

If anyone is to be slain by sword, by sword is that one to be slain.

Here is the perseverance and the faith of the saints.[163]

¹¹And I saw another beast coming up out of the earth, and it had two horns like a lamb's, and it spoke like a dragon. ¹²And it acts with all the authority of the first beast in its presence. And it makes the earth and all dwelling on it worship the first beast,[164] whose mortal wound was cured. ¹³And it is performing great signs, so that it even made fire come down from heaven to the earth in the presence of humans. ¹⁴And it is misleading those dwelling upon the earth through the signs which were given it to do before the beast, saying to those dwelling on the earth to make an image to the beast that has the sword wound and lived. ¹⁵And it was allowed[165] to give breath to the image of the beast so that the image of the beast would even speak[166] and have whoever did not worship the image of the beast be killed. ¹⁶And it had all people—the small and the great, the rich and the poor, and the free and the slave—be given a mark on their right hand or forehead,[167] ¹⁷so that no one can even buy or sell except one having the mark, the name of the beast or number of its name.[168]

¹⁸Wisdom is here: let one having knowledge calculate the number of the beast, for the number of a human: and his number is six hundred sixty-six.[169]

14 ¹And I looked, and behold the lamb was standing on Mount Zion, and with it a hundred and forty-four thousand who had his name and the name of his Father written on their foreheads. ²And I heard a sound from heaven like the sound of many waters and the sound of great thunder claps, and the sound I heard was like harpists playing their harps. ³And they are singing as if a new

---

163. This parallels Jer 15:2: "Those who are for pestilence, to pestilence, and those who are for the sword, to the sword; those who are for famine, to famine, and those who are for captivity, to captivity" (RSV).

164. In Asia, cultic officials required that religious honors be addressed to the emperor—W. Harrington, *Revelation*, 143.

165. "Mysteriously, even the beast operates within a divine plan; God is wholly sovereign"—ibid.

166. "Speaking statues were engineered in various ways, e.g., by hiding somebody in a hollow statue or by use of ventriloquism"—ibid.

167. According to Ford, *Revelation*, 215, branding appears on defeated populations, slaves, and soldiers.

168. Rather than an imperial cornucopia, the beast limited who could benefit from commerce—Friesen, "Myth and Symbolic Resistance." It seems that at least in Pergamum (Rev 2:13–16) Christian artisans who wished to earn a livelihood had to join pagan guilds. Moreover, the coins in use bore the image, name, and insignia of the emperor—W. Harrington, *Revelation*, 143–44.

169. "It is reasonable to believe that the emperor is Nero, much in mind throughout Revelation. It is scarcely coincidental that the Greek *Nerōn Kaisar*, transliterated into Hebrew script (*nrwn qsr*), gives 666. It is noteworthy that the Latin form *Nero Caesar* (in Hebrew script *nrw qsr*) gives 616, which occurs as a variant reading"—ibid., *Revelation*, 144.

song before the throne, before the four live beings and the presbyters; and no one could learn the song but the hundred and forty-four thousand, who were purchased from the earth. ⁴These are those who were not defiled with women, for they are chaste.[170] These are those who follow the lamb wherever he goes. They were purchased from humans as the first-fruit for God and the lamb, ⁵and falsehood is not found in their mouth. They are unblemished.[171]

⁶And I saw another messenger flying in mid heaven, holding eternal good news to announce to those dwelling on the earth and to every nation, tribe, tongue, and people, ⁷saying in a loud voice, "Fear God and give Him glory, because the hour for His judgment has come, and bow down to the One who made heaven, earth, sea, and springs of waters."

⁸And a second other messenger followed, saying, "She fell, the great Babylon fell,[172] who made all the nations drink from the wine of the wrath of her fornication."

⁹And a third other messenger followed them, saying in a loud voice, "If anyone worships the beast and its image, and accepts the mark on the forehead or on the hand, ¹⁰that one will also drink from the wine of God's wrath, which has been poured undiluted in the cup of His anger, and will be tormented by fire and sulfur before the holy messengers and before the lamb. ¹¹And the smoke from their torment will rise forever and ever, and those worshiping the beast and its image will have no rest day and night—also if anyone accepts the mark of its name. ¹²Hence is the persistence of the saints, those keeping the commandments of God and the faith of Jesus."

¹³And I heard a voice from heaven saying, "Write this: 'Blessed are the dead who died in the Lord from now on. Yes, says the spirit, so that they shall rest from their labors; for their works accompany them.'"

¹⁴And I looked, and behold there was a white cloud, and sitting on the cloud was one like a son of humanity, having on his head a golden crown and in his hand a sharp sickle. ¹⁵And another messenger came out from the sanctuary, crying out in a loud voice to the one sitting on the cloud, "Use your sickle and reap, for the hour for reaping has come, for the harvest of the earth has become ripe."[173] ¹⁶And the one sitting on the cloud cast his sickle on the earth, and the earth was harvested.

¹⁷And another messenger came out from the sanctuary which is in heaven, also having a sharp sickle. ¹⁸And there was another messenger from

---

170. W. Harrington, *Revelation*, 146–47, and Ford, *Revelation*, 234–35, present several interpretations: 1) The 144,000 comprise an army of heaven in a holy war, in which soldiers preserve ceremonial chastity, in the manner of David's forces in 1 Sam 21:5. 2) The 144,000 comprise a priesthood that abstained from sexual relations for liturgical purposes—Exod 19:15; 1 Sam 21:4. 3) The sexual relations are taken metaphorically to refer to idolatry.

171. "Unblemished," ἄμωμοί, is a Levitical term meaning "flawless" and hence fit as a sacrifice—W. Harrington, *Revelation*, 147; Ford, *Revelation*, 235.

172. Referring to Rome, John cites Isa 21:9, which exclaims that Babylon has fallen.

173. Joel 3:13: "Put in the sickle, for the harvest is ripe. Go in, tread, for the winepress is full" (RSV).

the altar, having authority over the fire, and it called out with a loud voice of the one having the sharp sickle, saying, "Use your sharp sickle and gather in the bunches of the grapevines of the earth, for its clusters are ripe." ¹⁹And the messenger cast its sickle onto the earth and gathered in the grape vines of the earth and cast them into the great wine press of the wrath of God. ²⁰And the winepress was tread outside the city, and blood came out from the winepress up to the bridles of the horses, sixteen hundred stadia[174] away.

15 ¹And I saw another great and amazing sign in heaven: seven messengers having seven final plagues, for the wrath of God was completed with them.

²And I saw something like a glassy sea mixed with fire,[175] and standing on the glassy sea were those who were victorious over the beast, over its image, and over the number of its name; they were holding harps of God. ³And they are singing the song of Moses[176] the servant of God, and the song of the lamb, saying:

> Great and wondrous are your works,
> > Lord, God, almighty;
> Just and truthful are your ways,
> > King of the nations.
> ⁴Who would not fear you, Lord,
> > And glorify your name?
> For you alone are holy,
> > For all nations shall come
> > And worship before you.
> For your just deeds appeared.[177]

⁵And after these I looked, and the sanctuary of the tent of testimony appeared in heaven, ⁶and the seven messengers who were holding the seven plagues came out from the sanctuary, wearing clean, glowing linen and with golden belts round their chests. ⁷And one of the four live beings gave the seven messengers seven golden bowls full of the wrath of God, Who lives forever and ever. ⁸And the sanctuary was filled with smoke[178] from God's glory and power, and no one could enter into the sanctuary until the seven plagues of the seven messengers would end.

16 ¹And I heard a loud voice from the sanctuary saying to the seven messengers, "Go and pour out the seven bowls of the wrath of God onto the earth."

---

174. "Outside the city" was the place of the crucifixion of Jesus. 1,600 stadia would be about 200 miles—W. Harrington, *Revelation* 156.

175. Ford, *Revelation*, 253, calls this "heavenly fire"; she cites Ezek 1:4, 13, 27.

176. Exod 15:1b–18.

177. W. Harrington, *Revelation*, 159, describes the canticle as a "mosaic of Old Testament phrases."

178. Smoke or a cloud appears in theophanies: Exod 40:35; Isa 6:4, Ezek 10:4—ibid., 161.

²And the first one came and poured out its bowl onto the earth; and there was a harmful and evil wound[179] on the people who had the mark of the beast and who worshiped its image.

³And the second poured out its bowl on the sea; and it became blood[180] like death, and every breath of life that was in the sea died.

⁴And the third poured out its bowl onto the rivers and springs of the waters; and it became blood.[181] ⁵And I heard the messenger of the waters saying,

> You are just, O Holy One Who is and Who was,
> > For You passed judgment on these,
> ⁶For they shed the blood of saints and prophets,
> > And You gave blood to them to drink;
> They deserve it.

⁷And I heard the altar speaking:

> Yes, Lord God Almighty,
> > Your judgments are trustworthy and just.

⁸And the fourth poured out its bowl upon the sun; and it was allowed to burn the people with fire. ⁹And the people were burned by an intense heat, and they blasphemed the name of God, who had authority over these plagues, and they did not repent to give Him glory.

¹⁰And the fifth poured out its bowl on the throne of the beast.[182] And its kingdom darkened;[183] they bit their tongues out of distress, ¹¹and they blasphemed the God of heaven from their distress and from their wounds,[184] and they did not repent of their deeds.

¹²And the sixth poured out its bowl upon the great Euphrates River; and its water dried up, so that the way of the kings from the rising sun was prepared.[185] ¹³And I saw three unclean spirits leaping[186] like frogs[187] out of the

---

179. This may be intended to correspond to the sixth plague in Egypt in Exod 9:10.

180. This may correspond to the first plague in Egypt in Exod 7:17–21.

181. This is a second correlate of the first plague in Egypt, in Exod 7:19–24. The lack of agreement between the singular verb and the plural subject led to variations in several important manuscript witnesses—Metzger, *Textual Commentary*, 755.

182. W. Harrington, *Revelation*, 165, notes the throne of the beast is Rome.

183. This may correspond to the ninth plague in Egypt in Exod 10:21.

184. These would be the wounds mentioned in Rev 16:2.

185. This is another allusion to a Parthian invasion—W. Harrington, *Revelation*, 166. Ford, *Revelation*, 263, cites Herodotus, *Histories*, 1:191, who reports that Cyrus walked across the drained bed of the Euphrates as he went to conquer Babylon; there is an allusion to this in Isa 44:27–28.

186. "Leaping": There is no verb here; "leaping" is implied.

187. W. Harrington, *Revelation*, 166, sees these as analogous to the locusts in Rev 9:1–11. John

mouth of the dragon, out of the mouth of the beast, and out of the mouth of the false prophets; ¹⁴for they are spirits of demons making signs, who go out upon the kings of the whole world to assemble them to the war of the great day of God almighty.¹⁸⁸ ¹⁵"Behold I am coming like a thief."¹⁸⁹ Blessed are they keeping vigil and keeping their garments so that they will not be walking naked and others seeing their embarrassment.¹⁹⁰ ¹⁶And it assembled them in the place that in Hebrew is called "Armageddon."¹⁹¹

¹⁷And the seventh poured out his bowl on the air; and a loud voice came out of the sanctuary from the throne, saying, "It is done." ¹⁸And there were lightning flashes, sounds, and thunder, and there was a great earthquake unlike what had occurred since humanity came upon the earth, so great a quake was it. ¹⁹The great city was in three parts, and the cities of the nations fell. And Babylon¹⁹² the great was remembered before God to give her the cup of the wine of the wrath of his anger. ²⁰And every island fled, and mountains were not found. ²¹And great hail stones weighing about a talent¹⁹³ fell down from heaven onto the people. And the people blasphemed God from the plague of the hail, because a plague of such is an exceedingly great one.

17 ¹And one of the seven messengers who were holding the seven bowls came and was speaking with me, saying, "Come, I will show you the verdict on the great harlot who sits over many waters,¹⁹⁴ ²with whom the kings of the earth fornicated and those dwelling on the earth became drunk on the wine of her fornication. ³And it brought me in spirit to a wilderness. And I saw a woman¹⁹⁵ sitting on a red beast, it being full of names of blasphemy and having seven heads and ten horns. ⁴And the woman was clothed in purple and red,¹⁹⁶ and adorned with purple, precious gems, and pearls, and she was holding a golden cup in her hand full of abominations and the unclean things

---

may have intended this plague to correspond to that narrated in Exod 8.

188. The "great day" of the Lord is language found in Joel 2—W. Harrington, *Revelation*, 166.

189. See 1 Thess 5:2, Matt 24:42, and Luke 12:39–40. John's allusion is to an early Christian saying.

190. The first clause is in the singular in the Greek, only the second in the plural. While the Greek uses the contrast between singular and plural to designate the difference in parties referred to, I introduce "others" and put the first clause into the plural to avoid the English pronoun problem. Harrington, *Revelation*, 166, relates this verse to the admonition to the Church at Laodicea to buy from the Lord "white garments to put on to cover the same of your nakedness"—Rev 3:18. Ford, *Revelation*, 163, however, prefers an explanation from John Lightfoot: The officer on duty at the Temple was to see that the guards kept awake. If they were asleep he was to beat them, and if they were asleep a second time he was to burn their clothes.

191. A plain in Palestine that was the site of many battles and disasters.

192. The great city, Babylon the Great, refers to Rome—W. Harrington, *Revelation*, 168.

193. Nearly 94 pounds each. The seventh plague in Egypt in Exod 9:24-25 consisted of hail and lightning.

194. What the waters are is explained in verse 15, below.

195. This woman stands in contrast to the one described in Chapter 12—W. Harrington, *Revelation*, 171.

196. Imperial colors.

of her harlotry,[197] ⁵and on her forehead had been written a name, with hidden meaning: "Babylon the great, mother of harlots and of the abominations of the earth." ⁶And I saw the woman drunken from the blood of the saints and from the blood of the martyrs of Jesus. And seeing her I wondered a great deal.

⁷And a messenger said to me, "Why are you surprised? I will tell you the secret of the woman and the beast which is carrying her and has seven heads and ten horns: ⁸The beast that you see was and is not, and is about to come up from the abyss, and it is going off into extinction. And those dwelling on the earth, whose names since the creation of the cosmos have not been written in the book of life, will be amazed to see the beast, because it was and is not and will be back. ⁹Here let the mind have wisdom: The seven heads are seven hills on which the woman is seated. They are also seven kings: ¹⁰Five have fallen, one is, another is not yet come, and when he comes he must remain a little. ¹¹And the beast which was and is not, is also an eighth and one of the seven,[198] and he is going into extinction. ¹²And the ten horns that you saw are ten kings who did not yet receive a kingdom, but for an hour they are receiving authority like kings with the beast.[199] ¹³These have a single purpose, and they will give their power and authority to the beast. ¹⁴They will make war against the lamb, and the lamb will defeat them, for the Lord of Lords is also King of Kings, and those with him are called, chosen, and faithful."

¹⁵And he says to me, "The waters that you saw, where the harlot sits, are peoples, crowds, nations, and tongues. ¹⁶And the ten horns that you saw and the beast, these will detest the harlot, and will make her depopulated and will eat her flesh and will consume her in fire; ¹⁷for God gave it to their hearts to effect His purpose and to serve one purpose and give their kingdom to the beast, until the words of God are fulfilled. ¹⁸And the woman whom you saw is the great city that has sovereignty over the kingdoms of the earth."

18 ¹After these things, I saw another messenger descending from heaven possessing great authority, and the earth was illuminated by its glory. ²And it called out in a powerful voice, saying:

> Babylon the great was falling, was falling,[200]
>> And became the dwelling place of demons
> And prison of every unclean spirit
>> And cage of every unclean bird
>>> And pen of every unclean and detested beast[201]

---

197. All these are terms routinely used of idolatry.

198. Nero all over again.

199. One can only speculate who these are. W. Harrington, *Revelation*, 172, understands them to be future emperors. I would suggest they are puppet kings in the empire.

200. Isa 21:9: "Fallen, fallen is Babylon . . ." (RSV).

201. "Prison," "cage," and "pen": All three words translate the same Greek word, φυλακὴ. Strangely,

³Becasuse all the nations have drunk from the wine of the wrath of her harlotry:

> Both the kings of the earth fornicated with her
>
> And the merchants of the earth became rich from the strength of her luxury.

⁴And I heard another voice from heaven saying:

> Come out from her,²⁰² my people,
>> Lest you share in her sins,
>
> And from her plagues,
>> Lest you get them;
>
> ⁵For her sins were heaped up to the sky
>> And God remembered her injustices.
>
> ⁶Render to her as she rendered,²⁰³
>> And pay back double according to her works.
>
> In the cup in which she mixed,
>
> Mix twice over for her:
>
> ⁷As much as she glorified herself and luxuriated,
>> Give her as much torment and sorrow.
>
> For she says in her heart,
>
> "I sit as queen,
>
> And I am not a widow,
>
> And I will know no sorrow."²⁰⁴
>
> ⁸Therefore one day the plagues will possess her,
>> Death, sorrow, and famine,
>
> And she will be consumed by fire,
>> For the Lord God who is judging her is powerful.²⁰⁵

⁹And the kings of the earth who fornicated with her and lived in luxury will weep and mourn over her when they see the smoke from her fire. ¹⁰Standing far off out of fear of her torment. They will be saying:

---

RSV has "dwelling place," "haunt," and "haunt." *Das neue Testament* has "demons dwelling in her and she is a nesting place for evil spirits and repulsive, fatal, winged beasts."

202. This resembles Isa 52:11, among other texts.
203. See Jer 50:29.
204. See Isa 47:7–8.
205. See Jer 50:34.

> Woe, woe to you, great city,
>
>> Babylon, powerful city,
>
> For your judgment came in one hour.

¹¹And the merchants of the earth weep and grieve over her, because no one buys their cargo any more, ¹²a cargo of gold, silver, precious stone, pearls, fine linen, purple, silk, scarlet cloth, every citron wood,[206] every ivory object, every object of precious wood, copper, iron, and marble, ¹³or buys[207] cinnamon, amomum,[208] incense, myrrh, frankincense, wine, oil, fine flour, wheat, cattle, and sheep; a cargo of[209] horses, carriages, and bodies; or buys[210] the life of humans.

> ¹⁴And your fruit of the soul's longing is gone from you,
>
> And all costly and glistening things are lost to you,
>
> They will never again find them.

¹⁵The merchants of these things, who were enriched by her, will stand off afar out of fear of her torment, weeping and grieving, ¹⁶saying:

> Woe, woe, to the great city,
>
> Robed in linen, purple, and scarlet,
>
> And adorned with gold, precious stone, and pearl,

¹⁷because in one hour such wealth was taken away. And every sea-captain, everyone who sails somewhere, sailors, and those who work the sea stood from a distance, ¹⁸and they cried out when they saw the smoke from her fire. They were saying, "What city was like the great city?" ¹⁹And they threw dust on their heads[211] and were crying out, weeping and grieving, saying,

> Woe, woe to the great city,
>
>> All those owning ships grew rich from her,
>>
>> From her costly things on the sea,

---

206. "Citron wood," ξύλον θύϊνον: According to Ford, *Revelation*, 299, a tree that grew in North Africa and was used for making costly tables. It had grain that looked variously like peacock eyes, tiger stripes, or panther spots.

207. "Or buys": This is supplied because the list of items changes from genitives that are dependent on "cargo" to accusatives, thereby establishing a series beginning with "cargo" and continuing with other nouns.

208. An Indian spice plant—Arndt and Gingrich, *Greek-English Lexicon*, 47, article on ἄμωμον.

209. "A cargo of": This is supplied because the list of items reverts to the genitive case.

210. "Or buys": This is supplied because the final item is in the accusative case.

211. Ezek 27:29–31: "The mariners and all the pilots of the sea stand on the shore and wail aloud over you, and cry bitterly. They cast dust on their heads and wallow in ashes; they make themselves bald for you, and gird themselves with sackcloth, and they weep over you in bitterness of soul, with bitter mourning" (RSV).

because in one hour it was taken away. ²⁰Rejoice over her, heaven, saints, apostles, and prophets, because God rendered a verdict against her for you. ²¹And one mighty messenger lifted a stone that was like a huge millstone and cast it into the sea, saying:

> Thus Babylon the great city
>> Will be thrown down with violence
>> And not be found any more.
> ²²And the sound of lyre players and musicians,
>> Flute players and trumpeters
>> Will not be heard in you anymore,
> And no artisan of any trade
>> Will be found in you anymore,
> And the sound of the mill
>> Will not be heard in you anymore,[212]
> ²³And the light of the lamp
>> Will not shine in you anymore,
> And the voice of bridegroom and bride
>> Will not be heard in you anymore;
> Because your merchants were the big shots of the world,
>> Because all the nations were misled by your sorcery,
> ²⁴And on her was found the blood of the prophets and saints,
>> And of all the butchered ones on the earth.

19 ¹After these things, I heard something like a loud voice of a great crowd in heaven, saying:

> Alleluia!
> Salvation, glory, and power be our God's,
>> ²Because His judgments are trustworthy and just;
> For He condemned the great harlot,
>> Who corrupted the earth with her harlotry,
> And He avenged His servants' blood
>> Which was on her hands.

³And again they proclaimed:

---

212. W. Harrington, *Revelation*, 183, cites Jer 25:10: "Moreover, I will banish from them the voice of mirth and the voice of gladness, the voice of the bridegroom and the voice of the bride, the grinding of the millstones and the light of the lamp" (RSV).

Alleluia!

Her smoke rises forever and ever.

⁴And the twenty-four presbyters and four live beings fell and worshiped God, Who was seated on the throne. They were saying: "Amen! Alleluia!" ⁵And a voice came out from the throne, saying:

Praise our God,
> All you His servants

And those who hear Him,
> The small and the great.

⁶And I heard something like the sound of a great crowd, the sound of many waters, and the sound of mighty thunder, saying:

Alleluia,

For the Lord, our God almighty,
> Has begun to reign.

⁷Let us rejoice and be glad,[213]
> And let us give Him glory,

For the wedding of the lamb came
> And his bride readied herself;

⁸And it is granted to her to be robed
> With shining and clean linen,

For the linen is the saints' just deeds.

⁹And the messenger[214] says to me, "Write, Blessed are they who have been called to the wedding banquet of the lamb." And it says to me, "These words of God are genuine." ¹⁰And I fell before his feet to worship it. And it says to me, "Do not do that; I am a fellow servant of you and of your brothers and sisters who hold the testimony of Jesus; worship God. For the witness of Jesus is the spirit of prophecy."

¹¹And I saw heaven opened, and behold a white horse, and seated on it one who was called faithful and trustworthy, and he judges and makes war by means of justice. ¹²And his eyes are like flames of fire, and on his head are many crowns; he had a name that had been written, which no one but he knew, ¹³and he wore a cloak that had been dipped in blood, and he has been called[215] "Word

---

213. Fekkes, "His Bride Has Prepared," notes that this and the subsequent bridal passage depend on Isa 61:10 and 54:11–12.

214. The verb has no expressed subject; "the messenger" is supplied.

215. "He has been called": literally, "his name has been called. . . ."

of God." ¹⁴And the armies of heaven, clothed in clean linen, followed him on white horses. ¹⁵And a sharp sword came out from his mouth, so that he would trample the nations with it, and it will be he who tends them with an iron rod; and he will tread the winepress of God almighty's wrath and anger.²¹⁶ ¹⁶And he had the name written on his cloak at the thigh,²¹⁷ "King of Kings and Lord of Lords."

¹⁷And I saw one messenger standing in the sun, and it was calling out in a loud voice, saying to all the birds flying in the middle of the sky, "Come, gather at the great feast of God,²¹⁸ ¹⁸so that you may eat the flesh of kings, the flesh of military tribunes, the flesh of the mighty, the flesh of horses and those seated on them, and the flesh of all the free and slaves, and of the small and the great." ¹⁹And I saw the beast and the kings of the earth and their armies assembled to make war against the one seated upon the horse and against his army. ²⁰And the beast was seized, and with it the false prophet who made signs before it by which he mislead those who accepted the mark of the beast and those who worshiped its image; the two were thrown alive into the lake of fire which burned in sulfur. ²¹And the remainder were slain by the sword of the one sitting upon the horse, the sword that came out of his mouth, and all the birds were fed with their flesh.

20 ¹And I saw a messenger descending from heaven, holding the key to the abyss and a great chain in his hand. ²And it seized the dragon, that ancient serpent, who is Devil and Satan, and it chained him for a thousand years, ³and it cast him into the abyss,²¹⁹ locked and sealed it over him so that he would not mislead the nations until a thousand years would be completed; after that it is necessary to let him loose for a little while.

⁴And I saw thrones,²²⁰ and on them sat those to whom judging was assigned, and I saw²²¹ the souls of those who had been beheaded on account of their witness about Jesus and on account of the word of God, and who neither worshiped the beast or its image and did not accept the mark on the forehead and on their hand; and they lived and ruled with the Messiah a thousand years. ⁵The rest of the dead did not live until the thousand years would be fulfilled. This is the first resurrection. ⁶Blessed and holy is one who has a share in this first

---

216. Isa 63:2–3: "Why is thy apparel red and thy garments like his that treads in the wine press? 'I have trodden the winepress alone, and from the peoples no one was with me; I trod them in my anger and trampled them in my wrath; their lifeblood is sprinkled upon my garments, and I have stained all my raiment'" (RSV).

217. "Cloak at the thigh": literally, "on the cloak and on his thigh."

218. This "forms a terrifying contrast to the divine banquet intimated in 3:20 . . . "—Ford, *Revelation*, 315.

219. "The abyss is the prison of demonic spirits before their final relegation to the 'lake of fire'"—W. Harrington, *Revelation*, 196.

220. The scene appears to be based on Dan 7:9–27.

221. "I saw": The repetition of "I saw" is supplied to clarify the grammatical structure of the verse.

resurrection. The second death has no power over them, but they will be priests of God and of the Messiah, and they shall rule with him for the millennium.

⁷And when the thousand years are fulfilled, Satan will be released from his prison, ⁸and he will set out to mislead the nations in the four corners of the earth, the nations of Gog and Magog,²²² to array them for war; their number will be as the sand of the sea. ⁹And they ascended to the open space of the earth and encircled the camp of the saints and the beloved city. And fire descended from heaven and consumed them; ¹⁰And the devil, who misleads them, was cast down into the lake of fire and sulfur, where both the beast and the false prophet were being tormented day and night forever and ever.

¹¹And I saw a great white throne and the one sitting on it, from whose face earth fled and heaven fled, and no place was found for them. ¹²And I saw the dead, those great and those small, standing before the throne, and books were opened;²²³ and another was opened, the book of life; and the dead were judged from what had been written in the books, according to their works. ¹³And the sea gave up the dead who were in it, and death and hell gave up the dead who were in them, and the dead²²⁴ were judged, each according to their works. ¹⁴And death and hell were cast into the lake of fire. This is a second death, the lake of fire. ¹⁵And if anyone is not found inscribed in the book of life, that one is cast into the lake of fire.

21 ¹And I saw a new heaven and a new earth,²²⁵ for the first heaven and the first earth went away, and there was no more sea. ²And I saw the new holy city, Jerusalem, descending out of heaven from God, prepared as a bride adorned for her husband. ³And I heard a loud voice from the throne saying, "Behold, God's dwelling place is with the humans, and God will dwell with them, and they will be his peoples, and God himself is with them as their God,²²⁶ ⁴and He shall

---

222. Ezek 38:2–6: "Son of man, set your face toward Gog, of the land of Magog, the chief prince of Meshech and Tubal, and prophesy against him and say, Thus says the Lord God: Behold, I am against you, O Gog, chief prince of Meshech and Tubal; and I will turn you about, and put hooks into your jaws, and I will bring you forth, and all your army, horses and horsemen, all of them clothed in full armor, a great company, all of them with buckler and shield, wielding swords; Persia, Cush, and Put are with them, all of them with shield and helmet; Gomer and all his hordes; Beth-togarmah from the uttermost parts of the north with all his hordes—many peoples are with you" (RSV). Gog is a type of an aggressive king, derived from Gyges, a seventh century BCE king of Sardis—Hemer, *Letters to the Seven Churches*, 131.

223. Dan 7:10 similarly speaks of books being opened in a depiction of a judgment in heaven.

224. "The dead": No subject is specified for the verb, "were judged," but obviously the dead are being judged, not the sea and the personifications of death, and hell. Death and hell, personified, meet their fate in the next verse.

225. Isa 65:17: "For behold, I create new heavens and a new earth; and the former things shall not be remembered or come into mind" (RSV).

226. "As their God": Some manuscript witnesses lack this phrase, and some that include it have a word order that would emphasize "their," suggesting "as a God Who is theirs" as a translation. See Metzger, *Textual Commentary*, 763–64. Ezek 37:27: "My dwelling place shall be with them; and I will be their God, and they shall be my people" (RSV); John consistently changes the wording of passages to which he alludes to include all nations rather than Israel alone.

remove every tear from their eyes, and there will be death no longer; there will no longer be grief, clamor, and toil; for the former things were removed.

⁵And the One seated on the throne said, "Behold I am making all things new." And He says, "Write, for these words are trustworthy and true." ⁶And He said to me, "Done! I am the Alpha and the Omega, the beginning and the end. I will give to those who are thirsting a gift from the springs of the water of life.²²⁷ ⁷The victor shall inherit these new things,²²⁸ and I will be his God and he will be My son. ⁸But to the timid, the unfaithful, those who detest, those who murder, fornicators, magicians, idolaters, and all liars—their share will be in the lake that is burning with fire and sulfur, which is the second death.

⁹And one of the seven messengers, who held the seven bowls that were filled with the seven last plagues, came and spoke with me, saying, "Come, I will show you the bride, the wife of the lamb." ¹⁰And it brought me in spirit to the great high mountain, and he showed me the holy city,²²⁹ Jerusalem, descending out of heaven from God, ¹¹containing the glory of God. Her radiance was like a precious stone, being as transparent as a jasper stone; ¹²she had a large high wall, with twelve gates, and at the gates twelve messengers, and names written over them are the names of the twelve tribes of the sons of Israel; ¹³three gates were from the east, three gates were from the north, three gates were from the south, and three gates were from the west; ¹⁴and the wall of the city has twelve foundation stones, and on them are the twelve names of the twelve apostles of the lamb.

¹⁵And the one speaking with me held a gold measuring rod for him to take the dimensions of the city, her gates, and her walls.²³⁰ ¹⁶And the city is laid out as a square, and her length the same as the width. And he measured the city with the rod at twelve thousand stadia;²³¹ the length, width, and her height were equal. ¹⁷And he measured her wall—one hundred forty-four cubits;²³² the human measure is the messenger's. ¹⁸And the material of her wall is jasper, and the city pure gold, like clear glass. ¹⁹The foundations of the walls of the city has been adorned with every precious stone:²³³ the first foundation jasper, the second sapphire, the third chalcedony,²³⁴ the fourth emerald, ²⁰the fifth sardonyx,

---

227. Jer 2:13 refers to the fountain of living waters.

228. "New": In the Greek, what is inherited is designated only by the demonstrative, literally "these." The only proximate plural object is "all things" in verse 5, literally simply "all." The translation here repeats "new" from verse five to clarify the antecedent.

229. Ezek 40:2: The Lord "brought me in the visions of God into the land of Israel, and set me down upon a very high mountain, on which was a structure like a city opposite me" (RSV).

230. Such a measurement undertaking also appears in Ezek 40.

231. About 1,500 miles—W. Harrington, *Revelation*, 214.

232. A cubit is about eighteen inches, but John goes on to say that he was not using the messenger's cubit but the human one, the distance from an elbow to the tip of the forefinger.

233. Isa 54:11: " . . . I will set your stone in antimony, and lay your foundations with sapphires. I will make your pinnacles of agate, your gates of carbuncles, and all your wall of precious stones" (RSV).

234. According to Arndt and Gingrich, *Greek-English Lexicon*, 874, article on χαλκηδών, it is uncertain what modern designations would correspond to *chalcedony*.

the sixth carnelian, the seventh chrysolite, the eighth beryl, the ninth topaz, the tenth chrysoprase, the eleventh jacinth, the twelfth amethyst.[235] 21And the twelve gates were twelve pearls, each one of the gates was from one pearl apiece. And the main street of the city was pure gold, like transparent glass.

22And I saw no sanctuary in her, for the Lord God Almighty is her sanctuary, as is the lamb. 23And the city has no need of the sun or moon to illuminate her, for God's glory illuminated her,[236] and the lamb is her lamp. 24And the nations walk by light from that glory.[237] And the kings of the earth bring their glory into her;[238] 25and her gates will not be closed daily, for there will be no night there;[239] 26and they will bring the glory and honor of the nations into her. 27And nothing profane, anyone performing an abomination, and no false person will enter her, but rather those who have been written in the lamb's book of life.

22:1And he showed me the river of the water of life, bright as crystal, coming from the throne of God and of the lamb.[240] 2In the middle of her[241] main street and of the river, from here and from there,[242] a tree of life bearing twelve harvests, yielding its harvest monthly, and the leaves of the tree were for the healing of the nations. 3And no longer will anything be accursed. And the throne of God and of the lamb will be in her, and his servants will worship him, 4and they shall look upon his face, and his name will be on their foreheads. 5And there will be night no longer, and they will not have need of the light of the lamp and the light of the sun, because the Lord God will shine upon them, and they shall reign for ever and ever.

6And he said to me, "These words are reliable and true, and the Lord God who inspires the prophets sent His messenger to show His servants what

235. John's enumeration of stones does not correspond to any known list of stones in late Judaism, nor does it correlate with specific tribes, apostles, zodiac signs, or geographical directions. He may well have selected the stones for the way they sounded in recitation—Reader, "Twelve Jewels." W. Harrington, *Revelation*, 214, suggests that John supplies the list of stones simply to establish a contrast with the jewels of the harlot in 17:4.

236. Isa 60:19: "The sun shall be no more your light by day, nor for brightness shall the moon give light to you by night; but the Lord will be your everlasting light, and your God will be your glory" (RSV).

237. "That glory": The Greek has simply a feminine genitive pronoun, whose antecedent is "glory."

238. Isa 60:3: "And nations shall come to your light, and kings to the brightness of your rising" (RSV).

239. Isa 60:11: "Your gates shall be open continually; day and night they shall not be shut . . . " (RSV). See also Zech 14:7.

240. Ezek 47 also has water flowing, but from the Temple. See also Joel 3:18 and Zech 14:8.

241. "Her," i.e, Jerusalem's. Some translators do not begin a new paragraph at 22:1, given the continued use of the feminine pronoun for the city.

242. In his recitation of the passage, John may have used gestures to clarify the image. Alternatively, the translation can read, "In the middle of her main street, and on both sides of the river . . . " would be a closer parallel to Ezek 47:12, though Ezekiel has "all kinds of trees" (RSV), so that some would be on one side and some on the other. The complete Ezek 47:12 reads: "and on the banks, on both sides of the river, there will grow all kinds of trees for food. Their leaves will not wither nor their fruit fail, but they will bear fresh fruit every month, because the water for them flows from the sanctuary. Their fruit will be for food and their leaves for healing" (RSV).

must soon come about." ⁷And, "Behold, I am coming soon. Blessed is the one keeping the words of the prophecy from this book."

⁸And I, John, am the one hearing and seeing these things. And when I heard and saw, I fell to worship before the feet of the messenger who was showing me these things. ⁹And he says to me, "No, not that: I am a fellow servant of yours, of your brothers and sisters the prophets and of those who keep the words of this book. Worship God." ¹⁰And he says to me, "Do not seal up the word of this prophecy of this book, for the time is near.²⁴³ ¹¹Let the unjust do unjust works for now, and let the defiled defile for now, and let the just make justice for now, and let the holy be holy for now.

¹²"Behold, I am coming quickly, and my reward is with me²⁴⁴ to pay all according to their works.²⁴⁵ ¹³I am the Alpha and the Omega, the first and the last, the beginning and the end.

¹⁴"Blessed are those cleansing their robes, so that theirs will be the right to the tree of life and they might enter into the city by the gates. ¹⁵The dogs, sorcerers, fornicators, murderers, idolaters, and all who love and practice deceit will be outside. ¹⁶I, Jesus, sent my messenger to give these in testimony about the churches to you. I am the root and offspring of David, the star, the light of the dawn."

¹⁷And the spirit and the bride are saying, "Come." And let the one hearing say, "Come." And let the one who thirsts come, the one wishing to receive the gift, the water of life.

¹⁸I will give testimony to everyone who hears the words of prophecy from this book. If anyone adds to them, God will add to that person the plagues written about in this book. ¹⁹And if anyone takes away from the words of the book of this prophecy and from the things written in this book, God will take away that person's share from the tree of life and from the holy city.

²⁰The one giving witness to these things says, "Yes, I am coming soon." Amen, come Lord Jesus.

²¹May the grace of the Lord Jesus be with all.

---

243. This is the opposite of Dan 12:4, where Daniel is instructed to seal up the book until the end of time.

244. See Isa 40:10.

245. "All . . . their": The Greek is in the singular; it is translated in the plural to avoid the pronoun problem in English.

*Chapter 19*

# The Johannine Letters

## Introduction

MODERN BIBLES CONTAIN THREE letters of John, which are simply given the titles *First Letter of John*, *Second Letter of John*, and *Third Letter of John*. The titles are misleading in the sense that the text of the letters name no author other than "The Presbyter," and the numerical designations do not necessarily reflect the order in which the letters were written. Two letters, numbered second and third, respectively, are brief; the third appears to be a mere cover letter for the more extensive *First Letter of John*. That first letter is not really a letter at all but rather an essay. In terms of linguistic style, all three appear to be the work of the same author, and they betray an awareness on the part of the Presbyter of some people who were no longer affiliated with him. Their order of composition appears to be *The Second Letter of John*, *The First Letter of John*, and *The Third Letter of John*. The *Second Letter* covers, albeit briefly, some of the same points made in the *First Letter*, but it does not mention the *First Letter*; indeed The Presbyter says he had much to write but did not want to set pen to paper.[1] My guess is that the thinking evident in the *Second Letter* eventually led to the composition of the *First Letter*. The *Third Letter*, which seems to mention the composition of the *First*, would have been composed soon after the *First* as a cover letter.

The traditional attribution of the letters to John can be justified by thematic continuities in the *First Letter* with the *Revelation of Jesus Christ*, the author of which identified himself as John. For example, the author says that walking in darkness is tantamount to a lie, an untruth; and the blood of Jesus, he says, cleanses the followers from sin—two themes found in *Revelation*.[2] Of course, this does not establish as a fact that the individual named John who wrote *Revelation* wrote the three letters. In fact, one must ask why an author who calls himself "John" in *Revelation* would later refer to himself as "the Presbyter." The letters, however, appear to come out of the same rhetorical universe as *Revelation*, less the inflammatory denunciations of the Roman Empire. The opening

---

1. 2 John 12.
2. 1 John 1:6 and 7.

lines of the *First Letter* also have continuities with the Prologue to the *Fourth Gospel*, which usually bears the title *Gospel of John* in modern Christian Bibles. Consequently, if one can justify labeling the three letters "Johannine" because they share the same rhetorical universe as John's *Revelation*, and one can also label the *Fourth Gospel* "Johannine," even though it does not name its author, on the grounds that it shares the same rhetorical universe as the "Johannine" letters. Again, this does not mean that someone named John, who wrote *Revelation*, wrote the *Fourth Gospel*, though it does explain why that gospel is popularly called "The Gospel According to John."

The time and place of the composition of the three letters cannot be ascertained from the texts of the letters themselves. By associating them with *Revelation*, we can make the educated guess that they were composed in what is now western Turkey, about 95 CE. Assigning a date of composition to the *Fourth Gospel* is no easy matter; indeed, it is a complex document that appears to have resulted from a blending together of works that in turn were composed at various times and in various places. Associating the three letters with that gospel does not in itself provide further information. Give or take a decade or so, however, *Revelation*, the three letters, and the *Fourth Gospel* seem to be roughly contemporaneous with one another. Irenaeus, writing about 180 CE, says that the elders of Asia Minor—Polycarp of Smyrna and Papias of Hieropolis—told him that John, the disciple of the Lord, who was the "Beloved Disciple" of the Fourth Gospel and author of the epistles, published the latter in the reign of Trajan; that would be during the period 98–117.[3] There is considerable skepticism about the accuracy of Irenaeus's information about different early Christians named John in and around Ephesus, and whether any of them were John, Son of Zebedee, or the "Beloved Disciple."[4] For John, Son of Zebedee, to have been an adult fisherman about the year 30, he would have to have been born at least as early as 10 CE and would have been about ninety years old in the reign of Trajan. Irenaeus, however, does not say that John the Son of Zebedee *published* the letters. If we assume the Beloved Disciple was someone other than John the Son of Zebedee, he might, as a child of six or seven years, have leaned on Jesus at the Last Supper and lived to publish the Johannine letters as a septuagenarian. More likely, he could have written or dictated elements that were later incorporated into the fourth gospel.[5]

The purpose of the *Second Letter* is to acknowledge an affiliating of the recipient church, "elect lady," with the author's church ("The children of your elect sister greet you");[6] "I rejoiced much because I have found some of your children living by

---

3. Painter, *1, 2, and 3 John*, 41.

4. See R. Brown, *Gospel According to John (i–xii)*, lxxxviii–xcii.

5. *Das neue Testament*, 35, says that the *Second Letter of John* is the earliest extant Christian work, dating from about 50 CE; the editors evidently accept the identification of the Presbyter with the Presbyter John whom Eusebius (*Ecclesiastical History* 3:25:3) said Papias knew. The editors, ibid., 63, date the *First Letter of John* from about 55 CE, an early date that does not seem justified by the evidence.

6. 2 John 13.

the truth, as we received the command from the Father."[7] The affiliation pertains to "some" of the members; apparently there was a parting of ways insofar as some others did not follow what was accepted as truth by the author. Whatever the dynamics may have been in the divisions and alignments in question, they also involved a doctrinal issue; it was a matter of acknowledging the "Jesus the Messiah coming in flesh."[8] It was not the coming of Jesus the Messiah *as* (something like) flesh that was at issue, but his coming *in* the flesh; this seems to refer in the first instance either to the Resurrection or the Second Coming, not to the Nativity, though it could include that too.

The purpose of the *First Letter* is to establish a fellowship among a number of churches to whom the essay was directed, by their having in common a faith in the Incarnate Deity.[9] There is also a concern that the recipients of the essay remain with the churches that accept Jesus. Again, the author does not really distinguish the Nativity from the Resurrection or the Second Coming, but rather speaks of the Son of God being "made manifest."[10]

The *Third Letter* is a cover letter for the essay that is traditionally named the *First Letter*. In this cover letter the Presbyter addresses Gaius, who had provided hospitality to co-workers of the Presbyter. The church of which Gaius was a member had experienced some division over receiving those co-workers because of the opposition of one Diotrephes.[11] Apart from these references, we have no information on Gaius and Diotrephes.

## The Sociology of Converging and Diverging Tendencies

Georg Simmel, the famous late-nineteenth-century and early-twentieth-century German philosopher and sociologist, observed that in social life, oppression by others and feelings of depression within oneself together tend to increase if one surrenders to them quietly and without protest.[12] Establishing an interpersonal balance thus becomes critical, and doing so may necessitate some level of conflict behavior. Similarly, relationships among groups continue through time only when accompanied by forms of conflict, usually under the form of political or economic competition. "As little as antagonism by itself amounts to making a society, so little does it—borderline cases aside—tend to be absent as a sociological factor in processes of making one...."[13] In line with this thinking, one would expect a religion, such as the early Christian movement, that developed its identity around a belief, would unite best internally by

7. 2 John 4.
8. 2 John 7.
9. 1 John 1:3.
10. 1 John 3:8.
11. 3 John 9.
12. Simmel, *Sociology*, 231.
13. Ibid., 235.

emphasizing a contrast with another religion that had quite a different belief. It would hardly suffice for Christians to contrast their unique belief with others who could go along with it, neither enthusiastically affirming it nor opposing it in principle. Certainly the early Christians could acknowledge that they differed from the non-exclusionary cultural pantheon of the Roman and Hellenistic world, but a competitor or opponent religion that was more like themselves would have united the Christians far better. This could help us to understand the ancient opposition of Christians and non-Christian Jews to one another, which is a theme that turned up in the letters to the churches in the first part of John's *Revelation*, and it is an intellectual avenue with which to approach the Presbyter's heightened awareness of the parties that broke away from the churches that were affiliated with him. What I am suggesting here is that divergences within what had been a more amorphous, but undivided, Christian movement served as the occasion and motivating force for the effort to form alliances of churches, an effort that took literary form in the Johannine letters.

Sociologists have dealt with this dialectic of convergence within an identity group and divergence from an "other" in the sociology of tradition. It is both fortunate and unfortunate that the term *tradition* lends itself to various meanings. It is fortunate because one can draw insights from slightly different nuances of the term. It is unfortunate because the mere use of the term leaves any theoretical statement vague. Edward Shils addressed this situation by beginning with a "barest" meaning of tradition and then following that up with insightful nuances. The barest meaning is anything handed down from a past to a present.[14] However, what is interesting is the change and development inherent in the handing down: "Constellations of symbols, clusters of images, are received and modified. They change in the process of transmission; they change also while they are in the possession of their recipients. This chain of transmitted variants of a tradition is also called tradition...." Sometimes variations in a tradition come from its bearers rationalizing and making corrections within it; these changes are extensions beyond the state of mere transmission. At other times a charismatic innovator appears among the bearers of the tradition, personally bringing about changes. In yet other cases, conditions that are external to the bearers of the tradition occasion variation. There may be a syncretism when the center of a society expands outward, introducing its cultural traits into the social periphery.[15] John Pobee, for example, provides the example of indigenous African "traditional" religions facing western culture as introduced by foreign missionaries.[16] This bears some analogy to the imposition of the Roman imperial cult in the provinces. Or, traits originating in the periphery may find their way into the center; this was happening when Jewish religion and its Christian derivative found their ways into major cities in the Roman Empire.

Importantly, there may be resistance against rationalizing a tradition, against the influence of a charismatic innovator, against the introduction of cultural traits from

---

14. Shils, *Tradition*, 12.
15. Ibid., 13, 214, 228, 244.
16. Pobee, "Aspects of African Traditional Religion."

the power centers of a society, or against the introduction of cultural traits from the periphery or from a different periphery. Such seemingly traditionalistic resistance may be, to use Karl Mannheim's terminology, "conservative," innovations in themselves that people introduce in order to resist some other innovation.[17] For example, in the course of sorting out questionnaire responses from Hungarian youth during the Soviet era in Hungary, Ivan Varga found it necessary to distinguish between traditional religiosity and non-traditional, in addition to the categories of religious indifference and communist atheists. Traditional religiosity involved believing in systems of dogma, observing religious and moral commandments, believing in sanctions in the afterlife, and observing religious practices. Non-traditional religiosity involved belief in a creator God or supernatural being who could be uninvolved in the world.[18] Those having this latter kind of religiosity were unconsciously deists or pantheists who were relatively unconcerned with religious sanctions. Varga was conducting his study in a context in which the traditional religiosity had been grounded in the past while the non-traditional was newer. The situation from which the Johannine letters came was the inverse of this: Before the author's traditionalizing, the non-traditional religiosity was relatively amorphous, including polytheist, pantheist, and even deist elements. By traditionalizing, the Johannine author was giving greater form to a religious pursuit.

Danièle Hervieu-Léger has famously conceptualized the handing down of a *traditum* from the past through a process that involves change as a "chain of memory." She highlights the constituting of tradition in a present by conferring authority on elements that come from the past.[19] She would focus on concrete groups that have imaginary genealogies that map out a succession of generations from the past into the future. The generations need not be many; for example, in the early Christian movement they may have been only a few. A tradition in this sense would create an avenue of social identification within the group and as a way of excluding, externally, those who have no part in the genealogy. For the Johannine author, there already was an imaginary genealogy for the local, household church. What appears to be going on with the letters is the emergence of a new trans-local genealogy in the making. As one reads the letters, a dialectic of love and exclusion comes into view; the recipients of the letters are to observe the great commandment of love, but the discourse draws a sharp line between the in-group and others. Such a dialectic is understandable in terms of the formation of a new trans-local identity group with its distinct genealogy.

---

17. Mannheim, "Conservative Thought."

18. Varga, "Sécularisation de la jeunesse hongroise." Hervieu-Léger, *Religion as a Chain of Memory*, 20, similarly describes the state of present-day Europe, where the historical religious organizations are unable to stipulate beliefs and rule behaviors, even among their own adherents, amid a proliferation of beliefs and practices that freely borrow symbols and references from multiple supernaturalist systems. I would add that seemingly naturalist references, especially from psychology, appear in a syncretism with received religiosity as well.

19. Hervieu-Léger, *Religion as a Chain of Memory*, 87.

## English Translations

### 1. Second Johannine Letter

¹The Presbyter, to the elect lady and her children, whom I truly love, and not I alone but also all who know the truth, ²on account of truth that dwells within us and that will be with us forever. ³Grace, mercy, peace will be with us in truth and love from God the Father and from Jesus, Messiah, the Son of the Father. ⁴I rejoiced much because I have found some of your children living by the truth, as we received the command from the Father. ⁵And now let me ask you, lady, not as someone writing a new commandment for you but that which we have from the beginning: that we love one another. ⁶And love is this: that we walk according to his commandments; the commandment is this, as you heard from the beginning, the one that you walk by. ⁷For many deceivers went out into the world, who do not confess Jesus, Messiah coming in flesh; such is the deceiver and the anti-messiah. ⁸Take care for yourselves, lest you lose what we worked for,[20] but may rather receive a full reward. ⁹Anyone who sets out and does not remain with the teaching of the Messiah is not with God.[21] One who remains with the teaching is also with[22] the Father and the Son. ¹⁰If anyone comes to you and does not bring this teaching, do not receive into the home or greet such a person; ¹¹for the one welcoming such shares in that person's evil works.

¹²Having much to write you, I do not intend to do it with paper and ink, but I hope to be in your presence to converse, so that our joy may be completed. ¹³The children of your elect sister greet you.

### 2. First Johannine Letter

1 ¹That which was from the beginning,[23] which we heard, which we saw with our eyes, what we viewed and our hands touched[24] concerning the word of life—²and the life was made manifest, and we watched, and we are testifying and announcing to you the eternal life that was near the Father and was made

---

20. "We worked for": Many textual witnesses have "you worked for." See Metzger, *Textual Commentary*, 719.

21. "Not with God": literally, "does not have God." *Have* in this context means to have as having a friend.

22. Once more, "with" is literally "have" in the sense of having a friend.

23. This and the reference to the Word later on in the verse parallel the opening words of the Fourth Gospel, "In the beginning was the Word. . . . " The latter in turn is phrased so as to parallel Gen 1:1. The text of the *Letter* may be more primitive than that of the Gospel, the latter being worked upon to allude to Genesis.

24. Jensen, *Affirming the Resurrection*, 60, sees this as an allusion to the Resurrection because he does not read the letter as being about the Incarnation.

manifest to us—³what we saw and heard we are announcing to you also, so that you too may have fellowship[25] with us. But our fellowship is also with the Father and with his son Jesus, Messiah. ⁴And we write these things so that our joy may be completed.[26]

⁵And this is the message that we heard from him and announce to you, that God is light and in Him there is no darkness at all. ⁶If we said that we have fellowship with Him and are walking in darkness, we are speaking falsely and not acting truthfully; ⁷but if we are walking in the light as He is in the light, we have fellowship with one another, and the blood of Jesus His son cleanses us from all sin. ⁸If we said that we have no sin, we are deceiving ourselves and the truth is not in us. ⁹If we confess our sins, He is faithful and just, so that He will pardon our sins and cleanse us from every injustice. ¹⁰If we said that we did not sin, we are making Him a liar and His word is not with us.

2 ¹My children, I am writing these things to you so that you might not sin. And if anyone should sin, we have an advocate near to the Father, Jesus, just Messiah; ²and he is a sin-offering for our sins, not only for ours but also those of the whole world. ³And we know that we know Him by this, if we keep His commandments. ⁴Someone saying "I know Him" while not keeping his[27] commandments is a liar, and truth is not in that person; ⁵but whoever keeps his word, God's love is truly perfected in that person. We know that we are with him by this. ⁶Someone claiming to remain with him ought also to walk as he indeed walked.

⁷Beloved, I am not writing a new commandment to you, but an old commandment that you have from the beginning. The word that you heard is the old commandment. ⁸On the other hand I am writing you a new commandment, which is a real one in him and among you, for the darkness is led away and the true light is already manifest. ⁹Someone claiming to be in the light while hating a brother is still in the darkness.[28] ¹⁰Someone loving a brother remains in the light, and there is no stumbling stone there; ¹¹but one hating a brother is in the darkness and walks in the darkness and does not know where to go, because darkness blinds that person's eyes.

¹²I write to you, children, because your sins were forgiven through his name. ¹³I write to you, fathers, because you have known him from the beginning. I write to you, youths, because you have defeated the evil one. ¹⁴I wrote to you, little children,[29] because you have known the Father. I wrote to you,

---

25. Perkins, "Koinonia in 1 John 1:3–7," 635, identifies "fellowship," κοινωνία, as language referring to the formation of a group having a common purpose, a *societas* in Roman legal parlance. The letter thus refers to a formal relationship with the author and ultimately with God. The term appears two more times in the following sentences.

26. "Joy" is the feeling expected from unity in a purpose of a fellowship—ibid., 636.

27. At some point in the text, the third person masculine pronoun shifts from referring to God the Father to Jesus; it seems to be here.

28. "A brother": literally "his brother." This is also true of the following verses.

29. Verse 12 addresses "children," τεκνία; here verse 14 addresses "children" again, but with a

fathers, because you have known Him from the beginning. I wrote to you, youths, because you are strong and the word of God remains among you and you have defeated the evil one.

¹⁵Love neither the world nor what is in the world. If someone loves the world, the love for the Father is not within.³⁰ ¹⁶Because everything that is in the world—passion for the flesh, passion of the eyes, and pretense in life³¹—is not from the Father but is from the world. ¹⁷Both the world and its passion pass away, but doing the will of God remains forever.

¹⁸Little children,³² it is the last hour; and as you heard the anti-messiah is coming; and now many anti-messiahs have come to be. We know from this that it is the last hour. ¹⁹From us they went out, but they were not *of us*, for if they were of us, they would have remained with us. But so that they may be revealed that they are not all of us, ²⁰you all both have an anointing from the Holy One and know it.³³ ²¹I did not write this³⁴ to you because you did not know the truth but because you did know it and because every lie is alien to the truth.³⁵ ²²Who is the liar unless it is the one denying that Jesus is the Messiah? This is the anti-messiah, the one denying the Father and the son. ²³Everyone who denies the son does not have even the Father; one who confesses the son also has the Father. ²⁴Let what you knew from the beginning remain with you; if what you heard from the beginning remains with you, you will also remain with the son and with the Father.³⁶ ²⁵And this is the promise that He promised us, eternal life.

²⁶I wrote you these things about those misleading you. ²⁷And the anointing that you received from him remains with you, and you have no need for someone to teach you; but since his anointing teaches you about all and it is a truth and not a lie, and since it taught you, remain with it.

²⁸And now, children, remain with him, so that if he appears we will have confidence and not be embarrassed near him at his coming. ²⁹If you know

---

different term, παιδία, which is translated here as "little children." See Painter, *1, 2, and 3 John*, 185, and R. Brown, *Epistles of John*, 297–300.

30. "Within": literally, "in him."

31. "In life": the Greek simply has a genitive, "of life," which is not meaningful in English.

32. Παιδία.

33. Painter, *1, 2, and 3 John*, 198, and R. Brown, *Epistles of John*, 344, point out that "anointing," χρῖσμα, appears here and in verses 20 and 27 below, but nowhere else in the New Testament. He suggests that it may be a term used by the author's opponents and taken over to distinguish the opponents' anointing from the anointing of the Holy One. At the end of the verse, I add "it" because English requires an object for "know."

34. "This": The past tense of "write" is used repeatedly in this letter to refer to what is written earlier in the letter; "this" is introduced here to make it clear that the author is not referring to a previous letter.

35. "Alien to the truth": literally "not from the truth." The translation used is suggested by R. Brown, *Epistles of John*, 329.

36. Repeated uses of "with" in the translation are literally "in."

that he is just, you also know that everyone who acts justly is born from him. 3 ¹See what love the Father gave you, that we may be called children of God. And so we are. Therefore the world does not know us because it did not know him. ²Beloved, we are now children of God, and it has not been revealed yet what we will be. We know that if whenever he appears we will be like him, that we will see him as he is. ³And all having this hope for him make themselves sacred, just as he is sacred.[37]

⁴All who act sinfully also act lawlessly, and sin is lawlessness.[38] ⁵You also know that he was made manifest so that he would take sins away, and there is no sin in him. ⁶Everyone remaining with him does not sin; everyone sinning has not seen him or known him. ⁷Children, let no one mislead you; the one acting justly is just, as He is just. ⁸The one acting sinfully is from the devil, since the devil sins from the beginning. The son of God was made manifest for this, to destroy the devil's works. ⁹Everyone begotten of God does not act sinfully because His posterity remains with Him; and that posterity cannot sin because it has been begotten by God. ¹⁰The children of God and the children of the devil are manifest by this: everyone not acting justly is not from God, especially the one not loving one's brother.

¹¹For this is the message that you heard from the beginning, that we should love one another, ¹²not as Cain was of the evil one and slaughtered his brother. And for what reason did he kill him? Because his works were evil and those of his brother just. ¹³And do not be surprised, brothers and sisters, if the world hates you. ¹⁴We know that we have passed from death over to life because we love the brothers and sisters; one not loving remains in death. ¹⁵One hating one's brother or sister is a murderer, and you know that every murderer does not have eternal life remaining within.[39] ¹⁶We know love by this, that he laid down his life for us; and we ought to lay down our lives for the brothers and sisters.[40] ¹⁷Now whoever have the goods of the world and see a brother or sister in need and shut off their compassion, how does the love of God remain in them?[41] ¹⁸Children, let us not love in word or speech but deed and truth ¹⁹as well; by that shall we know that we are from the truth. And we will assure our heart before Him ²⁰because God is greater than our heart if our heart would condemn, and He knows all. ²¹Beloved, if our heart would not condemn, we have confidence in God, ²²and whatever we request we receive from Him because we keep His commandments and do what is

---

37. "All . . . themselves": the Greek is in the singular but is translated in the plural to avoid the English pronoun problem.

38. "All . . .": The singular Greek is again rendered in the plural, this time to avoid confusion over the antecedent of "he" in the next verse.

39. "Within": literally, "in him."

40. "Our" is supplied.

41. This is in the singular in the Greek but his translated in the plural to avoid the English pronoun problem.

pleasing before Him. ²³And this is His commandment, that we trust the name of His son Jesus, Messiah, and love one another, as Jesus⁴² gave the commandment to us. ²⁴And those who keep his commandments remain with him and he with them; and by this we know that he remains among us, from the Spirit of which he gave us.

4 ¹Beloved, do not trust every spirit, but examine whether spirits are from God, because many false prophets have gone out into the world. ²You know the Spirit of God by this: Every spirit that confesses Jesus Messiah having come in flesh is from God, ³and every spirit that does not confess Jesus is not from God; and that one is the anti-messiah whom you have heard is coming and is already now in the world. ⁴Children, you are of God, and you have defeated them,⁴³ for he who is in you is greater than the one who is in the world. ⁵They are from the world; therefore they speak from the world and the world listens to them. ⁶We are of God; one who knows God hears us; one who is not of God does not hear us. From this we know the Spirit of truth and the spirit of deceit.

⁷Beloved, we love one another because love is from God, and everyone who loves is begotten by God and knows God. ⁸One who does not love does not know God, because God is love. ⁹The love of God was made manifest among us by this, that God sent His only son into the world so that we might live through him. ¹⁰The love is by this: not because we loved God but because He loved us and sent His son as expiation for our sins. ¹¹Beloved, if God so loved us, we too ought to love one another. ¹²No one has seen God; if we love one another, God remains among us and His love is accomplished among us.

¹³We know that we remain with Him and He with us by this: that He gave to us from His spirit. ¹⁴And we have seen and bore witness that the Father sent the son as savior of the world. ¹⁵God remains with whoever confesses that Jesus is the son of God, and that person remains with God. ¹⁶And we have known and have trusted the love that God has in us.

God is love, and one who remains in love remains in God and God remains in that person. ¹⁷Love has been perfected with us by this: that we may have confidence on the day of judgment that we are also in this world in the way he is. ¹⁸There is no fear with love, but complete love drives fear out, for fear has to do with punishment, but one who is afraid has not been made perfect by love. ¹⁹We love, because He loved us first. ²⁰If anyone says, "I love God," and hates a brother or sister, that person is a liar. For while not loving the brother or sister whom one has seen, one cannot love God whom one has not seen. ²¹And we have this command from Him, that the one loving God would be loving one's brother or sister also.

5 ¹Everyone who believes that Jesus is the Messiah has been begotten of God, and everyone loving the One begetting also loves what is begotten from

---

42. "Jesus": "he" in the Greek. The nearest potential antecedent before the pronoun is "Jesus." The commandment in the Johannine tradition is found, for example, in John 13:34.

43. "Them": the antecedent would be the false prophets.

Him. ²We know that we love the children of God by this: when we love God we act according to His commandments. ³For the love of God is this, that we keep His commandments; and His commandments are not burdensome, ⁴because everyone who has been begotten of God defeats the world; and the victory defeating the world is this: our faith. ⁵And who is the one defeating the world but the one believing that Jesus is the son of God?

⁶This is the one coming through water and blood: Jesus, Messiah, not by water only but by water and by blood; and the one giving witness is the spirit, because the spirit is truth. ⁷For there are three witnesses: ⁸the spirit, the water, and the blood, and these three are unanimous.⁴⁴ ⁹If we accept the witness of humans, God's witness is greater because this is God's testimony: that He has testified about His son. ¹⁰One having faith in the son of God has the testimony within:⁴⁵ One not having faith in God has made Him a liar for not having had faith in the testimony that God has given about His son. ¹¹And the testimony is this: that God gave us eternal life, and this life is in His son. ¹²One having the son has life; one not having the son of God does not have life.

¹³I wrote these things to you so that you may know that you have eternal life when having faith in the name of the son of God. ¹⁴And the confidence that we have concerning him is this: that if we ask for something according to his will, he hears us. ¹⁵And if we know that he hears us whatever we request, we know that the things requested that we had requested we have from him.

¹⁶If seeing one's brother or sister sinning a sin that is not unto death, one will ask, and for that one He will give life to those sinning not unto death. There is sin unto death; I am not saying to make entreaties about that. ¹⁷Every wrongdoing is a sin, and there is sin not unto death.⁴⁶

¹⁸We know that the one who has been begotten from God does not sin, but the one begotten from God provides protection,⁴⁷ and the evil one does not touch that person. ¹⁹We know that we are of God, and that the whole world is placed with the evil one.⁴⁸ ²⁰But we know that the son of God is present and gave us an understanding so that we know the One Who is true, and we are with the One Who is true, with His son Jesus, Messiah. He is the true God and eternal life. ²¹Children, guard yourselves from the idols.

---

44. "Unanimous": literally, "into the one." RSV translates it as "these three agree." R. Brown, *Epistles of John*, 569, as "of one accord," and Painter, *1, 2, and 3 John*, 300, as the almost literal "in the one."

45. Literally, "in himself."

46. Much has been written about the meaning of "sin unto death" and "sin not unto death"; R. Brown, *Epistles of John*, 612–19, provides a summary. The most likely meaning comes from the context of the letter itself; the author has spoken of those who had seceded from the Johannine community as not having life and as walking in darkness. He is telling his readers that he is not encouraging them to pray for the secessionists—R. Brown, *Epistles of John*, 618–19; Painter, *1, 2, and 3 John*, 319. RSV has "mortal sin," and *Das neue Testament* is similar, with "tödlich."

47. "Provides protection": literally, "protects him."

48. "Is placed with the evil one": literally, "reclines in the evil one."

## 3. Third Johannine Letter

1 ¹The Presbyter, to the beloved Gaius, whom I love in truth.

²Beloved, I wish that you are doing well in all things and are in good health, just as your soul is doing well. ³For I rejoiced greatly when brothers came and testified about your trustworthiness, since you conduct yourself with trustworthiness. ⁴I have no greater joy than this,[49] that I heard of my children conducting themselves with trustworthiness.

⁵Beloved, you act faithfully whatever you do for the brothers, strangers at that! ⁶They testified before the church about your love. You will do well sending them on[50] in a manner worthy of God. ⁷For they set out in behalf of the name, receiving nothing from the gentiles. ⁸So we ought to receive such people as guests so that we would become co-workers in the truth.

⁹I wrote something to the church; however, Diotrephes, loving to be first among them, does not accept us.[51] ¹⁰Therefore, if I come, I will call attention to his deeds—his making unjustified accusations against us with evil words, and not satisfied with that he also does not receive the brothers and forbids those who intend to and expels them from the church.

¹¹Beloved, do not imitate what is evil but what is good. One who acts lovingly is of God; one acting wickedly has not seen God.[52] ¹²Demetrius gets a testimonial from all and from trustworthiness itself; and we too give him a testimonial, and you know that our testimony is true.

¹³I had much to write to you, but I do not want to write to you with ink and pen.[53] ¹⁴But I hope to see you soon, and we will speak face to face. ¹⁵Peace to you. The friends greet you. Greet the friends by name.

---

49. "This": literally, "these." There is no obvious rationale for the plural form.

50. "Sending them on," προπέμψας: this is a technical expression referring to supplying travelers with what they may need.

51. Malherbe, "Inhospitality," 226, sees this verse as referring to a letter of recommendation the presbyter had written on behalf of the traveling brothers. Gaius is commended for receiving them. Margaret Mitchell, "Diotrephes," argues that ἐπιδεχεσθαι should be translated as "receive," not "accept the authority of." My understanding is that 1 John is what the Presbyter wrote to the church, and that Diotrephes does not accept any affiliation with the Presbyter.

52. Horvath, "Early Ecumenical Creed?" perceptively sees this verse as a statement of the basic principle behind the letter.

53. "You" is in the singular in this sentence. The Presbyter had much to write to Gaius, in addition to what was written in 1 John to the church in general.

*Chapter 20*

# First Pseudepigraphic Letter of Peter

## Introduction

FOR CENTURIES COMMENTATORS HAD taken the ascribed authorship of *First Peter* at face value, but modern scholars generally do not. The content of the letter parallels Pauline tradition at many points as well as general Christian terminology and doctrine; there is nothing particularly Petrine about it.[1] The prose doesn't reflect a Palestinian fisherman dictating in Greek as a second language, but rather Greek classical rhetorical training.[2] Quotations from the Hebrew scriptures do not come directly from the Hebrew but generally from the Septuagint Greek translation. There are no references to the earthly life of Jesus. There are no references to Paul, who would have been in Rome at the same time as Peter. There are, however, references to presbyters, church officials, thus suggesting some organizational development likely to have occurred after the time of Peter and Paul.

A reference in the letter suggests it was sent from a Roman church: "The co-elect church in Babylon greets you, also my son Mark."[3] *Babylon* was the code name for Rome after the year 70, when Roman forces destroyed Jerusalem as Babylonian forces had centuries earlier; "the co-elect (church) in Babylon" would be a Roman Christian congregation or the collective Church in Rome. As noted in the introduction of the chapter on the *Gospel of Mark*, someone named Mark appears to have been Peter's translator in Rome and the one who composed that gospel. Judging from style, the author of the *Gospel of Mark* is not the author of *First Peter*. The same section of the letter says, "I wrote to you briefly, sending by Silvanus, faithful brother as I deem him."[4] This does mean that someone named Silvanus authored the letter or took dictation

---

1. Horrell, "Product of a Petrine Circle?"

2. Achtemeier, 1 *Peter*, 1–6, who also points out that Peter is described as unlettered in Acts 4:13.

3. 1 Pet 5:13. See Elliott, *Conflict, Community, and Honor*, 24–25, for a similar view of the place of composition; he proposes 73–92 CE as the possible span of dates of composition. Achtemeier, 1 *Peter*, 2 and 33, notes that the persecution in Asia Minor described in the letter postdated the lifetime of Peter; he suggests, p. 50, a range of possible dates of composition of 80–100 CE.

4. 1 Pet 5:12.

for it; by convention the Greek "by Silvanus,"[5] indicates that the named individual, Silvanus, carried the letter from Rome to the recipients;[6] the expression was used that way, for example, by Ignatius,[7] numerous secular papyri, and evidently by Polycarp in the Greek behind the extant Latin of his *Letter to the Philippians*.[8] It is possible that the Silvanus who brought the letter to the recipients was the same Silvanus who preached with Paul and Timothy and appears as a contributing author in *First Thessalonians*.[9] If he were in his twenties in Paul's time, he would be in his fifties around the year 90.[10]

The letter is addressed to "the sojourners of the dispersion: Pontus, Galatia, Cappadocia, Asia, and Bithynia."[11] *Sojourners* translates παρεπιδήμοις, which can mean "people staying in a strange place," "strangers," "exiles," "sojourners," or "resident aliens." Their precise status in the named northwestern provinces, in what is now Turkey, is not clear.[12] That they are "of the dispersion" does not necessarily indicate the Jewish Diaspora from Palestine, though it could include that; it could indicate the place to which people being dispersed had gone. Indeed, the five named provinces are in apposition to "of the dispersion," suggesting a simple geographical meaning. Since converts from pagan cults are included in the recipients,[13] the recipients were not exclusively Diaspora Jews. The mention of "sojourners" is usually interpreted to refer simply to Christians, who were not at home in this world. The addressees are described as going through trying times; the author offers them encouragement. The trying times need not have been official persecution, though Roman officialdom may have been involved in persecuting Christians when the latter were denounced to them.[14]

## The Early Christian Movement: Not Quite an Entrenched Sect

The sociology of religion summarizes a great deal of information about particular religious groups by means of typologies in the church/sect tradition. It was Max Weber who formalized the procedure of using pure type;[15] pure types were hypothetical, extreme rational meanings that could be used as yardsticks for purposes of characterizing real cases. Thus, there may be no pure democracy in the world, but one could

---

5. διὰ Σιλουανοῦ.

6. Richards, "Silvanus Was Not Peter's Secretary"; Senior, "1 Peter," 5.

7. Ignatius, *Philadephians* 11:2 and *Smyrnaeans* 12:1.

8. The Latin reads "scripsi per": Polycarp, *Philippians* 14:1.

9. 2 Cor 1:19; 1 Thess 1:1.

10. In contrast, the parallels with Pauline theology inspired the date 50–55 CE in *Das neue Testament*, 53.

11. 1 Pet 1:1.

12. Senior, "1 Peter," 8–10, makes this point, disagreeing with Elliott, *Home for the Homeless*, who would have them be Christian resident aliens.

13. See 1 Pet 4:3–4.

14. Senior, "1 Peter," 7.

15. Weber, *Economy and Society*, 6.

use the conceptual type *democracy* to see how much any given regime approximates it. For Weber, a sect is neither necessarily small nor created by seceding from a more established religious entity.

> Rather, the sect is a group whose very nature and purpose precludes universality and requires the free consensus of its members, since it aims at being an aristocratic group, an association of persons with full religious qualification. The sect does not want to be an institution dispensing grace, like a church, which includes the righteous and the unrighteous and is especially concerned with subjecting the sinner to Divine law. The sect adheres to the ideal of the *ecclesia pura* (hence the name "Puritans"), the *visible* community of saints, from whose midst the black sheep are removed so that they will not offend God's eyes.[16]

Precisely because a sect would be voluntary, it cannot enter into an alliance with a political regime and remain true to its ethic.[17] Consequently, sects become opponents to governments to the extent that governments intrude into the workings of everyday life.

In actual use of "sect" as a type in empirical research, an oppositional stance toward the social environment seemed more important than voluntariness, especially in modern nation states where government and religion are separate. If all religions are voluntary, those that are "sects" are the ones that reject the world and its power structures. Accordingly, Benton Johnson defined sects as religious groups that reject the social environment in which they exist, and churches as groups that accept their social environments.[18] But what if the rejection of the environment, especially the political environment, goes so far as not seeking to so much as oppose the government? That seems to be the case with the author of *First Peter*, who unlike John, the author of *Revelation*, does not rail against Rome and its Empire. William Swatos describes the "entrenched sect" in his five-part typology of religious groups that also includes "church," "denomination," "dynamic sect," and a transitional form, the "established sect."[19] The entrenched sect, existing in and rejecting a world that would have an established religion,

> . . . is the church's nemesis. It has its archetype in the individual dissenter within a monopolistic system. . . . Depending upon the degree of monopolism, the entrenched sect may appear as a persecuted underground, subject to criminal sanctions ranging from quite mild to capital, or a determined minority excluded legally and/or socially from the cultural and political life of the larger society. The unique mark of the entrenched sect is that it does not seek "equal ground" with the church. It is "against the world" and either seeks to replace the present church, which it identifies with "the world," or ignores

---

16. Ibid., 1204.
17. Ibid., 1208.
18. B. Johnson, "On Church and Sect," 542.
19. Swatos, "Monopolism, Pluralism, Acceptance, and Rejection." The typology that Swatos developed also appears in the sociology of religion text on which he collaborated: Christiano, Swatos, and Kivisto, *Sociology of Religion*, 92.

the ongoing social system entirely, looking to "another world" that may be of several types....[20]

This is not quite the stance of *First Peter*, whose author would seemingly desire converts from the established polytheism and emperor-cult but does not appear to want to be established as part of "the world." The author of the letter does not want to replace the present church. Moreover, at this juncture in history, the established religious system does not seem to be all that interested in being established; it will tolerate the Christians if no one takes the trouble to denounce them. In response, *First Peter* does not oppose the state and does not ignore it, but encourages the Christians to go along with the entire system of power—from obeying laws to co-operating with slavery and the household power structure. Yet it is not a matter of an "established sect" insofar as there is no ongoing transition to one of the other types. For this reason, the stance taken by *First Peter* is not quite that of an entrenched sect, but it is not yet that of an established sect.

## Levels of Inclusiveness

It is a sociological commonplace to recognize the difference between micro phenomena (individual- and small group-level), meso phenomena (organization- and community-level), and macro phenomena (societal). It is a matter of how much breadth or scope needs be taken into account before reaching the boundary of something social. An individual who is "cultured" can be understood in terms of the high culture of a civilization, but the quality of being "cultured" reaches a closure of sorts with the individual; one may consider a very different person who is not "cultured" in that sense but is a member of the same society, works in the same organization, or even is a member of the same family. Being "cultured" is an individual feature, albeit one existing necessarily in a dialectic of mutual implication with a whole civilization. An organization may have high or low morale, but any one of its members may be individually feeling blue or enjoying life in general quite apart from the organization. A member of a team lacking momentum, for example, may try to be a "spark-plug" or to "jump ship" for another team, and such individual predispositions may be related to the team-level phenomenon; nevertheless the state of the individual is not a replication of the state of the group. Similarly, a war-like society may have communities within it that are inwardly peaceable, or individual members who detest war. Émile Durkheim argued for the necessity of a science of society, *sociologie*, on the grounds that only a society-wide fact can explain the coming into existence of another society-wide fact; changes at the individual level would occur randomly, but for something like a crime wave or a change in fertility and suicide rates to occur, where individual actions trend

---

20. Swatos, "Monopolism, Pluralism, Acceptance, and Rejection," 181.

somewhat in concert rather than randomly, some other macro-level stimulus would have to be having a generalized effect.[21]

Some decades ago I authored a thought experiment in which I applied these three levels of inclusiveness[22] to the church/sect or typological tradition in the sociology of religion.[23] A given "mentality" (predisposition, attitude) may be borne by an individual, an organization, or a society, for example. Of course, it may also be borne by a couple, a small group, a community; but to keep the discussion simple I posed three embodiments of a mentality: individual, institutional, and societal. Taking the oppositional nature of the sect type with respect to its social environment, and the "integrationist" nature of the church and denomination types, we immediately have six possibilities: individual oppositional mentalities, individual integrationist ones, institutional oppositional, institutional integrationist, societal oppositional, and societal integrationist. But to what would the individual, organization, or society be opposed, or with what would these be at peace with or comfortable with? An organization, for instance, may be opposed to individuals involving themselves with the environment, or it would want itself as an organized entity to be opposed even if its members are very much involved with it, or it may be opposed to the broader society. So far the possible combinations would yield eighteen possible stances. But matters are quite different if the environment to which, say, an individual is opposed would be a monistic one, wherein uniformity is demanded, or a pluralist environment, wherein varieties of belief systems are permitted. Now we have thirty-six possible stances, with a potential technical vocabulary of thirty-six terms.[24]

It is not necessary to review all of the thirty-six types here; indeed, it would be confusing since various authors may use any given term with a different meaning in mind. Suffice it to note that *First Peter* represents a meso-level oppositional stance toward the first century social environment. That social environment tended to be monist; it allowed for plural deities and cults, but only under the imperial umbrella. In such a setting, *First Peter* would have the individual be detached from the world—acting within it, not withdrawing from it, but being detached from its system of rewards and punishments. *First Peter* would also have its communities, its congregations, separate from other organizations; this is something of an institution-level separatism. Unlike the *Revelation* by John, however, *First Peter* does not present much by way of a macro-level critique.

---

21. Durkheim, *Rules of Sociological Method*, 134.

22. Many sociologists speak of "levels of analysis," but I avoid this term in order to prevent what I am describing from being confounded with Georges Gurvitch's "paliers, niveaux, plans étagés ou couches en profondeur"—Gurvitch, "Sociologie en profondeur," 157.

23. Blasi, "Dialecticizing the Types."

24. Ibid., 166, with a glossary on 169–70.

## Trans-Local Organization

While earlier Christian works showed regional ecclesiastical organization, such as Paul's supervision over the churches he had founded, John's concern with the churches to which he directed letters in the first part of his *Revelation*, and the Presbyter's network with congregations, *First Peter* embodies a concern on the part of one or more authors in Rome with churches in provinces far to the east in present-day Turkey. The letter presents the image of the local Christian communities being "living stones" that are built up into a spiritual house.[25] While in our own time, identity, not only with symbolic materials, such as Christian writings and rituals, but with organizations, is readily possible because of electronic media, that such would occur in antiquity is a notable achievement.

In the case of the authentic Pauline letters, it was a matter of Paul's personal network. By the time of Luke's *Acts of the Apostles*, Paul's visits to Jerusalem and his consultations with the Jerusalem leadership could be interpreted as being in some sense official in that they resulted in letters that Luke cites. But with *First Peter* there is the assumption that one or more persons in Rome have a role to play in encouraging Christians in remote locations. At about the same time, the *Letter of the Romans to the Corinthians* (First Clement), 95 CE, embodied an effort on the part of Roman Christian leaders to admonish a remote church about factions and conflict. The relationship between the Roman leadership and other Christian communities would become a matter of controversy for centuries to come. What is sociologically important is the emergence of sufficient organizational structure for it to lead to controversy.

## Household Code

*First Peter* has a code for an *oikos,* or household.[26] The purpose of the code in this case is explicitly to mollify critics who would claim the Christians were undermining the political order by threatening to undermine household patriarchy; the verses leading up to the household code encourage the readers to be subject to every human institution for "this is the will of God: by doing good, muzzling the ignorance of foolish people."[27] There is less talk of reciprocal respect between husband and wife than in the household codes in *Colossians* and *Ephesians*, but the household code of *First Peter* does speak of a slave suffering unjustly under a master, something that was impossible according to Aristotle. As David L. Balch notes, Aristotle held that as dependents, slaves and minors could make no claim against masters and parents and hence could suffer no real injustice, only something analogous to it.[28] Moreover, *First Peter* speaks of wives being Christians even as their husbands "disobey the word"; and ancient

---

25. 1 Pet 2:4; see Senior, "1 Peter," 15.
26. 1 Pet 2:18—5:7.
27. 1 Pet 2:15.
28. Balch, "Early Christian Criticism"; Aristotle, *Nicomachaean Ethics* 5:6:9.

philosophers held that wives should adopt the religions of their husbands.²⁹ So while the author seeks to mollify critics who viewed the Christians from the perspective of the dominant patriarchal culture, as in the cases of the authors of *Colossians* and *Ephesians*, the author of *First Peter* only goes half way in doing so.

## English Translation

### First Pseudepigraphic Letter of Peter

1 ¹Peter, an apostle of Jesus, Messiah, to the sojourners of the dispersion of Pontus, Galatia, Cappadocia, Asia, and Bithynia, who were chosen ²according to the foreknowledge of God the Father, by the sanctification of the spirit to obedience and the sprinkling of the blood of Jesus, Messiah: may grace and peace be multiplied for you.

³Blessed be the God and Father of our Lord Jesus, Messiah, who according to His great mercy begot us anew into a living hope by the resurrection of Jesus, Messiah from the dead, ⁴into an imperishable, undefiled, and unfading inheritance, preserved in the heavens for you, ⁵who by God's power are being guarded through faith in a salvation that is ready to be revealed. At the end time ⁶you will rejoice in this, even if for a little while it is necessary to be made sad by various trials,³⁰ ⁷so that the assaying of your faith, a testing³¹ more precious than gold, which perishes and which is assayed by fire, may be found amidst praise, glory, and honor in the revelation of Jesus, Messiah, ⁸whom you love while not seeing, in whom, though not yet seeing, you will rejoice with an inexpressible and glorified joy, ⁹obtaining the outcome of your faith, the salvation of the living.³²

¹⁰It was for this salvation that the prophets, who were prophesying about the grace which was to be yours, sought, and about which they carefully inquired, ¹¹inquiring into who or when³³ the spirit of Messiah within them was indicating when giving witness in advance to the sufferings toward Messiah's and the glories subsequent to them. ¹²It was revealed to them because

---

29. 1 Pet 3:1; Balch, "Early Christian Criticism," cites Dionysius of Halicanarsus, *Roman Antiquities* 2:25:1, and Plutarch, *Advice to Bride and Groom* 140:D and 144:DE.

30. Martin, "Present Indicative," associates "at the end time" with verse 6 and would make the verb tense future in English. He supports this with an analysis of ancient belief that one cannot be happy and sad at the same time—Martin, "Emotional Physiology."

31. "A testing": The comparative adjective, "more precious," refers to "assaying," not to "faith"; "a testing" is supplied resumptively to make this clear.

32. "Of the living," ψυχῶν: RSV translates as "of your souls," but "your" stands between "faith" and "salvation" and is not adjacent to "souls." The expression "salvation of your soul" in English also distinguishes the soul as something separate from the living person on earth, which is foreign to the thought of the author of *First Peter*. See Senior, "1 Peter," 33, who provides the translation "salvation of your souls" and then clarifies its meaning. Martin, "Present Indicative," argues that "rejoice" should be in the future in English translation; he translates ψυχῶν as "of your lives."

33. Kilpatrick, "1 Peter 1:11," renders this "Who is the Messiah and when will he come?"

they were not serving themselves but you in these matters, which now are announced to you through those preaching the good news to you in the holy spirit sent from heaven, things at which the angels[34] long to steal a glance.

¹³Therefore, girding the loins of your minds, being self-controlled, hope completely in the grace brought you by the revelation of Jesus, Messiah. ¹⁴As children of obedience,[35] not conforming in ignorance to your prior desires ¹⁵but according to the Holy One who called you, become holy yourselves in your conduct, ¹⁶for it is written, "Be holy, because I am holy."[36]

¹⁷And if you call upon a Father who judges impartially according to the work of each,[37] conduct yourselves with fear during the time of your exile, ¹⁸knowing that[38] you were not redeemed from your futile inherited way of life with perishables—gold and silver—¹⁹but with the precious blood of Messiah, like that of an unblemished and spotless lamb,[39] ²⁰known beforehand prior to the creation of the world but at the end of the ages appearing for your sake, ²¹you who through him have faith in God, Who raised him from the dead and bestowed upon him glory, so that your faith and hope are in God.

²²Having purified your lives by obedience to the truth for a genuinely mutual affection, love one another fervently with pure hearts, ²³reborn not from perishable but imperishable seed, through the living and abiding word of God; ²⁴for:

All flesh is like grass,

    And all its glory is like a blossom of the grass;

The grass dries out

    And the blossom falls off;

²⁵But the word of the Lord remains forever.[40]

---

34. I have been translating ἄγγελος as "messenger," but here it is necessary to make it clear that the author has heavenly beings rather than the deliverers of messages such as the prophets of old in mind.

35. Obedience is conformity to the law of God; children of obedience are those who would identify with such a way of life—Senior, "1 Peter," 40.

36. Lev uses this refrain often, e.g. at Lev 11:44, 45, and 20:7, using the wording of the Septuagint but not its full expression, which usually adds "I the Lord your God" or something of that nature.

37. Ps 28:4: "Requite them according to their work . . ." (RSV).

38. Horrell, "Product of a Petrine Circle?" sees the following as a Christological creed that is not paralleled elsewhere in the New Testament. This would be an example of *First Peter*'s use of broad Christian tradition.

39. Ibid., sees this as an allusion to Isa 53:7: "he was oppressed, and he was afflicted, yet he opened not his mouth; like a lamb that is led to the slaughter, and like a sheep that before its shearers is dumb, so he opened not his mouth" (RSV). Alternatively, Senior, "1 Peter," 44, notes the emphasis on the pristine condition of the lamb and suggests that *First Peter* is using Passover imagery. Of course, one need not see the Isaiah passage as independent of the Passover imagery.

40. Isa 40:6–8, not following the Septuagint, which translates as follows: "All flesh is grass, and all glory of humans is like a blossom of the grass; the grass dries out, and the blossom falls off, but the word of God remains with us forever."

And this is the word that is being proclaimed to you.

2 ¹So putting away every evil, every deceit, pretense, and envy, and all defamatory speech, ²long for the pure spiritual milk like a newborn infant, so that you may grow with it toward salvation, ³since you tasted and came to know[41] that the Lord is good.[42] ⁴Coming to him—a living stone, rejected by society[43] but a valuable chosen by God—⁵let yourselves as living stones, a spiritual house, be built into a holy priesthood, offering through Jesus, Messiah, spiritual sacrifices acceptable to God. ⁶For there is this[44] in a scripture: "Behold I am placing on Zion a select precious cornerstone, and one who believes in him will not be put to shame."[45]

⁷Hence an honor to those who believe, but for those not believing: "The stone that the builders rejected became what is at the head of the corner."[46] ⁸And: "A stone in the way and a rock of stumbling."[47] Those stumbling are those disbelieving the word; they were destined for that.

⁹But you are a chosen lineage,[48] a royal priesthood, a holy nation,[49] a people worth preserving,[50] so that you may proclaim the wonders[51] of the One Who called you from darkness into His marvelous light. ¹⁰Before, you were not a people, but now you are a people of God.[52] You were not shown mercy, but now you are being shown mercy.[53]

---

41. "Tasted and came to know": The Greek term, αὐξηθῆτε, means both "tasted" (RSV and *Das neue Testament*) and "came to know."

42. Ps 34:8, using the Septuagint Ps 33:9 phrase "that the Lord is good." The full verse in the Septuagint translates as "Taste and see that the Lord is good. Blessed is the man who hopes in him."

43. Literally, "by humans." This appears to be an allusion to Ps 118:22–23: "The stone which the builders rejected has become the head of the corner. This is the Lord's doing . . . " (RSV). E. Best, "1 Peter II 4–10," sees verses 2:4–7 not as a hymn, as some scholars had, but allusions to the Septuagint version of the Hebrew Bible.

44. Literally, "For it contains in a scripture." Senior, "1 Peter," 54, suggests it is a stock phrase for introducing a citation.

45. The cited text is Isa 28:16, closer to the Septuagint than to the Hebrew. The Septuagint translates as follows: "Behold I am inserting into the foundation stones of Zion a costly stone, a select precious cornerstone amid her foundation stones, and one who believes in him will not be put to shame." The stone is evidently a metaphor for a personage; consequently one could believe in or trust such a one.

46. Ps 118:22, using the wording of Septuagint Ps 117:22.

47. Allusion to Isa 8:14, which Paul also cites in Rom 9:33; *First Peter* uses the vocabulary found in Romans, not that found in the Septuagint. This does not necessarily mean he is citing Romans; he may simply be repeating broad Christian tradition—Senior, "1 Peter," 55.

48. Isa 43:20 refers to "my chosen people" with the same wording in the Septuagint.

49. Exod 19:6 uses the expressions "royal priesthood" and "holy nation" with the same wording in the Septuagint, where they are repeated at Exod 23:22.

50. This appears to be an allusion to the Septuagint language of Isa 43:21, Exod 19:5, and Exod 23:22.

51. Allusion to Septuagint wording of Isa 43:21.

52. This parallels Hos 1:9.

53. This parallels Hos 1:6.

¹¹Beloved, I encourage you as aliens and exiles⁵⁴ to abstain from the passions of the flesh, which militate against the spirit, ¹²keeping your conduct among the nations good so that by it those defaming you as criminals, from observing the good deeds, will praise God on a day of visitation.⁵⁵

¹³Be subject to every human authority for the sake of the Lord, whether to a king as a superior, ¹⁴or to governors sent by him for the punishment of evildoers but approval for doers of good; ¹⁵for this is the will of God: by doing good, muzzling the ignorance of foolish people, ¹⁶as free people and not as people having freedom as a cover for evil but as slaves of God. ¹⁷Pay honor to all: love the fellowship, fear God, pay honor to the royal power.⁵⁶

¹⁸Household slaves, be subordinate to the masters with all fear, not only to the good and kind ones but also to the unjust. ¹⁹For this is a grace if, out of consciousness of God, someone endures the pain of suffering unjustly. ²⁰For what credit is it if you keep sinning and are beaten? But if you keep doing good and are suffering, this is a grace from God. ²¹For you were called to this because⁵⁷ Messiah also suffered for you, leaving you an example for you to follow in his footsteps, ²²who "committed no sin, nor was deceit found in his mouth."⁵⁸ ²³Who, reviled, did not revile in return; suffering, did not threaten, but handed himself over to the One who judges justly.⁵⁹ ²⁴Who bore our sins with his body on the cross, so that having died to sins we may live in justice. By whose wounds you were healed.⁶⁰ ²⁵For you were like sheep led astray,⁶¹ but now you turned to the shepherd and guardian of your souls.

3 ¹Likewise, wives, be subordinate to your own husbands, so that even if some disobey the word they will be gained without a word through the conduct of the wives ²when they observe your pure conduct maintained with reverence.⁶² ³Let yours not be the conspicuous braids of hair, donning of gold, or wearing of fashionable clothing, ⁴but let yours be the secret of the

---

54. "Aliens and exiles": The terms allude to Ps 39:12, Septuagint Ps 38:13.

55. "Day of visitation": The expression appears in Isa 10:3; the Septuagint Greek has "the day of the visitation."

56. "Pay honor to all," πάντας τιμήσατε: This imperative is in the aorist (completed action) tense, while the three that follow are in the present (continuing action). Horrell, "'Honor Everyone . . . ,'" 196–98, argues that the aorist was used as a summary headline for the imperatives in the present that follow. Accordingly, I place a colon after it, differing from RSV and *Das neue Testament*. Ibid., 200–05, goes on to show that different words are used pointedly for honoring God and honoring royal power; he argues that it is consistent with the Christian fellowship facing official state persecution.

57. Horrell, "Product of a Petrine Circle?" sees what follows, up to verse 25, as another Christological creed that is not paralleled elsewhere in the New Testament.

58. Isa 53:9, following the wording of the Septuagint, except "sin" replaces "lawlessness."

59. "Himself" needs to be supplied here.

60. "By whose wounds you were healed": Isa 53:5, changing the verb from first person plural to second person plural in the Septuagint text.

61. Allusion to Isa 53:6.

62. "Maintained" is supplied.

human heart in the imperishability of the humble and tranquil spirit, which is precious before God. ⁵For that is how the holy wives who hoped in God adorned themselves, subordinating themselves to their own husbands, ⁶as Sara obeyed Abraham, calling him lord;[63] you became her children to do good and not to fear any terror.[64]

⁷Likewise let husbands conduct their family life with understanding,[65] showing honor to the wife as the weaker vessel and as coheirs of the gift of life, so that your prayers will not be thwarted.

⁸And finally, let all be[66] like-minded, sympathetic, familially loving, compassionate, unassuming, ⁹not returning evil for evil or verbal abuse for verbal abuse, but on the contrary giving blessing, for you were called to inherit blessing for this. ¹⁰For

> Let one wishing to love life
>
> and see good days
>
> Keep the tongue from evil
>
> and lips from speaking in deceit,
>
> ¹¹Turn away from evil and do good,
>
>     seek peace and pursue it,
>
> ¹²Because the Lord's eyes are upon the just,
>
>     And His ears open to their entreaties,
>
> But the face of God is against those doing evil.[67]

---

63. Kiley, "Like Sara," observes that the only place Sara calls Abraham "lord" is Gen 18:12 (in the Septuagint version), where it is not a case of obedience and may have been an insult. He suggests that the reason for citing Sara is that in Gen 12 and 20 she obeyed Abraham and posed as his sister when they were in a foreign land—and Christians were metaphorically aliens in their world. Abraham's treatment of Sarah was unjust, and the author is encouraging the Christians to endure unjust treatment. Sly, "1 Peter 3:66b," however, notes that in Gen 12 and 20 it is Abraham who obeys Sara, not the other way around. Sly continues, the writings of Philo and Josephus show that those two writers found her making suggestions and Abraham listening to be scandalous. If writing with scripture in mind, *First Peter* was ignoring the scriptural evidence and molding Sara to the imagined ideal of the Hellenistic wife. Senior, "1 Peter," 83, argues that the reference is not to Genesis but to the Testament of Abraham, where Sara is "a model of obedience to Abraham . . . and an example of fearlessness and good deeds. . . ."

64. "Terror": No husband is to be feared as much as God, nor is any threat to the Christian to be deemed comparable to the fear of the Lord—Senior, "1 Peter," 83.

65. This felicitous translation is given by Reicke, *Epistles of James, Peter, and Jude*, 100. Senior, "1 Peter," 83, interprets "with understanding," κατὰ γνῶσιν, as a consciousness of the ways of God. RSV has "live considerately." *Das neue Testament* is closer to Reicke with "walk understandingly" (geht verständnisvoll).

66. "Let . . . be": The verb needs to be supplied.

67. Ps 34:12–16, with somewhat different grammatical forms but the same vocabulary as Septuagint Ps 33:13–17a.

¹³And what person will harm you if you become zealots for the good? ¹⁴But if indeed you suffer for justice's sake, blessed are you.[68] And do not fear with their fear or be disturbed, ¹⁵but sanctify the Lord,[69] the Messiah, in your hearts, ready always for a defense before anyone who asks you for a statement about the hope that is in you, ¹⁶but with gentleness and respect, having a good conscience, so that in case you are defamed those who revile your good conduct in Messiah will be embarrassed. ¹⁷For if it is the will of God, it is better to suffer doing good than doing evil. ¹⁸For[70] Messiah also suffered once for sins, the just for the unjust, so that he might bring God to you, put to death in the flesh but made alive in the spirit, ¹⁹by which, after going to the spirits in prison,[71] he also preached ²⁰to those who disobeyed when God's patience waited in the days of Noah when the ark was constructed, into which a few—that is, eight lives—came safely through water.[72] ²¹And this[73] is a symbol that Baptism is now saving you, not a removal of grime from the flesh but a pledge to God of a good conscience through the resurrection of Jesus, Messiah, ²²who, after going to heaven where messengers, authorities, and powers obey him, is at the right hand of God.

4 ¹Messiah having suffered in the flesh, then, you also, arm yourself with the same insight: that one who suffers in the flesh has refrained from a sin, ²to live in the flesh for the remaining time no longer for the passions of humans but for the will of God. ³For enough of the time past was given over[74] to accomplishing the will of the nations, having lived in sensuality, passion, drunkenness, revelry, carousal, and wanton idolatry. ⁴Blaspheming, they are astonished by this: your not running along in this same flood of dissipation. ⁵They will give an account to the One having in preparation a judgment of[75] the living and the dead. ⁶For to this purpose the good news was announced

---

68. See Matt 5:10.

69. Allusion to Isa 8:13.

70. Horrell, "Product of a Petrine Circle?" sees verses 3:18–22 as another Christological creed that is not paralleled elsewhere in the New Testament.

71. Senior, "1 Peter," 101–04, makes the case that the spirits in prison are those referred to in "Jewish traditions about Enoch (see Gen 5:24; these are found especially in 1 Enoch)," punished by confinement for promiscuous unions with daughters of humans (Gen 6:2). The resultant offspring were the evildoers who were punished by the Great Flood. "What significance then did these ancient spirits possess according to the books of Enoch? They were important as patrons of the kings and mighty men of the world and as such constituted the origin and source of heathenism. Several passages in First Enoch make it clear that their punishment in the flood was thought of as a prototype of the coming judgment of the heathen rulers and oppressors"—Reicke, *Epistles of James, Peter, and Jude*, 110.

72. Cook, "1 Peter III.20," 77, translates this as "into which a few, that is eight persons, came safely through water." "Came safely through" translates διεσώθησαν. The eight lives were Noah, his three sons Shem, Ham, and Japeth, and the four wives (Gen 7:6–7), 13.

73. "This": Cook, "1 Peter III.20," argues that the relative pronoun beginning the verse refers to the preceding clause.

74. "Was given over": This is supplied.

75. "Judgment of": In the Greek, this is a verb in the infinitive.

to the dead,[76] so that judged according to humans in the flesh, they might live according to God in the spirit.

⁷But the end of all things is near. So be prudent and self-controlled for prayer. ⁸Above all, have earnest love for one another, for love covers a multitude of sins. ⁹Be hospitable to one another without grumbling. ¹⁰Just as each received a gift, serve it to one another as good stewards of the varying gift of God. ¹¹If anyone talks, let it be as words of God;[77] if anyone serves, let it be as from the strength that God supplies, so that God would be glorified by everything through Jesus, Messiah, whose is the glory and power forever and ever. Amen.

¹²Beloved, do not be surprised at your[78] fiery ordeal occurring to test you, as though it were something strange[79] happening to you. ¹³Rather insofar as you share in the sufferings of the Messiah, rejoice, so that, gladdened, you may rejoice in the revelation of his glory. ¹⁴If you are reviled for the name of Messiah, blessed are you,[80] because the spirit of glory and that of God are resting upon you. ¹⁵But let none of you suffer as a murderer, thief, evildoer, or as a transgressor of social boundaries;[81] ¹⁶but if as a Christian, be not ashamed, but give glory to God in this name.[82] ¹⁷For the time has come[83] for the judgment to begin with the house of God;[84] and with us first, what will the end be for those disregarding the good news of God? ¹⁸And, "If the just is saved with difficulty, where will the godless and the sinner appear?"[85] ¹⁹So even those suffering in accord with God's will should entrust their lives to the faithful Creator by doing good.

5:¹So, as a fellow presbyter and witness to the sufferings of the Messiah and also as sharer in the coming glory to be revealed, I am exhorting the

---

76. Senior, "1 Peter," 116, proposes that this refers to the gospel being proclaimed to people who then converted but have died before the time of the letter.

77. "Words of God": Senior, "1 Peter," 121, notes that this phrase often refers to oracles in the Septuagint; so he translates it as "oracle of God."

78. Literally, "among you."

79. There is a play on words in Greek here: "surprised" in the preceding verse, ξενίζεσθε, is a verb form of the same stem as "strange," ξένου.

80. See Matt 5:11 and Luke 6:22.

81. "Transgressor of social boundaries," ἀλλοτριεπίσκοπος: J. Brown, "Just a Busybody?" maintains that the term refers to crossing boundaries relevant to the household code. An *allotriepiscopos* is one who watches over what are not one's own affairs. According to R. Brown, Xenophon and Philo use the term to refer to violating gender roles—e.g., women involving themselves in affairs outside the household, which they saw as a serious matter. RSV translates the term as "mischief-maker." *Das neue Testament* is closer to Brown's reading.

82. Horrell, "Label Χριστιανός," argues that the name *Christian* was a label attached to the followers of the way by outsiders, carrying some stigma with it. *First Peter*, he argues, embraced the term, as labeled groups often do, changing its valence from negative to positive and using it to reinforce identity.

83. "Has come" is supplied; there is no verb in the Greek text.

84. Jer 25:29; Ezek 9:6; and Mal 3:1–6 speak of the punishment by God beginning at the Temple in Jerusalem—Senior, "1 Peter," 132.

85. Prov 11:31, slightly abbreviating the wording of the Septuagint.

presbyters among you: shepherd the flock among you, pastoring them toward God, not out of compulsion but willingly, not out of greed but out of a readiness, ³not lording it over those entrusted to you but becoming examples for the flock. ⁴And when the chief shepherd appears, you will be awarded the unfading crown of glory. ⁵Likewise, you who are younger, be subordinate to the presbyters. And all clothe yourselves with humility, for God "resists the proud, but gives grace to the humble."[86] ⁶Be humbled, then, under the mighty hand of God, so that He may lift you up at the time, ⁷after casting your every care upon Him, for His concern is for you.

⁸Be sober, be watchful. Your adversary the devil is going about roaring like a lion seeking to swallow someone. ⁹Withstand him, steadfast in the faith, knowing the same kinds of sufferings are brought about for your brothers in the world. ¹⁰But once you have suffered a little, the God of every grace who called you by Messiah Jesus, to His eternal glory will Himself restore you, confirm you, strengthen you, establish you. ¹¹His is the power forever. Amen.

¹²I wrote to you briefly, sending by[87] Silvanus, faithful brother as I deem him. I was[88] exhorting and testifying that there is this true grace of God.[89] Stand fast in it. ¹³The co-elect church[90] in Babylon[91] greets you, also my son Mark. ¹⁴Greet one another with a kiss of love. Peace be to you all who are in Messiah.

---

86. Prov 3:34, following the wording of the Septuagint, where the subject is "The Lord," κύριος, not "God."

87. Richards, "Silvanus Was Not Peter's Secretary," makes the case that "I write by," γράφω διά, means "I send it by."

88. "I was" is supplied. A participial construction referring to "I" occurs here.

89. Alternatively, "that this is a true grace of God." It is unclear what the antecedent of "this" is.

90. "Church" is supplied; the Greek simply has a feminine adjectival form, "co-elect."

91. "Babylon," i.e. Rome.

*Chapter 21*

# The Pastoral Epistles

## Introduction

THERE ARE THREE LETTERS composed together in, as it were, a triptych, ascribed to Paul of Tarsus and addressed to Timothy in two instances, and to Titus in one instance. In modern Bibles they are presented as *First Timothy*, *Second Timothy*, and *Titus*. As with the other pseudonymous letters in the New Testament, their authors associate them with persons known to the Christian public. In the case of the two letters addressed to Timothy, the addressee was known from Luke's *Acts of the Apostles* as well as from the authentic letters of Paul. In the opening of *First Timothy*, the author deliberately makes the fictitious nature of the work evident by contradicting the information to be found in *Acts*. "Just as I urged you, when I was going to Macedonia, to remain in Ephesus . . . "; "And sending two of those assisting him to Macedonia, Timothy and Erastus, he stayed some time in Asia."[1] Toward the closing of *Second Timothy*, the author depicts Paul awaiting trial in Rome, saying that only Luke (the author of *Acts* who ended that work with Paul awaiting trial in Rome) remained with him; and he says that Titus went to Dalmatia. Titus would have been known to Christians from *Galatians* and *Second Corinthians*, and there is nothing in either letter to associate him with Dalmatia. In *Titus*, the author says "I left you in Crete . . ." even though nothing in the authentic letters of Paul associates Titus with Crete and *Acts* 27 makes it clear that Paul never set foot on that island.[2] As a further measure of obvious fictionalizing, *Second Timothy* depicts Paul asking for a cloak and books to be brought to him from Troas, even as he is on the verge of execution in far-away Rome.[3] Consequently we can infer that the Pastorals were written late enough for readers to have some familiarity with *Acts* and with the authentic Paulines *as a collection of*

---

1. 1 Tim 1:3a; Acts 19:21b. R. Collins, *Letters that Paul Did Not Write*, 97, points out the discrepancy.
2. Titus 1:5. See R. Collins, *Letters that Paul Did Not Write*, 97–98.
3. 2 Tim 4:13; Houlden, *Pastoral Epistles*, 33. One might infer that the author knew of relics, as it were, of Paul in the possession of a Christian community in Troas.

*letters*, and they were written in a way to call to mind the history and heritage of Paul as the author develops organizational and theological arguments.

The Pastorals depict Timothy and Titus as apostolic delegates over local church communities. Benjamin Fiore notes that this points to a second generation, post-apostolic supervisory system; he dates the pastorals to around 89–90 CE, a little earlier than I would.[4] He also notes that the author makes not being a recent convert a requirement for church office, something not thinkable for a disciple within Paul's lifetime.[5] Nevertheless, community functions, liturgy, and office titles are not as solidified as they are in the non-canonical *First Clement* (ca 96–97). While Fiore thus places the pastorals before *First Clement*, I think it could be contemporaneous with it, with the solidification of office titles and the like being more advanced in Clement's Rome than in the Pastorals' Asia Minor. In any event, the Christian movement reflected in the Pastorals is less solidified than its later reflection in the letters of Ignatius (ca 110–115), which were largely directed to Asian churches. J.L. Houlden observes that the Pastorals describe a settled church, not a hasty mission prior to an expected immanent Second Coming. He notes further that the vocabulary of the Pastorals resembles that of late first- and early second-century Christian and non-Christian writers, and that many words are shared with the *Gospel of Luke* and the *Acts of the Apostles*.[6]

Despite the obvious fictionalizing and evident late date of the Pastorals, some reputable scholars maintain that they were actually written by Paul. This is not the place to review the literature on the subject, but a few arguments against that position can be highlighted here. The Pastorals present themselves as letters from Paul to two people who had worked closely with him. Nevertheless, as Raymond Collins notes,[7] they begin with formal introductions, as if the recipient did not know the sender: "Paul, Apostle of Jesus the Messiah by command of God our savior and of Jesus the Messiah our hope, to Timothy a legitimate child in faith. . . ."[8] "Paul, an apostle of the Messiah, Jesus, by the will of God, in accordance with the promise of life which is in the Messiah, Jesus, to Timothy, a beloved child. . . ."[9] In the case of *Titus*, the address does not even seem to be directed to someone familiar with the Christian tradition: "Paul, slave of God, an apostle of Jesus the Messiah according to the faith of the elect of God and the knowledge of the truth that conforms to piety, as well as the hope for the eternal life that God, free from deceit, promised from eternity. And he made his word manifest in its own time through the preaching with which I was entrusted according

---

4. Fiore, *Pastoral Epistles*, 19. *Das neue Testament*, 743, opts for the year 75 CE, though such a conclusion seems grossly undetermined from the reasons the editors give.

5. See 1 Tim 3:6.

6. Houlden, *Pastoral Epistles*, 22–23, 2, 24–25.

7. R. Collins, *Letters that Paul Did Not Write*, 92–93.

8. 1 Tim 1:1–2a.

9. 2 Tim 1:1–2a.

to the command of our savior God. To Titus, genuine child in a common faith...."[10] One would hardly find such greetings in genuine letters between intimates.

The Pastorals also "lack many of the particles and shorter words that Paul commonly used—for example, 'again' (*palin*), 'as' (*hōste*), 'then' (*ara*), and 'wherefore' (*dia*). These omissions are significant because writers tend to use such short words almost unconsciously in their writings."[11] Moreover, the Pastorals use some of the words that also appear in the authentic letters of Paul to convey different meanings: In Titus 3:1 *archai* means human rulers rather than heavenly principalities.[12] The phrase *en Christō* means "Christian" in the Pastorals rather than "Christian existence."[13] The Pastorals see faith as a form of knowledge rather than, as in Paul's authentic letters, as trust; the Pastorals thus parallel the Greco-Roman idea of the salvific effects of knowledge and the actions that flow from knowledge.[14] Moreover, *First Timothy* cites the *Gospel of Luke* as scripture.[15]

*Second Timothy* differs in genre from the other two Pastorals; it is a testamentary statement, similar to Acts 20:17–38, which depicts Paul addressing the Ephesian elders. Another example of the genre is the apocryphal *Testament of the Twelve Patriarchs*. The literary genre uses the purported author as a model, includes exhortations to the addressee to carry on the tradition, warns of false teachers, affirms ultimate correctness, and predicts the author's impending death. *First Timothy* and *Titus*, in contrast, are "church order" statements. They "resemble official memoranda given in classical antiquity to subordinate officials on their assumption of a new position"; such memoranda were public documents meant to inform those over whom the new officers were appointed. The Pastorals differ from these, however, insofar as they specify qualities, behavioral patterns, and attitudes as well as duties.[16]

The letters have certain opponents in mind: the "circumcision faction" having "Jewish myths";[17] people who would like to be teachers of the Law;[18] people who favor dietary restrictions;[19] and people who prohibit marriage.[20] The author therefore continues Paul's argument against requiring circumcision of gentile Christians, but it is unclear what "Jewish myths" were at issue; they could have been ones that mainstream rabbinic Judaism rejected as well. The dietary restrictions could have been ones re-

---

10. Titus 1:1–4a.
11. R. Collins, *Letters that Paul Did Not Write*, 95.
12. See Rom 8:38.
13. R. Collins, *Letters That Paul Did Not Write*, 95–96.
14. Fiore, *Pastoral Epistles*, 7.
15. 1 Tim 5:18; see Luke 10:10.
16. Fiore, *Pastoral Epistles*, 8–10.
17. Titus 1:10 and 14.
18. 1 Tim 1:7.
19. Titus 1:15; 1 Tim 4:3.
20. 1 Tim 4:3.

lated to the Torah, but it could also have been a continuation of the debate over meat offered to idols. Prohibiting marriage appears to reflect a Hellenistic asceticism rather than anything Jewish. The author appears to be intent on drawing lines between what was in the tradition of the Messiah Jesus and what was not.

## The Sociology of Degradation Ceremonies

Lloyd Pietersen has made a noteworthy sociological analysis of the Pastorals as "degradation ceremony."[21] The concept "degradation ceremony" arose out of the labeling-theory tradition of the sociology of deviance, which holds that crimes and other deviant actions are not criminal or deviant themselves but are defined as such through social interaction in society. Once a deed is defined as deviant, a person who is identified as one who performs it comes to be defined as deviant as well. Affixing a label upon someone as deviant is an important social event, taking form in such official processes as trials and commitments to mental treatment facilities. Degradation ceremonies are public processes by which individuals or groups take on such negative labels. A degradation ceremony need not pertain to deviance alone; most notably, they may involve labeling the target as a member of an out-group. Thus a degradation process places the target at odds with an acceptable in-group, either by characterizing the target as deviant or as foreign or enemy. In Pietersen's analysis of the Pastorals, the status to be conferred on the target individuals or group is that of *enemy*.

Harold Garfinkel coined the expression *degradation ceremony*. He defined it as "any communicative work whereby the public identity of an actor is transformed into something looked on as lower in the local scheme of social types."[22] Thus the term applies not only to such formal processes as legal and medical findings but to gossip and literature as well. It presupposes a scheme of social inequality in which individuals and identity groups can be ranked in some sense. It is a matter of status ranking rather than economic or political standing, though status can affect those too. Status ranking refers to prestige, social estimation—as promoted or undermined by genealogy, public opinion, tradition, and even charisma.[23] The status so ranked is not peripheral to the social standing of an individual but central, a "master status." It becomes the most important thing to know about a person or group. In bringing about a change in such social standing, the perpetrator[24] may claim the target appears to be one thing but is

---

21. Pietersen, "Despicable Deviants."

22. Garfinkel, "Conditions of Successful Degradation," 420.

23. Weber, *Economy and Society*, 305–06. The concept is broader than the "honor/shame" outcome, on which so many scholars have been focusing in the past few decades; "honor/shame" is more tied to the immediate situational outcome.

24. Garfinkel used negative terms in describing the process and those who take part in it. To appreciate the reason for this, one should recall that Garfinkel was writing in the aftermath of the Army/McCarthy Hearings, in which Senator Joseph McCarthy tried to advance his political stature by denouncing harmless people as "Communists." Ironically, it backfired on him when he became the

another in reality, or the target falsely operates as one kind of agent but is truly operating as another, or is appealing in trivial ways but dangerous in some important way. Status degradation involves moral indignation. "Moral indignation serves to effect the ritual destruction of the person denounced. Unlike shame, which does not bind persons together, moral indignation may reinforce group solidarities."[25] The creation of a moral solidarity in the in-group explains the appeal of degradation ceremonies. "Structurally, a degradation ceremony bears close resemblance to ceremonies of investiture and elevation."[26] To be successful, the denunciation in a degradation ceremony must not simply be about a person but about a *type* of person; the target becomes "one of those." And "one of those" needs be a moral category, not simply a category the audience does not prefer. Finally, the denouncer must speak for the collective, not as a private person.

Pietersen argues that the Pastorals embody a status degradation ceremony that transformed "insiders" into "outsiders." The author fictively assumed the persona of Paul in order to speak from tradition, much as a twenty-first century editorialist may assume the persona of Abraham Lincoln to write about preserving the union of a nation founded on principles if not always the reality of equality. Assuming the pseudonym of Paul the Apostle was more than a convention in the three letters, and addressing the letters to the similar personages, Timothy and Titus also served to enable the author to speak on behalf of the Christian collective. The targets who are denounced in terms of types by the Pastorals are members of the faith community, whom the author describes as people who had made a shipwreck of their faith and who will depart from the faith.[27] As Pieteren reads the three letters, they have the form of church order statements in order to enable the author to speak for the collective, but their point is to turn the author's targets into outsiders.

## The Greater Oikos

The Pastorals envisage the wider Christian movement in organizational terms. The movement never did develop into a unified entity since the eastern churches never recognized a primacy on the part of the Roman church; but if carried to its logical conclusion and implemented, the organizational form outlined in the Pastorals would tend in that direction—albeit with Ephesus rather than Rome at the pinnacle of the structure. The whole of the Church would be analogous to a household or *oikos*,[28] with the *episkopos* becoming the analog to the *paterfamilias*, governing with the presbyters, the heads of the separate households. Some households were undoubtedly

---

target of a similar degradation ceremony.

25. Garfinkel, "Conditions of Successful Degradation," 421.
26. Ibid.
27. 1 Tim 1:19, 4:1.
28. McGinn, *Jesus Movement*, 293.

headed by women; so when the instructions speak of correcting a household head or other household members, they specify by gender: "Do not rebuke an older man but urge him as you would a father, younger men as brothers, ²older women as mothers, younger women as sisters, with all propriety."[29] There are also instructions about deacons—men, but by exception also women.[30] Still other instructions are about widows.[31] The *episkopos* would be concerned with all of these.

The greater *oikos* is precisely what the Roman Empire was supposed to be. Here we have the countercultural Christian movement tending toward the same form as that of the Empire. Sociologically conceptualized, this is a case of a tendency toward organizational isomorphism. Amos Hawley famously articulated an organizational principle of isomorphism: "Units subject to the same environmental conditions, or to the environmental conditions as mediated through a given key unit, acquire a similar form of organization."[32] Most of the literature on formal organization focuses on modern bureaucracy, but a few modern processes can be found relevant to ancient organization. The formation and development of organizations has come to be termed *structuration*. Structuration tends to occur, among other times, when organizations interact and when there are patterns of domination or coalition. Hence the more the Christian movement had transactions with the government of the Empire, such as when its members were denounced and tried, the more the movement itself needed to take on some structure. For example, if a church member were arrested, the church would need to assemble resources to provide for that member's dependents, pay bribes and fines, and develop networks to provide refuge out of town. All such activities require some kind of a command structure. The structure needs to be legitimate in the minds of the wider membership, and the pattern of legitimate governance known to the members was that of the *oikos*. Consequently, in the same way that the Roman Empire organized itself legitimately after the pattern of the *oikos*, so did the Christian movement. When a given pattern, in this case the *oikos*, reaches a certain threshold of prevalence, beyond which adoption provides legitimacy rather than improves performance, it may be said to be predicated upon a myth and have something of a ceremonial existence.[33] The command structure can thus expand beyond the point at which it became necessary.

---

29. 1 Tim 5:1–2, my translation; the RSV fails to show the common linguistic parallel between the male presbyter and the female presbyters. Fiore, *Pastoral Epistles*, 101, reads the two references to elders as not referring to officers but to age designations, but one must ask why the Pastor would take the trouble to make age and gender distinctions here if it were not a matter of offices or positions.

30. 1 Tim 3:8–12.

31. 1 Tim 5:3–16.

32. Hawley, "Human Ecology," 334.

33. Mayer and Rowan, "Institutional Organizations"; Dimaggio and Powell, "Iron Cage Revisited."

THE PASTORAL EPISTLES

# English Translations

## First Letter to Timothy

1 ¹Paul, Apostle of Messiah Jesus by command of God our savior and of Messiah Jesus our hope, ²to Timothy a legitimate child in faith: Grace, mercy, peace from God the Father and Jesus the Messiah our Lord.

³Just as I urged you, when I was going to Macedonia, to remain in Ephesus[34] to instruct some persons not to teach a different doctrine ⁴or pay attention to myths and endless genealogies, which generate useless speculations rather than a household of God in faith, so I urge you now.[35] ⁵The purpose of the instruction is love from a pure heart, from a good conscience, and from a sincere faith. ⁶When some persons deviated from these, they turned to empty talk, ⁸wishing to be teachers of the law, without understanding either what they are saying nor what they are speaking so confidently about.

⁸But we know the law is good if someone applies it legitimately, ⁹knowing that the law is not set down for the just person but for the lawless, the undisciplined, the impious, sinners, the unholy, the godless, those who kill fathers and mothers, murderers, ¹⁰male prostitutes, pederasts, kidnappers,[36] liars, perjurers, and anything else that is opposed to the teaching that is wholesome according to the good news of the glory of the blessed God with which I was entrusted.

¹²I am thankful to Messiah Jesus, our Lord, who strengthened me, because he regarded me faithful, placing in ministry me, ¹³one who formerly disparaged, persecuted, and mistreated; but I was granted mercy because in ignorance I acted with mistrust; ¹⁴and the grace of our Lord overflowed with faith and the love which is in Messiah Jesus. ¹⁵The saying is trustworthy and worthy of full acceptance: "Messiah Jesus came into the world to save sinners"; I am the first of them. ¹⁶However, I was granted mercy through him, so that with me, the foremost, Messiah Jesus showed universal forbearance as a model of those about to trust in him for eternal life. ¹⁷And to the immortal, invisible, only God, King of the ages, be honor and glory forever and ever. Amen.

¹⁸I entrust this instruction to you, son, Timothy, according to the prophecies leading up to you, so that you may wage the good campaign with them, ¹⁹having a trustworthy and good conscience, which some, rejecting, suffered shipwreck concerning the faith. ²⁰Hymenaeos and Alexander[37] are among them, whom I handed over to Satan to be disciplined so that they not blaspheme.

---

34. As noted in the introduction, this contrasts Acts 19:22.

35. "So I urge you now": This is implied by the opening "just as" in verse 3 and needs to be supplied; see Fiore, *Pastoral Epistles*, 40.

36. A kidnapper, ἀνδραποιστής, is a stock character in denunciations, referring to a kidnapper who sells the victims as slaves, sometimes subjecting young males to cosmetic makeovers to market them as homoerotic sex objects—Harrill, "Vice of Slave Dealers."

37. Hymenaeos and Alexander appear to be the prime targets of the "degradation ceremony" embodied in the Pastorals.

2 ¹So I urge, first of all, petitions, prayers, requests, thanksgivings be made for all people, ²for kings and all who are in authority, that we may lead a tranquil and peaceful life in all piety and holiness. ³This would be good and pleasing before God our savior, ⁴who wishes all people to be saved and to come to knowledge of the truth. ⁵For there is one God, and one mediator of God and humans, the human Messiah Jesus, ⁶the one giving himself as a ransom for all, giving³⁸ testimony in his own times. ⁷For this I was appointed preacher and apostle—I am telling the truth, I am not lying—teacher of the gentiles with fidelity and truth.

⁸So I wish that men in every place to pray, lifting prayerful hands without ire and argument; ⁹and likewise that women dress in respectable apparel, with reverence and moderation, not with braids and gold, pearls, or costly clothing,³⁹ ¹⁰but wear⁴⁰ what is fitting for women proclaiming the worship of God.

During good works,⁴¹ ¹¹let a woman learn in silence whenever in a subordinate status.⁴² ¹²Now I do not permit a woman to teach or domineer over a man, but to be in silence. ¹³For Adam was formed first, then Eve;⁴³ ¹⁴and it was not Adam who was misled, but the woman, deceived, came into a transgression. ¹⁵But she will be saved through childbearing if the children remain in faith, love, and holiness with self-control.⁴⁴

---

38. The second "giving" is supplied.

39. Verses 8 and 9 appear to be allusions to 1 Cor 1:10 and 11:10, respectively. In the former verse, Paul cautions against dissension. In the latter verse, he advised that women "prophesying" in the assembly should wear hair coverings for respectability, even if outside the assembly they were mere slaves; covering the hair was what women with some status could do. Here, the Pastor warns against women going too far, wearing costly raiment, which would defeat the equalizing effect of all women being entitled to dress respectably.

40. "Wear": This is supplied, repeating the verb κοσμεῖν in verse 9, where it is translated as "dress."

41. "During good works": The United Bible Societies Greek and RSV edit this as part of the preceding sentence, but it does not really make sense there. In this translation it is associated with the following sentence. The sentence takes up a new topic; so I re-paragraph it accordingly.

42. "Whenever in a subordinate status": literally, "in every subordination."

43. Gen 2:21–22; 1 Cor 11:8–9.

44. According to Waters, "Saved through Childbearing," this is an allusion to Gen 3:16: "To the woman he said, 'I will greatly multiply your pain in childbearing; in pain you shall bring forth children, yet your desire shall be for your husband, and he shall rule over you'" (RSV). He goes on to suggest that the childbearing is metaphorical since the children are the virtues: faith, love, holiness, and self-control. Such a reading does not follow grammatically, since the virtues would be both the subject of the clause ("if they remain . . . ") and the object of the proposition ("in"). Rather, the subject of the concluding clause would be related to "childbearing"; hence I supply "the children" as the subject. This seems to be an allusion to Gen 3:15: God "will put enmity between" the serpent or devil and Eve, and between the serpent's seed and her seed, and the latter "shall bruise" the serpent's head and the serpent "shall bruise his heel" (RSV). The Pastor is not reading the Genesis verse as an explanation of serpents' crawling on their bellies, which is what that verse was probably about originally, but as providing types in salvation history. Thus it says womankind will be saved through offspring, not an individual woman.

3 ¹This saying is trustworthy: If anyone aspires to be a bishop, he desires a good work. ²So it is necessary for the bishop to be irreproachable, a husband of one wife, temperate, prudent, respectable, hospitable, apt at teaching, ³not quarrelsome, but gentle, peaceable, not greedy, ⁴managing his own house well, keeping children in control with all respectfulness. ⁵Now if someone does not know how to manage his own household, how will he care for the church of God? ⁶Not a new convert, lest puffed up he fall under the devil's verdict. ⁷But he must also have a good recommendation from outsiders, lest he fall into the reproach and snare of the devil.

⁸Similarly deacons should be worthy, not insincere, not given to much wine, not greedy, ⁹keeping the mystery of the faith in a clear conscience. ¹⁰And they should be examined first, then being blameless they may serve. ¹¹Likewise women[45] should be worthy, not slanderers,[46] sober, faithful in everything. ¹²Let deacons be husbands of one wife, managing children and their own household well, ¹³for those serving well as deacons obtain standing and much confidence in themselves by faith in Messiah Jesus.

¹⁴I am writing these things to you while hoping to come to you soon. ¹⁵But if I delay, they are for you to know how it is necessary to conduct yourself in the household of God, which is the church of the living God, a pillar and mainstay of the truth. ¹⁶And the mystery of piety is surely great:

> Who was made manifest through flesh,
>> Was vindicated through the spirit,
>> Was seen through messengers,[47]
> Was preached amidst the nations,
>> Was believed amidst the world,
>> Was taken up amidst glory.

4 ¹Now the spirit says expressly that some will become apostates from the faith in the later ages, occupying themselves with erring spirits and demonic teachings, ²through the pretense of liars who have been seared in their own conscience, ³who prohibit marriage, would have you abstain from foods that God created for sharing with thanksgiving among the faithful and those understanding the truth ⁴that every creation of God is good and nothing rejected that was received with thanksgiving, ⁵for it is made holy by the word of God and by prayer.

---

45. These would appear to be female deacons. No feminine word meaning "deaconess" seemed to be in use; in Rom 16:1 Paul uses a masculine form, deacon, for Phoebe "our sister." So to refer to deaconesses here, the author speaks of "women" in the context of a discussion of deacons. Fiore, *Pastoral Epistles*, 81, also understands this to be a reference to female deacons.

46. Same word as "devils."

47. "Through messengers," ἀγγέλοις could be translated "by messengers," but the parallel structure of the verse favors an instrumental sense.

⁶Setting forth these things to the brothers and sisters, you would be a good minister of Messiah Jesus, trained in the statements of the faith and the good teachings that you have followed. ⁷But avoid profane myths and old women's tales.[48] Rather, train[49] yourself for piety; ⁸for "Bodily exercise is advantageous for a few things, but piety is advantageous for all things, holding out the promise of life now and to come."[50] ⁹This saying is trustworthy and worthy of universal acceptance. ¹⁰For we strive and struggle for this because we have hoped in a living God Who is a savior of all people, especially the faithful.[51]

¹¹Command and teach these things. ¹²Let no one look down on[52] your youth, but become a model for the faithful by word, manner of life, love, fidelity, purity. ¹³Until I come, turn your mind to the public reading, exhortation, teaching. ¹⁴Do not neglect the gift that was given you through prophecy with the laying on of the presbyter's hands. ¹⁵Take care of these things, immerse yourself[53] in them, so that your progress would be evident to all. ¹⁶Look to yourself and to the teaching; be persistent with them, for when doing this you will save both yourself and those listening to you.

5 ¹Do not rebuke an older man but urge him as you would a father, younger men as brothers, ²older women as mothers, younger women as sisters, with all propriety.[54]

³Give honoraria to widows who are truly widows.[55] ⁴But if a widow has children or grandchildren, first let them learn to show piety toward their own household and give recompense to the parents, for this is pleasing before God. ⁵But one who is truly a widow and has been left alone has hoped in God and remains in supplications and prayers night and day. ⁶But one who lives luxuriating has died. ⁷Instruct these too, so that they would be irreproachable. ⁸But if anyone does not provide for dependents and especially those in the household,[56] that one denied the faith and is worse than an unbeliever. ⁹Let a widow be enrolled who is at least sixty years old, a wife of one husband, ¹⁰at-

---

48. "Old women's tales," γραώδεις μύθου: Fiore, *Pastoral Epistles*, 92, suggests that some of the tendencies the Pastor is warning against were related to female celibacy as championed in the *Acts of Paul and Thecla*.

49. "Train," γύμναζε: It is interesting that the Pastor uses this athletic term derived from the Greek practice of men exercising naked, which would be objectionable from a Jewish cultural perspective. It is hard to imagine Paul, for example, making such a recommendation using such language.

50. Fiore, *Pastoral Epistles*, 93, in his comment on the following verse, identifies this verse as an adage, employing words that are unusual for the New Testament.

51. "Especially," μάλιστα: H. Kim, "Interpretation of μάλιστα," argues that this term means "especially" every time it is used in the Pastorals.

52. This may be based on 1 Corinthians 16:11, though different Greek words are used.

53. "Immerse yourself": literally, be.

54. "Older man . . . older women," πρεσβυτέρῳ . . . πρεσβυτέρας.

55. Fiore, *Pastoral Epistles*, 102, argues that this should be translated, "Give honoraria," since the passage is about supporting the widows.

56. "Especially," μάλιστα: See note at 4:10.

tested by good works, if she parented, was hospitable, washed the feet of saints, helped the oppressed, was devoted to every good work. [11]But deny younger widows, for when they rebel against the Messiah they want to remarry,[57] [12]and have the condemnation of surrendering the prior pledge; [13]and while they are idle they also learn to go from house to house, not only idle but also gossipy and meddlesome; they learn[58] to talk about what they should not. [14]Thus I want the younger women to marry, parent, manage homes, give to an adversary no pretext for abusing us, [15]for some already turned away following Satan. [16]If any faithful woman[59] has widows, let her aid them and not let the church be burdened so that it can aid the true widows.

[17]The presbyters who govern well should be deemed worthy of double pay, especially[60] those laboring by word and teaching; [18]for the scripture says, "You shall not muzzle an ox when it is threshing,"[61] and "The worker is worthy of his pay."[62] [19]Do not entertain an accusation against a presbyter unless it is supported by two or three witnesses. [20]Reprove those sinning before all so that the others too would have fear. [21]I charge you, before God, Messiah Jesus, and those chosen as messengers, that you observe these things without discrimination, not acting out of partisanship. [22]Impose hands upon no one hastily or join in another's sins; keep yourself pure.

[23]From now on do not drink water only, but a little red[63] wine because of the stomach and your many ailments.[64]

[24]The sins of some people are public, leading those following them to judgment also; [25]in the same way good public works, having a different effect, cannot be hidden.[65]

6 [1]Let those who are under the yoke as slaves regard their masters as worthy of honor so that the name and teaching of God would not be defamed. [2]And those having believing masters should not despise them, because they

---

57. Literally, "marry," but as widows that would amount to violating the requirement of marrying only once.

58. "They learn" is supplied because the infinitive is dependent on the earlier "they learn."

59. The author assumes that younger dependent women would be under the supervision of the mistress of the household—Fiore, *Pastoral Epistles*, 107.

60. "Especially," μάλιστα: See note at 4:10.

61. Deut 25:4, using the vocabulary but not the word order of the Septuagint. 1 Cor 9:9 also cites the verse, but using different wording.

62. This quotes Luke 10:7, not the parallel at Matt 10:10. In saying this statement is from scripture, the author is citing Luke as a published work; this reinforces a late date of the Pastorals, well after the death of Paul of Tarsus.

63. "Red": literally, colored.

64. This seems to be a recommendation against an asceticism that would have one abstain from wine. In an environment in which water is rarely pure, abstaining from wine, which Epictetus recommended as a way of controlling one's passions (Fiore, *Pastoral Epistles*, 113 cites him), would be imprudent.

65. This is a very cryptic statement, presumably an adage that leaves much to be implied. A difficulty that is not resolved in this translation or the RSV and that in Fiore, *Pastoral Epistles*, is a lack of gender agreement between "sins" and "public."

are brothers; but rather serve them because those devoting themselves to good work are trustworthy and beloved.

Teach and encourage these things. ³If anyone teaches a heretical doctrine and does not turn to statements that are sound, those of our Lord Jesus, Messiah, and to teaching according to piety, ⁴that one has become conceited, understanding nothing, but has a morbid craving for controversy and disputes about words, from which comes jealousy, discord, defamation, evil suspicions, ⁵irritations of people who have been destroyed in mind and defrauded of truth, thinking piety to be a source of gain. ⁶There is great gain, however, in piety-with-contentment, ⁷for we brought nothing into the world, so that we can bring nothing out of it. ⁸But having sustenance and shelter, let us be content with these. ⁹But those wanting to be rich will fall into temptation, snares, and many foolish and harmful passions that will plunge people into ruin and destruction. ¹⁰For the love of money is the root of all evil; when striving for it some go astray from the faith and pierce themselves with many woes.

¹¹But you, God's person, flee such things. Rather, pursue justice, piety, faith, love, patience, gentleness. ¹²Struggle in the good contest of faith, grasp eternal life, to which you were called and pronounced the good confession before many witnesses. ¹³I instruct you before God, Who gives life to all, and before Messiah Jesus, who testified to the good confession before Pontius Pilate, ¹⁴that you keep the commandment,[66] spotless and irreproachable, until the appearance of our Lord Jesus, Messiah, whom the blessed and only Sovereign will reveal in His own time, the Sovereign Who is King of the ruling kings and Lord of the ruling lords, ¹⁶the only One possessing immortality and unapproachable light, Whom no human has seen or can see, to Whom be honor and power forever. Amen.

¹⁷Instruct those who are rich in the present age not to be haughty or to have put hope in the uncertainty of wealth, but in God Who grants us everything in abundance for enjoyment; ¹⁸instruct them to do good, to be rich in good works, to be generous, liberal, ¹⁹laying a good foundation for the future so that they may grasp the essence of life.

²⁰O Timothy, guard what was entrusted, turning away from godless chatter[67] and counter theses of what is falsely termed "knowledge"; ²¹some, professing that, stray from the faith.

Grace be with you.[68]

---

66. "The commandment": The Greek expression translated a common rabbinic one for almsgiving—Eubank, "Almsgiving."

67. "Godless chatter" can also mean "worldly" chatter. Ford, "Note on Proto-montanism," 343, renders it "silly chatter" and suggests it might refer to an abuse of glossolalia, but "silly" seems to stretch the meaning of the Greek.

68. "You" is in the plural.

## The Pastoral Epistles

## Second Letter to Timothy

1 ¹Paul, an apostle of Messiah Jesus by the will of God, in accordance with the promise of life which is in Messiah Jesus, ²to Timothy, a beloved child: Grace, mercy, peace from God the Father and Messiah, our Lord Jesus.

³I give thanks to God, Whom I serve, as did the ancestors, with a clear conscience, as I continuously remember you night and day in my prayers, ⁴longing to see you, having called to mind your tears, so that I may be filled with joy, ⁵seizing the memory of the genuine faith within you, which first dwelt in your grandmother Lois and your mother Eunice,[69] and I have been convinced that it is in you as well. ⁶For this reason I remind you to rekindle the gift of God that is in you from the laying on of my hands; ⁷for God did not give us a spirit of timidity but of power, love, and self-discipline. ⁸So do not be ashamed of the testimony of our Lord or of me, His prisoner, but join in suffering for the good news about the power of God, ⁹Who was saving and calling us with a holy calling, not according to our works but according to His own resolve and gift that He gave us in Messiah Jesus before all ages, ¹⁰but made manifest now through the manifestation of our savior Messiah Jesus, making death powerless and bringing into the light life and immortality through the good news, ¹¹for which I was appointed herald, apostle, and teacher. ¹²For this reason I also suffered those things, but I am not ashamed, but I know to Whom I have been faithful, and I have been convinced that He is able to guard what has been entrusted to me until that day. ¹³Have the example of sound discourses that you listened to from me with the faith and love which is in Messiah Jesus. ¹⁴Guard the good that has been entrusted to you through the holy spirit, who is dwelling among us.

¹⁵You know about all those people in Asia turning away from me, including Phygelus and Hermogenes.[70] ¹⁶May the Lord grant mercy to the household of Onesiphorus,[71] because he refreshed me frequently and was not ashamed of my handcuffs, ¹⁷but arriving in Rome he was seeking me out diligently and found me. ¹⁸May the Lord grant for him that he find mercy from the Lord on that day. He also provided services in Ephesus, of which you are more aware than I.[72]

---

69. These two names do not appear elsewhere in the New Testament. Acts 16:1 says simply that Timothy was the son of a Jewish woman who was a believer and a father who was a Greek. The author has an independent tradition about the family of Timothy.

70. These two persons are mentioned in no other place in the New Testament. Presumably they or their descendants were contemporaries of the Pastor who are being subjected to a degradation ceremony. The verse can be translated to say that all in Asia turned against Paul, but that is contradicted in the next sentence.

71. This name appears only here and at 2 Tim 4:19, where he is greeted. The end of verse 1:18 associates him with Ephesus. One might infer that his descendants were allies of the Pastor.

72. "Provided services": literally, "served." In English it is necessary to provide a noun so that "of which" would have a referent. At the end of the sentence, "I" is supplied to go with the comparative "than."

2 ¹You, then, my child, be strong with the grace that is in Messiah Jesus, ²and the things you heard from me through many testimonies. Entrust these things to faithful people who are competent for teaching others as well. ³Share in the suffering as a good soldier of Messiah Jesus. ⁴No one serving in an army becomes entangled in the affairs of civilian life, so that he would please the one who formed the army; ⁵and if an athlete competes[73] he is crowned only if he competes according to the rules. ⁶It is necessary for the laboring farmer first to share in the harvest. ⁷Understand what I am saying, for the Lord will grant you insight into everything. ⁸Remember Jesus, Messiah, raised from the dead, from the lineage of David, according to my good news; ⁹for it I am suffering to the point of imprisonment as a criminal, but the word of God has not been fettered. ¹⁰Therefore I am enduring it all for the elect, so that they also may attain salvation, which is in Messiah Jesus, along with eternal glory. ¹¹This saying is trustworthy:

For if we die with him, we will also live with him;[74]

¹²If we endure, we will also reign with him;

If we deny him, that one will deny us;[75]

¹³If we trust him not, that one will remain faithful,[76]

    for he cannot deny himself.

¹⁴Remind them of these things, when bearing witness before God, lest they dispute over what is to no one's advantage and the ruin of those hearing.[77] ¹⁵Hasten to present yourself to God as one who is proven, an unabashed worker, clearing the way straight to the statement of the truth. ¹⁶And avoid profane chatter; for it will proceed all the more to impiety, ¹⁷and the utterance of it will spread like gangrene; Hymenaeus and Philetus[78] are like this; ¹⁸they deviated from the truth, saying that the resurrection has already occurred, and they are causing the faith of some to fail. ¹⁹Actually God's firm foundation stands, having this legend:[79] "The Lord knows who are his," and "Let everyone who calls on the name of the Lord keep away from wrongdoing." ²⁰But in a

---

73. "Athlete competes": literally "someone competes." The verb, ἀθλῇ, implies participating in an athletic contest.

74. "Him" is supplied, based on the demonstrative pronoun in the last member of verse 12.

75. This appears to be related to the Q saying, which is adapted in Matt 10:32–33 ("So everyone who confesses me before people, I will also confess before my Father Who is in the heavens. ³³But whoever denies me before people, I will also deny before my Father Who is in the heavens") and Luke 12:8–9.

76. This may be based on Rom 3:3–4.

77. I am paragraphing this verse with the preceding and taking everything from verse 1 to this point as one paragraph. This differs from the United bible Societies Greek, RSV, and *Das neue Testament*.

78. Hymenaeus is also mentioned in 1Tim 1:20; Philetus is mentioned only here. They appear to be subjects of the Pastor's degradation ceremony.

79. "Legend": literally, seal. The image seems to be that of a legend or inscription in a seal.

large household there are not only gold and silver vessels but also wooden and clay ones, and those that are for presentable purposes and those that are not. ²¹So if someone cleanses oneself from it,⁸⁰ one will be a vessel for a presentable purpose, sanctified, useful to the master, made ready for ever good work. ²²But flee youthful craving, and pursue justice, faith, love, peace, along with those who call on the Lord with a clean heart. ²³And avoid foolish and uneducated discussions, knowing they spawn disputes; ²⁴it is not necessary for a slave of the Lord to fight, but to be gentle toward all, skillful in teaching, not vengeful, ²⁵correcting with courtesy those resisting; perhaps God might give them a conversion toward a recognition of truth, ²⁶and they might sober up from the devil's snare, after being taking prisoner by him for his purpose.

3 ¹And be aware of this, that hard times will come in the last days; ²for there will be selfish people, avaricious, braggarts, haughty, slanderous, disobedient to parents, ungrateful, unholy, ³unloving, defamers, dissolute, brutal, not philanthropic, ⁴traitors, rash, conceited, pleasure loving rather than devout, ⁵having the forms of piety but resisting its imperative: resist these too. ⁶For from such are those creeping into households and captivating silly women⁸¹ who are overwhelmed by sins, drawn by various passions, ⁷ever learning but never able to come to a recognition of the truth. ⁸But in the way Jannes and Jambres opposed Moses,⁸² so also they resist truth, people who are mentally destroyed, not qualified in matters of the faith. ⁹However, they will not prevail over more, for their ignorance will be plain to all, as that of those two also became plain to all.⁸³

¹⁰But you followed my teaching, way of life, resolve, fidelity, steadfastness, love, patience, ¹¹persecutions, and sufferings, that came upon me in Antioch, in Iconium, and in Lystra, the persecutions that I have borne, and the Lord rescued me from it all. ¹²And for sure all piously wishing life in Messiah Jesus, will be persecuted. ¹³But evil people and sorcerers will proceed to worse, misleading and misled. ¹⁴But you, keep to what you learned and been convinced of, knowing those by whom you were taught, ¹⁵and because you know the holy scriptures from early childhood, which are able to instruct you for salvation through fidelity in Messiah Jesus. All scripture⁸⁴ is God-inspired and suitable for teaching, for reproof, for improvement, and for training in justice, ¹⁷so that a person who is of God may be effective, equipped for every good work.

---

80. "It": In the Greek the word is in the plural—"those." It seems to refer to "idle chatter," which in the Greek is also in the plural.

81. There is obvious stereotyping here. Fiore, *Pastoral Epistles*, 167, points to the presumption that women are more susceptible to deception.

82. In rabbinic texts, these are two magicians of Pharaoh—ibid., 168.

83. Literally, as that of theirs also became. The Pastor is continuing the comparison with Jannes and Jambres, whose serpents Moses' serpent ate.

84. "All scripture," πᾶσα γραφὴ, can mean either the whole of scripture or each scriptural passage. In context, it means the whole of scripture, for one would not use a blessing found there, for example, to correct a wayward individual.

4 ¹I am entreating you before God and Messiah Jesus, who is about to judge the living and the dead: ²preach ¹both his coming and the kingdom; ²be in charge of the word in season, out of season,⁸⁵ reprove, censure, encourage, with all patience and every doctrine. ³For it will be a time when they will not put up with a teaching that is healthy but according to their own desires accumulate ear-tickling teachers, ⁴and they will turn ear away from the truth and turn ear toward myths. ⁵But you be sober in everything, suffer hardship, do the work of the evangelist, fulfill your service. ⁶For I am already offered up as a libation, and the season of my departure has arrived. ⁷I competed in the noble contest, I have finished the course, I have kept the faith. ⁸The rest is stored up for me, the crown of justice, which the Lord, the just judge, will award me on that day, but not me alone but also all those who have loved his manifestation.

⁹Hasten to come to me quickly, ¹⁰for Demas, loving the present age, deserted me,⁸⁶ and he has gone to Thessalonica, Crescens to Galatia,⁸⁷ Titus to Dalmatia.⁸⁸ ¹¹Luke alone is with me.⁸⁹ Come and take Mark with you, for he is helpful to me in ministry;⁹⁰ ¹²and I sent Tychicus to Ephesus.⁹¹ ¹³When you come, bring the cloak that I left behind with Carpus in Troas, as well as the scrolls, especially the parchments.⁹² ¹⁴Alexander the metalworker did great

---

85. I am associating the imperative, "preach," with the double accusative preceding it in Greek in verse 1 and the single noun, also in the accusative, "the word," with the next imperative, "be in charge of." This differs from RSV and *Das neue Testament*. Malherbe, "'In Season out of Season,'" 242, observes that "in season, out of season," εὐκαίρως ἀκαίρως, leaving out any conjunction between the two adverbs, was intended to be a striking phrase. He goes on to interpret it in terms of the usual translation, however.

86. A Demas is named by Paul in Phlm 24 as a fellow worker. Col 4:14 mentions a Demas sending greetings. While the Pastor will begin naming early Christians in this section to create a sense that a community of moral support is no longer present, the negative reference to Demas here probably does not refer to the Demas mentioned in Phlm and Col, since the latter appears to know of no defection on the part of "its" Demas. It seems likely that this Demas is a contemporary of the Pastor and migrant to Thessalonica who is being subjected to a degradation ceremony.

87. Crescens is mentioned nowhere else in the New Testament.

88. Titus is known from 2 Cor and Gal, but the Pastor appears to have no further knowledge of him. Here he reports his going to Dalmatia, on the Adriatic coast, but in the *Letter to Titus* he has him going to Crete.

89. Again we have a name from Phlm 24 and Col 4:14. The Pastor may have in mind the author of Luke/Acts.

90. The Pastor is probably again taking a name from Phlm 24, and possibly from Col 4:10. He may have thought Mark was the same person as John Mark in Acts or the Mark associated in legend with Peter (1 Pet 5:13) and as Peter's translator who was responsible for the *Gospel of Mark*. Either way, or both, the Pastor appears to have an intent of bringing facets of the Christian movement together in the face of his opponents, for while Paul would have no more to do with John Mark (Acts 15:37–40) and had had his tensions with Peter (Gal 2:11), the Pastor depicts Paul and "Mark" together.

91. Tychicus is known from Acts 20:4, Col 4:7, and Eph 6:21; in both Col and Eph he brings or accompanies the fictive letter. Eph 6:21 explicitly says (the fictive) Paul sent him to Ephesus, which the Pastor repeats.

92. According to Fiore, *Pastoral Epistles*, 185, "Ambrosiaster, *Commentary on the Second Letter to Timothy* (CSEL 81 3:317) identifies the cloak as the distinctive garment of a Roman citizen. . . . "

harm to me;⁹³ the Lord will repay him according to his deeds. ¹⁵You also be on guard against him, for he opposed what we said very much.

¹⁶At my first defense,⁹⁴ no one was standing beside me, but all abandoned me. Let it not be counted against them. ¹⁷But the Lord stood by me and strengthened me, so that the announcing may be finished and all the nations hear it. ¹⁸The Lord will deliver me from every evil work and save me for his heavenly kingdom; to Him be the glory forever and ever. Amen.

¹⁹Greet Prisca and Aquila, and the house of Onesiphorus.⁹⁵ ²⁰Erastus remains in Corinth, but I left Trophimus in Miletus, ailing.⁹⁶ ²¹Hurry to come before winter. Euboulus, Pudens, Linus, and Claudia and all the brothers and sisters greet you.⁹⁷ ²²The Lord be with your spirit, and grace be with all of you.⁹⁸

## Letter to Titus

1 ¹Paul, slave of God, an apostle of Jesus, Messiah according to the faith of the elect of God and the knowledge of the truth that conforms to piety, ²as well as the hope for the eternal life that God, free from deceit, promised from eternity. ³And He made his word manifest in its own time through the preaching with which I was entrusted according to the command of our savior God. ⁴To Titus,⁹⁹ genuine child in a common faith: Grace and peace to you from God the Father and our savior, Messiah Jesus.

⁵I left you in Crete for this, to further correct what remains to be corrected and appoint in each town presbyters, as I instructed you, ⁶if someone is blameless, a husband of one wife, having trustworthy children, not under accusation of dissipation or undisciplined. ⁷For it is necessary that the bishop as a minister of God be blameless, not arrogant, not quick-tempered, not

---

Carpus is otherwise unknown in the New Testament; he may well have been a contemporary of the Pastor in Troas who had a Pauline relic. The reference to scrolls and parchments may refer to the Jewish Scriptures and the earlier Christian literature. "Especially," μάλιστα: H. Kim, "Interpretation of μάλιστα," maintains that this Greek term means "especially" every time it is used in the Pastorals.

93. Alexander, whom the Pastor mentions in 1 Tim 1:20, is again made the object of the degradation ceremony.

94. The Pastor is depicting Paul writing during the time that his trial was taking place in Rome.

95. Prisca (or Priscilla) and Aquila are known from Acts, 1 Cor, and Rom 16. References to them are part of the fictive setting for the letter. Onesiphorus is likely a contemporary and ally of the Pastor; see above 1:16.

96. Erastus is known from Acts 19:22 and Rom 16. This greeting, too, is part of the fictive setting.

97. Fiore, *Pastoral Epistles*, 188, observes that this list of four people sending greetings along with Paul's contradicts the statement at verse 16 that Paul had been abandoned. Again, this is part of the Pastor's making the stage-settingan obvious fiction.

98. "Your spirit" is in the singular, referring to Timothy and his spirit; "all of you" translates a plural "your."

99. Titus is known from 2 Cor and Gal. "Genuine," γνησίῳ, also means "legitimate."

drunken, not pugnacious, not greedy, ⁸but welcoming, loving what is good, self-controlled, just, devout, disciplined, ⁹holding himself fast to the doctrine of the trustworthy word, so that he would be able to encourage by means of teaching that is sound, and correct opponents.

¹⁰For there are many who are undisciplined, are idle talkers, and are deceivers, especially those of the circumcision;¹⁰⁰ ¹¹it is necessary to silence those who, for the sake of a shameful gain, are bringing about the downfall of whole households by teaching what they ought not. ¹²Someone, one of the Cretans' own prophets, said, "Cretans are always liars, evil beasts, idle gluttons."¹⁰¹ ¹³This testimony is true. For this reason, correct them severely, so that they would be sound in the faith. ¹⁴Pay no attention to Jewish myths and the commands of people who are turning away from the truth. ¹⁵All things are clean for the clean, but for those who have been made impure and for the unfaithful nothing is clean, but both their mind and conscience are defiled. ¹⁶They declare they know God, but they repudiate Him in His works,¹⁰² since they are abominable, disobedient, and unsuitable for any good work.

2 ¹But you, say what is fitting for instruction that is sound: ²that older men be sober, dignified, prudent, sound in the faith, in love, and in perseverance, ³older women likewise worthy of reverence in conduct, not slanderers, not enslaved to much wine, teachers of what is good, ⁴so that they would bring the young women to be loving toward their husbands, loving towards their children, prudent, good, subordinate to their own husbands, so that so that the word of God not be defamed. Likewise encourage younger men to be reasonable; ⁷present yourself as a model of good deeds in all things, through incorruptibility in teaching, probity, ⁸speech beyond reproach in soundness, so that someone from the other side would be embarrassed, having nothing bad to say about us. ⁹Slaves are to be subject to their own masters in everything, to be pleasing, not contradicting, ¹⁰not pilfering, but demonstrating every good faith, so that by everything they may do credit to the teaching about our savior God.

¹¹For the grace of the savior God appeared to all people, ¹²instructing us so that, rejecting the impiety and worldly passions of humanity, we may also live in the present age with justice and piety, ¹³expecting the great hope for and appearance of the glory of the great God and our of our savior Jesus, Messiah, ¹⁴who gave himself for us so that we may be redeemed from all

---

100. "Especially," μάλιστα: H. Kim, "Interpretation of μάλιστα," maintains that this Greek term means "especially" every time it is used in the Pastorals. The circumcision party need not necessarily be ethnically Jewish; they could have been early Christians who wanted to follow the Law as found in the scriptures. The Pastorals date from a time where there had been a break between the Christian movement and Judaism.

101. Fiore, *Pastoral Epistles*, 204, says that Clement of Alexandria in *Stromata* 1:14 (Migne Patrologia Graeca 8:757c) "identifies the author of the quotation as Epimenides, but he does not give the title of the work. Jerome cites the text as *De oraculis*." Fiore goes on to cite the statement, "All Cretans are liars," in numerous sources.

102. An alternative translation: "by their works." The Greek simply has "in/by works."

lawlessness and that he may cleanse a chosen people for himself, a zealous one for good works. ¹⁵Say these things, encourage, and set them forth with every command; let no one look down upon you.

3 ¹Remind them to be subordinate to rulers, authorities, to be obedient, to be ready for every good work, ²to defame no one, to be peaceable, yielding, showing courtesy toward all people. ³For we too were once foolish, disobedient, misled, serving various passions and pleasures, living in evil and envy, hateful, despising all. ⁴"But when the goodness and benevolence of God our savior appeared, ⁵he saved us not through works of justice that we did but according to his mercy, through the bath of rebirth and renewal of the holy spirit, ⁶which he poured out upon us abundantly through Jesus, Messiah, our savior, ⁷so that made just by that grace we would become heirs according to the hope in eternal life." ⁸The statement is trustworthy, and I wish you to speak confidently about these things, so that those who have come to believe in God will be concerned about good works. These are good and beneficial for people; ⁹but avoid foolish controversies, genealogies, contention, and disputes about laws, for they are useless and empty. ¹⁰Avoid a divisive person after a first or second warning, ¹¹knowing that such is perverted and sins, being self-condemned.

¹²When I will send Artemas to you, or Tychicus,¹⁰³ hasten to come to me in Nicopolis,¹⁰⁴ for I have decided to winter there. ¹³Escourt Zenas the lawyer and Apollo with haste, so that nothing will be lacking for them.¹⁰⁵

¹⁵All those with me greet you. Greet those who love us in faith. Grace be with all of you.

---

103. Artemas appears nowhere else in the New Testament. Tychicus appears at Acts 20:4, Col 4:7, and Eph 6:21, as well as above in 2 Tim 4:12. The Pastor seems to be recognizing Artemas as an ally, and Tychicus would be part of the scenery. The verb "will send" is in the future, not the subjunctive; the implication is that the true author, the Pastor, is already sending Artemas somewhere (Crete?), perhaps bearing the three-part essay.

104. Nicopolis, located near the western coast of Greece, was the capital of Epirus. It fit into no known travel itinerary of Paul. At the time the Pastorals were probably written, it was the residence of Epictetus, who settled there after Emperor Domitian (81–96) exiled all philosophers from Rome.

105. Zenas appears nowhere else in the New Testament; he was probably someone the Pastor wanted to recognize as an ally. As with Artemas in the previous verse, Zenas is paired with a name from earlier Christian literature—Apollo (Acts 18:24 and 19:1; 1 Cor 1:12, 3:4–6, 3:22, 4:6, and 16:12).

*Chapter 22*

# Pseudepigraphic Letter to the Thessalonians
## *(Second Thessalonians)*

### Introduction

MODERN BIBLES CONTAIN A letter, "Second Letter of Paul to the Thessalonians," invariably placed after *First Thessalonians*. Doubts about the authenticity of this second *Thessalonians* first arose in the modern era because an eschatological section in it is inconsistent with the eschatological perspective in *First Thessalonians*.[1] How could one letter that says the End Times are to come about soon have been written by the same person who says the End Times are not near because a "lawless one" must first have his sway for a time? Raymond Collins offers a brief overview of the fascinating history of the controversy over the authenticity of the letter.[2] All the internal evidence in the letter points to it being a later work modeled after the authentic *First Thessalonians*. Not only is there the eschatological perspective differing from that of Paul, but that eschatology appears to be based either on the *Revelation from Jesus the Messiah* or the traditions behind it, or from Isaiah chapter 66, not from any Pauline source.[3] The second *Thessalonians* has a vocabulary that is somewhat different from Paul's, and it manages that achievement even while duplicating a number of sentences from *First Thessalonians*.[4] The views of the addressees of the two letters appear to be different; that of *First Thessalonians* was troubled by the fact that the End had not yet come, while that of the second believed that it had come already. Moreover, the second letter shows none of the personal warmth of *First Thessalonians*. The second letter reflects a situation where letters claiming to have been written by Paul are circulating: "I, Paul, write this greeting with my own hand. This is the mark in every letter of mine; it is

---

1. 2 Thess 2:1–12; 1 Thess 4:13—5:11.
2. R. Collins, *Letters that Paul Did Not Write*, 209–14.
3. See Aus, "God's Plan and God's Power," and Aus, "Relevance of Isa 66:7."
4. Schmidt, "Syntactical Style," used a computer program to find syntactical features in the second *Thessalonians* and the authentic Pauline letters; he found that the second *Thessalonians* is closer in style to Col and Eph than to the authentic Paulines.

the way I write"—a statement Collins suggests protests too much.[5] And, " . . . we beg you brethren not to be shaken in mind or excited, either by spirit or by word, or by letter purporting to be from us, to the effect that the day of the Lord has come."[6] Paul was not a famous personage in his lifetime; people writing in his tradition would not yet be modestly writing essays using his name rather than their own yet.[7] Despite the weight of this evidence, the issue of the (in)authenticity of this letter has been highly controverted in the modern literature. There are many scholarly commentaries that accept the work as authentic and articles in scholarly journals that interpret its obscure passages by looking at word usages in the authentic Pauline letters.

Other than situating the letter late in the era of pseudepigraphic Pauline literature, there are few clues relating to its actual author, date, and place of composition, or audience. Chapter 2, verses 2b and 3a, appear to depend on *First Timothy* 4:1, which would suggest a time of composition after the publication of the Pastorals. The fact that it is presented as a letter to the Thessalonians does not guarantee that Christians in Thessalonica were its actual intended readership; it was simply modeled on *First Thessalonians* in a number of respects. The letter's opening and closing duplicate those of *First Thessalonians*, and verbal fragments appear to be borrowed from that letter. Collins points out that the second letter replicates the structure of the first, even duplicating an unusual double thanksgiving found in the first:[8]

A. Letter Opening
   1. Prescript
   2. Thanksgiving

B. Letter Body
   1. Second Thanksgiving
   2. Benediction

C. Letter Closing
   1. Paraenesis
   2. Peace Wish
   3. Greetings
   4. Benediction

---

5. 2 Thess 23:17.
6. 2 Thess 2:2.
7. Aarde, "Struggle against Heresy," notes that while Paul cites the authority of the Lord—words of the Lord—the second *Thessalonians* and other post-Pauline letters cite Paul's apostolic authority.
8. R. Collins, *Letters That Paul Did Not Write*, 218–19.

The letter's author acknowledges and sympathizes with the End Time concerns of the readership, and the latter appears to be under persecution of some kind. One learns that

> ... the community is undergoing hard times at the hands of people who will undergo divine punishment (1:4–10). The afflictions are interpreted as signs of the end-time and have led to further apocalyptic agitation within its ranks. In fact the author speaks of doomsday preachers who are active within the community via ecstatic pronouncements, extended preaching, and use of a letter allegedly by Paul.[9]

Persecution, apart from that of Nero, is usually associated with the nineties in Asia Minor.

## Populism

People generally use the expression *populism* to refer to political elites pandering to the unlearned masses. Thus, modern dictators, such as Adolf Hitler and Josef Stalin, opposed too much sophistication in the arts since sophistication would bypass the masses. In democracies, politicians may affirm their disbelief in biological evolution, appeal to widespread prejudices against ethnic or sexual minorities, or insist that tax cuts solve all economic problems—all in order to secure the votes of the less intellectual of their potential constituents. Our interest here is not such a manipulation of the populous by elites, but a perspective shared by the unlettered and by those lettered who are barely above the unlettered in station. The lettered populists, proletaroid intellectuals, are literate but not esteemed by the elite or able to influence the elite. They may, for example, be scribes rather than scholars. In antiquity, their worldview may not have differed appreciably from that of any other skilled slave or hireling. Such people might dismiss the discourse and literature of intellectuals who are retained in the households of the wealthy or powerful as out of touch with the realities of everyday life. This is the kind of perspective that characterizes the second Thessalonian letter, as will be shown below.

Sociology has not treated this populist worldview very much. It has focused on more militant forms of more lowly positioned people who oppose and even hate those positioned over them. The emergence of class consciousness among workers, for example, has been a particular interest for the Marxian tradition of social thought; Georg Lukács, for example, wrote of a class being "ripe for hegemony" when its interests and consciousness enable it to organize the whole of society in accordance with its objective interests.[10] Class consciousness in that sense would inspire a collective

---

9. Richard, *First and Second Thessalonians*, 28.
10. Lukács, *History and Class Consciousness*, 52.

endeavor to take control of the entire society. The early American sociologist Edward Alsworth Ross, quite apart from the Marxian tradition, wrote of resentment:

> Resentment in its lower forms is an instinct; but in its higher forms it is simply the egoistic side of the sense of injustice. The more one recoils from *doing* an unjust action, the more he resents *suffering* such an action. On its altruistic side, the sense of justice lessens aggression by inspiring respect for the claims of others. On its egoistic side, it lessens aggression by prompting to the energetic assertion of one's own claims.[11]

Closely related to resentment is what the German social philosopher Max Scheler called *ressentiment*, borrowing the word from Friedrich Nietzsche. *Ressentiment* arises if powerful feelings of revenge, envy, the impulse to detract, spite, pleasure at another's misfortune, or malice must be suppressed because one is unable to act upon them because of weakness or fear.[12] Unlike class consciousness and resentment, *ressentiment* is not an insight into a true situation but a distortion of values; one devalues whatever somebody who is more favorably placed than oneself, or even placed over oneself, may possess. People sometimes summarize the phenomenon as "sour grapes," taking the punchline from the fable of Aesop.

In his treatment of "reference groups," Robert K. Merton noted that people "act in a social frame of reference yielded by the groups of which they are a part."[13] If one's associates in a group dress informally, for a trivial example, one would be more likely to do so oneself. But beyond that commonplace observation, people " . . . frequently orient themselves to groups *other than their own* in shaping their behavior and evaluations. . . . "[14] Thus, rather than conform to the fashions and values of a group to which one belongs, one may select some other, contrasting group for one's own orientation instead. What occurs in a way that is analogous to *ressentiment*, however, is that one can make a point of being *un*like a group, either a group to which one belongs or a group to which one does not belong, and which one wishes to be different from in an explicit way. Merton refers to such groups as "negative reference groups." An individual would be motivated to reject the ways of the negative reference group, not merely rejecting its norms, but forming counter-norms.[15] If we propose a situation in which ancient slaves and marginal freepersons take their masters and patrons as a negative reference group and sense some irritation at the fashions, behaviors, opinions, and worldviews of masters and patrons as a whole, we have the kind of "populism" that would apply to the second Thessalonian letter.

---

11. Ross, *Social Control*, 37.
12. Scheler, *Ressentiment*, 43–78.
13. Merton, *Social Theory and Social Structure*, 288.
14. Ibid.
15. Ibid., 354.

The letter's author expresses displeasure at some in the community "living in idleness."[16] "And we command you in the name of our Lord Jesus, the Messiah, brothers and sisters, to avoid any brother or sister going about idly...."[17] "¹¹For we hear of some going about idly among you, not working but networking."[18] Moderns may be tempted to understand a passage about idle people to refer to an underclass, analogous to street people pan handling in modern cities. One commentator has observed, however, that in antiquity elite people, not slaves and free laborers, were idle;[19] however, he did not take his observation far enough. He wanted the translation to read "disorderly lives" rather than "living in idleness." The Greek allows such a translation, but the context does not:

> For you yourselves know how one ought to imitate us: that we were not idle among you or eating bread from anyone without paying, but working by labor and exertion night and day in order not to burden anyone of you—not that we did not have the right, but in order that we ourselves would give an example for you to imitate us. For when we were with you, we also commanded this of you: that if someone does not want to work, let that person not eat.[20]

The author was concerned with people who were idle, not lacking in discipline. So if the letter's author would have the readers distance themselves from the idle, the negative reference group consists of those in a superior position: masters and patrons. Sheila E. McGinn and Megan T. Wilson-Reitz explain that the idle were upwardly mobile social climbers rather than some hypothetical jobless poor. In their view the author is reproaching social climbers for accepting the worldview that would lead them to despise labor, and for hanging around the elite as part of an entourage of clients.[21]

So a negative reference group for the author and other populists who would share in the author's perspective consisted of the stratum of masters and patrons. The letter, however, is not only about working; it presents a view of the End Times. The author rejects assembling to meet the coming Jesus, being shaken in mind, citing a statement in the spirit or citing a purported letter of Paul.[22] The author insists that the Day of the Lord has not already come and will not come soon. The agitation that the author rejects would be a fancy in which masters and clients were taken up at the time. From the perspective of the everyday world of the author, one should be concerned instead with the practical everyday world of working people.

---

16. ἀτάκτως περιπατοῦντος.
17. 2 Thess 3:6a.
18. 2 Thess 3:11.
19. Russell, "The Idle in 2 Thess."
20. 2 Thess 3:7–10.
21. McGinn and Wilson-Reitz, "Welfare Wastrels or Swanky Socialites."
22. 2 Thess 2:1, 2:2.

*Pseudepigraphic Letter to the Thessalonians*

# English Translation

## Pseudepigraphic Letter to the Thessalonians

[Textual material that is taken over from *First Thessalonians* is in *italics*, and that taken over from the Septuagint version of *Isaiah* 66 is underlined.]

1¹*Paul, Silvanus, and Timothy, to the assembly of Thessalonians, grace and peace be with you in God* our *Father and the Reverend Jesus, Messiah:* ²*Grace and peace be with you from God our Father and the Reverend Jesus, Messiah.*

³We must *always give thanks to God concerning you*, brothers and sisters, as is fitting, because your faith increases abundantly and the love of each one of all of you for one another is growing, so that we boast of you in the churches of God about your steadfastness and faith amidst all the persecutions of you and afflictions that you endure—⁵evidence[23] of God's just judgment, for your being considered worthy of God's kingdom, for which you are also suffering, ⁶since it was just for God to return[24] affliction to those afflicting you ⁷and relief to you who are afflicted, along with us, through the revelation from heaven of the Reverend Jesus with his mighty messengers, ⁸rendering in a flame of fire, punishment[25] on those who do not know God and do not heed[26] the good news of the our Reverend Jesus, ⁹those who will undergo eternal destruction far from the presence of the Lord and far from his glory and power, ¹⁰when he comes to be glorified among his saints and wondered at among all the faithful on that day, because our testimony to you was believed. ¹¹For this we also always pray concerning you, that our God will find you worthy of the call and fill every desire for goodness and work of faith with power, ¹²that the name of our Reverend Jesus be glorified[27] by you, and you by it, according to the gift of our God and the Reverend Jesus, Messiah.

2¹Now concerning the coming of our Reverend Jesus, Messiah, and our assembling with him, brothers and sisters, we request that you ²not be either quickly disturbed in mind or frightened, either on account of a spirit, statement, or letter written as if from us,[28] as though the day of the Lord has come.

---

23. "Evidence," ἔνδειγμα, appears nowhere else in the New Testament; it is taken to be a synonym of ἔνδειξις, "sign," "omen," or "proof." Bassler, "Enigmatic Sign," relates the passage to a contemporaneous Jewish theology of suffering, wherein present suffering by the pious is a chastisement or atonement whereby they are made worthy of their future existence. Thus the afflictions of the elect are a sign of God's righteous judgment.

24. Isa 66:4.

25. Isa 66:15.

26. Isa 66:4. The Septuagint parallels with a different grammatical form: καὶ οὐχ ὑπήκουσαν, "they did not heed."

27. Isa 66:5.

28. "Written" is implied here—see Blass and DeBrunner, *Greek Grammar*, 219–20, especially #425(4). While this phrase reveals that the author knew of Pauline pseudepigrapha, it is not clear that the reference is to *First Thessalonians*, though the addressees of that letter seem to have thought that

³Let no one deceive you under any guise; for unless the apostasy comes first²⁹ and the personage of lawlessness be revealed, that son of perdition, ⁴the one <u>standing in opposition</u>³⁰ and exalting himself over everything called a god or object of worship, so that he installed himself in the <u>Sanctuary</u>³¹ of God, proclaiming himself to be a god. ⁵Do you not remember that when I was still with you I said all this to you? ⁶And you know what is maintaining restraint now,³² so that he may be revealed in his own season. ⁷For the mystery of wickedness³³ is at work now; only He is restraining it at present until it is removed.³⁴ ⁸And then the <u>wicked one</u>³⁵ will be revealed, whom the Reverend Jesus with the breath of his mouth will do away with and render powerless at the appearance of the wicked one's³⁶ coming, ⁹whose coming is through the power of Satan, with every might, sign, and false portent, ¹⁰and every unjust deceit for those perishing. Rather than their being saved they did not accept the love of truth. ¹¹Therefore God is also sending them a delusional influence for them to believe what is false, ¹²so that all those who do not believe in the truth but delight in injustice may be condemned.

¹³But *we* must *give thanks to God* always concerning you, brothers and sisters beloved of the Lord, because God chose you from the first³⁷ for salva-

---

the End Times were imminent. In modeling the letter after *First Thessalonians*, the author is implicitly accepting it. The author's inspiration may well have come from 1 Thess 5, which holds that the times and seasons of the last days are unknown, that the Day of the Lord will come like a thief in the night.

29. Verse 2b to this point in verse 3 seems to reflect 1 Tim 4:1, which the author would agree with.

30. Isa 66:6, where it is a plural standing in opposition.

31. Isa 66:6, though it refers to the voice of the Lord in the Sanctuary; the opponent would be there implicitly.

32. "What is maintaining restraint," τὸ κατέχον: What it is that the readers are assumed to know is ambiguous. Commentators have looked to Paul's usage and theology for clues (e.g., O. Betz, "Der Katechon," but such a procedure is predicated upon the assumption that 2 *Thessalonians* is an authentic Pauline letter. Aus looks to Isa 66 to interpret the reference. Isa 66:18–21 provides the background: The Lord will gather all the nations, and these will bring the Israelis' brothers and sisters as an offering to Jerusalem—Aus, "God's Plan and God's Power." Aus, "Relevance of Isa. 66:7," 264–65, notes there was a delaying factor (Isa 66:9) analogous to birth pangs (Isa 66:7). ὁ κατέχων does not appear in the Septuagint version of Isaiah 66, but would translate the Hebrew 'ṣr, "restrain." Barrnouin, "Problems de traduction," translates ὁ κατέχων as "tient gardé," take custody.

33. "Mystery of wickedness": According to the analysis made by Furfey, "Mystery of Lawlessness," the mystery of wickedness is secret in general but knowable to the faithful, is in rebellion against God's law, is associated with the Antichrist but is not the same entity as the Antichrist, and is continually operative but for the time being under restraint.

34. Again, Aus, "God's Plan and god's Power," sees this as an allusion to Isa 66:9 in the Hebrew, with 66:18–21 as background.

35. Isa 66:3.

36. "The wicked one's coming": The Greek uses a possessive pronoun rather than "wicked one's."

37. "Chose . . . from the first," εἴλατο . . . ἀπ' ἀρχῆς; this is a well attested reading that the editorial committee of the United Bible Societies rejected in favor of one that employed phraseology that is more common in the Pauline literature—Metzger, *Textual Commentary*, 636–37. The committee's reasoning seems predicated on the authenticity of the second *Thessalonian* letter as a work of Paul.

tion in holiness of spirit and faithfulness of truth, ¹⁴to which He was calling you through our good news,³⁸ for obtaining the glory of our Lord Jesus, the Messiah. ¹⁵So stand firm now, brothers and sisters, and take hold of the traditions that you were taught whether through our speech or through our letter.³⁹ ¹⁶Now may our Lord Jesus, Messiah, himself, and God our Father, Who loves us and gives eternal comfort and good hope by grace, ¹⁷comfort your hearts and strengthen them in every good work and word.

3 ¹Finally, *brothers and sisters, pray for us*, that the word of the Lord may progress and triumph,⁴⁰ as it already has for you, ²and that we may be rescued from abnormal and evil people; for not all have the faith. ³But the Lord is faithful; He will strengthen you and protect you from the evil one. ⁴And we have been made certain about you by the Lord, that you are doing and will do what we commanded. ⁵And may the Lord lead your hearts to God's love and to the steadfastness of the Messiah.

⁶And we command you in the name of our Lord Jesus, the Messiah, brothers and sisters, to avoid any brother or sister going about idly and not according to the tradition that they received from us. ⁷For you yourselves know how one ought to imitate us: that we were not idle among you ⁸or eating bread from anyone without paying, but working by labor and exertion night and day in order not to burden anyone of you—⁹not that we did not have the right, but in order that we ourselves would give an example for you to imitate us. ¹⁰For when we were with you, we also commanded this of you: that if someone does not want to work, let that person not eat. ¹¹For we hear of some going about idly among you, not working but networking.⁴¹ ¹²And we command and encourage such people by the Reverend Jesus, Messiah, to eat their own bread, working in quiet. ¹³And you, brothers and sisters, do not grow weary when doing good things. ¹⁴And if anyone does not obey our words through this letter, take note of that person, do not associate with that person, so that such

---

If I were to opt for the committee's selection, I would translate it as " . . . God harvested you as first fruits. . . . " My choice of readings is in agreement with RSV, while that of the UBS committee's choice is followed by *Das neue Testament*.

38. There is a minor textual issue: The United Bible Society text includes καὶ, "and," between "which" and "he," putting it in brackets to indicate they were uncertain about it. The Deutsche Bibelstiftung edition of the same Greek text (*Novum Testamentum Graece* 1979) indicates in the textual apparatus that omitting the word is well attested. I omit it in the translation.

39. This may be a reference to *First Thessalonians*.

40. "That the word of the Lord may progress and triumph . . . ": Dewailly, "Course et gloire de la parole," argues that one should not pass over this verse too quickly. First, "word," ὁ λόγος, would be a term from Christian catechetical tradition, with Hebrew Bible echoes. "Speed on," τρέχῃ, is not a burst of speed, as in an athletic contest (as it is often translated), but a progression. And "be glorified," δοξάζηται, draws upon a divine attribute, not merely human acclaim.

41. The Greek makes a play on "working" (ἐργαζομένους), with the second term (περιεργαζομένους) meaning to interfere, be officious, or be a busybody. RSV uses the last of these meanings. The probable referent—loitering about an influential person in waiting to be sent as a client on some errand—suggests the contemporary word *networking*.

a person would be ashamed; ¹⁵and do not regard that person as an enemy, but warn as you would a brother or sister.

¹⁶Now may the Lord of peace Himself give you peace always and in every way. May the Lord be with all of you.

¹⁷The greeting with my own hand, Paul's, which is the sign on every letter; I write in this way. ¹⁸*May the grace of our Lord Jesus, Messiah, be with* all of *you.*

## Chapter 23

# The Johannine Gospel

### Introduction

SOME COMMENTATORS USE THE title *Fourth Gospel* rather than *Gospel According to John* because it is not at all clear that John, Son of Zebedee, was the author. The gospel in question, however, seems to be related to the letters of someone commonly referred to as "John," where the author refers to himself as the Presbyter. The *Revelation of Jesus the Messiah*, written by an author named "John," especially the section with letters to specific churches in Asia Minor, also seems to be related to the Presbyter's letters. Whatever the actual authorship of the gospel might have been, there was a community associated with this literature that is traditionally called *Johannine*. Consequently, we can call the gospel the *Johannine Gospel*. This gospel has all the appearances of going through a number of stages of development, and there may have been one author common to each stage, different authors at each stage, or one author for several stages with a different person responsible for the final version. The last possibility appears to be the most likely because someone respected a received text enough to publish it without making changes that would have removed inconsistencies and breaks in the narrative.

### Date of Final, Published Edition

The likelihood of stages of composition occurring over a period of time makes it difficult to fix a date on the material, since internal evidence may reflect some stage of development that is earlier than the final one. The one bit of evidence found in the text that helps set a possible date consists of references to an expulsion from the synagogue.[1] John 9:22, 35 is an anachronistic account of fear of the Judean authorities on the part of the parents of the man born blind whom Jesus cured; they say they feared being put out of the synagogue. John 12:42 says many Judean notables believed in Jesus but did not declare it out of fear of being excluded from the synagogue. John 16:2 is an allusion in Jesus' farewell discourse, to his followers being excluded from

---

1. John 9:22, 35; 12:42; and 16:2.

the synagogue in the future.² Some have taken these passages to refer to the *Birchath ha-Minim*, which was formulated against Jewish Christians; it was introduced under the presidency of R. Gamaliel II (ca 80–90) at Jamnia and composed by Shemuel ha-Qatan.³ It was a negative blessing, i.e. a curse, which no crypto-Christian in the assembly would utter.⁴ The writings of Justin Martyr (ca 114–165) clearly show that Christians in the second century saw the curse as a problem:

> . . . and now you reject those who hope in Him, and in Him who sent him . . . cursing in your synagogues those that believe on Christ.⁵

> . . . those of the seed of Abraham who live according to the law, and do not believe in this Christ before death, shall likewise not be saved, and especially those who have anathematized and do anathematize this very Christ in the synagogues. . . .⁶

> But if you curse Him and them that believe in Him. . . .⁷

There are discourses in the gospel that use abstract language, and that feature made the gospel popular among Gnostics in the third century, a group of spiritual thinkers who oriented themselves in an other-worldly direction and sought to apprehend the divine through mystical experiences. Early in the twentieth century commentators saw these discourses as Hellenistic and late. The discovery of such abstract discourse in the Qumran materials ("Dead Sea Scrolls," mostly from before the Common Era) has disproven that hypothesis.⁸ Consequently, other kinds of evidence have received renewed scrutiny. The discovery and analysis of the Rylands Papyrus 457 from Egypt, usually identified as $P^{52}$, tended to lead commentators toward an earlier date. Taken alone, however, $P^{52}$ only expands the range of possible dates for the composition of the *Johannine Gospel*; the papyrus is judged to have been written anywhere from 135 CE to early in the 200's.⁹ When considered along with two other papyri, however, the bearing of $P^{52}$

---

2. Manns, *John and Jamnia*.
3. Carroll, "Fourth Gospel and the Exclusion."
4. Whitacre, *Johannine Polemic*, sees a contradiction between the Johannine community consisting of ethnic Jews who would find the curse a problem and the author of the gospel finding it necessary to translate such terms as Rabbi (John 1:38) and Messiah (John 1:41). He does not take into account the stages through which the text was developed, with the composition of the community becoming more gentile and less Jewish over time. *Das neue Testament und frühchristliche Schriften*, edited by Berger and Nord, 313, ignores the curse and maintains, on the grounds of an absence of any mention of the destruction of Jerusalem combined with knowledge of the death of Peter, that the gospel was written in 68 or 69 CE.
5. Justin, *Dialogue with Trypho*, chapter 16.
6. Ibid., chapter 47.
7. Ibid., chapter 95.
8. R. Brown, *Gospel According to John (i–xii)*, xliii; and "Dead Sea Scrolls," 8.
9. Nongbri, "Use and Abuse of $P^{52}$."

on the dating of the gospel increases. Bodmer Papyrus II ($P^{66}$) and Bodmer Papyrus XV ($P^{75}$) date from about 175 to 225; $P^{52}$ and $P^{75}$ have textual variations of the gospel that resemble the readings of the fourth-century Codex Vaticanus (B), while $P^{66}$ has variations that resemble the fourth-century Codex Sinaiticus (א). As Raymond Brown noted, it takes time for the copying and recopying of a text to produce such variations.[10] Taken together, the three papyri move the known variations in the text of the *Johannine Gospel* back into the late second century and lead one to presuppose a development before then. Similarly, Heracleon (active around 170 or earlier, in Rome) and Origen (ca 184/185–253/254) appear to have had different variations in their texts of the gospel.[11] It is also notable that someone as early as Heracleon wrote a commentary on the *Johannine Gospel*, a commentary that Origin would criticize.

An early Christian writer, Papias (ca 100–200 CE), seems to have used the *Johannine Gospel*. In his Prologue, Papias lists seven disciples of Jesus, six of whom also appear in the Gospel of John. He gives the six in the same order as they appear in John 1:35–51 and 21:2. The mathematical probability of listing six names by chance in the same order as someone else is miniscule; in all probability Papias, a very early personage, was using the gospel.[12]

Another early Christian writer, Irenaeus of Lyons (died 202), working on an antignostic tract about 175–185, mentions the origins of the gospels in passing:

> Matthew also issued a written Gospel among the Hebrews in their own dialect, while Peter and Paul were preaching at Rome, and laying the foundation of the Church. After their departure, Mark, the disciple and interpreter of Peter, did also hand down to us in writing what had been preached by Peter. Luke also, the companion of Paul, recorded a book of the gospel preached by him. Afterwards, John, the disciple of the Lord, who also had leaned upon His breast, did himself publish a Gospel during his residence at Ephesus in Asia.[13]

Irenaeus's report is for the most part imprecise about dates; those familiar with Greek will take "while Peter and Paul were preaching" in a logical rather temporal sense. In fact, Irenaeus probably had the traditional order of the gospels from a Codex in mind: first Matthew, then Mark, then Luke. However, when it came to the *Johannine Gospel*, Irenaeus says "afterwards"; that gospel was written after the others, which would make it after 90 or so. Irenaeus believed the author, John, lived in Ephesus into the reign of Trajan (98–117).[14]

---

10. R. Brown, *Gospel According to John (i–xii)*, lxxx–lxxxiii. Recently, Nongbri, "Reconsidering the Place of Papyrus Bodmer XIV–XV," reviews the evidence and suggests the dating of $P^{75}$ is not secure.

11. Ehrman, "Heracleon, Origen, and the Text."

12. O'Connell, "Note on Papias's Knowledge."

13. Irenaeus, *Against Heresies*, 3:1. Hengel, *Johannine Question*, 137n, refers to a dissertation by Klaus Thornton that proposes that Irenaeus's information came from a list of writings in the community library in Rome: "It bears a striking similarity to the information about authors in ancient library catalogues."

14. R. Brown, *Gospel According to John (i–xii)*, lxxxvi.

Martin Hengel points out that a Roman presbyter, Gaius (between 180–220) rejected the *Johannine Gospel*, attributing it to Cerinthus, who was considered a heretic who flourished around 100.[15] This is significant because Gaius deemed the work to be that old. Hengel also points to Ptolemy, a disciple of Valentinus a generation before Irenaeus' time, referring to John, the Lord's disciple, as the author of the Prologue of the *Johannine Gospel*; this too points to a second-century writer considering the gospel to be early.[16]

In light of all the evidence, it is safe to assume that the *Johannine Gospel*, though containing earlier material, was published in the form that we now have between 100 and 110 CE.[17]

## Author/Source

As with the other canonical gospels, the author does not self-identify by name. P[66], which dates from about 175 to 225, carries the inscription, in Greek, "Gospel according to John." Candidates by that name include John, the son of Zebedee, and brother of James, John the Presbyter, and John Mark. Acts 4:13 describes Peter and John in Jerusalem as illiterate and common people who had been with Jesus. Just as Peter's tradition was put into written form by Mark, John's could have been written down by someone. But Peter and John are said not only to be illiterate and common, but *anthropois*, not youths; if John were a responsible adult of about 30 in the year 35 or so (and Paul remembers him as a leader),[18] he would have been 65 at the time of the destruction of Jerusalem and 95 at the turn of the century. Like Peter, moreover, John was a Galilean, and the *Johannine Gospel* focuses on Jerusalem, not Galilee. If John the Son of Zebedee was a Galilean, John the Presbyter, whom Papias distinguished from John the disciple,[19] has not been associated by any evidence with any region other than Asia Minor, but the author of the gospel refers to witnessing events in Jerusalem.[20] The Presbyter's association with Asia Minor does associate him with the publication

---

15. Hengel, *Johannine Question*, 6.

16. Ibid., 8. The Ptolemny in question was probably the teacher by that name executed by the Romans in 155—Ibid. It is sometimes noted that Ignatius does not refer to John being in Ephesus; ibid., 14–15, says this is so because in context Ignatius meant to refer to founders and martyrs, such as Paul and Peter, not to a contemporary who was still alive. It is tempting to make something of the theory that Irenaeus knew Polycarp who knew John of Ephesus, but Irenaeus would have been quite young while Polycarp was still alive, and Irenaeus says that Polycarp knew John but does not say he was taught by John—ibid., 15.

17. R. Brown, *Gospel According to John (i–xii)*, lxxx, sees this decade as the latest possible date, as opposed to the most likely.

18. Gal 2:9.

19. Hengel, *Johannine Question*, 16–21.

20. John 19:35. Keener, *Gospel of John*, 96–97, maintains that Eusebius misinterpreted Papias in attributing to him a distinction between two Christian personages named "John."

## The Johannine Gospel

of the gospel, however. John Mark's home was in Jerusalem;[21] he may have been from a Levitical family, since his cousin Barnabas was a Levite, and that family may have served some Temple function.[22] If John Mark was responsible for this gospel, he would not be the Mark who was responsible for fashioning Peter's preaching into the *Gospel of Mark*. However, the tradition in Acts has John Mark and Barnabas going to Cyprus, not Asia Minor, and then John Mark drops out of the picture.[23] Other possible candidates have been suggested, but with much speculation—for example, James H. Charlesworth makes a case for the Beloved Disciple being the apostle Thomas.[24]

The author, at least at some stage of the development of the gospel, was an eye witness to the piercing of Jesus' side[25] and refers at times to "the disciple whom Jesus loved" and at other times to "another disciple." Most reasonably, these can be understood as one and the same person. The anonymous disciple, along with Andrew, begins as a disciple of John the Baptist (this gospel never calls that prophetic figure "the Baptist") and begins to follow Jesus.[26] As Jesus is under arrest and taken to the residence of the high priest, the anonymous disciple is said to be known to the high priest and able to persuade a maid/porter to admit Peter into the courtyard.[27] The disciple whom Jesus loved leans against Jesus' chest during the Last Supper.[28] He stands near the cross, and Jesus gives Mary to him as his mother.[29] Mary Magdalene runs to Peter and the disciple whom Jesus loved, telling them Jesus' body was missing.[30] He is in a boat fishing with Simon Peter and others, and he recognizes Jesus on the shore.[31] Jesus says the disciple whom Jesus loved may survive until Jesus returns, and a confusion to the effect that the disciple would not die was thereby created.[32] In 21:24, the writer tells the reader that this disciple is the source of the things that have been related.[33] Raymond Brown suggests that the principal author in the earlier stages of the composition of the gospel is this anonymous disciple, and that his self-references are simply "the other disciple," while a later redactor inserted the term "the disciple whom Jesus loved."[34]

---

21. Acts 12:12.
22. See Acts 4:36.
23. See Acts 15:39.
24. Charlesworth, *Beloved Disciple*.
25. John 19:35.
26. John 1:35.
27. John 18:15–16.
28. John 13:23–26.
29. John 19:24–27.
30. John 20:2–10.
31. John 21:7.
32. John 21:20–23.
33. John 21:24. See R. Brown, *Gospel According to John (i–xii)*, xciii–xcv.
34. R. Brown, *Gospel According to John (i–xii)*, xciv.

I would not insist that only "The Twelve" were at the Last Supper with Jesus, as does Brown; no gospel says anyone was excluded, least of all a child who often kept the company of Peter.[35] Consequently, I do not favor John, son of Zebedee, as the strongest candidate, as did Brown on the grounds that he was one of the Twelve. Nor do I exclude John Mark on the grounds that he was not one of the Twelve. John the Presbyter can also not be eliminated, simply on the grounds that we do not know whether or not he had been in Jerusalem at an early age and migrated later to Ephesus and environs. All three could have been the basic source.

What is important about the biography of the author (or source) is not his name, but that he was an eye witness to many of the events narrated in the gospel. Raymond Brown points to a number of passages that appear to be historically accurate.[36] There is the description of the Samaritans' theology, their worshiping on Mount Gerizim, and the location of Jacob's Well (chapter 4). There is the description of the Pool of Bethesda (chapter 5).[37] There are descriptions of feasts—Passover (chapter 6) and Tabernacles (chapers 7–8). There are details about Jerusalem—the Pool of Siloam (John 9:7), the Portico of Solomon as a shelter in winter (10:22–23), and the stone pavement of Pilate's Praetorium (19:13). There is also an interesting but incidental reference to a particular Jerusalem spot in John 5:2: "There is in Jerusalem by the sheep a pool . . . " (my literal translation from the Greek). "Sheep" here is an adjective preceded by a definite article.[38] There was a Sheep Gate in Jerusalem,[39] but by the time of the Johannine narrative it appears to have been simply called "The Sheep." If John 5:2 were written for a largely gentile audience in Ephesus some thirty years after the destruction of Jerusalem, the writer would use the imperfect tense and would, the way modern translators do, supply "gate"; but the text reads "There is in Jerusalem by the sheep. . . . " This is evidently a wording from an earlier stage in the development of the gospel by someone who knew the pre-destruction Jerusalem.[40]

So the account in the *Johannine Gospel* originates from a disciple of Jesus, who was largely oriented to Jerusalem. It ends up being published in Ephesus some seventy years later. The redactor of the final version respected the text, leaving many incongruities in it; one would presume that the redactor revered the source, at times referring to

---

35. Ibid., xcvi.

36. Ibid., xlii.

37. Wallace, "John 5:2," argues against the accuracy of the gospel's description, but he does so largely by pointing out what archaeological evidence is not there, not with any evidence that is inconsistent with the gospel account. It turns out that archaeologists had begun to debate the evidence. In his reading of the gospel text itself, he points to the use of the present tense in a work published after the destruction of the site, ignoring the likelihood that the redactor/publisher may have retained the wording of an earlier text out of respect.

38. τῇ προβατικῇ.

39. See Neh 3;1 and 32; 12:39. The Septuagint (2 Esd 13:1) translates it as the Sheep Gate, τὴν πύλην τὴν προβατικήν.

40. Broer, "Knowledge of Palestine."

him as the "Beloved Disciple." The Beloved Disciple evidently produced a text, either penning or dictating it, before the redactor worked on it for publication. We know that the Romans destroyed and depopulated Jerusalem in 70, and that followers of Jesus had left the city beforehand; had they not they would have been taken as slaves to Rome or elsewhere. Obviously, a migration from Jerusalem or environs to Ephesus had taken place. Logically, the earliest phase of composition could have taken place, alternatively, in Jerusalem, in some temporary locale before the migration to Ephesus, or in Ephesus. What is interesting sociologically is the fact of migration, to which we will return below. Where the writing began to take place is of lesser importance.

Harry and Paul Eberts associate the *Gospel of John* with the Hellenist faction that emerged early on in the Christian movement in Jerusalem.[41] This is certainly possible, but the salience of such faction identifications at the relatively late date of the gospel's composition argues against it.

## Composition of the Text

Tom Thatcher identifies four different theories that have been proposed for the composition of the *Johannine Gospel*: The "oral tradition theory" would have oral traditions gathered separately into the synoptic gospels and into the fourth gospel. The "written source theory" would have oral tradition gathered separately into a Signs Source of miracle narratives and a Passion Narrative, and then these two written documents merged into a Signs Gospel, which the fourth Evangelist combined with a gnostic sayings source. The "synoptic dependence theory" would have oral Jesus traditions written into the synoptic gospels and perhaps some other written sources, and merged into the fourth gospel. The "developmental theory" would have oral Jesus traditions shaped by a community over time.[42] The oral tradition theory and the synoptic dependence theories are obviously mutually exclusive; one may not be true without the other being untrue. They also exclude the other two theories. The four approaches are discussed below out of Thatcher's order: first, third, second, fourth.

If the first, "oral tradition" theory were true, one would have expected a much more coherent narrative in the *Johannine Gospel*. It would be analogous to the *Gospel of Mark*, where seams are visible but the result nevertheless relates a story that progresses smoothly from scene to scene. One would not have concluding passages such as John 20:30, which is followed by more text. Nor would one find first-hand testimony, such as John 19:35, written some seventy years after the reported events.

D. Moody Smith reviews the discussion of the third, "synoptic dependence" theory, noting that the question of the dependence of the fourth gospel on the other three has been discussed for centuries.[43] At first glance, the theory seems simple, but matters

41. Eberts and Eberts, *Early Jesus Movement and Its Gospels*, 208.
42. Thatcher, "Introduction."
43. Smith, *John Among the Gospels*; see also Smith, *Johannine Christianity*, 97–105.

become much more complicated when it is realized that the other three gospels had undergone developmental processes. Some commentators speak of predecessor versions of Mark, with a narrative of a Galilean ministry, a passion narrative, and resurrection accounts being stitched together. Thus where John differs from Mark, it can be explained away by a theory of redaction on the part of Mark. Then Matthew and Luke, as is well known, used the *Gospel of Mark* as a source, as well as a sayings source ("Q"). Any differences between the fourth gospel and the two later synoptic gospels could be explained away by referring to redaction of Mark's text, or Q by Matthew and Luke, or for that matter redaction by an editor of Q of earlier forms of the sayings. What I draw from this is that, while the theory would explain away differences between the fourth gospel and the others and focus on similarities, it is equally possible to explain away similarities in terms of oral traditions common to both John and the synoptic gospels. Indeed, Matthew and Luke are said to have their unique traditions ("M" material and "L" material). One is struck by the indeterminate nature of the evidence and inferences to be drawn from the evidence. The conclusions of those who adhere to the theory are underdetermined. Aside from the impossibility of disproving a theory with so many loopholes and escape hatches, there is the fundamental question of how much of a similarity is evidence of dependence and how much dissimilarity is evidence of independence. In a well-executed study of Mark 8:22–26 and John 9:1–41 (the cure of a man born blind), Thomas Brodie is impressed by a few fragmentary similarities while in contrast I am struck by considerable dissimilarities; "fundamental ingredients" as Brodie terms them, should be more pervasive in a work than they appear to be in his study.[44] It seems, from my perspective, that some oral tradition found its way at the early stages of the development of both the *Gospel of Mark* and the *Johannine Gospel*; the two gospels, after all, came out of the same movement that we call "Christian."

To dwell a little further on the "dependence theory," if the fourth evangelist depended on one of the synoptic gospels rather than jot down oral traditions as he or she heard them, and first-hand memories as they came to mind, we would expect to find fragments that are arranged into a scene or discourse in an earlier gospel to be similarly arranged in the fourth gospel. Raymond Brown investigated precisely that possibility. He found three major scenes that include parallels with the fourth gospel: The Agony in the Garden,[45] the Trial before Caiphas,[46] and the Temptations of Jesus.[47] In each case, the fragments that are paralleled in the fourth gospel are scattered in various places. Brown goes further in drawing his conclusion than disconfirming the dependence theory; he maintains that a case can be made for the basic historicity of the *Johannine Gospel* and for theological reorganization on the part of the synoptic gospels.[48]

44. Brodie, *Quest for the Origin*, 31–33.
45. Matt 26:36–46; Mark 14:32–42; Luke 23:40–46.
46. Matt 26:59–68; Mark 14:55–65; Luke 22:66–70.
47. Matt 4:1–11; Mark 1:12–13; Luke 4:1–13.
48. R. Brown, "Incidents That Are Units in the Synoptic Gospels," 160.

The second, "written source" theory has enjoyed a great deal of attention. Logically, it is compatible with and even suggested by the developmental theory. However, investigators have tended to opt for one or the other. The search for sources in the fourth gospel has been a staple of research in New Testament studies for decades.[49] In the middle of the twentieth century, Rudolf Bultmann's theory of a "signs source" that was blended with a "sayings source" received most attention. The term "signs source" comes from the text of the gospel itself, which begins numbering signs (miracles) but, in its present form, includes signs that are not numbered and in fact interrupt the numbering. Building on Bultmann's theory, Robert Fortna and Urban von Wahlde independently essayed reconstructions of the Signs source.[50] From one point of view, the fourth evangelist had access to sayings as any Christian would; the fourth gospel's discourses were often exegeses on a saying, not separate essays imported by the evangelist.[51] Focusing instead on the proposed signs source versus a sayings/discourse source, one could look for stylistic differences between the proposed two parts of the gospel; Ruckstuhl affirms that his inquiries revealed no stylistic differences between the two sources as identified by Bultmann, by Fortna, or by Willem Nicol.[52] Felton and Thatcher conducted a more sophisticated study of minute stylistic patterns that would differentiate Fortna's signs source from other narrative sections and from sayings/discourse sections. They found differences, which they say confirms the existence of the signs source that Fortna had identified.[53]

As noted above, the fourth, "developmental" theory is not a true alternative to the second, "written source" theory. However, the best known proponent of the developmental approach, Raymond R. Brown, wrote his two-volume commentary on the *Johannine Gospel* after Ruckstuhl's studies seemed to show stylistic commonalities in Bultmann's purported signs source and sayings/discourse source, but before the Felton/Thatcher validation of the Fortna signs source model. On the basis of Ruckstuhl's data, he rejects the Bultmann signs source/sayings source model. Theoretically one can accept the developmental theory and either a) reject all source theories, b)

---

49. Urban von Wahlde, *Earliest Versions*, 21–24, cites efforts to reconstruct the text of sources by Hans Heinrich Wendt, Julius Wellhausen, Wilhelm Wilkens, Maria-Émile Boismard and Arnaud Lamouille, Emanuel Hirsch, Rudolf Bultman, D. Moody Smith, and Willem Nicol.

50. Fortna, *Fourth Gospel*; von Wahlde, *Earliest Versions*. Incidentally, without looking for a Signs Source, some years ago I endeavored to separate out portions of sources in the *Johannine Gospel* on the basis of breaks, duplications, and seams as well as obvious stylistic patterns, arranging the results in separate columns, all in preparation for a sociology of the Johannine community—Blasi, *Sociology of Johannine Christianity*; Keener, *Gospel of John*, 37, says of this work that it "adopts a sociological approach to identifying sources, but unconvincingly presses too far behind the extant texts." He may be right that I pressed too far behind the extant texts, but sociology does not identify sources and I did not attempt to use the discipline to do so. Rather, I used features of the text itself for that purpose, and then used sociological models to interpret the resultant source texts.

51. Lindars, "Traditions Behind the Fourth Gospel."

52. Ruckstuhl, "Johannine Language and Style."

53. Felton and Thatcher, "Stylometry and the Signs Gospel."

reject the Bultmann source theory but accept one or more alternative source theories, or c) be open to most source theories. The central contention of the developmental theory is that the traditions that ended up in the *Johannine Gospel* were fashioned by a Johannine community's experiences over time. For traces of early experiences to be retained, it actually implies the traditions retaining some fixed, probably written, form prior to the final version of the gospel. An advantage of the developmental theory is that passages that seem close to a Judeam setting (e.g. Jerusalem in the time of Jesus) and distant from "the Jews" can be included in the same gospel.[54]

The most influential developmental theory of the composition of the *Johannine Gospel* for some time has been that of Raymond Brown.[55] A first phase saw a body of non-synoptic traditional material pertaining to the works and words of Jesus. It is notable that Brown did not propose separate sources for works (what Bultmann had called "signs") and words. A second phase saw decades of use of the traditional material in preaching; a Johannine school of preachers gave a unifying stamp but not a stylistic or narrative uniformity to its body of literature. In the third phase, an evangelist organized the material into a consecutive gospel, in which Jesus replaces the various Jewish feasts; some of the material from phase 2 was not included. In the fourth phase, the evangelist re-edited the material one or more times to meet the needs of different occasions, such as objections from disciples of John the Baptist and Christians who still belonged to synagogues. The excommunication of the latter was another occasion that required re-editing. In the fifth, final stage, a redactor reinserted material from the second phase that the evangelist had not used in the various editions of the gospel. Some of the newly included material consisted of variants of material already in the text. The redactor did not feel free to rewrite, but instead simply inserted material where it fit thematically. At this phase, the insertion of the Lazarus motif (chapters 11–12) occasioned the relocation of the Temple incident narrative to chapter 2. The final redactor may have been responsible for the addition of chapter 21 and the writing and insertion of the prologue. In a later study Brown renumbers the five phases to two, adds a third in which the *Letters of John* are written, and adds a fourth phase for the different trajectories of the adherents of the author of the letters into a union with the wider Christian church, and the opponents of the author of the letters into a secession and eventually Gnosticism.[56]

Birger Olssen proposes an alternative developmental theory. The Johannine sector of what we now call the Christian movement began in Jerusalem from about 40 to 70 CE.

> From here comes the disciple of Jesus who formed the Johannine group . . . ,
> an eyewitness but not one of the twelve, "the disciple whom Jesus loved". Like

---

54. R. Brown, *Gospel According to John (i–xii)*, and R. Brown, *Gospel According to John (xiii–xxi)*. The inclusion of both kinds of passage is a problem for Stegemann and Stegemann, *Jesus Movement*, 225–26.

55. *Gospel According to John (i–xii)*, xxxiv–xxxix.

56. R. Brown, *Community of the Beloved Disciple*.

John the Baptist he probably came from priestly circles. He "was known to the high priest" (Jn 18:15) and "his" Gospel is saturated with priestly, cultic categories: the image of Jesus, the emphasis on purification, the big feasts, etc. The opponents of Jesus in John are to a great extent the high priests.[57]

A second phase is situated beyond the Jordan, about 70–90 CE. This phase is marked by the curses in the synagogue against such heretics as the Christians. A third phase is situated in Asia Minor, about 90–110 CE. An orientation toward universal salvation develops there. More Greeks join the community. 1 John 2:19 suggests there were some who could not accept the humanity of Jesus, and that issue occasioned a schism. Those remaining in the community around the Presbyter merged with the broader Christian movement. "The Johannine Christians recognized other traditions without giving up their own."[58]

## Particular Features

There are two features of the *Johannine Gospel* that the modern reader needs to appreciate in order to not find it confusing. The modern reader is tempted to read this gospel with the other three in mind, but the narrative is a different one even where there are parallels. This is in part because the evangelist used a different calendar from that of the other evangelists, and the liturgical practices regulated by that calendar left its impression on the Johannine narrative. In addition, the evangelist goes beyond the words and works of Jesus by using person-types to communicate his points. These person-types need not be characterized with historical accuracy for the evangelist to communicate his message by means of them, though his use of them does not preclude historicity.

First let us turn to the calendar. It is well known that the Last Supper/Passover Meal in the *Johannine Gospel* does not correspond in many respects to the narratives in the synoptic gospels, in particular the day of the week on which it occurs. Annie Jaubert explains that the Johannine community used a more ancient calendar than that used in the synoptic gospels and by the established Jerusalem priesthood, the Zadokite calendar, which is also reflected in the Qumran materials. She goes on to propose that the ancient custom of re-enacting Jesus washing the disciples feet on the Tuesday-to-Wednesday night came from the Johannine community, and also that the Tuesday-to-Wednesday evening corresponded to the Passover in the Zadokite calendar (1991:66).[59] The celebration of the appearance of Jesus on the Sunday after Passover makes sense as the second Sunday (John 20:26, "Eight days later") after the Tuesday-to-Wednesday Zadokite Passover. She also points to the first farewell discourse as not an ordinary hortatory farewell address; it is interrupted by questions.[60] During the Passover meal, it was the custom to ask questions

---

57. Olsson, "History of the Johannine Movement," 30.
58. Ibid., 33.
59. Jaubert, "Calendar of Qumran," 66.
60. John 13:31—14:31.

of the senior man present, usually the father. In the case of Jesus' discourse, the questions are by Simon Peter, Thomas, Philip, and Judas not Iscariot.[61] The focus is on Jesus going (Exodus). Jaubert traces the Passover theme further back in the thirteenth chapter of John: The meticulous account of Jesus' actions in washing the disciples' feet is a description of a Johannine ritual.[62] In John 13:10, it is presumed that Peter had bathed—an obligatory purification before the Passover meal. The fact that Jesus was performing a ritual purification during the meal resembles the practice that appears in the *Book of Jubilees* 21:16 and the *Testament of Levi* 18:2. Consequently, the astonishment the disciples display is not at the washing of their feet but at Jesus taking the role of a slave in doing it.[63]

Raymond Collins points to the use of person-types in the *Johannine Gospel*, calling it an "individualist approach."[64] He observes that the gospel describes different types of faith situation by highlighting individual persons:

1. John (the Baptist): one sent by God to give witness to Jesus.
2. Nathaniel: an authentic Israelite who recognizes Jesus as the Messiah.
3. Nicodemus: the nonbeliever.
4. The Samaritan Woman: one crossing the boundary separating Jewish Christians and Samaritan Christians, but also as a minister who leads others to belief.
5. The Herodian official: a person who believes in the word that gives life.
6. The lame man who is cured but ultimately stays in the Jewish community.
7. The man born blind who, once cured, defends Jesus and is cast out of the synagogue.
8. Philip: disciple who at first misunderstands and a Greek disciple who leads others to Jesus.
9. Lazarus: the disciple who has died but will be raised.
10. Martha: the firm believer looking forward to resurrection.
11. Judas Iscariot: one whom Satan has entered.
12. Mary the mother of Jesus: The one who faithfully awaits the messianic times.
13. Mary Magdalene: Believer in the resurrected Jesus.
14. Thomas: One who recognizes the divinity of Jesus.
15. Peter: Representative of the disciples.
16. The Beloved Disciple: The believer *par excellence*, whose testimony had special significance for the Johannine movement.

---

61. John 13:36; 14:5; 14:8, 14:22.
62. John 13:4–5, 12. Jaubert, "Calendar of Qumran," 70.
63. Jaubert, "Calendar of Qumran," 72.
64. R. Collins, "Representative Figures."

This literary device makes any historical reconstruction of events in the life of Jesus more difficult than it would otherwise be, but it also has a sociological significance that will be pointed out below.

## The Sociology of Religion and Migration

The sociological study of migrant religion began early in the history of the sociology of religion. The famous 1895 *Hull-House Maps and Papers* included two such studies, though more from an ethnic than immigration perspective.[65] One early concern in the United States was whether immigrant religion helped or hindered "Americanization."[66] A depression-era controversial study from the "Chicago school" tradition of ethnography found that the second generation of immigrant Russian "Jumper" Christians in Los Angeles tended to go astray into juvenile delinquency and then adult criminality as the parents' old-world religion lost its grip over them.[67] That an immigrant religion could become weaker across generations suggests a methodological difficulty: If one studied an immigrant congregation, one would be studying those who had retained some level of participation in the religious life of the traditional faith, even as many others, perhaps a majority of the immigrant community, may not be involved any longer in the religion at all. Perhaps the communal bonds of a religion prevented the most religious from leaving the "old country," thereby making a representative study of migrants, as opposed to a congregation, a study of a fairly irreligious sample to begin with. Then among the second generation, assimilation into the receiving society might involve some de-ethnicizing, and that in turn may lessen even more what religiosity there may have been in the community, or some in the second generation may convert to some other religion than the one traditional for the ethnic group of their parents.

However unrepresentative a study of an immigrant congregation may be, it can nevertheless be an interesting study. The religion may be providing something socially as well as religiously valuable to its active members. Clearly, religion is not an isolated factor in the immigration process but is tied up with family and ethnicity.

> Religious rituals, with their symbolic re-enactment of and ties with tradition, often serve as primary mechanisms for the reproduction of culture. Because religious services among new immigrants are frequently performed in the native language, they become a link with traditional culture and can serve as a vehicle to reproduce ethnic identity. . . .[68]

An immigrant church or temple often provides ethnic communities with refuge from the hostility and discrimination of the larger society, as well as resources for economic

---

65. Zeman, "Bohemian People"; Zeublin, "Chicago Ghetto."
66. See Fry, *New and Old Immigrant*.
67. Young, *Pilgrims of Russian-town*.
68. Ebaugh and Chafetz, "Introduction," 39–40.

mobility and opportunities for social position and recognition within the community itself.[69] For example, a study of New York City Korean immigrant Christian churches noted that they provided fellowship for their members, maintained Korean culture, offered social services, and provided social status and positions for those in leadership positions.[70] Kmec found a similar pattern for mainland European immigrants to Ireland.[71] An ethnography of youth in a New York City Chinese immigrant congregation found that the congregation and its pastor provided a source for legitimating prosocial behavior, thereby compensating for the loss of authority on the part of parents; kinship ties had weakened in the process of migration and settlement.[72] That a congregation could serve as a substitute family in what, in fact, were a small number of cases reveals how important families could be in general; an interview study of "college aged" Asian American young adults, presumably more middle class and with fewer families under stress, revealed that their family heritage was crucial for the transmission of religious identity and practice.[73] For the older generation in the old country, religion might be taken for granted as part of the environing culture; but in the new pluralist society it is a different matter. But in contrast, when there are barriers to an immigrant group assimilating into a society, its ethnic religion may persist in stronger form than ever as an ethnic marker;[74] in such cases an old world religion may not weaken (further) once a group has undergone the migration process. Throughout the world of immigrant-receiving nations, second generation Muslims have been observed to seek purer forms of Islam than the folk versions of their parents. This leads one to suspect that across traditions the religion of the second generation will not be a carbon copy of that of the first. Sharon Kim's study of second generation Korean American churches in Los Angeles found that rather than replicate the insular ethnic churches of their parents they operated in English, used popular music forms, emphasized volunteering for ministries rather than depending on clergy, and were informal in attire; but unlike other American churches they stressed global issues, encouraged arts both in worship and as careers, and were communal in their value systems rather than individualistic.[75] It would be making too many assumptions to apply such concepts as youth culture and global consciousness to the Johannine community in first century Ephesus, but evidence of late redaction should not be thought of as the workings of the whims of an individual redactor.

By surveying a representative sample of immigrants in a society, one may find that migrants engage in their traditional religious practices less often after migration than they had before, despite the impression made by isolated studies of congregations. A

69. Hirschman, "Role of Religion."
70. Min, "Structure and Social Functions."
71. Kmec, "Religion as a Response."
72. Cao, "Church as Surrogate Family."
73. Park and Ecklund, "Negotiating Continuity."
74. Diel and Koenig, "Religiosität türkischer Migranten."
75. S. Kim, "Replanting Sacred Spaces."

major study of recent immigrants into the United States revealed that this has been the case for most groups, with the exception of Russians and Koreans.[76] A study of immigrants to the Province of Quebec did not stop at comparing pre- and post-migration religious practice, but also interviewed people three years after migration as opposed to six months after; it seemed that the decline, which occurred for all but Pentecostal immigrants, continued over time.[77] While the migration experience itself involved the breaking up of social involvements that supported religion, thereby no longer allowing it to exert its salutary effects on the immigrant population, the formation of ethnic concentrations, enclaves, is one phenomenon that works in the opposition direction.[78]

In approaching the relationship between religion and migration, it is necessary to consider the several phases of the migration process separately: 1) Deciding to migrate, 2) Preparing for the trip; 3) The journey; 4) Arrival; 5) Settlement; 6) Development of transnational linkages.[79] As suggested above, deep involvement in a religion may militate against deciding to migrate, except perhaps as a missionary. In early Christian phenomena, we must distinguish between the migratory behavior of such a figure as Paul of Tarsus and Christians who might have migrated for economic reasons. In preparing for a trip, there may be much "discerning of the spirit," especially in the case of a missionary, but the economic migrant may pray about the prospect of leaving home for a new life as well. The journey itself may involve brief stays with Christian households along the route through a pre-existing network of Christians—a system of what sociologists sometimes refer to as "loose connections." The moment of arrival may occasion some contact with Christians in the new setting, but again these would be loose connections that are not expected to be permanent. So some sustained involvement in a Christian community may or may not mark the stage of settlement in the new society. In the case of refugees, deciding to migrate and preparing for the trip may occur in a hurry; the journey itself may involve contacts with the loose network of Christians, but arrival and settlement may be a matter of chance rather than plan. Whether the Johannine community left Palestine as a migration for opportunity or as a refugee flight, its uniqueness, as reflected in its gospel, can be thought of in terms of a settlement apart from neighboring Christian communities in its new homeland, neighboring communities with which it was only loosely connected.

## Sociology of Calendars

One will not likely find a course in the sociology of calendars in any university catalog, but in specialized classes in sociological theory one might find readings about time. The present concern is not with the broad topic of the "sociology of time" but with calendar time.

76. Massey and Espinoza, "Effect of Immigration."
77. Connor, "Increase or Decrease?"
78. Connor, "International Migration."
79. Hagan and Ebaugh, "Calling Upon the Sacred."

The qualifier *calendar* suggests that there are other kinds of time as well; so it is necessary to distinguish among some kinds of time. Such a distinction among kinds of time runs throughout the sociological theory of the Austrian-American scholar Alfred Schutz, but he takes it up most directly in a study of the phenomenological philosophy of his one-time mentor Edmund Husserl.[80] Schutz begins with the observation that any conscious subject participates in several time dimensions. He mentions first our personal inner time, "the flux of immanent time." We live in an inescapable stream of consciousness. Second, while being wide awake in our stream of consciousness, we may remember that last Tuesday we prepared to do something last Wednesday—maybe on Tuesday we purchased tools for a project carried out on Wednesday or prepared notes on Tuesday for a presentation on Wednesday. Tuesday definitely came before Wednesday, but in our stream of consciousness we may have Wednesday in mind first and only as a later afterthought consider of what we did Tuesday. Thus there is an articulation between Tuesday and Wednesday that may follow some logic other than sequence. If our stream of consciousness is perfectly articulated with the before-and-after structure of this second realm of time, we are experiencing something like music. Then there is a third kind of time, the objective intersubjective time on which a number of us have developed a consensus—the Tuesday of any given week always comes before the Wednesday of that week. This is "calendar or 'social time.'"[81]

What is critical in calendar time is its shared nature. It becomes a clue to the social structure of a society or social situation when it is shared with some people but not others. The fact that the Qumran community shared a calendar among its adherents and did not share in the calendar used by the Jerusalem priesthood tells us something about the social location of the Qumran adherents in the larger Palestinian Jewish world. In the modern West we have an agreed-upon civil calendar, based on a sixteenth-century calendar reform accepted by Pope Gregory XIII, but also an associated western liturgical calendar that was designed to peg the date of Easter to lunar cycles while keeping that feast from migrating out of the climatic season of spring. But westerners are also conscious of the liturgical calendar of Eastern Christians, that of Jews, and that of Muslims.[82] By orienting ourselves to a particular calendar, especially one that is other than the civil calendar, we are aligning ourselves with a particular portion of society. While still in Palestine, the Johannine community was doing that when it observed the Zadokite calendar. When it carried that practice over into the time of its settlement in Ephesus, it was still "giving off" an impression, perhaps that of simply being different from other Christians; but any stance vis-à-vis the Jerusalem priesthood would be, at best, a memory. Rather, it may have had a salience in the community's stance toward the Ephesian Jewish community.

80. Schutz, "Edmund Husserl's Ideas."

81. Ibid., 29; Schutz and Luckmann, *Structures of the Life-World*, 47.

82. Some are also conscious of the former Soviet Union not accepting the Gregorian reform of the calendar until 1929, which explains why the 1917 revolution in pre-Soviet Russia, known as the October Revolution, was commemorated in November.

## The Sociology of Saints

As noted above, the *Johannine Gospel* communicates faith stances by depicting a number of personages at different junctures in its narrative. Some of these are recognized as saints in the Christian West—Mary Magdalene, John the Baptist, and Peter, for example. There is also the inverse—Judas Iscariot as a prototypical traitor—but the usual social phenomenon is the evolution of the saint with an associated cultus of some kind. Two millennia after the beginning of the Jesus movement most saint traditions come to us in relatively established and fixed forms. It is the emergence of more recent saints that would most resemble the literary use of personages in the *Johannine Gospel*. Archbishop of San Salvador Oscar Romero, for example, acquired great posthumous charisma after he was assassinated by a right-wing faction in the Salvadoran military. A study of two locally respected holy men in India, where Hindu practice allows for the divinization of deceased people, showed that respected decedents could come to be cultivated in a relatively short time.[83] As an aspect of local folk religions, shrines set up in honor of saints can become sites at which people seek favors, quite independently of official priestly theologies; in Nepal and India, for example, both Muslims and Hindus have been observed to seek favors from Muslim saints.[84] There is no evidence that a phenomenon of that nature had developed in connection with the fourth gospel, but some other aspects of saint cults do appear to be quite relevant.

Where there are migrations of people from locales where there are folk-religious cults of saints, to places that are metropolitan and more cosmopolitan, the migrants often renew the saint cultus in their new homelands. Olga Odgers suggests that the cult of patron saints of distant local homelands enable people to maintain continuities across spatial separations.[85] The renewal of the saint cults, with shrines within churches or with parades (sometimes quite independently from clergy) represent creative efforts to make everyday life in the new setting meaningful. This would be a function[86] of such a cultus for the migrating generation. For a later generation, perhaps for a major proportion of the intended audience of the *Johannine Gospel*, the focus on Palestinian personages from the time of Jesus could serve a different function, analogous to a function identified by Agathe Bienfait for the many saints whom Pope John Paul II canonized. These, Bienfait maintains, linked the personal charisma of the individual saints to the office charisma of the organized Catholic Church.[87] They amounted to in-

---

83. Sharma, "Immortal Cowherd."
84. Gaborieau, "Le cult des saints."
85. Odgers, "Construcción del espacio."
86. By *function*, we mean a purpose that may not be fully explicated in people's consciousness. The sociological recognition of such functions is not the same thing as a full functionalist theory, wherein a social entity is described as having needs that must be met in order to persist through time. A function is also quite different from psychological functions, which are categories of psychic behavior.
87. Bienfait, "Zeichen und Wunder." On personal charisma and office charisma, see Weber, *Economy and Society*, 114.

stances of repersonalizing the office charisma. When the leadership of the Johannine church in Ephesus came to be borne by a second, perhaps non-immigrant generation, for example after the death of the Beloved Disciple, the literary use of respected personages from the Palestinian era would satisfy such a function.

## Church Mergers

As noted above, hypothetical trajectories of the history of the Johannine community propose its merger, or at least a merger of the more orthodox part of it, into the broader Christian movement. One can consider the Johannine community from the perspective of schism, since there is evidence of tension from the split from synagogue Judaism in the *Johannine Gospel*,[88] but we discuss schism elsewhere in this volume. The question of a merger arises because there is no evidence of a long-term separate existence for a Johannine church, and the broader Christian movement accepted the *Johannine Gospel* and uses it to this day. In North America, churches whose origins had been separate in Europe for geographical and linguistic reasons have merged; consequently one no longer finds separate Norwegian, Danish, Swedish, German, Finish, and Icelandic churches, but rather Lutheran churches that differ from one another in theology or on the basis of new world rather than old world geography. The European nationalities and languages had simply ceased to be salient. One study traced a succession of mergers of Presbyterian churches in the United States, all having a Scottish ancestry. The doctrinal issues that had led to the formation of separate denominations in Scotland ceased to be salient in the United States in the 1950s. However, the denomination that existed largely in the American South did not join the largely northern merger Presbyterian Church that had been created in 1955; the literature at the time stressed doctrinal liberalism as the rationale for not joining, but statistical analyses showed that delegates who voted against merging tended to be whites from counties that were heavily African American, from counties that were not urban, and from counties that were relatively prosperous. At the time, racial integration was a vigorously debated political issue.[89] It was not until about three decades later that the Presbyterian denomination based in the South merged with the rest of the Presbyterian Church. While doctrinal issues cannot be dismissed, aspects of social context are relevant to mergers and non-mergers as well.

In a general discussion of church mergers, Alan Black cites differences in such factors as age, socio-economic status,[90] levels of education, ethnic backgrounds,[91] geo-

---

88. Blasi, *Sociology of Johannine Christianity*, 92–93.

89. Dornbusch and Irle, "Failure of Presbyterian Union."

90. Black, "Marriage Model of Church Mergers"; Mann, "Canadian Church Union," 174, points to the lower class standing of the Canadian Baptists and the higher class standing of the Anglicans as one of the factors working against their participating in the merger that created the United Church of Canada.

91. Mann, "Canadian Church Union," 174, also points to the English identity of the Anglican Church, especially its clergy, as working against merging into the UCC.

graphical concentration, values, beliefs,[92] lifestyles, and previous experiences with church unions[93] as potential barriers to mergers. He had modern Western democratic settings in mind,[94] but counterparts of these factors could have been at work in the Johannine community in Ephesus. Rather than age, per se, generation from the immigrant experience in Ephesus may have been relevant. Instead of socio-economic status, it would be a matter of slave status, leading family of a household, or free workers. Rather than educational attainment, it would be whether those who were literate were Hellenistic or Jewish in their intellectuality. The ethnic identities in question would similarly be Greek and Jewish. It is not clear how much variation in values there might have been among early Christians, but beliefs evidently differed insofar as passages of the *Johannine Gospel* stress the humanity and physicality of Jesus, both before and after Easter. There were clearly differences over whether marriage or celibacy should be encouraged in early Christianity, but that does not appear to be a key issue in the *Johannine Gospel*. Finally, there may have been earlier involvements with followers of John the Baptist and with Samaritans, but whether these were attempted church unions can only be guessed.

Once a merger occurs, there is often a fraction of one of the merging churches that opposes the whole idea and splits off to become a new church. For example, a large part of the Canadian Presbyterian membership split off and formed a new Presbyterian church rather than join the United Church of Canada, partly on the basis of Scottish identity; those who favored the merger were content to see their opponents go their own way because they wanted to avoid further rancor, and they wanted to enter the United Church with strong and unified congregations.[95] A focused study of a South Carolina Methodist congregation that would not join the merged Methodist Church in 1939 showed that prior tensions among leading families were largely responsible, with one family in favor of the union and others opposed.[96] The suggestion that some left the Johannine community to join the gnostic trajectory when the community merged with the broader Christian movement is consistent with all this, and one would expect prior rivalries to be relevant. And those who favor merging tend to liken the church to a human body in their rhetoric;[97] we have the vine-and-branches

---

92. Templeton and Demerath, "Presbyterian Re-formation," point to differences in belief leading some congregations to opt out of an American Merger of Presbyterians; those that saw the merged denomination as too liberal opted out.

93. The three churches that merged to form the United Church of Canada had each been formed from prior unions, involving some forty different bodies. Thus the final merger was not an isolated event but a lengthy process—Silcox, *Church Union in Canada*, 25; see his chart of the unions on page 469.

94. A general study of American Protestant organizational consolidations focuses on factors that would similarly be most relevant to the modern world but not relevant to the first century Hellenistic context—such factors as a broad ecumenical movement and the pursuit of efficiency—Chaves and Sutton, "Organizational Consolidation." The modern environment also raises such issues as the governmental regulatory environment and subcultural issues of organizational identity.

95. Mann, "Canadian Church Union," 179; Silcox, *Church Union in Canada*, 293.

96. Tuberville, "Religious Schism."

97. Black, "Organizational Imagery."

metaphor and the wish that all might be one.[98] One outcome of a merger is that union becomes a goal rather than a mere method; consequently admission to the church may be made easier than prior to a merger.[99]

There is one more pattern that may be relevant to a merger of the Johannine community into the broader Christian movement. The Protestant churches in Belgium, representing a small fraction of the population, began as a diverse set of independent congregations. A number of them entered into what was termed a union of churches in 1839, largely to form a mechanism through which the Belgian government could pay their clergy (Union de Eglises Protestantes Evangéliques de Belgique). Some churches that the government did not recognize, and whose clergy it did not pay, also joined the Union. The Union became a denomination in 1957, despite the variety of theologies and worship patterns within it: the Eglise Evangélique Protestante de Belgique. The Methodists, who originated from American Methodist missionaries and had been nominally under a bishop in Geneva, joined the new church in 1968, abandoning the episcopal form of organization. The remnants of the Dutch Reformed Church in Belgium experienced a liberal/conservative divide, with the former joining the Union in the nineteenth century and the latter forming the Classe de Belgique des Gereformeerde Kerken in 1894. There was also a denomination formed out of revivals in 1849, the Eglise Chrétienne Missionaire de Belgique, later renamed the Eglise Réformée de Belgique in 1970. The three denominations that were thus formed from earlier mergers again merged in 1978, forming the Eglise Protestante Unie de Belgique, largely on the basis of prior cooperation in a federation, in foreign missions, and in a common theology school. What is interesting is that the theological and practical variety that existed from the beginning persists, albeit within one church.[100] Unification did not mean uniformity, at least not over decades. It is an open question how different and for how long the Johannine community was different from other Christian communities.

## Translation

### The Johannine Gospel

1 ¹In Genesis there was speaking, and the speaking was to God, and the speaking was God.[101] ²This was to God in the beginning. ³Through him[102] all things

---

98. John 15:5 and 17:21.

99. Silcox, *Church Union in Canada*, 449.

100. Dhooghe, "Le protestantisme en Belgique." It should be noted that there is also a wide variety of Protestant churches outside the merger denomination.

101. The usual translation is "In the beginning was the word," but that misses the allusion to Gen 1:1 and makes the phrase "to God" unnatural.

102. "Him": αὐτοῦ: "speech" or "word" is masculine in Greek, and here it can be understood to be personified.

came to be, and apart from him nothing came to be that has come about.[103] ⁴In him was life, and the life was people's light. ⁵And the light shines in the darkness, and the darkness did not overcome it.[104]

[⁶A man named John came to be sent by God. ⁷He came for testimony, so that he may give testimony about the light, so that all would believe through it. ⁸He was not the light, but to testify about the light. ⁹The true light, which shines on all people, was coming into the world.][105]

¹⁰He was in the world, and the world came to be through him, and the world did not know him. ¹¹He came into his own,[106] and his own people did not accept him.[107] ¹²But to those who accepted him he gave the ability to become children of God—to those believing in his name—¹³those who were born not from blood, from the will of flesh, or from the will of a man, but from God.[108] ¹⁴And the speech became flesh and dwelt among us, and we[109] saw his glory, glory as the only begotten from the Father, full of grace and truth. [¹⁵John testifies about him and has cried out, "This was the one about whom I said, 'One coming after me has ranked above me, because he was before me.'"] ¹⁶For we all received from his fullness one gift in place of another.[110] ¹⁷For the law was given through Moses, grace and truth came about through Jesus, the Messiah.

[¹⁸No one has ever seen God; the only begotten of God, who was in the bosom of the Father, makes Him known.][111]

103. "That has come about": R. Brown, *Gospel According to John (i–xii)*, 6, and others, arguing from the balance of strophes in poetic form, would associate this with verse 4: "... came to be. That which has come to be in him was life...." The translation follows the RSV because associating it with verse 4 would reduce creation to living entities alone—not something the Evangelist had any reason to say.

104. "Overcome," κατέλαβεν, can also mean "seize," "master," and "understand." The evangelist may have intended all of these.

105. An abrupt switch to a narrative about John the Baptist begins with verse 6. R. Brown, *Gospel According to John (i–xii)*, 3, places this interruption in parentheses, noting that some commentators end the interruption at the end of verse 8 and make 9 resume the poetic prologue—ibid., 9. This is one of many such jumps in the *Johannine Gospel*, and New Testament scholars routinely take them as evidence of juxtapositions of textual material from different sources. Elsewhere, Blasi, *Sociology of Johannine Christianity*, 33, I have suggested that originally insertions such as John 1:6–9 appeared as marginalia or text written on some different part of the page from what comes before; by being read to a room of scribes in order to duplicate it, the physical separations of source material would have been lost.

106. "His own," is in the neuter plural; the meaning seems to be that he came into his own creations.

107. "His own people": literally "his own," but in the masculine plural—see R. Brown, *Gospel According to John (i–xii)*, 10.

108. "Those who" is in apposition to the "those who accepted him."

109. Tenney, "Footnotes," 364, sees this as one among many "footnotes," this one alluding to the author. Others will be pointed out below. Such notes are important because they indicate the work of a redactor rather than a source's.

110. This would refer to a new dispensation replacing that of the Law. Tenney, "Footnotes," sees "we" as another note alluding to the author.

111. This appears to be an insertion, but it is not part of the narrative about John the Baptist, from which previous interruptions came.

¹⁹And this is the testimony of John, when the Judeans sent priests and Levites from Jerusalem to ask him, "Who are you?"¹¹² ²⁰And he acknowledged—and did not deny—and he acknowledged, "I am not the Messiah." ²¹And they asked him, "Who, then? Are you Elijah?" And he says, "I am not." "Are you the prophet?" And he answered, "No." ²²Then they said to him, "Who are you? That we may give an answer to those who sent us. What do you say about yourself?" ²³He said, "I am 'a voice crying: Straighten the roadway of the Lord in the desert,' as the prophet Isaiah said."¹¹³ ²⁴And there were those sent from the Pharisees, ²⁵and they questioned him and said to him, "Why then do you baptize if you are not the Messiah, Elijah, or the prophet?" ²⁶John answered them, "I am baptizing with water; in your midst one has been standing whom you do not know, ²⁷who is coming after me, the strap of whose sandal I am not worthy to loosen." ²⁸These things occurred in Batanaea,¹¹⁴ beyond where John was baptizing in the Jordan.

²⁹The next day he sees Jesus coming to him and says, "Look! The lamb of God who takes away the sin of the world. ³⁰He is the one about whom I said, "A man is coming after me who ranked above me because he was before me. ³¹And I had not known him, but I came baptizing with water that he may thereby be made known to Israel." ³²And John was giving testimony, saying, "I have seen the spirit coming down like a dove from heaven, and it stayed on him; ³³and I had not known him, but He who sent me to baptize with water told me, 'On the one you see the spirit coming down and resting on, that is the one baptizing with the holy spirit.' ³⁴And I have seen, and I have given testimony that he is the son of God."¹¹⁵

³⁵The day after that John had been standing, as well as two of his disciples, ³⁶and having seen Jesus walking he says, "Look! The lamb of God!" ³⁷And the two disciples heard him speaking, and they followed Jesus. ³⁸But Jesus, turning and seeing them following, says to them, "What do you seek?" And they said to him, "Rabbi," (which translated means *teacher*),¹¹⁶ "where are you staying?" ³⁹He says to them, "Come and see." Then they went and saw where he

---

112. This might be a continuation of the narrative in verse 6. "Judean," Ἰουδαῖοι, is usually translated as "the Jews." As in many other passages in the New Testament, this word is used for the authorities in Jerusalem. Some manuscript witnesses add "to him" after "sent."

113. Isa 40:3; the Greek wording differs from the Septuagint as well as from the synoptic parallels (Mark 1:3, Matt 3:3, Luke 3:4).

114. Most translators take the Greek, Βηθανίᾳ, to refer to Bethany, a town near Jerusalem that was not across the Jordan. According to Brownlee, "Whence the Gospel?" 168–69, who notes the text does not say it was a town, it was probably Batanaea in the highlands of Transjordania. Origen, who in his travels was unable to locate a Bethany by the Jordan, adopted the reading Bethabara, which he seems to have found in a few copies circulating in his day, ca 200—Metzger, *Textual Commentary*, 199. Neither Bethany nor Batanaea is at the Jordan; so John would not have been baptizing (verse 26) there.

115. Some commentators find a textual variant supported by few manuscript witnesses more likely original: "that he is the elect one"; see R. Brown, *Gospel According to John (i–xii)*, 57.

116. Tenney, "Footnotes," 364 points to this as a translation footnote.

stays, and they stayed with him that day; it was about the tenth hour.[117] [40]One of the two who heard through John and were following him was Andrew, the brother of Simon Peter. [41]Right away he found his own brother Simon and says to him, "We have found the Messiah" (which is translated, the *Anointed One*).[118] [42]He led him to Jesus. Seeing him, Jesus said, "You are Simon the son of John. You shall be called *Kephas*" (which is translated *Rocky*).[119]

[43]The next day he wanted to go out to Galilee, and he found Philip. And Jesus says to him, "Follow me." [44]Now Philip was from Bethsaida,[120] from the town of Andrew and Peter. [45]Philip finds Nathanial and says to him, "We found the one Moses wrote about in the law and the prophets wrote about, Jesus son of Joseph, from Nazareth." [46]And Nathanial said to him, "Can anything good be from Nazareth?" Philip says to him, "Come and see." [47]Jesus saw Nathanial coming to him and says about him, "Look, truly an Israelite in whom there is no guile."[121] [48]Nathaniel says to him, "From where do you know me?" Jesus answers and said to him, "Before Philip called you, I saw you under the fig tree." [49]Nathanial answers him, "Rabbi, you are the son of God; you are the king of Israel." [50]Jesus answers and said to him, "Because I told you that I saw you down at the fig tree you believe? You shall see greater than this."

[51]*And he says to him,*

*"Amen. Amen I say to you, you shall see heaven opened and the messengers of God ascending and descending above the son of humanity."*[122]

2[1]And on a Tuesday there was a wedding in Cana of Galilee, and the mother of Jesus was there.[123] [2]Now Jesus himself was invited to the wedding,

117. I.e., about 4:00 p.m. Fortna, *Fourth Gospel*, 6, points to this as gratuitous factual detail in the narrative that the redactor left in because of a reluctance to rewrite received tradition.

118. In Greek, "the Anointed One" is *Christos*. Tenney, "Footnotes," 364, identifies this as a translation footnote; Fortna, *Fourth Gospel*, 6, points to it as evidence of the redactor inserting an explanatory parenthesis.

119. Tenney, "Foonotes," 364, identifies this as a translation footnote. Kephas means "rock" in Aramaic, but the word used here to translate *Kephas* is *Petros*, "Rocky," not *petra*, "rock"—R. Brown, *Gospel According to John (i–xii)*, 76. Hereafter I render it "Peter."

120. The site of BethSaida, 1.5 miles north of the Sea of Galilee, has been found, but most of the ruins are from before the New Testament era. The tetrarch Herod Philip, who ruled 4 BCE to 33/34 CE, rebuilt the settlement around 30 CE and designated it a city; he renamed it "Julia" in honor of Augustus' daughter—Laughlin, *Fifty Major Cities*, 59–61.

121. O'Neill, "Son of Man," citing Philo *On the Change of Names*, 381, points out that *Israel* meant "He who sees God." Ibid., 376, sees this as an allusion to Gen 28:12; "The Son of Man is seen as the stone at Bethel upon which Jacob had his dream, and which he later set up and anointed with oil as an altar."

122. This is the first of the double Amen sayings that either the evangelist or the redactor worked into the narrative. I am putting them into italics and setting them apart. The saying alludes to Gen 28:12, concerning Jacob: "And he dreamed that there was a ladder set upon the earth, and the top of it reached to heaven; and behold, the angels of God were ascending and descending on it!" (RSV)

123. R. Brown, *Gospel According to John (i–xii)*, 98, identifies Khirbet Qânâ, nine miles north of Nazareth, as the likely place, not Kefr Kenna, which is often pointed out to pilgrims; and he notes that "mother of X" is a dignified way of referring to someone's mother. As I read the narrative, the wedding

as well as his disciples. ³And when the wine ran short the mother of Jesus says to him, "They have no wine." ⁴And Jesus says to her, My lady, what is that to us? My hour has not yet come." ⁵His mother says to the servers, "Do whatever he tells you." ⁶Now there were six stone water jars there, set for the Jews' purification, amounting to two or three measures.¹²⁴ ⁷Jesus says to them, "Fill the water jars with water." And they filled them to the brim. ⁸And he says to them, "Now ladle some out and bring it to the head waiter." And they brought it. ⁹And as the head waiter tasted the water-become-wine—and he did not know where it was from, but the servers who had ladled the water knew¹²⁵—the head waiter calls the bridegroom ¹⁰and says to him, "Everyone sets out the good wine first, and when they have drunk freely the rest;¹²⁶ you have kept the good wine up to now." ¹¹Jesus made this beginning of the signs in Cana of Galilee and made his glory evident, and his disciples believed in him.¹²⁷

¹²After this he went down to Capernaum, and also his mother, the brothers, and his disciples, and they stayed there not many days.¹²⁸

¹³And it was near the Passover of the Judeans,¹²⁹ and Jesus went up to Jerusalem. ¹⁴And he found those selling oxen, sheep, and doves and the money changers, seated in the Temple precincts. ¹⁵And making a whip from cords he drove all out from the Temple precincts, also the sheep and oxen, and he poured out the coins of the money changers and overturned the tables, ¹⁶and he told those selling doves, "Take these away from here, do not make my Father's house an emporium." ¹⁷His disciples recalled that it is written, "Zeal for Your house will consume me."¹³⁰ ¹⁸Then the Judeans responded and said to him, "What sign have you to show us, since you do such things?" ¹⁹Jesus replied and said to them, "Destroy this sanctuary and I will raise it in three days." ²⁰Then the Judeans said to him, "This shrine was built in forty-six years, and you will raise it in three days?" ²¹But he was saying that about the shrine of his body. ²²Then when he

---

celebration would have already been going on for some days (see verse 10); if it began the previous Wednesday, according to a custom later codified in the Mishnah (see ibid., 98), it would be depicted as nearing its conclusion the following Tuesday.

124. A measure was about nine gallons. Fortna, *Fourth Gospel*, 6, points to the reference to the size of the jars as gratuitous factual detail in the narrative that the redactor left in because of a reluctance to rewrite received tradition.

125. Tenney, "Footnotes," 364, and Fortna, *Fourth Gospel*, 6, point to this as evidence of a redactor inserting an explanatory parenthesis.

126. R. Collins, "Proverbial Sayings," 137–39, sees this as a use of a traditional proverb.

127. Tenney, "Footnotes," 364, identifies this as a summarizing note.

128. Hedrick, "Vestigial Scenes," 357, sees this as "a vestige of a completely independent scene." His impression is that the author composed by attaching plotted scenes to settings, and unused settings appear as vestigial settings such as this one—ibid., 364. More such settings will be noted below.

129. In general, this gospel narrates from the perspective of a different calendar from that of the Jerusalem authorities; hence it specifies the Passover of the Judeans.

130. Septuagint Ps 68:10 (Ps 69:9), with the verb in the future rather than the past.

## The Johannine Gospel

was raised from the dead, his disciples recalled that he was saying such things, and they believed the scripture and the statement that Jesus made.[131]

[23] Now while he was in Jerusalem during the Passover festival, many believed in his name, seeing his signs, which he was performing. [24] But Jesus himself did not entrust himself to them because he knew everything [25] and had no need for anyone to give him testimony about human nature; for he himself knew what was in humanity.[132]

3 [1] Now there was a man from the Pharisees, Nicodemus by name, a ruler of the Judeans. [2] He came to him at night and said to him, "Rabbi, we know that you, a teacher, have come from God, for no one can perform the signs you do unless God is with him."[133]

> [3] Jesus replied and said to him,
>
> "Amen. Amen I say to you, unless you are born again, it is not possible for you to see the kingdom of God."

[4] Nicodemus says to him, "How can a person, being an adult, be born again? Is it possible to enter into his mother's womb a second time and be born?"[134] [5] Jesus answered,

> "Amen. Amen I say to you, unless you are born of water and spirit, it is not possible to enter into the kingdom of God."

[6] "What is born of the flesh is flesh, and what is born of the spirit is spirit. [7] Do not be surprised that I said to you, 'You must be born again.' [8] Wind[135] blows where it wills, and you hear its sound, but you do not know where it coming from and where it is going. Thusly is everyone born from the spirit." [9] Nicodemus answered and said to him, "How can such things be?" [10] Jesus answered and said to him, "You are a teacher of Israel and you do not know these things?"

> [11] Amen. Amen I say to you that we are saying what we know about, and what we have seen we give testimony about, and you do not accept our testimony.

[12] If I speak of things on earth to you and you do not believe, how would you believe if I speak to you of the things of heaven?"[136]

---

131. Tenney, "Footnotes," 364, sees this as a memory of disciples inserted into the narrative.

132. Ibid., identifies verses 24 and 25 as an explanatory footnote.

133. "We know": Nicodemus is depicted as speaking for the Sanhedrin, evidently at a time after Jesus had performed works in Jerusalem—R. Brown, *Gospel According to John (i–xii)*, 135. Much of the scene and the double Amen statements appear to be unrelated to this introduction; it seems to be an inserted narrative with the double Amen statements in turn inserted into it.

134. "Nicodemus says to him . . .": Because of the insertion of the double Amen saying, which appears to interrupt the narrative, it was necessary for the redactor to insert the question Nicodemus poses.

135. "Wind," τὸ πνεῦμα, is the same word as "spirit." R. Collins, "Proverbial Sayings," 139–40, sees what follows as a traditional proverb.

136. "You" here and in verse 11 is in the plural; Nicholson, *Death as Departure*, 65, suggests that it is in the plural to contrast the understanding of the community with the understanding of those

¹³"No one indeed goes up to heaven except he who has come down from heaven, the son of humanity.¹³⁷ ¹⁴And as Moses lifted up the serpent in the wilderness, in this way must the son of humanity be lifted up ¹⁵so that everyone who believes in him would have eternal life, ¹⁶for God loved the world in this way; therefore He gave the only begotten son so that all who believe in him would not perish but have eternal life. ¹⁷For God did not send the son into the world to condemn the world but that the world would be saved through him.¹³⁸ ¹⁸One who believes in him is not condemned, but one who does not believe has already been condemned for having not believed in the name of the only begotten son of God. ¹⁹Now this judgment is due to the fact that the light has come into the world and people loved darkness rather than light, for their works were evil. ²⁰For everyone engaging in what is evil hates light and does not go into the light lest the deeds be exposed; ²¹but one doing truth¹³⁹ comes into the light so that the deeds may be made manifest because they are carried out in God."

²²After these things Jesus, as well as his disciples, came to the land of Judea, and he was staying there with them and baptizing.¹⁴⁰ ²³Now John was also baptizing, at Aenon near Salim, because water was plentiful there.¹⁴¹ And people came and were baptized. ²⁴For John had not yet been cast into prison. ²⁵So a controversy about purification arose between John's disciples and a Judean. ²⁶And they went to John and said to him, "Rabbi, he who was with you beyond the Jordan, about whom you have testified, behold he is baptizing and all are going to him." ²⁷John answered and said, "A human cannot receive even one thing unless it is given from heaven. ²⁸You yourselves testify of me that I said 'I am not the Messiah,' rather 'I am sent before him.' ²⁹The bridegroom is the one who has the bride, but the bridegroom's best man, standing and hearing him, rejoices at the festive dinner at the sound of the bridegroom.¹⁴² So has my joy been made total. ³⁰He must increase, but I must decrease."

---

whom Nicodemus is made to represent.

137. It is unclear whether this discourse is part of the scene with Nicodemus or a theological reflection inspired by it. "Goes up" is in the perfect tense in the Greek; Pierce and Reynolds, "Perfect Tense-form," cite a grammatical theory the makes the aspect of the perfect tense primary and its temporal reference secondary; thus it translates here in the present because the emphasis is on the "present effects" traditionally associated with the present tense.

138. Gundry and Howell, "Sense and Syntax," 39, discuss translating this part of the discourse. Tenney, "Footnotes," 364, labels verses 16–21 a footnote presenting a theological discussion.

139. R. Brown, *Gospel According to John (i–xii)*, 135, explains this expression as a Semitism that is also found in the Septuagint Greek.

140. Hedrick, "Vestigial Scenes," 357–58, sees this as a vestige of a completely independent source that is contradicted at John 4:2 by the redactor.

141. On the possible geographical sites of Aenon and Salim, see R. Brown, *Gospel According to John (i–xii)*, 151. The text seems to place John there, but not Jesus, who is said to be in Judea. Thus Aenon and Salim need not be in Judea. Of the sites Brown mentions, two are near the Jordan, making the reference to plentiful water superfluous. A third is in Samaria: four miles east-southeast of Schechem is the town of Sâlim, and eight miles northeast of Sâlim is modern 'Ainûn, which today has no water.

142. The best man, literally "friend of the groom," prepares the banquet and rejoices at the sound

³¹He coming from above is above all;¹⁴³ he who is from the earth is of the earth and speaks from the earth. He coming from heaven is over all. ³²He bears witness to what he has seen and heard, and no one accepts his testimony. ³³He who accepts his testimony certified that God is truthful.¹⁴⁴ ³⁴For he whom God sent speaks the words of God, for the spirit does not provide in delimited quantities. ³⁵The Father loves the son and has placed all in his hands. ³⁶One who believes in the son has eternal life, but one heedless of the son will not see life; rather God's anger remains on him.

4 ¹When Jesus learned that the Pharisees heard that Jesus was making more disciples and baptizing more than John ²(though Jesus himself did not baptize; rather it was his disciples), ³he left Judea and left for Galilee again.¹⁴⁵ ⁴Now it was necessary¹⁴⁶ for him to travel through Samaria. ⁵So he came to a city of Samaria called Sychar,¹⁴⁷ near the field that Jacob gave his son Joseph. ⁶Now Jacob's well was there. So then Jesus, wearied from the journey, sat on the well. It was about the sixth hour.¹⁴⁸

⁷A woman of Samaria came to draw water. Jesus says to her, "Give me some to drink," ⁸for his disciples had left for the city to buy some food. ⁹So the Samaritan woman says to him, "Why are you, a Jew, asking me, a Samaritan woman, for a drink? (for Jews have no dealings with Samaritans.)¹⁴⁹ ¹⁰Jesus replied and said to her, "If you recognized the gift of God and who it is saying to you, 'Give me some to drink,' you would have asked him and he would have given you living¹⁵⁰ water." ¹¹The woman says to him, "Sir, you have no bucket and the cistern is deep; so how do you have living water? ¹²Are you greater than our father Jacob, who gave us the cistern and drank from it himself, as well as his sons and livestock?" ¹³Jesus answered and said to her, "Everyone who drinks from this water will thirst again, ¹⁴but whoever should drink from the water that I will give will never thirst again, but the water I will give will become a well within that person

---

of the bridegroom's party arriving.

143. Tenney, "Footnotes," 364, labels 3:31–36 a footnote presenting a theological discussion. It seems to be a reflection upon the preceding scene, much as 3:13–21 was a reflection on the scene with Nicodemus.

144. "Certified," ἐσφράγισεν: The word means, literally, to affix a seal onto. R. Brown, *Gospel According to John (i–xii)*, 158, suggests the translation "certified."

145. Tenney, "Footnotes," 364, labels this as an explanatory footnote; Hedrick, "Vestigial Scenes," 358, observes that it contradicts John 3:22. The reasoning for leaving Judea is not entirely clear. One may surmise that the evangelist means Jesus wanted to avoid the Pharisees in Judea making invidious comparisons between him and John the Baptist.

146. It was not absolutely necessary since there was an alternative route. R. Brown, *Gospel According to John (i–xii)*, 169, but necessary in the sense that he had to go through Samaria to follow the route he had chosen.

147. Jerome equated Sychar with Schechem—R. Brown, *Gospel According to John (i–xii)*, 169.

148. I.e., about noon, an unusual time for the woman, soon to be introduced into the scene, to be performing the chore of fetching water; that would normally be done in the morning or evening—ibid.

149. Tenney, "Footnotes," 364, identifies this as a note citing a custom.

150. The text is playing on the expression, "living water," ὕδωρ ζῶν, which also means "flowing water."

springing up into eternal life." ¹⁵The woman says to him, "Sir, give me this water so that I will not thirst or come here to draw water."

¹⁶He says to her, "Go call your husband and return here." ¹⁷The woman answered and said to him, "I do not have a husband." Jesus says to her, "You spoke well, 'I have no husband'; ¹⁸for you had five husbands, and the one you have now is not your husband. You have spoken the truth." ¹⁹The woman slays to him, "Sir, I see that you are a prophet. ²⁰Our fathers worshiped on this mountain; and you Jewish people[151] say the place where it is necessary to worship is in Jerusalem." ²¹Jesus says to her, "Believe me, madam, that the hour is coming when you Samaritans[152] will worship the Father neither on this mountain nor in Jerusalem. ²²You Samaritans[153] worship One Whom you do not know; we worship One we know, because salvation is from the Jewish people. ²³But the hour is coming, and it is now, when the genuine worshippers will worship the Father in spirit and truth; for the Father indeed is seeking such to worship him. ²⁴God is a spirit, and it is necessary for those worshiping Him to do so in spirit and truth." ²⁵The woman says to him, "I know that a messiah" (which means the Anointed one)[154] "is coming; when he comes, he will announce everything to us." ²⁶Jeus says to her, "I am he, the one speaking to you."

²⁷And at that his disciples came, and they were shocked that he was speaking with a woman,[155] though no one said, "What do you want with him?"[156] or "Why are you talking with her?" ²⁸Then the woman left her water jar and went into the city and says to the people, ²⁹"Come see someone who told me everything I have done. Is he perhaps the Messiah?" ³⁰They came out from the city and went to him.

³¹Meanwhyile the disciples were urging him, "Rabbi, eat." ³²But he said to them, "I have food to eat that you do not know about." ³³So the disciples were saying to one another, "Did someone bring him something to eat?" ³⁴Jesus says to them, "My food is that I do the will of the One Who sent me and complete His work. ³⁵Do you not say, 'Four months now and the harvest comes?' Look, I tell you, lift your eyes and see the fields, because they are white, almost at the harvest. ³⁶The reaper is already receiving pay and gathering fruit for eternal life, so that sower and reaper alike rejoice. ³⁷For the saying on this is true: 'One is

---

151. Literally, "you" in the plural.

152. Literally, "you" in the plural.

153. Literally, "you" in the plural

154. "Anointed one," the Christ. Tenney, "Footnotes," 364, identifies that this as a translation note.

155. That was something that a man did not do in public—R. Brown, *Gospel According to John (i–xii)*, 173.

156. "With him": supplied; the literal reading is "What do you want?"

the sower and another is the reaper."¹⁵⁷ ³⁸I sent you to harvest what you have not worked over; others have worked over it, and you came upon their work."¹⁵⁸

³⁹Now many of the Samaritans from that city believed in him because of the statement of the woman testifying, "He told me all that I did."¹⁵⁹ ⁴⁰So as the Samaritans came to him, they urged him to stay with them, and he stayed there two days, ⁴¹and many more believed through his speaking; ⁴²and they were saying to the woman, "We no longer believe because of your say so, for we heard him ourselves, and we know that he is truly the savior of the world."

⁴³And after the two days he went from there to Galilee. ⁴⁴(For Jesus himself testified that a prophet has no honor in his own country.)¹⁶⁰ ⁴⁵Then when he did come to Galilee, the Galileans welcomed him, having seen all that he did in Jerusalem at the feast, for they too went to the feast.¹⁶¹

⁴⁶Then he came again to Cana of Galilee, where he made the water into wine. And there was a royal official¹⁶² whose son was ill in Capernaum. ⁴⁷Hearing that Jesus came from Judea to Galilee, he went to him and asked that he come down and heal his son, who was about to die. (⁴⁸Then Jesus said to him, "Unless you people see signs and wonders, you will not believe at all!"¹⁶³) ⁴⁹The royal official says to him, "Sir, come down before my son dies." ⁵⁰Jesus says to him, "Go, your son lives." The man believed what Jesus said to him and left. ⁵¹Now as he was still going down his slaves met him saying that his boy was alive. ⁵²Then he inquired from them that hour at which he recovered. They told him, "Yesterday at the seventh hour the fever left him."¹⁶⁴ ⁵³The father knew it was that hour that Jesus said to him, "Your son lives"; and

---

157. R. Collins, "Proverbial Sayings," 140–41, points to verses 35 and 37 as uses of a traditional proverb.

158. J.A.T. Robinson, "The 'Other,'" based on the association of Samaritans and the followers of the Baptist, explains that the "others" who sowed and worked are the missionaries of John the Baptist.

159. R. Brown, *Community of the Beloved Disciple*, 187, notes that this is a case of a woman preaching.

160. This seems to be a side note that Tenney, "Footnotes," did not identify. R. Collins, "Proverbial Sayings," 141–43, suggests it is a traditional proverb. It actually contradicts what follows in verse 45, a fact that has been a matter of commentary since antiquity—R. Brown, *Gospel According to John (i–xii)*, 187. If we view the work of the evangelist as preaching material, the verse would be a note to cue in a discussion of the superficial nature of acceptance of the gospel on the basis of signs, or miracles (see John 2:23–25). The redactor would have left it in out of a disinclination to rewrite the received text.

161. Hedrick, "Vestigial Scenes," 358, sees this as a vestige of a completely independent source.

162. This would presumably be an administrator or soldier in the service of Herod Antipas, Tetrarch of Galilee and Perea.

163. "You people": the second person verbs "see" and "believe" are in the plural. Following R. Brown, *Gospel According to John (i–xii)*, 190, the translation indicates this by supplying "people." Fortna, *Fourth Gospel*, 5, observes that this does not quite fit in the narrative. Indeed, it appears to be a lesson that one might draw from it. One might see it as another side note that was worked into the narrative at some point in the development of the text; hence the translation has it in parentheses.

164. The seventh hour would be 1:00 in the afternoon. Fortna, *Fourth Gospel*, 6, sees this as a gratuitous factual detail that the redactor did not rewrite out of respect for the original narrative.

he believed as well as his whole household. ⁵⁴Now again, Jesus worked this second sign while coming from Judea into Galilee.¹⁶⁵

5 ¹After these things there was a feast of the Judeans, and Jesus went up to Jerusalem. ²Now there is near the sheep gate in Jerusalem a pool, called in Hebrew Bethsaida,¹⁶⁶ having five porticos. ³A number of the sick, blind, lame, and paralyzed lay in them.¹⁶⁷ ⁵Now there was a certain man there, ailing thirty-eight years. ⁶Seeing him lying there, and knowing that he had already been there a long time, Jesus says to him, "Do you want to be healed?" ⁷The ailing man said to him, "Sir, I have no one to plunge me into the pool when the water stirs; but when I come another goes down before me."¹⁶⁸ ⁸Jesus says to him, "Rise, take up your mat, and walk." ⁹And he was healed immediately, and he took up his mat and walked.

But it was the Sabbath on that day. ¹⁰So the Judeans were saying to the man who had been healed, "It is the Sabbath, and it is not permitted for you to carry your mat." ¹¹And he answered them, "But he who healed me said to me, 'Take your mat and walk.'" ¹²They asked him, "Who is the person who was saying to you, 'Take and walk?'" ¹³But he did not know who it was who healed him, for Jesus withdrew, there being a crowd in the place. ¹⁴Afterwards Jesus found him in the Temple precincts and said to him, "See, you became healthy; sin no more, lest something worse happen to you."¹⁶⁹ ¹⁵The man left and announced to the Judeans that it was Jesus who made him healthy. ¹⁶And therefore, because he did these things on the Sabbath, the Judeans began to persecute Jesus. ¹⁷But Jesus responded to them, "My father is working even now; I am also working." ¹⁸Consequently the Judeans sought even more to kill him, for he not only loos-

---

165. Tenney, "Footnotes," 364, sees this as a summary note. Many commentators suggest that the order of chapters 5 and 6 had been reversed and that chapter 6 should follow here—see R. Brown, *Gospel According to John (i–xii)*, 235–36.

166. Texts vary on the name; well attested readings also include *Bethzatha* and *Bethesda*.

167. Some manuscript witnesses add "awaiting the movement of the water, ⁴for each season an angel of the Lord went down in the pool and troubled the water. Then whoever stepped in first after the troubling of the water was healed of whatever kind one was held back by, no matter what." Metzger, *Textual Commentary*, 209, describes verse 4 as a gloss.

168. The ailing man's response does not answer Jesus' question. The commentaries that address this problem try to explain it away by saying the sick man did not know who Jesus was or that he could perform a cure (e.g. Lagrange, *Évangile selon Saint Jean*, 136–37; Haenchen, *John*, 245; Morris, *Gospel according to John*, 269; Maloney, *Gospel of John*, 168). Granted that point, the response still does not answer Jesus' question. Some revising of the narrative had taken place, presumably prior to the final redaction since the redactor left received texts unchanged, even if they created difficulties. A clue as to what happened in the earlier revision is found in verse 14, where Jesus says " . . . sin no more. . . . " One may hypothesize that the original narrative had explained, in the narrative voice or in the voice of a bystander, the man's condition in terms of him having sinned grievously; indeed the man does turn out to be something of a rascal, reporting Jesus to the authorities. The evangelist rejects the idea that there is any causal connection between sin and sickness at John 9:3; he may have deleted the sin explanation and inserted Jesus' question. The man's statement, left in as a curious response to Jesus' question, could have been part of his own explanation of his condition.

169. As noted above, the connection between sin and illness is rejected in John 9:3.

ened the Sabbath but also called God his own father, making himself equivalent to God. ¹⁹Then Jesus answered and was saying to them,

> *Amen. Amen I say to you,*¹⁷⁰ *the son cannot do anything on his own, unless he sees the Father doing it. For whatever He does, the son likewise also does.*¹⁷¹ ²⁰*For the Father loves the son and shows him all that He does, and will show him greater works than these so that you may be amazed.* ²¹*For just as the Father raises and enlivens the dead, so also does the son enliven those whom he wishes.* ²²*For the Father does not even judge anyone, but He has handed over all judgment over to the son,* ²³*so that all would honor the son as they honor the Father. One who does not honor the son does not honor the Father Who sent him.*
>
> ²⁴*Amen. Amen I say to you, one hearing my word and believing in Him Who sent me has eternal life, and will not come under condemnation but has passed over from death into life.*
>
> ²⁵*Amen. Amen I say to you, the hour is coming and it is now, that the dead will hear the voice of the son of God, and those who listened will live.* ²⁶*For just as the Father has life in Himself, so also has He handed it over to the son to have life in himself.* ²⁷*And He handed authority over to him to pass judgment, because he is a son of humanity.* ²⁸*Do not be surprised at this, for the hour is coming in which all those in the tombs will hear his voice.* ²⁹*And those who did good will come forth to the resurrection of the living, but those who practiced evil to a resurrection of damnation.*

³⁰"I cannot do anything by myself; I make a judgment as I hear, and my judgment is just, for I do not seek my will but that of the One Who sent me.¹⁷² ³¹If I were to testify about myself, my testimony might not be truthful; ³²but Another is testifying about me, and I know that the testimony that He is giving about me is true.

³³"You have sent people to John, and he has testified truthfully. ³⁴But I am not receiving the testimony from a man; rather I say these things so that you might be saved. ³⁵He was the light, shining and lit, and you wished to exult for a time in his light. ³⁶But I have testimony greater than John's; for the works that the Father handed over to me for me to complete, the works that I do—they testify, concerning me, that the Father has sent me. ³⁷And the Father Who sent me, He has testified about me. Neither did You listen to His voice, ever; nor did you see His form, ³⁸and you do not have His word remaining within you, for you do not believe in the one He sent. ³⁹You search

---

170. In the double Amen passages that follow, the terms that refer to God the Father are capitalized and those that refer to the son are not, simply to keep it clear to what the pronouns are referring. No claims about Trinitarian theology are to be implied.

171. R. Collins, "Proverbial Sayings," 143–45, sees this as a use of a traditional proverb.

172. This seems to be what was originally introduced by verse 19a; it is predicated on a miracle having been performed.

the scriptures, because you suppose you have eternal life in them; and they are what testify about me. ⁴⁰And you do not want to come to me to have life.

⁴¹"I do not accept praise from people, ⁴²but I knew you—that you do not have the love of God within yourselves. ⁴³I have come in the name of my Father, and you do not accept me. If others should come in their own name, you would accept them¹⁷³ ⁴⁴When you accept praise from one another and do not seek the praise of the only God, how can you believe? ⁴⁵Do not suppose that I will accuse you before the Father; Moses, in whom you hoped, is your accuser. ⁴⁶For if you believe Moses, you would believe me, for he wrote about me. ⁴⁷But if you do not believe his writings, how might you believe my words?"

6 ¹Afterwards, Jesus went across the Sea of Galilee, of Tiberias.¹⁷⁴ ²Now a large crowd followed him because they saw the signs that he worked for those who were ill. ³But Jesus went up a mountain and sat there with his disciples.¹⁷⁵

⁴Now it was near Passover, the feast of the Judeans. ⁵Raising his eyes then and seeing that a large crowd is coming to him, Jesus says to Philip, "Where will we buy bread so that they may eat?" ⁶But he was saying this testing him, for he knew what he was about to do.¹⁷⁶ ⁷Philip answered him, "Two hundred denarii worth of bread will not be enough for them so that each would get a little." ⁸One of his disciples, Andrew the brother of Simon Peter, says to him, ⁹"There is a lad here who has five barley loaves and two little fish; but what are they for so many?" ¹⁰Jesus said, "Make the people lie down." Now there was much grass in the place. So men numbering about five thousand lay down. ¹¹Then Jesus took the loaves and, after giving thanks, distributed them to those reclining, and likewise from the little fish, as much as they wanted. ¹²Now when they were satisfied, he says to his disciples, "Gather up the leftover pieces lest any are lost." ¹³So they gathered them up, and twelve baskets of fragments were full from the five barley loaves that were more than enough for those who had eaten. ¹⁴Then the people, seeing the sign that he had worked, were saying, "This is truly the prophet who is coming into the world." ¹⁵Then Jesus, realizing that they were about to come and seize him in order to make a kingdom, withdrew again to the mountain by himself.

¹⁶Toward evening his disciples went down to the sea, ¹⁷and climbing into a boat they began going across the sea to Capernaum. (And it was already dark, and Jesus had not come to them yet.) ¹⁸And with a great wind blowing, the sea is aroused. ¹⁹When they had rowed about twenty-five or thirty stadia¹⁷⁷ they see Jesus walking on the sea and nearing the boat, and they were afraid.

---

173. "Them": this is in the singular in the Greek; the number is changed to avoid the English pronoun problem.

174. The lake was known as both the Sea of Galilee and, later, the Sea of Tiberias.

175. Hedrick, "Vestigial Scenes," 359, sees this as a vestige of a completely independent source.

176. Tenney, "Footnotes," 364, lists this as a note explaining the mind of Jesus.

177. About three or four miles.

²⁰But he says to them, "It is I, do not be afraid."¹⁷⁸ ²¹Then they wanted to take him into the boat, and immediately the boat was on land at the destination.

²²The next day the crowd that stayed across the sea saw that there was only one boat there and that Jesus did not go with his disciples into the boat but only his disciples left. ²³But skiffs came from Tiberias close to the place where they ate the bread when the Lord gave thanks.¹⁷⁹ ²⁴Then when the crowd saw that Jesus is not there, nor his disciples, they climbed into the skiffs and went to Capernaum, looking for Jesus. ²⁵And when they found him on the other side of the sea they said to him, "Rabbi, when did you come here?" ²⁶Jesus answered them and said,

> *Amen. Amen I say to you, you are not looking for me because you saw signs but because you ate from the loaves and were satisfied.*

²⁷"Do not work for the nourishment that perishes but the nourishment that lasts into eternal life, which the son of humanity will give you, for the Father, God, set a seal on him." ²⁸ Then they said to him, "What should we do to do the work of God?" ²⁹Jesus answered and said to them, "This is the work of God: that you believe in the one whom He sent." ³⁰Then they said to him, "Then what sign do *you* perform, so that we may see and believe you? What do you do? ³¹Our ancestors ate the manna in the wilderness, as it is written, 'He gave them bread from heaven to eat.'"¹⁸⁰ ³²Then Jesus said to them,

> *Amen. Amen I say to you, Moses did not give you bread from heaven, but my Father will give you genuine bread from heaven.*

³³"Indeed, the bread of God is that¹⁸¹ coming down from heaven and giving life to the world." ³⁴Then they said to him, "Sir, give us this bread all the time." ³⁵Jesus said to them, "I am the bread of life. One coming to me will not hunger at all, and one believing in me will not thirst all the time. ³⁶But I told you that you saw me and do not believe. ³⁷All that the Father might give me will come to me, and I will not cast out whatever comes to me,¹⁸² ³⁸for I have not come down from heaven to do my will but the will of the One who sent me. ³⁹And this is the will of the One who sent me, that I not send away any of what He gave me but raise it on the last day. ⁴⁰For this is the will of my Father: All who see the son and believe in him should have eternal life, and I will raise him on the last day."

---

178. "It is I," Ἐγώ εἰμι, the same expression that begins the "I am" sayings and suggests the divine name.

179. Tenney, "Footnotes," 364, lists this as an explanatory note.

180. Ps 78:24 (Septuagint Ps 77:24), with a slightly different word order from the Septuagint.

181. "That," could also be translated "the one." Jesus intends "the one" while the audience hears "that."

182. "All" and "whatever" are in the neuter singular, but both words obviously refer to people. Blass and Debrunner, *Greek Grammar*, 76, #138, says, "The neuter is sometimes used with reference to persons if it is not the individuals but a general quality that is to be emphasized." This usage extends into the following verses.

⁴¹Then the Jews[183] were murmuring[184] about him because he said, "I am the bread coming down from heaven," ⁴²and they were saying, "Is he not Jesus the son of Joseph, whose father and mother we know? How is it that he is saying now, "I have come down from heaven?" ⁴³Jesus answered and said to them, "Do not murmur among one another. ⁴⁴No one can come to me without the Father who sent me drawing one, and I will raise that one up on the last day. ⁴⁵It is written in the prophets, 'And all shall be taught by God.'[185] Everyone who hears from the Father and learns, comes to me. ⁴⁶Not that anyone has seen the Father; only the one who is from God has seen the Father."

⁴⁷*Amen. Amen I say to you, the one believing has eternal life.*[186]

⁴⁸"I am the bread of life. ⁴⁹Your ancestors ate the manna in the desert and died. ⁵⁰This bread is what is coming down from heaven, so that anyone who would eat of it would not also die. ⁵¹I am the living bread that came down from heaven.[187] If anyone eats from this bread, that one will live forever; but the bread that I will give is also my flesh for the life of the world." ⁵²Then the Jews began to argue among themselves, saying, "How can he give us his flesh to eat?" ⁵³Then Jesus said to them,

*Amen. Amen I say to you, unless you eat the flesh of the son of humanity and drink his blood, you do not have life within you.*

⁵⁴"One who eats my flesh and drinks my blood has eternal life, and I will raise that one up on the last day. ⁵⁵For my genuine flesh is nourishment, and my genuine blood is drink. ⁵⁶One who feeds on my flesh and drinks my blood remains in me and I in that one. ⁵⁷As the living Father sent me and I live through the Father, that one who feeds on me will live through me. ⁵⁸This is the bread that is coming down from heaven, not as the ancestors ate and

---

183. This is a different narrative, which either the evangelist or the redactor has inserted into the present location. From one perspective, it marks the first instance where Galileans are called "the Jews," revealing a different vocabulary; the scene would be in or near Nazareth, where the household of Jesus would be known. An alternative view would have this be a text written in a locale such as Ephesus, where the distinction between Judean authorities and Galileans would have had little meaning; the references to the family of Jesus would be a well-developed counter tradition against the Christian movement.

184. "Murmuring": R. Brown, *Gospel According to John (i–xii)*, 270, cites Exod 16:2, 7, 8, where the gathering of the sons of Israel murmur against Moses and Aaron after receiving the manna. The Septuagint uses a slightly different Greek word, διεγόγγυζεν, in the singular, while here a plural, "the Jews," are the subject and the verb lacks the prefix: Ἐγόγυζον. An earlier draft of the narrative may well have followed the wording in Exodus more closely.

185. Isa 54:13, according to the Septuagint: "And all your sons (will be) taught by God. . . ."

186. The "hook" on which this double Amen saying hangs is the next verse, verse 48.

187. This appears to be a different version of the preceding discourse—R. Brown, *Gospel According to John (i–xii)*, 285.

died; the one eating this bread will live forever." ⁵⁹He said these things when teaching in the synagogue in Capernaum.¹⁸⁸

⁶⁰Then,¹⁸⁹ many of his disciples, listening, said, "This statement is hard; who can listen to it?" ⁶¹But Jesus, aware that his disciples were murmuring about this, said to them, "Are you scandalized by this? ⁶²What if you see the son of humanity ascend to where he was before? ⁶³The one giving life is the spirit; the flesh is of no benefit. The words that I have spoken to you are spirit and are life. ⁶⁴But there are among you some who do not believe." For Jesus knew from the outset some were not believing and one is the one who would betray him.¹⁹⁰ ⁶⁵And he was saying, "This is why I have said to you that no one can come to me unless it is granted to that one by the Father."

⁶⁶At this many of his disciples left him and afterwards no longer traveled with him. ⁶⁷Then Jesus said to the twelve, "Do you wish to go too?" ⁶⁸Simon Peter answered him, "Lord,¹⁹¹ to whom shall we go? You have words of eternal life, ⁶⁹and we have believed and have known that you are the holy one of God." ⁷⁰Jesus answered them, "Did I not choose you twelve? Yet one of you is a devil." ⁷¹He was speaking of Judas, son of Simon the Iscariot,¹⁹² for he, one of the twelve, was about to hand him over.

7 ¹And afterwards, Jesus was traveling about in Galilee, for he did not want to go about in Judea since the Judeans were seeking to kill him. ²Now the feast of the Judeans, Tabernacles, was near.¹⁹³ ³Then his neighbors¹⁹⁴ said to him, "Leave here and go to Judea so that your disciples¹⁹⁵ will also see the works you perform. ⁴For no one who acts in secret and seeks to be before the public. If you do such things, show yourself before the world." ⁵For his neighbors did not believe in him.¹⁹⁶ ⁶Then Jesus says to them, "My time is not yet here, but the time for you is always suitable. ⁷For the world is unable to hate you, but it hates me because I testify about it, that its works are evil. ⁸You

---

188. Tenney, "Footnotes," 364, lists this as a note identifying a setting.

189. This seems to resume the narrative from verse 50—R. Brown, *Gospel According to John (i–xii)*, 299.

190. Tenney, "Footnotes," 364, lists this as a note explaining the mind of Jesus.

191. Normally, the address, κύριε, could translate as "sir," but given the context, it is tantamount to a declaration of faith; so here it is rendered "Lord."

192. The pattern of the name suggests that Judas was the son of a man named Simon who was from Kerioth, a Judean village—R. Brown, *Gospel According to John (i–xii)*, 298. Since many Judeans migrated to Galilee (Root, *First Century Galilee*, 29) it does not follow that Judas was not a Galilean. Tenney, "Footnotes," 364, lists this verse as an explanatory note.

193. Tenney, "Footnotes," 364, lists this as a note identifying a setting.

194. "Neighbors," οἱ ἀδελφοὶ; see Arndt and Gingrich, *Greek-English Lexicon*, 16, article on ἀδελφός, #4.

195. The disciples in this instance are evidently not those who already traveled with Jesus but hypothetical new Judean disciples.

196. "Neighbors," οἱ ἀδελφοὶ; see ibid. Tenney, "Footnotes," 364, lists this verse as an explanatory note.

go up to the feast; I am not going up to this feast since my time has not been fulfilled." ⁹And saying these things he himself remained in Galilee.

¹⁰But as his neighbors¹⁹⁷ went up to the feast, he too went up, not openly but in secret. ¹¹And the Judeans were looking for him at the feast and saying, "Where is he?" ¹²And there was much murmuring about him in the crowds. Some were saying, "He is a good one," but others, "No, he misleads the crowd." ¹³No one was speaking very openly about him out of fear of the Judeans.

¹⁴But when the feast was already half over Jesus went up to the Temple precincts and began teaching. ¹⁵Then the Judeans were amazed, saying, "How does he know writing, untaught?" ¹⁶Then Jesus answered them and said, "My teaching is not mine but that of the One who sent me. ¹⁷If someone wishes to do His will, he will know about the teaching, whether it is from God or whether I am speaking on my own. ¹⁸One speaking on one's own is seeking personal glory; but one seeking the glory of the One who sent one, such a one is truthful and has no wrongdoing within. ¹⁹Did Moses not teach you the law? Yet not one of you keeps the law: Why are you seeking to kill me?" ²⁰The crowd answered, "You are possessed; who is seeking to kill you?" ²¹Jesus answered and said to them, "I performed one work, and all of you are shocked ²²by that. Moses gave you circumcision—not that it is from Moses but from the ancestors—and you circumcise a man on the Sabbath. ²³If a man receives circumcision on the Sabbath to not break the Law of Moses,¹⁹⁸ should you be angry that I make a whole man healthy on the Sabbath? ²⁴Do not judge by appearance, but judge with an honest judgment."

²⁵Then some of the Jerusalemites were saying, "Is this not the one they are seeking to kill? ²⁶And here he is speaking openly and no one is saying anything to him. Perhaps the authorities actually know that he is the Messiah? ²⁷But we know where he is from, and when the Messiah comes no one knows where he is from."¹⁹⁹ ²⁸Then Jesus, teaching in the Temple precincts, cried out and said, "Do you know me and know where I am from? I did not indeed come on my own, but you do not know the One Who actually sent me. ²⁹I know Him, for I am from the One who sent me." ³⁰Then they tried to arrest him, but no one laid a hand on him because his hour had not yet come. ³¹Now many from the crowd believed in him, and they were saying, "When the Messiah comes, will he work more signs than he has?"

³²The Pharisees heard the crowd murmuring such things about him, and the chief priests and the Pharisees sent officers to arrest him. ³³Then Jesus said, "I am with you yet a little while, and I am going to the One Who sent

---

197. "Neighbors," οἱ ἀδελφοὶ; see Arndt and Gingrich, *Greek-English Lexicon*, 16, article on ἀδελφός, #4.

198. The Law required circumcision on the eighth day after birth; if birth took place on a Sabbath, so did circumcision—R. Brown, *Gospel According to John (i–xii)*, 312. See Gen 17:12.

199. There was theory of a "hidden messiah" in antiquity—R. Brown, *Gospel According to John (i–xii)*, 53, citing a statement of "Trypho" in Justin, *Dialogue,* 8:4 and 90:1.

me. ³⁴You will look for me and not find me, and where I am you cannot go." ³⁵Then the Judeans said to themselves, "Where is he about to go that we will not find him? Is he about to go to the diaspora among the Greeks and teach the Greeks?²⁰⁰ ³⁶What does he mean by, 'You will look for me and not find me, and where I am you cannot go'?"

³⁷Now on the major last day of the feast Jesus stood up and cried out, saying, "If anyone thirst, come to me, and let ³⁸anyone who believes in me ³⁷drink.²⁰¹ ³⁸As the scripture said, 'Rivers of living water will flow out from within him.'"²⁰² ³⁹Now he said this about the spirit that those who believed in him were going to receive. For there was not yet a spirit since Jesus was not yet glorified.²⁰³

⁴⁰Then some in the crowd who heard these words were saying, "This is truly the prophet."²⁰⁴ ⁴¹Others were saying, "This is the Messiah." But others were saying, "But is the Messiah coming from Galilee? ⁴²Did the scripture not say that the Messiah is coming from the seed of David, and Bethlehem was the town David came from?" ⁴³Then a division over him developed in the crowd. ⁴⁴And some of them wanted to arrest him, but no one laid a hand on him.

⁴⁵Then the officers went to the chief priests and Pharisees, and the latter said to them, "Why did you not bring him?" ⁴⁶The officers answered, "Never did anyone speak as did this man." ⁴⁷The Pharisees answered them, "Have you also been misled? ⁴⁸Have any of the rulers or Pharisees believed in him? ⁴⁹But this crowd, which does not know the law, is accursed." ⁵⁰Nicodemus, the one

---

200. "Among the Greeks," τῶν Ἑλλήνων: R. Brown, *Gospel According to John (i–xii)*, 314, takes this as a genitive of direction; see Blass and Debrunner, *Greek Grammar*, 92, #166. It cannot be translated "of the Greeks" because the Diaspora consisted of Jews, not Greeks.

201. There is a debate in the literature whether "(any)one who believes in me" is the subject of "drink," as translated above, or whether it goes with the following verse; for a summary, see R. Brown, *Gospel According to John (i–xii)*, 320–21). The second approach would make the believer rather than Jesus the source of the flowing waters in the next verse, but as Brown points out another Johannine work, Rev 22:1, "shows a river of living water flowing from the throne of God and of the Lamb (i.e. Christ)." How one understands verse 37 also affects how one understands verse 38.

202. The pronoun (αὐτοῦ) refers to the one believing, according to Fee, "Once More." Hence, "The one believing in me—as the scripture said—from within will flow living water." Menken, "Origin of the Old Testament Quotations," however, argues for the pronoun referring to Jesus. Hence "He who believes in me, for him, as scripture has said, rivers of living water shall flow from his (i.e., Jesus') inside." Marcus, "Rivers," suggests that the passage being cited is Isa 12:3: "With joy you will draw water from the wells of salvation." The Isaiah passage, he says, is associated in rabbinic literature with the Feast of Tabernacles, the setting in which John has Jesus speaking. Menken, "Origin of the Old Testament Quotations," however, suggests that Ps 78:16 may be the citation: ""He made streams come out of the rock, and caused waters to flow down like rivers." He also points to Zech 14:18 from the Septuagint: "and on that day living water will come out from Jerusalem." To explain "from within" or "from the insides" he points to Ps 114:8: "who turns the rock into a pool of water, the flint into a spring of water"; in Hebrew *spring* is a homonym for "intestine, insides," which is κοιλία in Greek, the word found in the gospel passage. R. Brown, *Gospel According to John (i–xii)*, 321–23, discusses these possibilities as well as others.

203. Tenney, "Footnotes," 364, lists this as an explanatory note.

204. Here "some" has to be supplied.

from among them who earlier came to him,[205] says to them, [51]"Does our law judge people without first hearing from them and learning what they do?"[206] [52]They answered and said to him, "Are you also from Galilee? Inquire and see that no prophet will rise up from Galilee."[207]

8 [12]Jesus was speaking to them again, saying, "I am the light of the world. One following me will not walk in darkness but will have the light of life." [13]Then the Pharisees said to him, "You are testifying on your own behalf. Your testimony is not true." [14]Jesus answered and said to them, "If indeed I testify on my own behalf, my testimony is true since I know where I came from and where I am going; but you know neither where I come from nor where I am going. [15]You judge according to the flesh; I am judging no one. [16]And if *I* were to judge, my judgment is true because it is not I alone but I and the Father Who sent me. [17]And even in your law it is written that the witness of two persons is true.[208] [18]I am testifying on my own behalf and the Father Who sent me is testifying about me." [19]Then they were saying to him, "Where is your father?" Jesus answered, "You know neither me nor my Father; if you knew me, you would also know my Father." [20]He was saying these words while teaching in the treasury area in the Temple precincts,[209] and no one arrested him because his hour had not yet come.

[21]Another time he said to them, "I am going and you will look for me, and you will die in your sin. Where I am going you cannot come." [22]Then the Judeans were saying, "Is he killing himself, since he is saying, 'Where I am going you cannot come'?" [23]And he was saying to them, "You are from below; I am from above. You are from this world; I am not from this world. [24]I said then that you will die in your sins, for if you do not believe that I am, you will die in your sins." [25]Then they were saying to him, "Who are you?" Jesus said to them, "I told you from the first what I am also saying to you now.[210] [26]I have

---

205. Tenney, "Footnotes," 364, lists this as a note identifying a person.

206. Verse 51 is in the singular in the Greek and is translated in the plural to avoid the pronoun problem in English.

207. John 7:53—8:11 is not found in the earliest textual witnesses of the *Johannine Gospel*—Metzger, *Textual Commentary*, 219–22. A separate chapter will be devoted to it.

208. Deut 17:6 and 19:15; both passages pertain to testimony about the commission of crimes.

209. Tenney, "Footnotes," 364, lists this as a note identifying a setting.

210. Establishing the Greek for this verse has been a text critical problem—Metzger, *Textual Commentary*, 223–24; R. Brown, *Gospel According to John (i–xii)*, 347–48. Funk, "Papyrus Bodner II," and Förster, "Überlegungen zur Grammatik von Joh 8.25," present the reading from P[66], which dates from about 200 in codex form and which is used for the present translation: Εἶπεν αὐτοῖς ὁ Ἰησοῦς, Εἶπον ὑμῖν τὴν ἀρχὴν ὅ τι καὶ λαλῶ ὑμῖν. "Jesus said to them, 'I told you from the first what I am also saying to you (now).'" RSV has a cryptic shorter reading: "Even what I have told you from the beginning"; *Das neue Testament* has, translating roughly, "Just what I say from the first the whole time now" (Davon spreche ich doch schon die ganze Zeit). Caragounis, "What Did Jesus Mean?" would translate καὶ as "precisely" rather than "even" or "also." His translation is "[I am] from the beginning!—precisely what I have been saying to you"; however he admits in a note that "from the beginning" is connected with "I am saying," not the implicit "I am."

much to say about you and to condemn; but He who sent me is trustworthy, and I heard from Him the things I am saying to the world." [27]They did not understand that he was speaking to them of the Father.[211] [28]Then Jesus said to them, "When you lift up the son of humanity, then you will understand that I am, and that I do nothing on my own but talk about things as the Father taught me. [29]And He Who sent me is with me; He has not left me alone, for I always do what is pleasing to Him."

[30]When he was saying these things, many believed in him. [31]Then Jesus was saying to the Judeans who had believed him, "If you remain with my word, you are truly my disciples, [32]and you will know the truth and the truth will make you free." [33]They replied to him, "We are descendant of Abraham and have never enslaved anyone;[212] how is it you say, 'You will become free?'" [34]Jesus answered them,

*Amen. Amen I say to you that everyone who commits sin is a slave of sin.*

[35]"Now the slave does not stay in the household for eternity; the son stays for eternity. [36]If then the son frees you, you are really free. [37]I know you are descendent of Abraham."

"However, you[213] seek to kill me because my word gets nowhere with you. [38]I speak of what I have seen in the presence of the Father; you then should do what you heard from the Father." [39]They replied and said to him, "Our father is Abraham." Jesus says to them, "If you are children of Abraham, you should be doing the works of Abraham. [40]But now you are seeking to kill me, someone who has told you the truth that I heard from God. Abraham did not do that. [41]You perform the works of your own father." Then they said to him, "We were not born illegitimately; we have one Father, God." [42]Jesus said to them, "If God were your father, you would love me, for I came forth from God and am here; for I have not come on my own, but He sent me. [43]For what reason do you not understand my speech? Is it because you cannot listen to my word? [44]You are from your father the devil, and you wish to act on the desires of your father. He was a killer from the beginning, and he did not stand by the truth since truth was not within him. When he speaks falsehood, he speaks from his own since he is a liar and father of falsehood.[214] [45]But I speak the truth; you believe me not. [46]Who from your number convicts me of sin? If I speak the

---

211. Tenney, "Footnotes," 364, sees this as a note of the memory of the disciples.

212. Such a statement assumes the topic under discussion is the treatment of Judeans by Judeans; Lev 25:39–46 distinguishes between an Israelite working off a debt owed to another Israelite and the enslavement of a foreigner.

213. At some point Jesus begins addressing Judeans who did not believe in him, distinct from those addressed in verse 31. I think the shift in addressee occurs here, and paragraph it accordingly, because the preceding verses, which describe making people permanent members of the household, make more sense addressed to the Judeans who believed in Jesus. An ancient presenter would shift tone at this juncture.

214. "Of falsehood": literally "of it."

truth, why do you not believe me? ⁴⁷One who is from God listens to the words of God. For this reason you do not listen: you are not from God."²¹⁵

⁴⁸The Judeans answered and said to him, "Do we not say correctly that you are a Samaritan and are possessed?" ⁴⁹Jesus answered, "I am not possessed; rather I honor my Father, and you dishonor me. ⁵⁰But I do not seek my glory; there is One seeking it, and condemning."

> ⁵¹*Amen. Amen I say to you, if anyone should keep my word, that one will not see death forever.*

⁵²Then the Judeans said to him,²¹⁶ "Now we know that you are possessed. Abraham died, also the prophets, and you say, 'If anyone would keep my word, that one will not taste death forever.' ⁵³Are you greater than our father Abraham, who died? And the prophets, who died? What do you make yourself out to be?" ⁵⁴Jesus answered,²¹⁷ "If I glorify myself, my glory is nothing; it is my Father who is glorifying me, whom you say, 'He is our God.' ⁵⁵And you do not know Him, but I know Him. And if I were to say that I do not know Him, I would be a liar like you; but I know Him and keep His word. ⁵⁶Your father Abraham rejoiced that he might see my day, and he saw it and was glad." ⁵⁷Then the Judeans said to him, "You are not yet fifty years old, and you saw Abraham?"

> ⁵⁸*Jesus said to them,*
>
> *Amen. Amen I say to you, before Abraham came to be, I am.*

⁵⁹Then they took up stones to throw at him, but Jesus hid himself and left the Temple precincts.

9 ¹And coming he saw a man blind from birth. ²And his disciples asked him, "Rabbi, who sinned, this man or his parents, that he would be born blind?" ³Jesus answered, "Neither did he nor his parents sin, but it was to make the works of God be made manifest in him. ⁴It is necessary for us to work the works of the One who sent me while it is still day; night is coming, when no one can work.²¹⁸ ⁵When I am in the world, I am the world's light." ⁶After saying these things he spat on the ground, made clay from the spittle, smeared²¹⁹ his clay onto the eyes

---

215. Translating this verse has long been a problem. Förster, "Die syntaktische Funktion," argues for, "From this it follows: You do not hear, therefore you are not of God." RSV has "He who is of God hears the words of God; the reason why you do not hear them is that you are not of God." *Das neue Testament* has "One who comes to me can understand God's words. You cannot understand me because you do not come to me from God" (Wer von Gott her kommt, der kann Gottes Worte verstehen. Ihr könnt mich nicht verstehen, weil ihr nicht von Gott her kommt).

216. This is not continuing the narrative and discourse from verse 50, but rather is an insertion cued in by verse 48; the double Amen statement in turn was cued in by this verse.

217. This is the continuation of the narrative and discourse from verse 50.

218. R. Collins, "Proverbial Sayings," 145–46, sees this as a use of a traditional proverb.

219. "Smeared," ἐπέχρισεν, also means "anointed."

⁷and said to him, "Go wash in the pool of Siloam" (which means "Sent").²²⁰ Then he left and washed, and he went seeing. ⁸Then neighbors and those seeing that he had been a beggar before were saying, "Is this not the man who sat and begged?" ⁹Some said, "He is." Others said, "No, but he looks like him." He himself said, "I am." ¹⁰Then they were saying to him, "How then were your eyes opened?" ¹¹He answered, "The man called Jesus made clay and smeared my eyes and said to me, "Go to Siloam and wash. Then going and washing, I began seeing." ¹²And they said to him, "Where is he?" He says, "I don't know."

¹³They bring him, who was once blind, to the Pharisees. ¹⁴Now it was the Sabbath on the day Jesus made the clay and opened his eyes.²²¹ ¹⁵Then the Pharisees too were asking him again how he came to see. And he said to them, "He put clay on my eyes, and I washed, and I see." ¹⁶Then some of the Pharisees were saying, "This man is not from God because he does not keep the Sabbath." But others were saying, "How can a sinful man perform such signs?" And there was a division among them. ¹⁷Then they spoke to the blind man again: "What do you say about him, since he opened your eyes?" And he said, "He is a prophet."

¹⁸Then the Judeans did not believe it that he had been blind and gained sight, until they summoned the parents of the man who had gained his sight, ¹⁹and they asked them, saying, "Is this your son, whom you say was born blind? How then doe she see now?" ²⁰Then his parents answered and said, "We know that this is our son and that he was born blind; ²¹but how he sees now we do not know, or who opened his eyes we do not know. Ask him; he is of age. He can speak for himself." ²²His parents said these things because they feared the Judeans, for the Judeans already agreed that anyone who professed him to be the Messiah would be put out of the synagogue. ²³Therefore his parents said, "He is of age; ask him."

²⁴Then they summoned the man who had been blind a second time and said to him, "Give glory to God;²²² we know that this man is a sinner. ²⁵Then he answered, "Whether he is a sinner, I do not know. I know one thing: that I was blind and now I see." ²⁶Then they said to him, "What did he do to you? How did he open your eyes?" ²⁷He answered them, "I told you already and you did not listen. Why do you want to hear it again? Do you also want to become his disciples?" ²⁸And they reviled him and said, "You are a disciple of that man, but we are disciples of Moses. ²⁹We know that God has spoke to Moses, but we do not know where this man is from." ³⁰The man answer and said to them, "Now this is amazing: you do not know where he is fr and he opened my eyes. ³¹We know that God does not listen to sinners if someone is devout and acts on His will, He listens to that one. ³²It h been heard from the beginning of time that someone opened the someone born blind. ³³If this man is not from God, he would not be a

---

220. Tenney, "Footnotes," 364, identifies this as a translation note.
221. Ibid.: This as a note identifying a setting.
222. This is a swearing-in formula—R. Brown, *Gospel According to John (i–x*

anything." ³⁴They answered and said to him, "You were born entirely in sin, and you are teaching us?" And they cast him out.

³⁵Jesus was hearing that they cast him out, and finding him he said, "Do you believe in the son of humanity?" ³⁶He answered and said, "And who is that, sir, so that I may believe in him?" ³⁷Jesus said to him, "You have seen him indeed, and he speaking with you is he." ³⁸And he uttered, "I believe, Lord!" And he worshipped him. ³⁹And Jesus said, "I came in judgment against this world, so that those not seeing may see and those seeing may become blind."²²³

⁴⁰Some from the Pharisees who with him heard these words and said to him, "Are we also blind?" ⁴¹Jesus said to them, "If you were blind, you have no sin; but now that you say, 'We see,' your sin remains."

> 10 ¹Amen. Amen I say to you, one who does not come through the gate into the sheep yard but is climbing over another way is a thief and bandit.

²"Now one who enters through the gate is a shepherd of the sheep. ³The gatekeeper opens for him, and the sheep listen to that one's voice; and that one calls his own sheep by name and leads them out.²²⁴ ⁴When he leads all his own out, he goes ahead of them, and the sheep follow him because they know his voice. ⁵But they do not follow a stranger at all but rather will flee from that one because they do not know the voice of strangers." ⁶Jesus told this similitude to them; but they did not understand what he was saying to them.²²⁵ ⁷then Jesus said again,

> Amen. Amen I say to you, I am the sheep gate. ⁸All who came before me are thieves and bandits; but the sheep do not listen to them.

am the gate; if anyone enters through me, that one will be saved and will and leave and find pasture. ¹⁰The thief does not come in except to steal, er, and kill; I come that they may have life and have to the full. ¹¹I am shepherd; the good shepherd lays down his life for the sheep.²²⁶ ¹²The hireling who is not even a shepherd, to whom the sheep do not belong, sees the wolf coming and leaves the sheep and flees, and the wolf seizes and scatters them, [13]because he is a hireling and is not concerned about the sheep. [14]I am the good shepherd, and I know mine and mine know me, [15]just as the Father knows me and I know the Father; and I lay down my life for the sheep. [16]I also have other sheep that are not from this yard; I must lead them, and they will listen for my voice and become one flock, one shepherd. [17]For this the Father loves me, that I lay down my life so that I may receive it back. [18]No one takes it from me, but I lay it down on my own. I have power to lay it down, and I have power to take it up again; I received this command from my Father."

[19]A division occurred again among the Judeans because of these sayings. [20]Now many of them were saying, "He has a demon and is out of his mind; why listen to him?" [21]Others were saying, "Such utterances are not those of a possessed person; can a demon open the eyes of the blind?"

[22]Then came the feast of Hanukkah[227] in Jerusalem. It was winter, [23]and Jesus was walking in Solomon's Portico in the Temple precincts.[228] [24]Then the Judeans surrounded him and were saying to him, "How long will you keep us in suspense?[229] If you are the Messiah, tell us plainly." [25]Jesus answered them, "I told you and you do not believe: The works that I do in the name of my Father testify on my behalf; [26]but you do not believe because you are not from my sheep. [27]My sheep listen to my voice, and I know them, and they follow me, [28]and I give them eternal life, and they shall never perish at all, and no one will seize them from my hand. [29]My Father, Who gave them to me, is greater than all, and no one can seize them from the hand of the Father. [30]I and the Father are one."

[31]Again the Judeans picked up rocks to stone him. [32]Jesus responded to them, "I showed you many good works from the Father: Are you stoning me for such as those?" [33]The Judeans answered him, "We are not stoning you for a good work but for blasphemy and because you, being a human, make yourself God." [34]Jesus answered them, "Is it not written in your law, 'I said, you are gods?'[230] [35]If it calls 'gods' those to whom the speech of God came, and the scripture cannot be done away with, [36]do you tell one whom the Father consecrated and sent into the world, 'You are blaspheming,' because I said, 'I am a son of God?'[231] [37]If I do not do the works of my Father, do not believe me;

227. Literally, "Rededication," commemorating the rededication of the Temple by Judas Maccabaeus in 165 BCE.

228. Tenney, "Footnotes," 364, lists these verses as a note identifying a setting.

229. Literally, "take up our life." "The use of this expression for suspense is not well attested . . ." —R. Brown, *Gospel According to John (i–xii)*, 403, but both Brown and RSV translate it that way.

230. Ps 82:6, following Septuagint Ps 81:6. Referring to it as "your law" suggests the dispute reflects a much later era, in which the Christian audience was not largely Jewish.

231. Hanson, "John's Citation of Psalm lxxxii," argues that the argument given by Jesus does not rely only on the part of Ps 82 quoted, but the rest of the Psalm to follow. The argument would be, "(I)f to be addressed by the pre-existent Word justifies men in being called gods, indirect and mediated

³⁸but if I do them, even if you do not believe me, put faith in the works so that you may know and understand that the Father is in me and I in the Father." ³⁹Then they were seeking again to arrest him, and he eluded their grasp.

⁴⁰And he went again beyond the Jordan to the place where John was first baptizing, and he stayed there.²³² ⁴¹And many came to him and were saying that while John worked no sign, all John was said about this one was true. ⁴²And many believed in him there.

11 ¹Now someone was ailing, Lazarus from Bethany,²³³ of the village of Mary and Martha her sister.²³⁴ ²(Now it was Mariam²³⁵ who anointed the Lord with myrrh and wiped his feet with her hair; her brother Lazarus was ailing.) ³Then the sisters sent word to him, saying, "Sir, the one whom you love is ailing." ⁴But when he heard this, Jesus said, "This sickness is not about a death but the glory of God, so that the son of God may be glorified through it." ⁵Now Jesus loved Martha, her sister, and Lazarus. ⁶When he heard that he was ill, he remained where he was for two days. ⁷Then after that he says to the disciples, "Let us go back to Judea." ⁸The disciples say to him, "Rabbi, the Judeans are seeking to stone you now, and you are going back there?" ⁹Jesus answered, "Are there not twelve hours of daylight? If people walk in the day, they will not stumble because they see the light of this world. ¹⁰But if people walk in the night, they stumble because the light is not in it."²³⁶ ¹¹He said these things, and later he says to them, "Our friend Lazarus has fallen asleep; however I am going so that I may wake him." ¹²Then the disciples said to him, "Sir, if he has fallen asleep he will recover."²³⁷ ¹³But Jesus was speaking about his death. They presumed that he was talking about sleep in the sense of resting. ¹⁴So then Jesus told them plainly, "Lazarus died, ¹⁵and I am happy on your account, that you may believe, since I

---

though that address was, . . . far more are we justified in applying the title Son of God to the human bearer of the pre-existent Word, sanctified and sent by the Father . . . "—ibid., 161. The Psalm reads: "I say, 'You are gods, sons of the Most High, all of you; nevertheless, you shall die like men, and fall like any prince.' Arise, O God, judge the earth; for to thee belong all the nations!" (RSV) See Hanson's response to critics, "John's Citation of Psalm lxxxii Reconsidered." Neyrey, "'I Said: You Are Gods,'" pursues the same argument, but using a midrashic exposition of the Sinai theophany, which argued that the Israelis heard God and did not die, and hence were like gods—i.e., deathless. But once they set up a golden calf and worshiped it, their punishment was that they would die like humans. "If Israel, who became holy, may be called *god*, then it is not blasphemy of Jesus, whom God consecrated and sent as his apostle into the world, is called *god* and *Son of God*"—ibid., 659.

232. Hedrick, "Vestigial Scenes," 360, sees this as a vestige of a completely independent narrative.

233. Bethany, just east of Jerusalem, is present day El ʿAzariyeh—R. Brown, *Gospel According to John (i–xii)*, 422.

234. Burkett, "Two Accounts," explains the *aporias* in John 11:1–44 by proposing two source accounts that were merged together, one featuring Mary and one featuring Martha.

235. Verse 2 uses the Hebrew form of Mary while verse 1 uses the Hellenized form. Tenney, "Footnotes," 364, lists this as a note identifying a person.

236. The Greek is in the singular; it is translated in the plural to avoid the pronoun problem in English. R. Collins, "Proverbial Sayings," 146–49, sees this as a use of a traditional proverb.

237. "Recover," σωθήσεται, could also be rendered "saved."

was not there. But let us go to him." ¹⁶Then Thomas, who is called the Twin, said to the fellow disciples, "Let us go too, that we may die with him."

¹⁷Arriving, Jesus found that he was already four days in the tomb.²³⁸ ¹⁸Now Bethany was near Jerusalem, about fifteen stadia away.²³⁹ ¹⁹And many of the Judeans had come to Martha and Mariam to console them over their brother. ²⁰Then Martha went to meet Jesus when she heard that he was coming; but Mariam was seated in the home. ²¹Then Martha said to Jesus, "Sir, if you were here my brother would have never died; ²²but I also know now that whatever you ask of God, God will give you." ²³Jesus says to her, "Your brother will rise." ²⁴Martha says to him, "I know that he will be raised in the resurrection on the last day." ²⁵Jesus said to her, "I am the resurrection and the life: one who believes in me will live even if dying, ²⁶and everyone who lives and believes in me shall never die at all. Do you believe this?" ²⁷She says to him, "Yes, Lord;²⁴⁰ I have come to believe that you are the Messiah, the son of God who is coming into the world."²⁴¹

²⁸And after saying this she left and called Mariam her sister, saying secretly, "The teacher is here and is calling you." ²⁹And when she heard she rose quickly and went to him. Now Jesus had not yet come into the village, but he was still in the place where Martha met him.²⁴² ³¹Then Judeans who were with her in the house and consoling her, seeing Mariam rise and go out quickly, followed her, supposing she was going to the tomb to cry there. ³²Then, when Mariam came where Jesus was, seeing him she fell at his feet, saying to him, "Lord, if you were here my brother would never have died." ³³Then Jesus, when he saw her crying and the Judeans accompanying her crying, was moved in spirit and was disturbed, ³⁴and he said, "Where did you place him?" They said to him, "Sir, come and see." ³⁵Jesus wept. ³⁶Then the Judeans were saying, "See how he loved him." ³⁷But some of them said, "Could he who opened the eyes of the blind man have done something so that this man would not die?"

³⁸Then Jesus, moved within himself again, came to the tomb. Now it was a cave, and a stone lay upon it. ³⁹Jesus says, "Take the stone away." Martha, the sister of the deceased, says to him, "Sir, it smells now, for it is the fourth day." ⁴⁰Jesus says to her, "Did I not say to you that if you believe you would see the glory of God?" ⁴¹Then they took away the tone. And Jesus lifted up his eyes and said, "Father, I thank You for hearing me. ⁴²And I know that You hear me always; but because of the crowd standing around I spoke, so that they may

---

238. "This detail is mentioned to make it clear that Lazarus was truly dead. There was an opinion among the rabbis that the soul hovered near the body for three days but after that there was no hope of resuscitation"—R. Brown, *Gospel According to John (i–xii)*, 424.

239. About one and three fourths miles—ibid., 434. Tenney, "Footnotes," 364, lists this as a note identifying a setting.

240. "Lord," κύριε, can also mean "sir," but in the context of a profession of faith would be "Lord."

241. R. Brown, *Community of the Beloved Disciple*, 190–91, notes that in the *Johannine Gospel* it is Martha, not Peter, who declares Jesus to be the Christ, the Son of God.

242. Tenney, "Footnotes," 364, lists this as a note identifying a setting.

believe that You sent me." ⁴³And having said that he called out with a loud voice, "Lazarus, come out." ⁴⁴The man who had died came out, bound hand and foot with bandages and his face wrapped in a facecloth. Jesus says to them, "Untie him and let him go."

⁴⁵Then many of the Judeans, who came to Mariam and saw what he had done, believed in him. ⁴⁶But some of them went to the Pharisees and told them what Jesus did. ⁴⁷Then the chief priests and the Pharisees convened the Sanhedrin, and they were saying, "What do we do, since this man performs many signs? ⁴⁸If we leave him be, all will believe in him, and the Romans will come and take away both our place and nation." ⁴⁹But one of them, Caiaphas, who was high priest in that year, said to them, "You know nothing. ⁵⁰Do you not think that it is better for you that one man die for the people and the whole nation not perish?" ⁵¹(Now he did not say this on his own, but being high priest in that year he was prophesying that Jesus was about to die for the nation, ⁵²and not for the nation only but that the scattered children of God may also be gathered into one.)²⁴³ ⁵³From that day, then, they planned to kill him.

⁵⁴Then Jesus no longer walked about openly among the Judeans, but he went from there to the region near the desert, to the city called Ephraim;²⁴⁴ he stayed there with the disciples.

⁵⁵Now it was near the Judeans' feast of Passover, and many went up to Jerusalem from the region in order to purify themselves before the Passover.²⁴⁵ ⁵⁶Then they were looking for Jesus and saying to one another while standing in the Temple precincts, "What do you think: Will he so much as come to the feast?" ⁵⁷Now the chief priests and the Pharisees had given orders that anyone who might know where he is should reveal it, so that they would arrest him.

12 ¹Then six days before the Passover Jesus came to Bethany, where Lazarus was, whom Jesus raised from the dead. ²They held a dinner for him there, and Martha served,²⁴⁶ and Lazarus was one of those reclining with him. ³Then Mariam, taking a pound of precious genuine nard perfume, anointed Jesus' feet and wiped his feet with her hair;²⁴⁷ and the house was filled with the fra-

---

243. Ibid. lists this as an explanatory note.

244. The exact location is unclear—R. Brown, *Gospel According to John (i–xii)*, 441.

245. Ibid., 445, cites Josephus, *Jewish War* 1:11:6, #229, about country people purifying themselves at Jerusalem before a feast: "Herod went to Samaria which was rife with communal agitation, and after restoring order, he returned at the head of his troops to Jerusalem for a festival. Malichus, alarmed at his approach prevailed on Hyrcanus to send Herod orders forbidding him to bring aliens among the people during their purification."

246. R. Brown, *Gospel According to John (i–xii)*, 447, notes this would be at night after the close of the Sabbath. He also notes, *Community of the Beloved Disciple*, 187, that Martha is said to *diakonein*, serve. By the time the *Johannine Gospel* was published, the office of *diakonos* existed and people were appointed to it with a laying on of hands (Acts 6:1–2). Thus the passage in its final form was meant to be understood as referring to women deacons.

247. The anointing of feet is something done in preparation for a burial; normally one would not anoint a living person's feet—R. Brown, *Gospel According to John (i–xii)*, 454. Brown explains the wiping of feet with hair as a contamination from the traditional narrative of the sinful woman wiping

grance of the perfume. ⁴But Judas Iscariot, one of his disciples, who was about to hand him over, says, ⁵"Why was this perfume not sold for three hundred denarii[248] and given to the poor?" ⁶Now he did not say that because he cared for the poor but because he was a thief and, keeping the money box, he pilfered what was put in.[249] ⁷Then Jesus said, "Allow her, so that she may attend to it for the day of my burial; ⁸for you have the poor with yourselves always, but you do not have me always."

⁹Then a large crowd[250] of the Judeans knew that he was there, and they came not only to see Jesus but also Lazarus, whom he raised from the dead. ¹⁰But the chief priests planned to kill Lazarus, ¹¹because on his account many of the Judeans were going over to Jesus and believing in him.

¹²The next day the large crowd that was coming to the feast, hearing that Jesus was coming to Jerusalem, ¹³was taking the palm branches of the phoenix palms[251] and went out to greet him; and they were crying out, "Hosanna: blessed by the name of the Lord is he who is coming!"[252] and "King of Israel!" ¹⁴But Jesus, finding a little donkey, sat on it—as it is written,

> Fear not daughter of Zion;
> Behold your king is coming,
>> Seated on the colt of a donkey.[253]

¹⁶His disciples did not understand these things at first, but when Jesus was glorified, then they remembered that these things had been written about him and people did these things for him.[254] ¹⁷Then the crowd that was with him was testifying about when he called Lazarus from the tomb and raised him from the dead. ¹⁸Because of this the crowd was also greeting him since

---

tears with her hair, which found its way into Luke 7:38—ibid., 451.

248. Three hundred days' wages.

249. Tenney, "Footnotes," 364, lists this as an explanatory note.

250. "A large crowd": manuscript witnesses vary, with some including the definite article. The word order with the definite article would be very unusual Greek—Metzger, *Textual Commentary*, 237.

251. "Was": the verb is plural in the Greek. "The palm branches of the phoenix palms"—Hill, "Pleonasm or Prolepsis?" observes that φοῖνιξ, the Greek word for palm tree used in the text, also means "phoenix," the legendary self-regenerating bird, a symbol of resurrection. There is some question whether palm branches would be available in Jerusalem, unless imported for some purpose, such as the Feast of Tabernacles, as opposed to Passover. R. Brown, *Gospel According to John (i–xii)*, 456–57, deems it impossible to specify at what feast a procession of the kind described might have taken place.

252. Ps 118:26a, using the wording of Septuagint Ps 117:26a. It can also be understood to say "Blessed is he who is coming in the name of the Lord!" which would express the evangelist's theological view of if not that of the Psalm.

253. Beginning with "Daughter of Zion," the citation is Zech 9:9, not using the wording of the Septuagint but citing loosely.

254. "People" is supplied to go with the verb. Tenney, "Footnotes," 364, lists this verse as a note of the memory of the disciples.

they heard that he had worked this sign.[255] [19]Then the Pharisees said to one another, "See, it is no use; look, the world follows after him."

[20]Now there were Greeks[256] who were among those going up to worship at the feast; [21]they approached Philip, then, who was from Bethsaida of Galilee, and they were asking him, "Sir, we wish to see Jesus." [22]Philip goes and talks to Andrew; Andrew comes, as well as Philip, and they talk to Jesus. [23]And Jesus answers them, "The hour has come for the son of humanity to be glorified."

> *Amen. Amen I say to you, unless the grain of wheat falling to the earth dies, only it remains; but if it die, it will yield much fruit.* [25]*One who loves one's life will lose it, and one who hates one's life in this world will secure it forever.* [26]*Anyone who would serve me should follow me, and where I am my servant will also be. The Father will honor anyone who serves me.*

[27]"Now is my soul troubled. And what should I say? Father, save me from this hour? But for this I came to this hour. [28]Father, glorify your name." Then came a voice from heaven: "I both glorified it and will glorify it again." [29]Then when the crowd standing by heard it, it was saying that it had thundered. Others were saying, "A messenger has spoken to him." [30]Jesus responded and said, "This voice did not come for me but for you. [31]Now is the judgment of this world, now the ruler of this world will be cast out. [32]And when I am lifted up from the earth, I will draw all to myself." [33]He was saying this, indicating by what kind of death he was about to die. [34]Then the crowd answered him, "We heard it said in the Law that the Messiah will remain forever,"[257] and, "How is it that you say that it is necessary for the son of humanity to be lifted up? Who is this son of humanity?" [35]Then Jesus said to them, "The light is among you for a little while. Walk while you have the light, lest the darkness come upon you; those who walk in the darkness do not even know where they are going.[258] [36]While you have the light, have faith in the light so that you become children of light." Jesus was saying these things, and upon leaving he hid himself from them.

[37]But after he had performed such signs before them, they did not believe in him, [38]so that the statement of Isaiah the prophet would be fulfilled, which says,

---

255. I understand this repetition to be the result of two versions of the narrative being blended together.

256. R. Brown, *Gospel According to John (i–xii)*, 466, suggests they are proselytes, since their being gentiles explains Jesus response below that the hour has come. It should be noted that Philip (verse 21) has a Greek name and that his origin was Galilee, where there was a mixed population.

257. Van Unnik, "Quotation from the Old Testament," reviews a number of texts that say the Messiah would remain forever. Ps 88:37 comes closest to the text, using the same wording in the Septuagint. McNeil, "Quotation," finds a Targum of Isa 9:5 closest; however, Chilton, "John XII 34," argues that such a haggadah could have circulated for generations before being applied to Isa 9:5, making a focus on that passage unwarranted.

258. The Greek has this clause in the singular; it is translated in the plural to avoid the pronoun problem.

> Lord, who believed our report?
>
> And to whom has the strength of the Lord been revealed?[259]

³⁹They were unable to believe because of something else Isaiah spoke of:

> ⁴⁰He has made their eyes blind
>
> And dulled their heart,
>
> So that they would not see with the eyes
>
> And not understand with the heart and turn around,
>
> And I shall heal them.[260]

⁴¹Isaiah said these things because he had seen his glory, and he was speaking about him. ⁴²Nevertheless, many of the rulers also believed in him, but they did not admit it because of the Pharisees, lest they be put out of the synagogue. ⁴³For they loved the opinion of humans more than the glory of God.[261] ⁴⁴And Jesus cried out and said,[262] "One who believes in me does not believe in me but in the One Who sent me, ⁴⁵and one who sees me sees the One Who sent me. ⁴⁶I have come into the world as light, so that everyone who believes in me would not remain in darkness. ⁴⁷And I do not condemn anyone who hears my words and does not keep them, for I came not to condemn the world but to save the world. ⁴⁸One who rejects me and does not accept my words has a self-condemnation; what I spoke is what condemns that person on the last day; ⁴⁹for I did not speak on my own, but the Father Himself Who sent me gave me a command, which I articulated and which I articulate now. ⁵⁰And I know that His command is eternal life. So I am speaking what and in the manner that my Father has told me to."

13 ¹Before the feast of the Passover Jesus, knowing that his hour came for him to pass from this world to the Father, having loved his own who were in the world, loved them to the end. ²And when dinner began, the devil having already put it in the heart of Judas son of Simon of Iscariot to hand him over,

---

259. Isa 53:1, following the wording of the Septuagint.

260. Isa 6:10, deviating from both the Septuagint Greek and the Masoretic Hebrew. The Septuagint reads, "The heart of this people has been dulled, and they hardly hear with their ears. And they closed their eyes, lest they see with the eyes and hear with the ears and understand with the heart and turn back, and I will heal them." The Hebrew reads, "Make the heart of this people fat, and their ears heavy, and shut their eyes; lest they see with their eyes and hear with their hearts, and understand with their hearts, and turn and be healed" (RSV). Other New Testament citations of the passage (Acts 28:26–27, Matt 13:13–15, and implicitly in Mark 6:12 and Luke 8:10) are closer to the Septuagint reading—see R. Brown, *Gospel According to John (i–xii)*, 485–86.

261. Tenney, "Footnotes," 364, identifies the whole of 12:37–43 as a note explaining the mind of Jesus as well as inserting a theological discussion. R. Brown, *Gospel According to John (i–xii)*, 484, proposes the reference to seeing the glory of God in verse 41 suggested "glory of God" in verse 43.

262. There is no narrative setting for the following discourse; commentators have suggested various places in the gospel to which it may be connected—see R. Brown, *Gospel According to John (i–xii)*, 490.

³Jesus,²⁶³ knowing that the Father had placed all things into his hands and that he came from God and was going to God, ⁴rose from the dinner and removed his robe, and taking a towel, he tied it around himself. ⁵Then he poured water into the wash basin and began to wash the disciples' feet and wipe them with the towel that he had tied around himself.²⁶⁴ ⁶Then he came to Simon Peter. "Sir," he says to him, "you will wash my feet?" ⁷Jesus answered and said to him, "You do not understand what I am doing now, but you will understand afterwards." ⁸Peter says to him, "You will never wash my feet at all!" Jesus answered him, "Unless I wash you, you have no part with me." ⁹Simon Peter says to him, "Sir, not only my feet but also hands and head." ¹⁰Jesus says to him, "One who has bathed need not, except to wash the feet; otherwise the whole is clean. And you²⁶⁵ are clean, but not all." ¹¹For he knew the one who was handing him over; that is why he said, "Not all of you are clean."²⁶⁶

¹²Then when he washed their feet and put his robe back on and reclined again, he said to them, "Do you know what I have done to you? ¹³You call me 'teacher' and 'Lord,'²⁶⁷ and you speak correctly, for I am. ¹⁴If then I, Lord and teacher, washed your feet, you too should wash one another's feet. ¹⁵For I have given you an example so that you should do as I did to you."

> ¹⁶*Amen. Amen I say to you, slaves are not greater than their masters or messengers greater than those who sent them.*²⁶⁸

¹⁷"If you understand this, blessed are you if you do it. ¹⁸I am not saying this about all of you; I know those whom I have chosen. But to fulfill the scripture: 'The one who is feeding on my bread raised his heel to me.'²⁶⁹ ¹⁹I am saying this to you now before it happens so that when it happens you may believe that I AM."

> ²⁰*Amen. Amen I say to you, one who accepts whomever I send accepts me, and one accepting me accepts the One who sent me.*

---

263. "Jesus": supplied; the Greek has no expressed subject of the verb "rose," but the implied subject is indicated by "him" at the end of verse 2.

264. Weiss, "Foot Washing," points to passages in the works of Philo that refer to foot washing as a preparation for offering a sacrifice. Philo, *Questions and Answers on Exodus Book I*, #2 cites a saying, "One should not enter with unwashed feet on the pavement of the Temple of God." Philo, *On the Life of Moses* II, 138, describes the priests washing their feet most especially, and their hands, " . . . as a symbol of their irreproachable life. . . . "

265. "You": This is in the plural and thus refers to those present for the dinner.

266. Tenney, "Footnotes," 364, lists this as a note explaining the mind of Jesus.

267. "Lord," Ὁ κύριος, is the expression used in lieu of the name of God in the Septuagint, but it could also be "master."

268. The double Amen statement is in the singular in the Greek; it is translated in the plural to avoid the English pronoun problem.

269. Ps 41:9, not following the Septuagint. R. Brown, *Gospel According to John (xiii–xxi)*, 554, notes that showing the bottom of one's foot to someone in the Near East is a mark of contempt.

²¹After saying these things, Jesus was troubled in spirit.

> *And he was testifying and said, "Amen. Amen I say to you, one of you will betray me."*

²² The disciples were looking at one another, at a loss over what he was saying. ²³One of his disciples, whom Jesus loved, was leaning on Jesus' breast.²⁷⁰ So Simon Peter nods to him to find out who it was he was talking about. ²⁵So leaning back on Jesus' chest he says to him, "Sir, who is it?" ²⁶Jesus answers, "It is the one for whom I will dunk a small piece of bread and to whom I will give it." Then dunking the small piece of bread²⁷¹ he gives it to Judas son of Simon of Iscariot. ²⁷And then, after the small piece of bread, Satan entered into him. Then Jesus says to him, "Do what you are doing quickly." ²⁸And none of those reclining knew what he talked to him about; ²⁹for some supposed, since Judas held the money box, that Jesus was saying to him, "Buy what we need for the feast," or to give something to the poor.²⁷² ³⁰Then taking the small piece of bread, he left immediately.

And night began. ³¹So when Judas²⁷³ left, Jesus says, "Now the son of humanity was glorified, and God was glorified in him,²⁷⁴ ³²and God will glorify him in Himself and will glorify him immediately. ³³Little children, I am with you a little while; you will seek me, and as I told the Judeans, 'Where I am going you cannot come'; and I am telling you now. ³⁴I am giving you a new commandment, that you love one another. As I loved you, you also should love one another. ³⁵All will know by this that you are my disciples, that you have love for one another."

³⁶Simon Peter says to him, "Sir, where are you going?" Jesus answered him, "It is not possible to follow me now to where I am going, but you will follow later." ³⁷Peter says to him, "Why is it not possible for me to follow now?"

> *"I will give up my life for you."* ³⁸*Jesus answers, "Will you give your life for me? Amen. Amen I say to you, the rooster will not crow before you deny me three times."*

---

270. Tenney, "Footnotes," 364, lists this as a note alluding to the author.

271. Many textual witnesses add "and took it"—Metzger, *Textual Commentary*, 241.

272. Tenney, "Footnotes," 364, lists this as a note of the memory of the disciples. Something might be purchased for the Passover meal. The meal in progress might have been the main meal of the day, not the Passover meal that would be held at night. Giving something to the poor might be observing a pre-Passover custom. There is considerable controversy over such details—R. Brown, *Gospel According to John (xiii–xxi)*, 576.

273. "Judas": Supplied; the Greek simply has the verb.

274. Many textual witnesses add "If God was glorified in him"—Metzger, *Textual Commentary*, 242.

**14** ¹"Do not trouble your heart; believe in God, and believe in me.²⁷⁵ ²There are many abodes in my Father's house. If not, would I tell you that I am going to prepare a place for you? ³And if I go and prepare a place for you, I will come again and bring you to myself, so that where I am you also would be. ⁴And you know the way where I am going."

⁵Thomas says to him, "Sir, we do not know where you are going. How can we know the way?" ⁶Jesus says to him, "I am the way, the truth, and the life; no one comes to the Father but through me. ⁷If you know me, you also know my Father; and from now you know Him and see Him."²⁷⁶

⁸Philip says to him, "Sir, show us the Father, and it will be enough for us." ⁹Jesus says to him, "I am with you for such a time and you do not know me, Philip? One who sees me sees the Father. How is it that you say, 'Show us the Father'? ¹⁰Do you not believe that I am in the Father and the Father is in me? The words that I say to you²⁷⁷ I do not say on my own. But dwelling in me, the Father is doing His works. ¹¹Believe²⁷⁸ me that I am in the Father and the Father is in me. But if not, believe through the works themselves."

*¹²Amen. Amen I say to you, one who believes in me will do the works that I do, and do greater than these, because I am going to the Father.*

¹³"And whatever you²⁷⁹ ask in my name, I will do, so that the Father may be glorified in the son. ¹⁴If you ask anything of me in my name, I will do it.

¹⁵"If you love me, keep my commandments. ¹⁶And I will ask the Father and He will give you another Paraclete to be with you forever, ¹⁷the Spirit of truth, whom the world cannot accept because it neither sees nor understands it.²⁸⁰ You understand it, because it remains with you and is in you. ¹⁸I will not leave you orphaned; I am coming to you. ¹⁹A little while and the world will no longer see me, but you will see me, because I live and you will live. ²⁰On that day you will understand that I am in my Father and you are in me and I am in you. ²¹Those who have my commandments and keep them are the ones who

---

275. The double Amen statement of 13:38 is often treated as Jesus' response to Peter's question about not being able to follow Jesus to where Jesus is going. However, verse 38 is manifestly about another topic, Peter's denial later in the narrative. I take it as an editorial sidebar, similar to the other double Amen statements. The fact that Jesus' response to Peter's question is in the plural ("do not trouble" and "your") could lead a reader to see it as a separate discourse, but also in his replies to Thomas (14:7) and Philip (14:10b) Jesus reverts to the plural, in effect making his replies instructions for all the disciples. The same pattern occurs with Jesus' reply to Peter—beginning in the singular in 13:36 and reverting to the plural in 14:1.

276. "You" is in the plural.

277. "You" is in the plural.

278. "Believe" is in the plural.

279. "You" resumes in the plural.

280. "It," αὐτὸ; the neuter pronoun agrees with Spirit, πνεῦμα, a neuter noun.

love me; and the ones who love me will be loved by my Father, and I will love and reveal myself to them."[281]

[22]Judas (not Iscariot)[282] says to him, "Sir, what has happened that you are about to reveal yourself to us and not to the world?" [23]Jesus answered and said to him, "If some love me and keep my word, my Father will also love them, and we shall come to them and make a dwelling with them.[283] [24]One not loving me will not keep my words; and the word that you[284] hear is not mine but that of the Father who sent me.

[25]I have spoken these things to you while remaining with you; [26]but the Paraclete, the Holy Spirit that the Father will send in my name, he will teach you everything and remind you of everything I said to you myself.[285] [27]I leave you peace, I give you my peace; not as the world gives do I give it to you. Do not trouble your hearts or be timid. [28]You heard me say to you, "I am going and am coming to you. If you love me, you should rejoice that I am going to the Father because the Father is greater than I. [29]I have spoken to you now before it happens so that when it happens you may believe. [30]I will no longer discuss many things with you, for the ruler of the world is coming. He holds nothing over me, [31]but so that the world may know that I love the Father, I also do as my Father commanded me. Get up, let us go out from here."

15 [1]"I am the true vine, and my Father is the vine-dresser.[286] [2]He Himself will remove every branch on me not bearing fruit, and He Himself will clear every one bearing fruit so that it will bear more fruit. [3]You are already clear because of the word that I have spoken to you.[287] [4]Stay on me, and I will stay among you. As the branch cannot bear fruit by itself if it does not stay on the vine, so you cannot if you do not remain in me. [5]I am the vine, you the branches. The one remaining on me and I in it, that one will bear much fruit, for apart from me you cannot do anything. [6]If any do not remain in me, they will be cast out and dry up like a branch, and some will gather them together and cast them into the fire, and they will burn.[288] [7]If you remain on me and my

---

281. "Those . . . ones . . . ones . . . them": The Greek is in the singular but is translated in the plural to avoid the English pronoun problem.

282. Possibly Judas the son of James (Luke 6:16; Acts 1:13)—R. Brown, *Gospel According to John (xiii–xxi)*, 641.

283. "Some . . . them . . . them . . . them": The Greek is in the singular but is translated in the plural to avoid the English pronoun problem.

284. "You" is in the plural.

285. "Myself": The textual witnesses are divided over whether ἐγώ appears at the end of the sentence, emphasizing the first person.

286. This is the beginning of a second version of the final discourse—R. Brown, *Gospel According to John (xiii–xxi)*, 656–57.

287. "You" is in the plural.

288. "Any . . . they . . . them" are in the singular in the Greek but translated in the plural to avoid the pronoun problem in English; however, "some will gather them up and cast" is in the plural in the Greek, with "some" supplied.

words remain in you, ask for whatever you wish and for you it will come to be. ⁸My Father was glorified by this: that you bear much fruit and be my disciples. ⁹As the Father was loving to me, I also loved you; you remained in my love. ¹⁰If you keep my commandments, you will remain in my love, as I have kept my Father's commandments and remain in His love.

¹¹"I have told you these things that my joy may be in you and your joy may be complete. ¹²This is my command, that you love one another as I loved you. ¹³No one has greater love than this: that one lay down one's life for one's friends. ¹⁴You are my friends if you do what I order you. ¹⁵I no longer call you slaves because slaves do not know what their master is doing;²⁸⁹ but I called you friends because everything I heard from my Father I made known to you. ¹⁶You did not choose me, but I chose you, and I appointed you to go and bear fruit, and your fruit will remain so that whatever you ask the Father in my name He will give you. ¹⁷I command you this, that you love one another.

¹⁸"If the world hates you, understand that it has hated me before you. ¹⁹If you are of the world, the world would love its own; but because you are not of the world but rather I myself chose you out of the world, the world hates you because of that. ²⁰Remember what I myself said to you: 'Slaves are not greater than their master.'²⁹⁰ If they persecuted me, they will persecute you also; if they kept my word, they will keep yours also. ²¹But they will do all these things to you on account of my name, since they do not know the One Who sent me. ²²If I had not come and spoken to them, they would not have had sin; but now they have no excuse for their sin. ²³One who hates me also hates my Father. ²⁴If I had not done the works among them that no one else did, they would have had no sin; but now they have both seen and hated both me and my Father. ²⁵However, this is so that the statement that is written in their law²⁹¹ may be fulfilled: 'They hated me for no reason.'²⁹²

²⁶"When the Paraclete whom I will send you comes from the Father, the spirit of truth that is coming out from the Father, he will testify about me; ²⁷and you also give testimony because you are with me from the beginning. 16 ¹I have said these things to you so that you will not stumble. ²They will excommunicate you; but the hour is coming that all who kill you will suppose they are offering worship to God.²⁹³ ³And they will do these things because they do not know the Father or me. ⁴However I have spoken these things to you

---

289. "Because slaves ... their": The Greek is in the singular but is translated in the plural to avoid the English pronoun problem.

290. The Greek is in the singular but is translated in the plural to avoid the English pronoun problem.

291. "Their Law" is to be taken in a broad sense to refer to all of the Hebrew scripture. One may infer from "their" that the evangelist's audience did not identify itself as Jewish.

292. Pss 35:19 and 69:4, using the vocabulary of Septuagint Pss 34:19 and 68:5 but not its participial constructions nor, for that matter, those of the Hebrew.

293. "All ... they": The Greek is singular, but the translation is plural to avoid the English pronoun problem.

so that when the hour for them comes you would remember them because of my telling you.

"Now I did not tell you these things at the beginning because I was with you. ⁵But now I am going to the One who sent me, and none of you is asking me, 'Where are you going?'[294] ⁶However, because I have said these things to you, sorrow has filled your heart. ⁷But I have told you the truth. It is good for you that I go away. For if I were not to go away, the Paraclete will not come to you. But if I go, I will send him to you. ⁸And when he comes he will convince the world about sin, justice and judgment: ⁹On the one hand about sin, because they did not believe in me; ¹⁰on the other hand about justice, because I am going to the Father and you will see me no longer; ¹¹then about judgment, because the ruler of this world has been condemned.

¹²"I still have much to say to you; however, you cannot bear it now. ¹³But the spirit of truth is coming; it will guide you with the whole truth. It will not speak on its own but will say what it will hear and will announce to you what is coming. ¹⁴It will glorify me since it will announce to you what it receives from what is mine. ¹⁵All that the Father has is mine; therefore I say that it will announce to you what it will receive from mine.

¹⁶"A little while and you will no longer see me, and again in a little while you will see me." ¹⁷Then some of his disciples said to one another, "Why is he saying to us, 'A little while and you will not see me, and again in a little while you will see me,' and, 'I am going to the Father'?" ¹⁸So they were saying, "What is this little while?[295] We do not understand what he is saying." ¹⁹Jesus knew that they wanted to question him, and he said to them, "You are discussing with one another about my saying, 'A little while and you will not see me, and again a little while and you will see me.'"

*²⁰Amen. Amen I say to you, you will weep and mourn, but the world will rejoice.*

"You will be distressed; however, your distress will turn into joy. ²¹When a woman gives birth, she feels pain because her hour has come; but when she gives birth to the child, she remembers the affliction no longer through the joy that a human is born into the world. ²²And so you have sorrow on the one hand now, but I shall see you again, and your heart shall rejoice, and no one will take your joy away from you. ²³And on that day you will not be asking me for anything."

*Amen. Amen I say to you, whatever you ask the Father in my name, He will give to you. ²⁴Up to now you did not ask for anything in my name; ask and you will receive, so that your joy would have been completed.*

---

294. The fact that this contradicts John 13:36 is evidence that the discourse is an alternative farewell address, not a continuation of the one that began in chapter 13.

295. Some manuscript witnesses add "that he is saying."

²⁵"I have spoken these things figuratively; the hour is coming when I will speak to you figuratively no longer but inform you about the Father plainly. ²⁶On that day you will ask in my name, and I will not tell you that I will ask the Father for you; ²⁷for the Father Himself loves you because you have loved me and you have believed that I came from God. ²⁸I came from the Father and I have come into the world; I am leaving the world again and going to the Father." ²⁹His disciples say, "See, now you are speaking plainly and saying no figure. ³⁰Now we know that you know everything and have no need for someone to inquire of you; by this we believe that you came from God." ³¹Jesus answered them, "You believe now? ³²Behold the hour is coming and has come that you will be scattered, each to your own home, and leave me alone; yet I am not alone since the Father is with me. ³³I have said these things so that you may have peace through me. You have affliction in the world; but have courage, I have conquered the world."

17 ¹Jesus said these things,²⁹⁶ and raising his eyes to heaven he said, "Father, the hour has come: Glorify Your son so that the son may glorify You, ²insofar as You gave him authority over all flesh, so that he may give to them all that You have given him, eternal life. ³And this is eternal life: that they should know You, the only true God, as well as the one You sent, Jesus the Messiah.²⁹⁷ ⁴I glorified You on earth, completing the work that You gave me to do; ⁵and now glorify me, Father, with the glory beside You which I possessed beside You before the world was.

⁶"I revealed Your name to the people of the world whom You entrusted to me. They were Yours, and You gave them to me, and they have kept Your word.²⁹⁸ ⁷Now they have known that all You have given me is from You, ⁸that You have given me the words I have given them, and they accepted and truly understood that I came forth from You, and they believed that You sent me. ⁹I myself ask, concerning them—I am not asking about the world but about those whom You entrusted to me, since they are Yours ¹⁰and all that are mine are Yours and Yours mine and by them I have been glorified; ¹¹and I am no longer in the world and they are in the world, and I am coming to You—holy Father, keep them by your name, which²⁹⁹ you gave me, so that they may be one as we are one. ¹²When I was with them I was protecting them with Your

---

296. R. Brown, *Gospel According to John (xiii-xxi)*, 744-45, sees this as a second independent discourse that the redactor inserted. He observes that by adding a prayer to the end of a farewell discourse, the redactor replicates the pattern of Deut.

297. Ibid., 741, notes that although the evangelist often has Jesus referring to himself in the third person as the son, referring to himself as "Jesus the Messiah" seems anomalous; Brown suggests that "Jesus the Messiah" Ἰησοῦν Χριστόν, is an insertion by the redactor.

298. Ibid., 743, notes that the temporal perspective seems to be that of the time of the evangelist rather than of the Last Supper.

299. "Which," ᾧ, is in the dative where one would expect the accusative relative pronoun; this seems to have led copyists to introduce variations into the text—Metzger, *Textual Commentary*, 249-50.

name, which You gave me;[300] and I guarded, and none of them was lost except, that the scripture would be fulfilled, the son of destruction.[301] [13]But now I am coming to You, and I say these things in the world so that they may have my joy made full within themselves. [14]I have given Your word to them myself, and the world hated[302] them since they are not of the world, just as I am not of the world. [15]I do not ask that You take them from the world but that You keep them from evil.[303] [16]They are not of the world, just as I am not of the world. [17]Consecrate them in the truth; Your word is truth. [18]As You sent me into the world, I also sent them into the world; [19]and I consecrate myself for them so that they may also be consecrated in truth.

[20]"But I make my request not about them alone but also about those who believe in me through their word, [21]that all would be one, as You, Father, are in me and I in You, that they may be also in us, that the world may believe that You sent me. [22]And I have given them the glory that You gave me, so that they may be one as we are one, [23]I in them and You in me, so that that they may be brought to completion in one, that the world may know that You sent me and loved them just as You loved me. [24]Father, I wish that where I am they, whom[304] You have given me, may be with me, so that they may see my glory, which You have given me, and that You loved me before the creation of the world. [25]Just Father, the world does not even know You, but I know You, and they knew that You sent me, [26]and I made Your name known to them, and I will make it known so that the love with which You loved me may be in them and I too in them."

18 [1]After saying these things,[305] Jesus went out with his disciples beyond the Kidron wadi[306] where there was a garden, which he as well as his disciples entered. [2]But Judas, who was betraying him, also knew the place, for Jesus often met there with his disciples. [3]Then Judas, taking the cohort[307] and the officers from the chief priests and Pharisees, comes there with lanterns, torches, and weapons. [4]Then seeing all that was coming toward him, Jesus went out and says

---

300. Again, "which," ᾧ, is in the dative where one would expect the accusative relative pronoun.

301. "The son of destruction," ὁ υἱὸς τῆς ἀπωλείας, may be an allusion to Isa 57:4—Freed, *Old Testament Quotations*, 97. Isa 57:4 in the Septuagint reads "Are you not children of destruction, a lawless seed?" οὐχ ὑμεῖς τέκνα ἀπωλείας, σπέρμα ἄνομον.

302. Again, the time perspective of the evangelist rather than the narrative—R. Brown, *Gospel According to John (xiii-xxi)*, 761.

303. "Evil," or, as ibid., 761, prefers, "the evil one." The parallel with the Lord's Prayer in Matt 6:13 is obvious.

304. "Whom": In the Greek this is a neuter singular relative pronoun associated with "wish," creating a temporary ambiguity that "they may be" clarifies, creating an emphasis in the process.

305. It is unclear whether this redactive connecting sentence originally referred to John 14:31, where Jesus says "Get up, let us go out from here," or whether it was added after the additional versions of Jesus' farewell address had been inserted—R. Brown, *Gospel According to John (xiii-xxi)*, 813.

306. "Wadi": The reference is to a valley where a stream runs in the winter—ibid., 806.

307. "Cohort," σπεῖραν: This would be a Roman contingent.

to them, "Whom do you seek?" ⁵They answered him, "Jesus the Nazorean."³⁰⁸ He says to them, "I am he."³⁰⁹ Now the one handing him over, Judas, stood with them. ⁶Then when he said to them, "I am he," they backed up and crouched. ⁷So he asked them again, "Whom do you seek?" and they said, "Jesus the Nazorean." ⁸Jesus replied, "I told you, I am he. So if you are looking for me, let those people go," ⁹so that the statement he made would be fulfilled: "I did not lose a single one from those whom you gave me."³¹⁰ ¹⁰Then Simon Peter, who had a sword, drew it and struck the chief priest's slave and cut off his right ear. Now the name for the slave was Malchus.³¹¹ ¹¹Then Jesus said to Peter, "Put the sword in the sheath. Am I not to drink the cup that my Father has given me?" ¹²Then the cohort and military tribune,³¹² and the officers of the Judeans apprehended Jesus, bound him, ¹³and led him first to Annas, for he was the father-in-law of Caiaphas, who was the high priest that year.³¹³ ¹⁴Now it was Caiaphas who counseled the Judeans that it was advantageous or one person to die for the people.³¹⁴

¹⁵Now Simon Peter as well as another disciple were following Jesus. Now the latter disciple was known to the high priest, and entered into the courtyard of the high priest³¹⁵ with Jesus, ¹⁶but Peter was standing outside the gate. Then the other disciple who was known to the high priest went in and spoke with the gatekeeper and led Peter in. ¹⁷Then the gatekeeping slave girl says to Peter, "Are you not also one of the disciples of this man?" He says, "I am not." ¹⁸Now slaves and officers stood nearby, having had prepared a fire because it was cold, and they were warming themselves. And Peter was also with them and warming himself.

---

308. There is a discussion over whether "Nazorean" refers to Nazareth or to one of several religious sects that went by similar names; when arresting someone the geographical origin of the person wanted makes the most sense—R. Brown, *Gospel According to John (xiii–xxi)*, 809–10.

309. Literally, "I am."

310. An inexact parallel to John 17:12. This seems to be an insertion into the original narrative—R. Brown, *Gospel According to John (xiii–xxi)*, 811.

311. Tenney, "Footnotes," 364, lists this as a note identifying a person. "Malchus," Μάλχος, is a Nabataean Arab name—Arndt and Gingrich, *Greek-English Lexicon*, 489–90, article on Μάλχος.

312. "Military tribune," χιλίαρχος, equivalent to the Roman "tribunus militum," means literally commander of a thousand. The narrative may be using the term less precisely, but it may well be that the narrative intends to convey the impression that the Romans were thinking in terms of a much more significant military threat than Jesus and his disciples, only one of whom raised a sword.

313. According to Josephus, *Antiquities* 18:2:1, #26, Annas (Hananyah) was appointed by the Roman prefect Quirinius in 6 CE and deposed by Valerius Gratus in 15, ibid., 18:2:2, #34. He remained powerful, for his five sons eventually became high priests, ibid., 20:9:1, #198. John is the only source for two details: Annas playing a role in the interrogation of Jesus, and Annas being the father-in-law of Caiaphas.

314. See John 11:49–51. Tenney, "Footnotes," 364, lists John 18:14 as a note identifying a person.

315. "High priest . . . high priest": The narrative follows the practice of referring to a former high priest, in this case Annas, with his former title, a convention also followed in the Mishnah—R. Brown, *Gospel According to John (xiii–xxi)*, 820.

¹⁹Then the high priest was asking Jesus about his disciples and about his teaching. ²⁰Jesus answered him, "I have spoken openly to the world. I always taught in a synagogue and in the Temple precincts, where all Jews gather,³¹⁶ and I said nothing in secret. ²¹Why are you interrogating me? Interrogate those who have heard what I said to them. Obviously, they know what I said." ²²Now after he had spoken, one of the officers standing by gave Jesus a slap, saying, "Is that the way to answer the high priest?" ²³Jesus answered him, "If I said something wrong, testify about the wrong; but if well, why do you hit me?" ²⁴Then Annas sent him, bound, to Caiaphas, the high priest.

²⁵Now Simon Peter was also standing, warming himself.³¹⁷ Then they said to him, "Are you not also one of his disciples?" He denied that and said, "I am not." ²⁶One of the high priest's slaves, a relative of the one whose ear Peter had cut off, says, "Did I not see you in the garden with him?" ²⁷Then again Peter denied it, and immediately a rooster crowed.

²⁸Then they led Jesus from Caiaphas to the Praetorium. Now it was daybreak, and they did not enter into the Praetorium, so that they would not defile themselves but would eat the Passover dinner.³¹⁸ ²⁹So Pilate went out to them and spoke: "What accusation do you bring against this man?"³¹⁹ ³⁰They answered and said to him, "If this one were not doing evil, we would not have handed him over to you." ³¹Then Pilate said to them, "You take him, and condemn him according to your law." The Judeans said to him, "We are not permitted to execute anyone," ³²so that the statement of Jesus would be fulfilled; he said, indicating the kind of death by which he was about to die. ³³Then Pilate went back into the Praetorium and called for Jesus and said to him, "You? Are you the King of the Judeans?"³²⁰ ³⁴Jesus answered, "Are you saying this on your own or did others tell you about me?" ³⁵Pilate answered, "I am not a Judean, am I? Your people and high priests handed you over to me. What did you do?" ³⁶Jesus answered, "My kingdom is not of this world; if my kingdom were of this world, my officers would be fighting for me not to be handed over to the Judeans. But then my kingdom is not here." ³⁷Then Pilate said to him, "So then, you are a king?" Jesus answered, "You are saying that I am a king. I was born and came into the world for this: to witness to truth. Everyone who is of the truth listens to my voice." ³⁸Pilate says to him, "What is truth?"

---

316. "Where all Jews gather": ibid., 826, suggests this is an insertion into the narrative to make it understandable to gentile readers.

317. Presumably, the scene is still at the courtyard of Annas.

318. This makes sense if it is recalled that Jesus and his disciples in the Johannine narrative seem to follow a different calendar from that of the Judean authorities.

319. The evangelist and redactor both assume the reader knows who Pontius Pilate was, an equestrian rank ruler of Judea 26–33 CE. The administrative title of his position had been prefect at one time but had been changed to procurator. Philo and Josephus portray him in a very negative light; Tacitus mentions the execution of "Christ" by Pilate—R. Brown, *Gospel According to John (xiii–xxi)*, 847.

320. The narrative does not explain how Pilate came to know of this accusation, but his emphasis on "you" suggests he expected a much more threatening personage than the one before him.

And after saying this he went out again to the Judeans and says to them, "I find no case here."[321] ³⁹But you have a custom that I will release one person to you at Passover; so do you wish me to release the king of the Jews to you?" ⁴⁰Then they shouted back, "Not him, but Barabbas." Now Barabbas was an insurrectionist.[322]

19 ¹So then Pilate took Jesus and scourged him.[323] ²And the soldiers, having woven a crown from thorns, put it on his head, and draped him in a purple robe,[324] ³and they were approaching him and saying, "Hail, king of the Jews"; and slapping him. ⁴And Pilate went back outside and says to them, "Look, I am bringing him out to you so that you may know that I find no case here."[325] ⁵Then Jesus came out, wearing the thorn crown and the purple garment. And he says to them, "Behold the man." ⁶Then when the high priests and the officers saw him, they cried out, saying, "Crucify! Crucify!" Pilate says to them, "You take him and crucify, for I find no case here." ⁷The Judeans answered him, "We have a law, and according to the law one must kill him, because he made himself a son of God."

⁸Then when Pilate heard this statement, he was more fearful.[326] ⁹and he went back into the Praetorium and says to Jesus, "Where are you from?" But Jesus gave him no answer. ¹⁰Then Pilate says to him, "Are you not speaking to me? Do you not know that I have authority to release you and I have authority to crucify you?" ¹¹Jesus answered him, "You have no authority at all over me except what was given you from above; therefore the one handing me over to you has the greater sin." ¹²From this time Pilate sought to release him.[327]

Now the Judeans were shouting, saying, "If you release him, you are no friend of Caesar. Everyone who makes himself king is speaking against Caesar."[328] ¹³Then, after hearing these statements, Pilate led Jesus out and sat on a judicial bench at a place called Stone Pavement, named *Gabbatha* in Aramaic.[329] ¹⁴Now it was the preparation day for the Passover, about the sixth

---

321. It does not seem likely that Pilate would trapes back and forth in and out of the Praetorium. The redactor appears to be weaving different trial narratives together. Here, "And after saying this" would be the redactor's transition between one narrative and another. The inserted narrative appears to extend to the end of 18:40.

322. Tenney, "Footnotes," 364, lists this as a note identifying a person.

323. This seems to resume the narrative that was cut off at "What is truth?"

324. The robe would be "purple" in the same way the thorns would be a crown—a mock substitute. Purple was rare and costly; they more likely used a Roman soldier's red cloak.

325. The logic is that torture elicited nothing from Jesus that constituted a legal case.

326. This seems to be another place where another trial narrative is being inserted. Pilate would have no reason to be particularly fearful of a reference to the Torah punishment for blasphemy (Lev 24:16), but he would have reason to be fearful of people demanding the release of an insurrectionist such as Barabbas.

327. After all, Jesus endorsed Pilate's authority, saying it came from above.

328. This sentence appears to continue the narrative from 19:7. "Now the Judeans were shouting, saying" would be the redactor's connective.

329. "The *bēma* or *sella curilis* would normally have stood in the forecourt of the procurator's

hour.³³⁰ And he says to the Judeans, "Behold your 'king.'" ¹⁵Then they called out, "Away! Take him away! Crucify him!" Pilate says to them, "Shall I crucify your 'king'?" The chief priests answered, "We have no king but Caesar." ¹⁶So for them he then handed him over to be crucified.³³¹

Then they took Jesus along; ¹⁷and bearing the cross himself he went out to what is called Skull Place, which is called Golgotha in Aramaic,³³² ¹⁸where they crucified him, and with him two others, one on each side, but Jesus in the middle. ¹⁹Now Pilate wrote a notice and put it on the cross;³³³ and it was written, "Jesus the Nazorean, king of the Judeans." ²⁰Then many of the Judeans read this notice, because the place where Jesus was crucified was near the city. And it had been written in Aramaic, Latin, and Greek. ²¹Then the chief priests of the Judeans were saying to Pilate, "Do not write, 'The king of the Judeans,' but 'He said, I am king of the Judeans.'" ²²Pilate answered, "What I have written, I have written."

²³Then the soldiers, when they crucified Jesus, took his clothing and divided them into four parts, a share for each soldier, also the tunic. But the tunic was seamless, in one piece from top to bottom. ²⁴So they said to one another, "Let us not divide it, but toss for whose it will be," so that the scripture may be fulfilled, which says, "They divided my clothing for themselves, and over my fine clothing they cast lots."³³⁴ On the one hand the soldiers did these things; ²⁵on the other Jesus' mother, his mother's sister, Mary the wife of Clopas, and Mary Magdalene stood by his cross.³³⁵ ²⁶Then seeing his mother as well as the

---

residence, elevated with steps leading to it so that the judge could look over the spectators. . . . (I)t was not absolutely necessary for the governor to sit on the judge's bench when passing sentence except in the case of capital sentences"—R. Brown, *Gospel According to John (xiii–xxi)*, 881. *Gabbatha* is an alternative name, not a translation.

330. Tenney, "Footnotes," 364, lists this as a note identifying a setting. The sixth hour would be noon.

331. "For them": One way to read the Greek is "he handed him over to them to be crucified" (RSV and *Das neue Testament*), but such a reading has difficulties: Later in the narrative (19:23) Roman soldiers, not the chief priests, crucify Jesus. Moreover, crucifixion was a Roman punishment; the Jewish punishment would have been stoning (Lev 24:16). Thus neither in the narrative is Jesus handed over to the chief priests nor historically is that likely to have happened. It is not at all unusual for the Dative, αὐτοῖς in this instance, to mean "for."

332. Tenney, "Footnotes," 364, identifies this as a translation note.

333. The suggestion is not that Pilate physically wrote out the notice and posted it himself but that he ordered that these things be done.

334. Ps 22:18, following the wording of Septuagint Ps 21:19.

335. The family and friends of someone who is being crucified would be kept at a distance; but once the condemned one is hanging on the crossbeam, they would be allowed closer. His mother Mary's sister could be the Salome of Mark 15:40, and she could be the mother of the sons of Zebedee (James and John) who is mentioned in Matt 27:56. Mary the wife of Clopas may be Mary mother of James and Joses, who is mentioned in Mark 15:40; Hegesippus (ca 150 CE, cited by Eusebius) says a Clopas mentioned in Luke 24:18 was the brother of Joseph, the reputed father of Jesus. James the son of Clopas and this Mary may be "James the Brother." R. Brown, *Gospel According to John (xiii–xxi)*, 904–06, reviews this scattered information and the suggestion that the *Johannine Gospel* does not mention the name of Salome because she was the evangelist's mother and the evangelist was maintaining anonymity by referring to himself as the disciple whom Jesus loved. If true, then the subsequent

disciple whom he loved standing by, he says to his mother, "Madam, behold your son." ²⁷Then he says to the disciple, "Behold your mother." And from then on the disciple accepted her among his own.

²⁸After this, seeing that all had been completed, Jesus, to complete the scripture, says, "I thirst."³³⁶ ²⁹There was a jar full of sour wine there; then placing a sponge full of the sour wine on hyssop, they pressed it to his mouth.³³⁷ ³⁰Then when he took the sour wine, Jesus said, "It is finished," and bowing the head he gave up the spirit.

³¹Then the Judeans, when it was the preparation day, lest the bodies remain on the cross on the Sabbath, which on that Sabbath was an important day,³³⁸ asked Pilate to break their legs and they be taken away.³³⁹ ³²Then the soldiers went and broke the legs of the first and the other crucified with him. ³³But coming to Jesus, when they saw he had already died, they did not break his legs, ³⁴but one of the soldiers stabbed his side with a lance, and blood and water came out immediately.³⁴⁰ ³⁵And he who watched has given witness, and his testimony is true, and he knows what he is saying is true, so that you too may believe.³⁴¹ ³⁶For these things happened that the scripture may be fulfilled,

---

narrative, in which Jesus asks the beloved disciple to accept his mother into his family, would make sense; she would be the beloved disciple's maternal aunt.

336. Bampfylde, "John XIX 28," 253, associates ἵνα τελειωθῇ ἡ γραφή with the preceding clause: After this, knowing that all had been finished for the scripture to be completed, he says, "I thirst." The scripture commonly cited in conjunction with this verse is Ps 22:15, "my strength is dried up like a potsherd, and my tongue cleaves to my jaws." The general parallel is evident, as the psalm continues: "thou dost lay me in the dust of death. Yea, dogs are round about me; a company of evildoers encircle me; they have pierced my hands and feet—I can count all my bones—they stare and gloat over me; they divide my garments among them, and for my raiment they cast lots" (RSV).

337. Sour wine was used to quench thirst. Left to ferment naturally, grape juice will alternate between wine and vinegar; sour wine would be somewhere in between these two states. The hyssop stalk, one to two feet in length, is left over after drying and removal of the leaves, which are used for aromatic and medicinal purposes. R. Brown, *Gospel According to John (xiii–xxi)*, 930, notes that in Exod 12:22 "hyssop was to be used to sprinkle the blood of the paschal lamb on the doorposts of the Israelite homes," and that Heb 9:18–20 "recalls that Moses used hyssop to sprinkle the blood of animals in order to seal the earlier covenant."

338. Tenney, "Footnotes," 364, lists this as a note identifying a setting. There is a reference to only one cross; it was common practice to suspend several convicts on one large crossbeam, notwithstanding later artistic depictions of three separate crosses.

339. Deut 21:22–23: "And if a man has committed a crime punishable by death and he is put to death, and you hang him on a tree, his body shall not remain all night upon the tree, but you shall bury him the same day, for a hanged man is accursed by God . . . " (RSV). Breaking the legs would hasten death by suffocation.

340. Ford, "'Mingled Blood,'" interprets blood and water mingling as satisfying a ritual requirement in the slaughter of the Pascal Lamb.

341. Since the Beloved Disciple is the only male member of the group of family and friends listed as standing by the cross (19:26), the assumption is that the evangelist is that disciple—R. Brown, *Gospel According to John (xiii–xxi)*, 936. Tenney, "Footnotes," 364, lists this as a note alluding to the author. There is a text critical issue in this verse (as well as John 20:31), with both the present subjunctive and aorist subjunctive forms of the verb *believe* well attested in the manuscript witnesses. Carson, "Syntactical and Text-critical," argues for the present subjunctive rather than the aorist, maintaining

## THE JOHANNINE GOSPEL

"None of its bones shall be broken."³⁴² ³⁷And again another scripture says, "They shall look upon the one they have pierced."³⁴³

³⁸Now after these things Joseph of Arimathea,³⁴⁴ who had been a disciple of Jesus but a secret one out of fear of the Judeans, asked Pilate if he could remove the body of Jesus; Pilate permitted it. Then he went and removed his body. ³⁹Now Nicodemus also went, he who had gone to him at night first, bringing a compound of myrrh and aloes, about seventy-five pounds.³⁴⁵ ⁴⁰Then they took Jesus' body and bound it with linen cloth and the perfumery, as is the custom of the Judeans for burying. ⁴¹Now there was a garden in the place where he was crucified, and in the garden a new tomb in which no one had yet been placed; ⁴²So they placed Jesus there because of the Preparation Day of the Judeans, for the tomb was nearby.³⁴⁶

20 ¹Now on Sunday, early³⁴⁷ while it was still dark, Mary Magdalene came to the tomb,³⁴⁸ and she saw the stone removed from the tomb.³⁴⁹ ²Then she

---

that the gospel was aimed at believers, whom the Evangelist wanted to continue in a believing state.

342. Exod 12:46, following the wording of the Septuagint, except for a different form of the future verb for "break," and the use of the possessive (its) rather than the phrase "from it." Rather than the verb form in Exod (συντρίψετε), the text replicates the future form from Ps 34:20 (Septuagint Ps 33:21 (συντριβήσεται). Tenney, "Footnotes," 364, lists this as an explanatory note.

343. Zech 12:10, following neither the Septuagint nor the Hebrew exactly. The Masoretic Hebrew has the Lord, "me," being pierced; the text is probably corrupt, and many alternative Hebrew texts have "him"—R. Brown, *Gospel According to John (xiii-xxi)*, 938. The complete verse reads, "And I will pour out on the house of David and the inhabitants of Jerusalem a spirit of compassion and supplication, so that, when they look on him whom they have pierced, they shall mourn for him, as one mourns for an only child, and weep bitterly over him, as one weeps over a first-born" (RSV).

344. Matt 27:57 describes Joseph of Arimathea as a rich man, and Luke 23:51 identifies him as a member of the Sanhedrin and Arimathea as a city of the Judeans. The location of Arimathea is uncertain; R. Brown, *Gospel According to John (xiii-xxi)*, 938, discusses the locations various scholars have proposed. The uncanonical *Gospel of Peter*, verse 3, describes Joseph as a friend of Pilate and Jesus who was present at the trial before Pilate and, realizing they were about to crucify Jesus, asked Pilate for the body—noted by ibid., 939.

345. About 100 Roman pounds, R. Brown, *Gospel According to John (xiii-xxi)*, 941.

346. Tenney, "Footnotes," 364, lists this as a note identifying a setting.

347. R. Brown, *Gospel According to John (xiii-xxi)*, 980, notes that the text follows the Roman reckoning of days when it uses the term "early," for the Jewish reckoning would begin the previous sundown.

348. Ibid., 981, cites a passage from the uncanonical *Gospel of Peter*, verses 50–54. It reads as follows: "Now at the dawn of the Lord's Day Mary Magdalene, a female disciple of the Lord (who, afraid because of the Jews since they were inflamed with anger, had not done at the tomb of the Lord what women were accustomed to do for the dead beloved by them), having taken with her women friends, came to the tomb where he had been placed. And they were afraid lest the Jews should see them and were saying, 'If indeed on that day on which he was crucified we could not weep and beat ourselves, yet now at his tomb we may do these things. But who will roll away for us even the stone placed against the door of the tomb in order that, having entered, we may sit beside him and do the expected things? For the stone was large, and we were afraid lest anyone see us. And if we are unable, let us throw against the door what we bring in memory of him; let us weep and beat ourselves until we come to our homes.'" Brown notes that Mary Magdalene not coming alone is probable, and in agreement with the synoptics, and that coming to mourn is also probable.

349. The *Johannine Gospel* had not mentioned in the burial narrative the stone rolled at the

runs and comes to Simon Peter and to the other disciple, the one whom Jesus loved, and says to them, "They have taken the Lord from the tomb, and we do not know where they put him."[350] ³Then Peter went out as well as the other disciple, and they went to the tomb.[351] ⁴Now the two were running together, and the other disciple ran ahead faster than Peter and came first to the tomb; ⁵and bending over he sees the linen cloths lying there, though he did not go in. ⁶Then Simon Peter also came, following him, and entered the tomb; and he saw the linen cloths lying there, ⁷and the cloth that had been over his head, not lying with the linens but rolled up apart in a place by itself. ⁸Then the other disciple, who had first come to the tomb, also entered and saw and believed; ⁹for they did not yet know the scripture that says he must rise from the dead.[352] ¹⁰Then the disciples went back home.

¹¹Now Mary stood outside at the tomb crying.[353] Then while she cried she leaned into the tomb, ¹²and she saw two messengers in white, sitting, one at the head and one at the feet where the body of Jesus had lain.[354] ¹³And they say to her, "Madam, why are you crying?" She says to them, "They took my Lord, and I do not know where they placed him." ¹⁴After saying these things she turned around and saw Jesus, standing, and she did not recognize that it was Jesus. ¹⁵Jesus says to her, "Madam, why are you crying? Whom do you seek?" Supposing that it is the gardener, she says to him, "Sir, if you carried him off, tell me where you put him, and I will take him." ¹⁶Jesus says to her, "Mary."

---

entrance to the tomb; Mark 15:46, Matt 28:2, and the passage from the *Gospel of Peter* quoted in the previous note, above, do.

350. The plural, "we do not know," has led to the suggestion that an earlier version of the narrative included other women, as in Luke 24:10–12; see Hartmann, "Die Vorlage der Osterberichte," 199. However, the subject of the verb, "we," can simply mean that Mary, Peter, and the other disciple did not know.

351. The narrative shifts from the singular (Peter was going out) to the plural (and they went); Hartmann, ibid., 200, would explain the problem by seeing references to the disciple whom Jesus loved as an insertion. "They went," Hartmann maintains, originally referred to Peter and Mary Magdalene. While Hartmann's theory is certainly possible, the pattern of a compound subject having a singular verb is fairly common in the Johannine narrative; I have been translating it, as here, with a clause in the singular followed by "as well as."

352. Tenney, "Footnotes," 364, sees this as an explanatory note. Hartmann, "Die Vorlage der Osterberichte," 204, however, sees it as part of the earlier version of the narrative, with the plural verb referring to Peter and Mary Magdalene. What scriptural passage or passages is meant is unclear. A candidate is Ps 16:9–10; R. Brown, *Gospel According to John (xiii–xxi)*, 987, adds Hos 6:2.

353. As the narrative stands, the reader is surprised that Mary Magdalene suddenly appears outside the tomb. As Hartmann, "Die Volage der Osterberichte," 197–98, reconstructs the narrative as it stood prior to the insertion of the Beloved Disciple into the scene, she would have been included in the plural "they went" in 10:3, and hence would have stayed at the tomb while Peter returned home. He sees the narrative of the appearance of the messengers (angels) as another insertion—ibid., 205.

354. The two angels "in white" (hence supernatural) mark off an empty space. The scene parallels a common one in the Roman Empire taken from the Egyptian Isis cult: Isis and her sister Nephthys flank a bier and assist Osiris in his resurrection. The scene was frequently employed in tombs by those seeking to secure their own afterlife. There are clear differences between the gospel scene and that of the Isis cult: the body of Jesus is absent, and the angels are not assisting Jesus in his overcoming of death—Hulster, "Two Angels."

Turning she says to him, in Aramaic, "Rabbouni" (which means "Teacher").[355] [17]Jesus says to her, "Do not cling to me, for I have not yet gone up to the Father. But go to my brothers and tell them, 'I am ascending to my Father and your Father, to my God and your God.'"[356] [18]Mary Magdalene went, announcing to the disciples, "I saw the Lord!" and the things he said to her.

[19]Then it was evening one day after the Sabbath, and the disciples were behind locked doors out of fear of the Judeans. Jesus came and stood in the middle and says to them, "Peace for you."[357] [20]And after saying this he showed his hands and side to them. Then the disciples, seeing the Lord, rejoiced. [21]Then Jesus said to them again, "Peace for you. As the Father sent me, I also am sending you." [22]And after saying this he breathed and says to them, "Receive the Holy Spirit: [23]Whatever sins you might forgive are forgiven them, whatever you might hold have been held."

[24]Now Thomas, one of the twelve, who is called the Twin, was not with them when Jesus came. [25]Then the other disciples were saying to him, "We saw the Lord." But he said to them, "Unless I see the marks[358] of the nails in his hands and poke my finger into the place of the nails and poke my hand in his side, I will not believe at all." [26]And after eight days his disciples were inside again, and Thomas was with them. Jesus comes when the doors had been locked, and he stood in the middle and said, "Peace for you." [27]Then he says to Thomas, "Reach out your finger here and see my hands, and reach out your hand and poke it into my side, and be not unbelieving but believing." [28]Thomas answered and said to him, "My Lord and my God." [29]Jesus says to him, "You have believed because you saw me; blessed are they not seeing and believing."

[30]Then on the one hand Jesus worked many other signs before his disciples, which are not written in this book. [31]On the other these have been written so that you may believe that Jesus is the Messiah, the Son of God, and so that believing you may have life in his name.[359]

---

355. Tenney, "Footnotes," 364, identifies this as a translation note. R. Brown, *Community of the Beloved Disciple*, 189, observes that apostolic authority came at the outset from seeing the risen Christ. In the *Johannine Gospel* Mary Magdalene, not Peter or the Beloved Disciple, sees the risen Christ.

356. Hartmann, "Die Vorlage der Osterberichte," 207, calls attention to "my brothers." This would appear to link the tradition to the Brothers in Jerusalem.

357. "Peace for you": This is not a mere greeting or a wish, but a solemn statement of fact—R. Brown, *Gospel According to John (xiii–xxi)*, 1021.

358. Textual witnesses vary: "the place," "the mark," "the marks." The Greek variations are very close in spelling: τὸν τόπον, τὸ τύπον, τοὺς τύπους. Ibid., 1025, reasons that the confusion would not have arisen unless there were two different words to begin with. Thus rather than use "place" twice, he accepts "mark" first and then "place" later in the sentence. The translation above accepts the plural of "place," as found in P[66]. The subsequent reference to nail marks does not mean the nails supported Jesus' body during the crucifixion; ropes likely did that. The nails would have kept the crucified from sliding his arms toward the head for better leverage.

359. Tenney, "Footnotes," 364, lists this as an explanatory note. There is a text critical issue in this verse (as well as John 19:35), with both the present subjunctive and aorist subjunctive forms of the verb "believe" well attested in the manuscript witnesses. Carson, "Syntactical and Text-critical," argues

21 ¹After these events Jesus revealed himself again to the disciples at the Sea of Tiberias.³⁶⁰ Now he appeared³⁶¹ as follows: ²Simon Peter, Thomas who was called the Twin, Nathanial from Cana of Galilee, the sons of Zebedee, and two others of his disciples were together. ³Simon Peter says to them, "I am going to fish." They say to him, "We too will go with you." They went out and boarded the boat, and during that night caught nothing. ⁴But when it was already dawn Jesus was standing on the shore; however, the disciples did not know it was Jesus. ⁵Then Jesus says to them, "Boys, are you catching any food?" They answered him, "No." ⁶So he said to them, "Cast the net on the right side of the boat, and you will find some." So they cast, and they were no longer able to haul in because of the quantity of the fish. ⁷Then that disciple whom Jesus loved says to Peter, "It is the Lord." So Simon Peter, hearing that it was the Lord, put on the outer garment, for he was naked, and cast himself into the sea.³⁶² ⁸But the other disciples came in the boat (for they were not far from land, but about a hundred yards off³⁶³), towing the net of fish. ⁹Then when they got out onto the land, they see a charcoal fire had been made and a fish on it and bread. ¹⁰Jesus says to them, "Bring some of the fish that you just caught." ¹¹Then Simon Peter went up and pulled the net onto the land, filled with one hundred fifty-three large fish; and although there were so many the net did not break. ¹²Jesus says to them, "Come, eat breakfast!" And none of the disciples dared to inquire of him, "Who are you?" knowing it was the Lord. ¹³Jesus comes and takes the bread, and he gave it to them, and likewise the fish. ¹⁴This was the third time Jesus appeared to the disciples after being raised from the dead.³⁶⁴

¹⁵Then when they had eaten breakfast, Jesus says to Simon Peter, "Simon son of John, do you love *me* more than these things?"³⁶⁵ He says to him, "Yes,

---

for the present subjunctive rather than the aorist, maintaining that the gospel was aimed at believers, whom the Evangelist wanted to continue in a believing state. The verses manifestly conclude the gospel, making the next chapter an added narrative.

360. No textual evidence suggests that the *Johannine Gospel* ever circulated without chapter 21; it appears to be a Galilean appearance narrative that the redactor added on following the Jerusalem narratives—R. Brown, *Gospel According to John (xiii–xxi)*, 1077–1082.

361. "Appeared," ἐφανέρωσεν, is the same word that is used transitively earlier in the verse and translated as "revealed." A fragment of the uncanonical *Gospel of Peter*, verses 58–60, provides an account that appears to lead up to the narrative of Chapter 21: " Now it was the final day of the Unleavened Bread; and many went out returning to their home since the feast was over. But we twelve disciples of the Lord were weeping and sorrowful; and each one, sorrowful because of what had come to pass, departed to his home. But I, Simon Peter, and my brother Andrew, having taken our nets, went off to the sea. And there was with us Levi of Alphaeus whom the Lord. . . . "

362. Tenney, "Footnotes," 364, lists ""for he was naked" as an explanatory note.

363. "Two hundred cubits." Ibid., lists "for they were not far from the land" as an explanatory note. Fortna, *Fourth Gospel*, 6, sees "but about a hundred yards off" as gratuitous factual detail retained by the redactor who was reluctant to remove anything from the received text.

364. Tenney, "Footnotes," 364, lists this as a summary note.

365. Ramelli, "Simon Son of John," supports the translation, "do you love *me* more than you love these things?" R. Brown, *Gospel According to John (xiii–xxi)*, 1103–04, points out that if the intent was

Lord, you know that I love you." He says to him, "Feed my lambs." [16]He says to him again a second time, "Simon son of John, do you love *me*?" He says to him, "Yes, Lord, you know that I love you." He says to him, "Tend my sheep." [17]He says to him a third time, "Simon son of John, do you love *me*?" Peter was grieved that he said to him a third time, "Do you love me?" And he says to him, "Lord, you know everything, you know that I love you." Jesus says to him, "Feed my sheep."

> [18]*Amen. Amen I say to you, when you were younger, you put your belt on yourself and walked where you wished; but when you grow old, you will extend your hands,*[366] *and another will tie you and lead you where you do not wish."* [19]*Now he said this, indicating by what kind of death he was to glorify God.*[367]

And after saying this he says to him, "Follow me."[368]

[20]Turning, Peter sees the disciple whom Jesus loved following, the one who also leaned back on his chest at the supper and said, "Lord, who is the one handing you over?" [21]Then seeing him, Peter says to Jesus, "Lord, what about him?" [22]Jesus says to him, "If I wish him to remain until I come, what is that to you? You follow me." [23]Then this saying went out to the brothers, that the disciple will not die. But Jesus did not say to him that he will not die, but, "If I wish him to remain until I come, what is that to you?" [24]This is the disciple who is testifying about these things and who was writing them down, and we know that his testimony is true. [25]Now there are also many other things that Jesus was doing, which, if they were written one by one, I do not think the world itself would have room for the books that would be written.[369]

---

to contrast Peter's love with that of the other disciples, "you" would have been explicitly stated with a pronoun rather than simply inferred, as it is, in the verb ending.

366. This is a formulaic reference to crucifixion—R. Collins, "Proverbial Sayings," 136–37.

367. Tenney, "Footnotes," 364, lists this as an explanatory note.

368. The double Amen insertion concerning Peter's death indicates that the redactor interpreted "Follow me" as an instruction to follow Jesus into death by execution, followed by resurrection.

369. Tenney, "Footnotes," lists these last three verses as notes alluding to the author.

*Chapter 24*

# Fragment on the Woman Accused of Adultery (John 7:53—8:11)

## Introduction

MODERN CHRISTIAN BIBLES INCLUDE a narrative in the *Johannine Gospel* about a woman accused of adultery and brought to Jesus. Some modern commentaries on that gospel skip this narrative altogether, some comment on it in an appendix, and some place their analysis of it in the sequence of numbered chapters at 7:53. The narrative does not appear in the most ancient Greek manuscripts of the gospel, though some later manuscripts do have it. Some place it elsewhere in the *Johannine Gospel* and some in the *Gospel of Luke*. The manuscript of the *Johannine Gospel* Desiderius Erasmus used as the basis for his 1516 edition of the Greek New Testament, the first produced on a printing press, was one that placed the narrative at 7:53, and early printed Bible translations, including the King James Version, used the Erasmus edition, commonly called the "textus receptus," as the Greek text to be translated.[1]

The style and vocabulary of the narrative do not appear to be Johannine, suggesting that the author was not in the Johannine circle.[2] According to Eusebius, the early Christian writer Papias "expounded another story about a woman who was accused before the Lord of many sins, which the *Gospel according to the Hebrews* contains."[3] On the one hand, this other story may not be the same one because the one that appears in modern Bibles does not say the woman was accused of many sins; on the other hand, Papias may have known of a different version of the same story. The *Apostolic Constitutions* 11:24,[4] dating from the third century, describes the same story as that found in modern Bibles; it was "used to caution bishops against too great severity in dealing with penitents."[5] Because the fragment is so short, there is not much text

---

1. Moore, "Commemorating 500 Years of the Greek New Testament in Print."
2. R. Brown, *Gospel According to John (i–xii)*, 335–36.
3. Eusebius, *Ecclesiastical History*, 3:29:17.
4. *Apostolic Constitutions* 11:24 = Syriac *Didascalia* 7.
5. Barret, *Gospel according to St. John*, 589.

to mine for clues about the date and place of origin of the narrative. Consequently, its placement here following the *Johannine Gospel* is not intended to imply any particular date for its composition.

## An Approach from the Sociology of Law

The famous sociologist and legal historian Max Weber distinguished public from private law, characterizing the latter as norms issuing from a state but regulating non-state conduct.[6] The narrative substantively concerns private law, but the salient issue is one of public law. By the time of Jesus of Nazareth, the Judean state was subordinate to the Roman Empire, and a stratum of intellectuals of upper-class origin comprised the legal experts who interpreted the Torah. Such a stratum furthered the rationalization of the legal system, replacing magical elements and negotiation with reasoned applications of codified legal principles.[7] In the narrative about the woman accused of adultery, there does not appear to be any question of a formal trial; rather "the scribes and the Pharisees" parade her before Jesus in order to trip him up. If he agrees with the stipulation of the Law that she should be executed (private law), he would be in trouble with the Romans for endorsing a lynching (contrary to public law). If he does not agree with the stipulation of the Law, he could be accused of being unpatriotic. He escapes the quandary by putting the matter back into the hands of the people accusing her: "Whoever among you is without sin, let him be the first to cast a stone at her." After the accusers leave the scene, he proceeds to speak with the accused on a personal basis. So what is the bearing of the Law on conduct, and how is it enforced?

The sociologist and legal theorist Georges Gurvitch applies his characteristic sociology in depth to law. He sets the most external aspect of law at one pole and the most subjective at another, and then describes some intermediary legal phenomena between those two poles. He proposes six levels in depth for law:

a) Organized law fixed in advance

b) Flexible organized law found ad hoc

c) Organized intuitive law

d) Fixed spontaneous law

e) Flexible spontaneous law, found ad hoc

f) Intuitive spontaneous law[8]

Organized law fixed in advance is the most external kind, involving specialists and a code of some kind. Intuitive spontaneous law involves parties arriving at a conclusion

---

6. Weber, *Economy and Society*, 641.
7. Ibid., 824.
8. Gurvitch, *Sociology of Law*, 178–80.

themselves, especially in a time in which organized law is absent. Between these poles one finds room for discretion, the absence of technical procedures, or technical procedures that predetermine outcomes without substantively mandating them, and even emergent outcomes from unique situations. The situation depicted in the narrative of the woman accused of adultery has echoes of organized law fixed in advance insofar as the literate stratum of experts were able to consult the Torah, but because of the Roman domination of Judea everything that had been fixed and organized was made relative and tentative. How much genuine authority the Judean authorities had was open to question. Nevertheless, it was not yet an entirely revolutionary situation; there were norms to live by. Decisions about the breach of inherited norms were not made with complete spontaneity. It was within this situation that there would have been room for the experts in received legal traditions to attempt to trip Jesus up.

## English Translation

### Fragment on the Woman Accused of Adultery

7 [53] And they went each to their[9] own house, 8 [1] but Jesus went to the Mount of Olives. [2] And at dawn he appeared again in the Temple precincts, and the whole people comes to him, and sitting he was teaching them. [3] Now the scribes and Pharisees brought a woman caught in adultery, and standing her in the middle [4] they say to him, "Teacher, this woman has been caught in the very act of adultery. [5] Now in the law Moses commands us to stone such women.[10] So what do you say?" [6] But they were saying this, testing him, so that they would have something with which to accuse him.[11] But Jesus, leaning down, began writing with his finger in the dirt. [7] And after they continued interrogating him, he stood up and said to them, "Let the one from among you who is

---

9. "Their": The Greek literally reads "his."

10. It is true that Lev 20:10 and Deut 22:22–24 specify a death penalty for adultery, but neither specifies stoning; moreover, both adulterers would be executed, but the accusers only speak of the woman—O'Day, "Study in Misreading," 632.

11. The accusers are saying nothing of a trial; rather, they were trying to implicate Jesus in a lynching if he answered one way, or in failing to uphold the Torah if he answered another way—Morris, *Gospel according to John*, 782. They showed no interest in the rule of law or in the situation of the woman—O'Day, "Study in Misreading," 632.

## Fragment on the Woman Accused of Adultery (John 7:53—8:11)

sinless first cast a stone."[12] ⁸And again, bending down, he wrote in the dirt.[13] ⁹Now those hearing began leaving, one by one, beginning with the elders, and he was left alone, and the woman was before him. ¹⁰And standing up, Jesus said to her, "Madam, where are they? Is no one condemning you?" ¹¹And she said, "No one, sir." And Jesus said, "And I am not condemning you. Go, and from now sin no more."[14]

---

12. This writing in the dirt has occasioned considerable puzzlement and speculation. Derrett, "Law in the New Testament," imaginatively proposed that Jesus was writing Exod 23.1b: "You shall not join hands with a wicked man, to be a malicious witness" (RSV). O'Day, "Study in Misreading," 636, argues that a concern with *what* Jesus writes is misguided; the text highlights the fact *that* he writes. She finds an explanation for the act of writing in Jer 17:13: "O Lord, the hope of Israel, all who forsake thee shall be put to shame; those who turn away from thee shall be written in the earth, for they have forsaken the Lord, the fountain of living water" (RSV). Manson, "Pericope De Adultera," 256, points out that it was Roman criminal procedure for a presiding judge to write down a sentence and then read it aloud: Jesus "stoops down and pretends to write down the sentence, after which he reads it out: 'whoever among you is without sin, let him be first to cast a stone at her.'"

13. One objection to Manson's interpretation is that it leaves no rationale for Jesus bending down to write again; however, Jesus may be threatening to say more because the woman's accusers failed to follow proper procedure by warning her before accusing her—Morris, *Gospel according to John*, 784. Among the many intriguing symbolic meanings for the writing on the ground suggested by Paul Minear, the most persuasive is that Jesus wrote twice to address two different cases, that of the accusers and that of the woman they accused—Minear, "Writing on the Ground," 30.

14. O'Day, "Study in Misreading," 636–37, argues that the structure of the narrative equates the standing of the accusers and the accused woman before Jesus, and that the point of the narrative is to be derived from that structural feature.

*Chapter 25*

# The Pseudepigraphic Letter of Jude

## Introduction

THE *LETTER OF JUDE* found in Christian Bibles is brief, generally neglected, but controversial. While it has a letter-like opening, it is not really a letter but an anti-heresy pamphlet.[1] The very possibility that the author was not one of several people named Judas, or Jude, mentioned elsewhere in the New Testament, occasions some of the controversy.[2] Apart from references to Judas Iscariot, the *Gospel of Mark* and the *Gospel of Matthew* list a Judas as a brother (possibly a step-brother) of Jesus.[3] The *Gospel of Luke* and the *Acts of the Apostles* list a Judas, son of James, as one of the twelve;[4] *Acts* also mentions a Judas called Barsabbas, an early Christian evidently from Jerusalem.[5] The *Johannine Gospel* narrates Judas (not Iscariot), a disciple, asking a question of Jesus at the Last Supper.[6] It is not clear which New Testament person named "Judas," if any, is ostensibly being identified in the opening of the letter: "Judas, slave of Jesus Christ, brother of James...." Most commentators understand "Judas" to be a pseudonym, though the author could be someone named "Judas" from a much later generation than the ones mentioned elsewhere in the New Testament. An important argument

---

1. Sellin, "Häeretiker," 208.

2. Bauckham, *Jude and the Relatives*, 177–78, concludes that Jude the brother of the Lord wrote the letter in the first century in Palestine. One must ask why Luke would not have known this and did not mention Jude, and why Jude figures nowhere in the recollections of Paul in *Galatians* about Christians involved in the deliberations over the circumcision of gentile converts. *Das neue Testament und frühchristliche Schriften*, edited by Berger and Nord, 682, also attributes the letter to a brother of Jesus and thus give it an early date of composition.

3. Mark 6:3; Matt 13:55. Bauckham, *Jude and the Relatives*, 31–32, reviews the ancient literature on the family of Jesus, concluding that "the Epiphanian view" (i.e., that the "brothers of the Lord" were stepbrothers, sons of Joseph by an earlier marriage) "has a better claim to serious consideration than is often nowadays allowed. The second-century tradition could preserve an accurate historical memory. On the other hand, it could be a legendary construct in favour of the perpetual virginity of Mary."

4. Luke 6:16; Acts 1:13.

5. Acts 15:22, 27, and 34.

6. John 14:22.

against any of the New Testament people named "Judas" writing the letter is that the letter itself refers to the apostles as belonging to an earlier generation;[7] indeed, it describes the Christian faith as something traditional and fixed and objectified.[8] Judas, one of the twelve, can be eliminated because the Judas whom Luke lists as one of the twelve had a father named "James," but the Judas of the letter has a brother named "James" and the ancient Jews did not give sons the first names of their fathers.[9] Judas, the relative of Jesus, had grandsons who were investigated under Emperor Domitian (reigned 81–96 CE); he let them go after discovering they were poor farmers who posed no threat to Rome.[10] If Jude the brother of Jesus were the author, the work would be very early since only grandsons survived into the era of Domitian.[11] Moreover, the Greek of the letter is fairly sophisticated; why would poor farmers have such a literate grandfather[12] or, alternatively, afford the services of that good of a scribe? Then there is the fact that the letter does not refer to Jesus as one would refer to an intimate relative, but with formulaic expressions.[13] Finally, one must ask why something written by a brother of Jesus would be given so little attention by the early Christians: "It is hard to conceive of all the curious sequences wherein a brother of Jesus managed to write a letter like this one—which then circulated on the edge of Christian literature with its authority being frequently doubted but which eventually made its way into the main circle of Christian texts."[14] In fact, even the ancients were skeptical about the letter; Eusebius mentions it in the same sentence as the *Letter of James*, where he describes the authenticity of both letters as being denied "since few of the ancients quote it" (the *Letter of James*), "as is also the case with the Epistle called Jude's, which is itself one

---

7. Jude 17; see Reicke, *Epistles of James, Peter, and Jude*, 190. Bauckham, *Jude and the Relatives*, 171, maintains that the verse refers to the "predictions" of the apostles being made beforehand, *not that the apostles were around beforehand, and that therefore the apostles could still be alive and active.* The Greek verb can be translated that way, but the translation of that verb is not the issue. The issue is how distant in the past were the apostles uttering their words or predictions. If it is necessary for the author of *Jude* to tell the readers to recall these predictions, one would think they would be not very recent. Bauckham also argues that verse 18 implies the readers themselves heard the apostles' predictions, and the RSV and *Das neue Testament* make it seem so: "They said to you...." However, the Greek does not really say that: ὅτι ἔλεγον ὑμῖν, "that they were saying to you...." The imperfect conveys the information that the action in question was progressive; if it were still in progress the present tense would have been used.

8. D. Harrington, "Jude and 2 Peter," 15 and 183.

9. Acts 1:13; Reicke, *Epistles of James, Peter, and Jude*, 190.

10. Eusebius, *Ecclesiastical History*, 3:9:1—3:20:6. Bauckham, *Jude and the Relatives*, 99–100, points out that they were investigated as a potential threat because they were descendants of David, not because they were relatives of Jesus. There must have been many thousands of descendants of David to investigate!

11. Reicke, *Epistles of James, Peter, and Jude*, 190.

12. D. Harrington, "Jude and 2 Peter," 183.

13. Ibid.

14. Donelson, "Gathering Apostolic Voices," 24–25.

of the seven called Catholic; nevertheless we know that these letters have been used publicly with the rest in most churches."[15]

The letter's author seems to be an ethnic Jew because the translations from the Hebrew Bible are from the Hebrew text and not from the Septuagint and the version of 1 *Enoch* cited seems to be the Aramaic original rather than the Greek translation.[16] He may well have once been a member of the "Brothers," the Christian community in Jerusalem led by James prior to the latter's execution by Hanan ben Hanan in 62 CE[17] and the destruction of the city by the Romans in 70, and hence identify himself as a "Brother of James."

A second controversy arises from the fact that there are close parallels between the *Letter of Jude* and the *Second Letter of Peter*. According to Bo Reicke, Jude 2 closely tracks Second Peter 1:2; Jude 3 tracks Second Peter 1:5; Jude 5a, Second Peter 1:12; Jude 5b–19, Second Peter 2:1—3:3, and Jude 24, Second Peter 3:14. These parallels are said to cluster in the middle chapter of *Second Peter*.[18] The logical possibilities are that the author of the *Letter of Jude* based that work on *Second Peter*, that both works used a common source text, or that the author of *Second Peter* based that letter on the *Letter of Jude*. Daniel Harrington reports that most commentators believe the *Letter of Jude* was a source for *Second Peter* because Jude 5–7 refers to events from the Hebrew Bible out of order while *Second Peter* puts them in chronological order; one could understand why the author of *Second Peter* would put the narrated events in order but not why the author of *Jude* would set about putting them out of order.[19] In supporting the dependence of *Second Peter* on *Jude*, Jeremy Hultin points out that it is hard to explain why the author of Jude would have drawn only from the middle section of *Second Peter*, passing over all the theologically rich material in the first and third chapters.[20] There is one other correction that appears in *Second Peter*; the author removes references to works that were not accorded canonical status. *Second Peter* was written at a time when the process of establishing a canon of Christian literature had begun while *Jude* seems to have been written prior to that process.

---

15. Eusebius, *Ecclesiastical History*, 2:23:23.

16. Bauckham, *Jude and the Relatives*, 136–37, 139.

17. Josephus, *Antiquities*, 20:9.

18. Reicke, *Epistles of James, Peter, and Jude*, 189–90. The clustering does not seem to be all that impressive to me. I have underlined the verbal parallels in the translation of 2 *Peter* in the next chapter.

19. D. Harrington, "Jude and 2 Peter," 162–63. Joubert, "Facing the Past," 59, and Watson, *Arrangement, Invention, and Style*, 52–53, undermine this argument by pointing out that the author of *Jude* orders the events in terms of increasingly horrible punishments: from natural death on earth, to capture in eternal chains until judgment day, to punishment by eternal fire. What creates the deviation from chronological order in *Jude* are the events from non-canonical sources, and ibid., 162, maintains that the author of *Jude* could have inserted them into the text of 2 *Peter* as readily as the latter remove them from *Jude*. I must disagree: why would an author introduce controverted evidence lessening the force of an argument? A later author, some time after the author of 2 *Peter*, would have no reason to do that.

20. Hultin, "Literary Relationship," 33. His argument seems to be over stated.

It is not possible to attach a specific date to the composition of the letter, but the very fact that it speaks of the apostles as belonging to an earlier tradition and refers to tradition would make it contemporaneous with the Gospel of John, somewhere between 100 and 110. Bo Reicke argues that a problem of lukewarm members well-off enough to be recruited away from the Christian movement, which the letter addresses, suggests a date decades after the time of Paul.[21] By the time of Eusebius (260/265–339/340 CE) the canonical status of the work was still disputed, and that would not have been the case if it were an early work. The letter appears in a third century papyrus, P[72].[22]

John Gunther makes a case for Alexandria as the place of composition.[23] He begins by eliminating Palestine and Syria: The letter was only brought into the Syrian canon in the sixth century; it was still in dispute in Palestine in the time of Eusebius. The libertinism that the letter criticizes was not an issue in Palestine or Syria, or in Jewish Christianity. Finally, the letter does not associate Jude with Jesus as a brother, something, Gunther argues, that would have happened in Palestine. He also maintains that the letter is not Roman: Neither *First Clement*, which was composed and issued on behalf of the Roman Church, nor the *Shepherd of Hermas*, a Roman work, deal with the problems *Jude* confronts. He explains away an unusual parallel between a line in the Roman writer, Justin Martyr's *Dialogue with Trypho* and the letter ("Jesus led your fathers out of Egypt") by arguing that such a statement could not have been from the *Letter of Jude* because the subject in the sentence, "Jesus," does not appear there in the letter. This is not at all persuasive 1) because the earliest and most geographically widespread manuscript witnesses in fact have "Jesus" and not "the Lord" or "God" as the subject;[24] 2) Justin need not have had the best manuscript if it had not read "Jesus"; and 3) Justin could have known the letter in Rome without quoting or paralleling it completely in this instance. Gunther does not appear to have succeeded in eliminating Rome as a possible place of composition. The case he makes *for* Alexandria begins with the letter's reference to the Enoch literature, which was popular in Egyptian Christian circles.[25] Then he points to a reference in verse 12 to waterless clouds, a phenomenon more characteristic of Alexandria than, for example, Rome.[26] He also points to metaphors in verses 12–13: reefs or sunken rocks on which ships run aground,[27] and wild waves of the sea casting up and carrying foam, filth, and refuse.

21. Reicke, *Epistles of James, Peter, and Jude*, 192.

22. Noted by Soards, "1 Peter, 2 Peter, and Jude," and also evident from the apparatus of the modern Greek editions of the New Testament.

23. Gunther, "Alexandrian Epistle."

24. Bartholomä, "Did Jesus Save?," 2.

25. Gunther, "Alexandrian Epistle," 550.

26. Ibid., 551–52.

27. Ibid., 551. The metaphor of hidden rocks, which Gunther also cites, is not as solid an example as the others since the term used also means "stains" and is probably to be taken in that sense in verse 12, where it appears.

Both of these metaphors correspond to ancient depictions of Alexandria's harbor.[28] Finally, he argues that doctrines that the letter attacks (the separation within the deity between a merciful and a law-giving person; using the enslavement of angels as an explanation for lustful behavior by humans) were characteristic of Egyptian sects—specifically, Carpocratianism and Cainitism.[29] Desjardins points out that Gnosticism, of which these two sects were early forms, was not marked by licentiousness and that the author of the *Letter of Jude* as well as that of *Second Peter*, with their world rejection, were more like the Gnostics than were the people they criticize.[30] On the whole, Gunther's arguments certainly lead one to see Alexandria as a likely place of composition, but it is not at all certain insofar as Rome remains a possibility.

Since we do not know the location in which the letter was written or that of the intended readership, we cannot say a great deal about the latter. Stephen Joubert notes that the linguistic content and ideology presupposes some familiarity with 1 *Enoch* and the *Assumption of Moses*,[31] which were not widespread in the ancient Christian movement.[32] The speech community in question is thus a distinct one—i.e., it deviates in content from the broader movement.

## The Sociology of Doctrinal Orthodoxy

The author of the *Letter of Jude* adheres to what is taken to be orthodox doctrine, as opposed to what is described as heresy. There is more than an ideological dimension to this orthodoxy since the author accuses the heretics of moral deviance as well. The focus here will be on doctrine, since that category can include teachings about morality as well as about Jesus, the nature of deity, and angels. This focus beyond deity-oriented beliefs that reaches to issues of moral conduct is not unique to *Jude*, of course, but the vehemence this letter exhibits about doctrinal and moral deviation calls for its being highlighted here. As a late work, *Jude* cannot be identified as the source of orthodox doctrines; indeed, precisely because they are orthodox or traditional indicates that the source of them was to be found in some prior experience. That prior experience may include experiences of people hearing Jesus of Nazareth in Galilee and Judea, but the

---

28. Strabo, *Geography,* 17:6:1; Josephus, *Jewish War,* 4:10:5. Gunther also points to parallels of language with other works (the letters of John, the *Johannine Gospel*, the *Letter of Barnabas*), which for purposes of his argument need to be accepted as Egyptian works—"Alexandrian Epistle," 552–53. Bauckham, *Jude and the Relatives*, 140, proposes that the four images from nature in Jude 12b–13 were inspired by 1 Enoch 2:1–5 and 80:2–8, but that does not seem likely since 1 Enoch 2:1–5 simply mentions astronomical and climate topics by broad categories instead of observable phenomena and 1 Enoch 80:2–8 is a simple recitation of end-time natural disasters.

29. Gunther, "Alexandrian Epistle," 554–55.

30. Desjardins, "Portrayal of the Dissidents."

31. Rather than the *Assumption of Moses*, it may have been the *Testament of Moses*, but Joubert's point is not undermined by that.

32. Joubert, "Language, Ideology, and the Social Context," 340.

gospels themselves do not present Jesus' discourses as a compendium of the doctrines of the Christian movement. There was a *process* in which early disciples articulated their best judgment as situations emerged and questions arose: " . . . I say, not the Lord, that. . . . "[33] These new judgments were perceived as logical, reasonable, or inevitable deductions, derivations, applications, and expansions of traditions received earlier, either from Jesus or from the Hebrew Bible. In the New Testament literature, they are frequently attributed to the Holy Spirit, the precise nature of which had not yet been explicitated.

Beginning with an originary subjective experience—either that of arriving at a cognition of a peculiarly Christian stamp or of a peculiarly Christian reception of a Jewish principle—we should trace the process that issues in a more or less fixed "orthodox" or "traditional" formulation, in order to understand the nature of doctrinal orthodoxy. The sociologists who described this kind of process were the Austrian American Alfred Schutz and his students at the New School in New York City, Peter L. Berger and Thomas Luckmann.[34] Schutz frequently spoke of the "stock of knowledge" available to an individual, group, or society. Humans orient themselves to their environing worlds not only on the basis of external stimulations but of retained clusters of past experiences and categories of interpretation, and these clusters and categories comprise the "stock of knowledge" at hand. A person's subjective stock of knowledge "consists only in part of 'independent' results of experience and explication. It is predominantly derived from elements of the social stock of knowledge."[35] That stock of knowledge in turn developed in the subjective experiences and explications of previous generations. The reception of previous generations' subjective experiences and explications does not result in a perfect copy of the latter, first because the earlier people change their experiences in the very act of articulating them (turning an experience into an object necessarily conveys it as no longer something experienced subjectively first-hand), second because what had been expressed in some manner in the past was selectively received by past generations according to what was relevant to their life-worlds, and thirdly because a present generation receives the objectified expressions that had been retained and transmitted according to the relevance structures of the present life-world. Such socially derived elements of knowledge "can be modified in more or less 'independent' processes of explication. They can, for example,

---

33. 1 Cor 7:12.

34. The principal thinker on the matters taken up here was Schutz, who had been made acutely aware of the precariousness of what was taken to be everyday knowledge by his experiences on the southern front between the Austro-German and the Italian forces in World War I, to which he set out as an impressionable youth, though an officer, and his return, as a veteran old before his time, to a depressed and demoralized Vienna. Schutz did not live long enough to complete a general statement of his sociology; Luckmann completed the work based on Schutz's notes—Schutz and Luckmann, *Structures of the Life-World*. Meanwhile, Berger and Luckmann published their own sociology of everyday knowledge, *Social Construction of Reality*, refashioning and extending Schutz's approach.

35. Schutz and Luckmann, *Structures of the Life-World*, 262.

be 'improved' before they are channeled back into the social stock of knowledge."[36] Schutz did not see "objectivation"—the embodiment of past subjective processes in the objects and events of the everyday life-world—as a neutral medium.

The process of objectivation involves the person who had the originary experience making "indications." The indication may be behavioral—e.g., reacting to a hot object by blowing on one's fingers. (Was Paul rolling his eyes while dictating his reference to speaking in tongues?) In a society without television and electronic video, verbal indications would be more predominant. Schutz emphasized that people manipulate indications; they exaggerate, hide some aspects, and shape them for purposes of easier reception. The indications themselves detach from the situations that engender them.[37] Then the indications require interpretation.[38] The very existence of systems of signs, languages, presupposes "a far-reaching detachment of subjective experiences from the spatial, temporal, and social" dimensions of everyday experience.[39] Once symbolized, what derived from the experiences becomes part of new "we-relations." People identify themselves with groups; they are Baptist Christians, Catholic Christians, Greek Orthodox Christians, Methodist Christians, etc., or perhaps only Christian loosely speaking. How they read the creation poem in *Genesis* will be affected by how they identify themselves and what systems of discourse come to them through their group networks and institutional apparatus. And the resultant stock of knowledge at hand for a given individual will not only differ from the originary subjective experience because of the fact of its mediation through indications and symbolic formulation, but it will also differ from the individual's own grasp of it since it is then fitted into a new (and changing) biographically unique relevance structure.[40]

Using one of Schutz's expressions, Berger and Luckmann speak of sedimentation: experiences that are retained in memory, and congeal in recollection as recognizable and memorable entities. Berger and Luckmann go on to describe intersubjective sedimentation, which occurs when several individuals share a biographical situation. Such can become "truly social" when intersubjective sedimentations become incorporated in a sign system of some kind.[41] Once so embodied, a sedimented experience can be transmitted across generations. This transmission often involves a social apparatus of specialized persons and procedures.[42] The issue then arises as to which persons and which procedures. Identifying who and how the transmission of tradition is to take place is a matter of "legitimation," a term taken from Weber's political sociology.

36. Ibid., 263.
37. Ibid., 267–69.
38. Ibid., 273.
39. Ibid., 279.
40. Ibid., 285.
41. Berger and Luckmann, *Social Construction of Reality*, 67.
42. Ibid., 70.

According to Berger and Luckmann, "Legitimation as a process is best described as a 'second-order' objectivation of meaning." It "produces new meanings that serve to integrate the meanings already attached to disparate institutional processes."[43] This means that in a given present generation, the contemporary experts make indications about objectivated contents from previous generations, using contemporary procedures. Legitimation is the process of identifying the institutionally acceptable indications from the past and second indications in the present. "The function of legitimation is to make ostensively available and subjectively plausible the 'first-order' objectivations that have been institutionalized."[44] This is what appears to be going on in the *Letter of Jude*.

## Boundary Maintenance

Boundary maintenance is a concept that comes from sociological functionalism. As described by Talcott Parsons, the persistence of any given social system of action depends on maintaining certain constancies of pattern.[45] The pattern is what keeps the system from blending into its environment and ceasing to exist as such. This becomes a matter of difference or separateness from a social environment; the difference may be static symbolic contents of some kind or a distinct trajectory of dynamics (change). Earlier than Parsons, Georg Simmel described boundary maintenance in terms of the "self-preservation of the group": the group needs to survive the turnover of its membership, perhaps by persisting on a particular territory.[46] Changes in the person of the authority in the group comprise a particularly delicate matter. Another threat to the continuity of a group identity is a reversal of a past decision.[47] Maintaining continuity involves the emergence of norms, of which there are three kinds: morality, honor, and law. Law brings about outer conformity through external means; morality effects loyalty through inner means; honor brings about outer conformity through inner means.[48] The *Letter of Jude* appears to make principal use of morality.

---

43. Ibid., 92.
44. Ibid.
45. Parsons, *Social System*, 482.
46. Simmel, *Sociology*, 443–541.
47. Ibid., 475.
48. Ibid., 476.

# English Translation

## Pseudonymous Letter of Jude

¹Judas, slave of Jesus, Messiah, a Brother of James, to those called, beloved in God the Father and preserved for Jesus, Messiah.⁴⁹ ²May mercy, peace, and love increase for you.

³Beloved, while engaged in writing to you in all eagerness about our common salvation, I have a need to write you, exhorting you to fight by the faith that was handed down to the saints once and for all;⁵⁰ ⁴for some people slipped in, who have been publicly sentenced to this condemnation before—ungodly, exchanging the grace of our God for sensuality and repudiating our only master and Lord, Jesus, Messiah.

⁵But I wish to remind you, though you know all this, that Jesus, once saving a people from the land of Egypt, then destroyed those not believing;⁵¹ ⁶and he has kept the angels in eternal fetters in darkness below until the judgment of the great day, who did not keep to their own domain but left their own habitation;⁵² ⁷likewise Sodom and Gomorra and the cities around them

---

49. In one possible interpretation, the author would be invoking the *Letter of James* and its practical, ethical faith rather than speculative focus of those whom the letter will go on to criticize—Sellin, "Häeretiker," 224.

50. Gunther, "Alexandrian Epistle," 547–48, notes that verse 3 suggests the author of the letter had been writing a more general treatise on Christianity but had to turn to this letter because of a crisis of some kind.

51. Jude 5 has a text critical problem. The subject could be κύριος, Lord; Ἰησοῦς, Jesus; or θεὸς, God, depending on which among conflicting ancient manuscript witnesses one accords the most weight. The United Bible Societies committee acknowledged the weight attestation supporting "Jesus" but considered it an impossibility—Metzger, *Textual Commentary*, 723–24, and has "Lord" in the text. RSV simply uses "he"; *Das neue Testament* has "God" (Gott). Bartholomä, "Did Jesus Save?" does not consider it impossible for "Jesus" to be in the original, but simply a result of a high Christology on the part of the author. If Jesus pre-existed in the deity, then his having a part in saving the Hebrews from slavery in Egypt is not impossible.

52. Gen 6:1–2: "When men began to multiply on the face of the ground, and daughters were born to them, the sons of God saw that the daughters of men were fair; and they took to wife such of them as they chose." "Sons of men" meant "angels." Reicke, *Epistles of James, Peter, and Jude*, 199, and D. Harrington, "Jude and 2 Peter," 196, point to a more elaborate version of the legend in 1 *Enoch*, an ancient Jewish work, the relevant portion of which dates from 300 BCE. 1 *Enoch* is held to be canonical by the Ethiopian Jews and the Ethiopian and Eritrean Tewahedo churches. A first relevant passage is from 1 Enoch 9: "Thou seest what Azazel hath done, who hath taught all unrighteousness on earth and revealed the eternal secrets which were (preserved) in heaven, which men were striving to learn: And Semjaza, to whom Thou hast given authority to bear rule over his associates. And they have gone to the daughters of men upon the earth, and have slept with the women, and have defiled themselves, and revealed to them all kinds of sins." Azazel and Semjaza are names of angels. A second relevant passage is from 1 Enoch 10: "And again the Lord said to Raphael: 'Bind Azazel hand and foot, and cast him into the darkness: and make an opening in the desert, which is in Dudael, and cast him therein. And place upon him rough and jagged rocks, and cover him with darkness, and let him abide there for ever, and cover his face that he may not see light. And on the day of the great judgement he shall be cast into the fire. And heal the earth which the angels have corrupted, and proclaim the healing of the earth.'"

indulging in immorality in the same way as them and going out after an alien flesh, provide an example of being punished justly by eternal fire.[53]

⁸Likewise, these also, though having visions, defile flesh on the one hand and reject bearers of lordship[54] on the other; they slander the glorious ones.[55] ⁹But Michael the archangel, when disputing with the devil, was discussing the body of Moses; he did not dare to convict him of blasphemy, but said, "May the Lord rebuke you."[56] ¹⁰Now these people do not know what they revile on the one hand, and on the other they are being corrupted by something they know in a nature-like way, in the manner of non-reasoning animals.[57] ¹¹Woe to them, for they went the way of Cain[58] and abandoned themselves to the

---

53. According to Sellin, "Häeretiker," 217, the example of the Sodomites points to a defilement that occurs if earthly beings climb up to what is of heaven. Its point is that one should not make out with the other kind of being, ἕτερα σάρξ. The sin, exemplified not only by the Sodomites but also in the other cases taken from tradition, is in the mixing of earthly life and heavenly life. Each should remain in is sphere—the angelic in heaven and the human on the earth. Sellin insists it has nothing to do with sexual morality among humans.

54. Often translated "dominions": a category of angels, they were thought of as bearers of God's ruling power.

55. According to Desjardins, "Portrayal of the Dissidents," 93–94, the "glorious ones," δόξαι, are church leaders. Sellin, "Häeretiker," 214–15, Bauckham, *Jude ad the Relatives*, 271, and D. Harrington, "Jude and 2 Peter," 197, maintain that the term refers to a category of angels. The two readings are not necessarily contradictory; earthly entities such as church leaders were thought to have angels that corresponded to them.

56. According to Bauckham, *Jude and the Relatives*, 143–44, and Joubert, "Facing the Past," 60, most commentators over the centuries have thought verses 9–10 were based on the *Assumption of Moses*, but they themselves maintain that it is based on the *Testament of Moses*. Only fragments of both works are extant, and Bauckham, *Jude and the Relatives*, 238, relies on a reconstruction of the text of the *Testament*. D. Harrington, "Jude and 2 Peter," 198, mentions the theory that the former work was part of the latter work's lost ending. The point of the narrative is that Michael did not have the authority to dismiss the devil's accusation against Moses—that Moses murdered an Egyptian and thus did not deserve an honorable burial—but left the matter to God (Bauckham, *Jude and the Relatives*, 274) by saying, "May the Lord rebuke you"—a formula that also appears in Zech 3:2, the wording in the Septuagint being almost identical.

57. "In a nature-like way," ψυχικός, refers to biological life; it contrasts the spiritual (verse 19), πνευματικός—Sellin, "Häeretiker," 218. RSV has "by instinct"; *Das neue Testament* has "as stupid cattle."

58. As is well known, Cain murdered his brother Abel (Gen 4:8); the suggestion here is that the intruders the author of *Jude* is condemning committed spiritual murder—D. Harrington, "Jude and 2 Peter," 199.

deceit of Balaam for a price,⁵⁹ and perish in the rebellion of Korah.⁶⁰ ¹²These people are stains in your agape feasts,⁶¹ feasting fearlessly together, tending to themselves; they are rainless clouds borne away by winds; late autumn fruitless trees, twice dead, uprooted; ¹³wild waves of the sea foaming up their own ignominy; straying stars for which the black of darkness has been reserved in eternity.⁶²

¹⁴Now Enoch, seventh generation from Adam, also prophesied about them, saying, "Look, the Lord came with his holy myriads ¹⁵to work judgment against all and punish every soul for the impiety of all their works they committed and for all the harsh things that the godless sinners said against him. ¹⁶They are grumblers finding fault, proceeding with their own passion, and their mouth speaks, puffed up, admiring personages for the sake of gain."

¹⁷But you, beloved, recall the words proclaimed in the past by the apostles of our Lord Jesus, Messiah, ¹⁸for they were telling you that at the end of time there will be scoffers proceeding with the ungodly ones' very own passions. ¹⁹They are factionalists, natural, having no spirit, ²⁰but you, beloved, believe, building yourselves on your most holy faith, proceeding in the Holy Spirit; ²¹keep yourselves in God's love, anticipating the mercy of our Lord Jesus, Messiah, unto eternal life. ²²And be merciful to those who are wavering, ²³and

---

59. In Num 22–24 the diviner Balaam is hired by the Moabite King Balak to curse the Israelites, but the Lord takes control of his tongue and, three times, a blessing came out. It is unclear that Balaam wanted a curse to come out, but in Num 31:16 the fact that Israelite men had sexual relations with Moabite women and joined in the worship of the latter's gods is blamed on Balaam's advice. Deut 23:3–5 summarizes the legend: "No Ammonite or Moabite shall enter the assembly of the Lord; even to the tenth generation none belonging to them shall enter the assembly of the Lord for ever; because they did not meet you with bread and with water on the way, when you came forth out of Egypt, and because they hired against you Balaam the son of Be'or from Pethor of Mesopotamia, to curse you. Nevertheless the Lord your God would not hearken to Balaam; but the Lord your God turned the curse into a blessing for you, because the Lord your God loved you" (RSV).

60. Korah led a rebellion against Moses in the desert (Num 16); Moses set up a test and punishment: "And Moses said, 'Hereby you shall know that the Lord has sent me to do all these works, and that it has not been of my own accord. If these men die the common death of all men, or if they are visited by the fate of all men, then the Lord has not sent me. But if the Lord creates something new, and the ground opens its mouth, and swallows them up, with all that belongs to them, and they go down alive into Sheol, then you shall know that these men have despised the Lord.' And as he finished speaking all these words, the ground under them split asunder; and the earth opened its mouth and swallowed them up, with their households and all the men that belonged to Korah and all their goods. So they and all that belonged to them went down alive into Sheol; and the earth closed over them, and they perished from the midst of the assembly" (Num 16:28–33 RSV).

61. "Stains," σπιλάδες, can also mean "hidden rocks" or "reefs"; Reicke, *Epistles of James, Peter, and Jude*, 205, translates the word with that meaning. RSV has "blemishes."

62. "Jude lists clouds as symbolic of the region of the air, trees for the earth, waves for the sea, and planets for the dark outer spaces and the nether regions, too, since they rise and descend in the heavens"—Reicke, *Epistles of James, Peter, and Jude*, 207.

save them, snatching them from the fire, but being merciful to them cautiously, hating even the garment[63] that has been stained by the flesh.

²⁴Now to the One Who is able to keep you from stumbling and place you unblemished before His glory in exultation, ²⁵to God alone our Savior, through Jesus, Messiah, our Lord, be glory, majesty, power, and authority, before the entire age, now, and for all time. Amen.

---

63. "Garment," χιτών: The χιτών is the garb of the wandering charismatic; see the journeying disciples—Mark 6:9b, Matt 10:10. The Cynic wandering philosophers took only a χιτών—Sellin, "Häeretiker," 223–24).

*Chapter 26*

# Second Pseudepigraphic Letter of Peter

## Introduction

SIMILAR TO THE CASE of the *Letter of Jude*, the *Second Letter of Peter* is a neglected book of the New Testament. We can associate it with the *Letter of Jude* for reasons other than neglect; it too is a late pseudonymous work written to correct tendencies faced by the Christian church,[1] and in fact it includes a section that parallels the *Letter of Jude*. There is also a reference to a body of Pauline letters and an allusion to the *Gospel of Matthew*. A few writers contest such evidence in order to maintain that Peter, one of the Twelve, authored the letter,[2] but the vast majority of scholars see *Second Peter* as the latest book of the New Testament, too late to have been written by the apostle Peter. Eusebius, writing in the fourth century, has the following to say about the letter: "But the so-called Second Epistle" (of Peter) "we have not received as canonical, but nevertheless it has appeared useful to many, and has been studied with other Scriptures."[3]

As was common in ancient literature, the author wrote in the name of a noted predecessor. While in the case of the *Letter of Jude* the author may have been a Jewish Christian in the Diaspora named Judas who had once belonged to the community of Brothers led by James in Jerusalem, here we definitely have an instance of pseudonymity. Consequently, there was some intent in selecting the pseudonym "Peter." One can well understand why a writer in Greece and Asia Minor would choose "Paul," the missionary founder of churches in those geographical areas, but why would a writer choose the name "Peter"? Peter had been martyred in Rome; so it is sometimes proposed that the author was in Rome or wanted the letter to be associated with Rome.[4] Since *First Peter* had been addressed to readers in Asia Minor, and the author

---

1. Whether the tendencies faced by the Christian church were internal or external is an open question. Talbert "II Peter and the Delay," maintains that the problem was an external gnostic sect that rejected the expectation of an End Time and held to an antinomian stance and a libertine life style.
2. E.g., Green, *Second Epistle General of Peter*.
3. Eusebius, *Ecclesiastical History*, 3:3:1.
4. Reicke, *Epistles of James, Peter, and Jude*, 145; Senior, *1 & 2 Peter*, 99.

of *Second Peter* actually refers to that letter,[5] the author *may* have intended this letter for churches in Asia Minor; however, that is not indicated in the opening address.[6] Indeed, it only begins as a letter; as in the case of *Jude* the work is simply following the Christian literary convention of opening as a letter. Most of the text takes the form of a farewell address, a testament fictively occasioned by the imminent death of Peter.[7] Another possible reason for selecting the pseudonym "Peter" would be to identify with a Petrine "school," not in the sense of a body of writers sharing a theology but writers having a common founding figure.[8]

The date of the letter is difficult to fix with precision, but there are clues. The apostolic generation had passed away.[9] Reference is made to a body of Pauline letters.[10] The author knows the Transfiguration narrative in the Matthean version.[11] Among the synoptics, only Matthew adds "with whom I am well pleased" to what the voice from the cloud says, and that is the version of the saying cited in *2 Peter*. Robert Miller points out that *2 Peter* uses almost identical vocabulary as *Matthew* in restating the saying.[12] The *Gospel of Matthew* dates from about 90 CE, 80 at the earliest; hence *2 Peter* would be later than that. As mentioned above, *2 Peter* makes a reference to *1 Peter*, which dates from about 90 CE; again *1 Peter* would therefore be later than that. And *2 Peter* has a central section that is dependent on the *Letter of Jude* (see the introduction to that letter), which dates from 100 to 110. *Second Peter* also has an allusion to the *Gospel of John*, concerning the predicted death of Peter, and that gospel similarly dates from 100 to 110.[13] Consequently, *Second Peter* must date from some time after 110/110. The letter is included in $P^{72}$, a papyrus from the 200s,[14] and the *Apocalypse of Peter*, a noncanonical work dating from about 135–140, refers to the letter;[15] so we can best think of it as an early second century work.[16]

---

5. 2 Pet 3:1.
6. Reicke, *Epistles of James, Peter, and Jude*, 145.
7. Ibid., 146; Neyrey, "Apocalyptic Use," 504; D. Harrington, "Jude and 2 Peter," 229.
8. Soards, "1 Peter, 2 Peter, and Jude," 3831.
9. Kraftchich, *Jude, 2 Peter*, 71, citing 2 Pet 3:4.
10. Ibid., 72, citing 2 Pet 3:15–16.
11. 2 Pet 1:17; Matt 17:5.
12. Miller, "Is There Independent Attestation?" The only difference occurs with "in whom," which is ἐν ᾧ in Matt 17:5 and εἰς ὃν in 2 Pet 1:17. Ibid., 624, sees these as interchangeable usages with εὐδοκέω; Arndt and Gingrich, *Greek-English Lexicon*, 319, article on εὐδοκέω agree.
13. 2 Pet 1:14; John 21:18–19.
14. Soards, "1 Peter, 2 Peter, and Jude," 3840.
15. Kraftchick, *Jude, 2 Peter*, 72.
16. *Das neue Testament*, 737, assigns it the date about 75 CE; it should be noted that they also give the date 50–55 to 1 Pet, which 2 Pet mentions, and they give the date 71 to Matt, which 2 Pet quotes. One would have to accept these latter two composition dates in order to give such an early date to *Second Peter*.

The Greek of 2 *Peter* differs from that of any other part of the New Testament. It is not the familiar direct Attic style but the "Asian" style "characterized by a loaded, verbose, high-sounding manner of expression leaning toward the novel and bizarre, and careless about violating classic ideals of simplicity."[17] Despite this linguistic elaborateness, the author and, presumably, the intended readership are world-denying; the author accuses the opponents of indulging in lust and being attracted to the world.[18] One thing that was important about the letter in antiquity was that the Greek was so different from that of *First Peter*, which was accepted as a work of the apostle, that it could not have been by the same person, even making allowances for a secretary or translator. Consequently, the work was not unqualifiedly accepted as scripture. As noted, Eusebius said it was not part of the canon, though it seemed to be a profitable read to many, and listed it a disputed work. Similarly the Muratorian Canon did not list the letter as scripture, and Origen considered it a disputed work.[19]

## The Sociology of Written Communication

*Second Peter* highlights written communication in a way that other New Testament works do not. Other works allude to previous writings, especially by citing passages of the Hebrew Bible. And they quote oral tradition, as when Paul writes out creedal, poetic, and ritual texts. As noted in the introductions to the *Gospel of Matthew* and the *Gospel of Luke*, those two books incorporated most of the *Gospel of Mark* and numerous sayings from "Q," reformulating them in the process. *Second Peter*, however, alludes to published Christian writings as authoritative, at a point in time in which they were fairly recent, not ancient materials as were the Hebrew Scriptures. Specifically, the author has in mind prophetic statements in recognized Christian writings. Following up the citation of Matthew's account of the Transfiguration, the author writes "Especially be aware of this: that no prophecy of scripture comes from a private interpretation; for prophecy was never borne by human will, but humans borne by the Holy Spirit spoke from God."[20] Moreover, the author warns against interpretations of the Christian writings that depart from the Christian community's shared knowledge. Specific reference is made to interpreting the writings of Paul: "as our beloved brother Paul also wrote you, according to the wisdom given to him, as speaking in all the letters indeed about these things in them, in which there are some things hard to understand, which the ignorant and unstable twist, as also the other scriptures, to their own destruction."[21]

A little-known facet of sociological theory addresses this kind of situation. In his general treatise on sociology, Georg Simmel included an "Excursus on Written

17. Reicke, *Epistles of James, Peter, and Jude*, 146–47.
18. Desjardins, "Portrayal of the Dissidents."
19. Eusebius, *Ecclesiastical History*, 3:3:1; ibid., 3:25:3:4; Kraftchick, *Jude, 2 Peter*, 71.
20. 2 Pet 1:20–21.
21. 2 Pet 3:15b–16.

Communication" within a chapter on secrecy.[22] He noted that the essence of writing is the opposite of secrecy; the general process of writing conveys rather than withholds knowledge. However, there is much that is *not* conveyed in writing that would normally be conveyed in speech.

> In an immediate presence every participant in interaction gives the other more than the mere contents of one's words; one thereby sees one's counterpart and plunges into the sphere of a state of mind that is not at all expressible in words, feels the thousand nuances in the emphasis and in the rhythm of its expression....[23]

The written form strips away much that contributes to a thought in the mind of the writer; it isolates a facet of a transitory thought and bestows a permanent form onto it. Thus while a given written communication is necessarily ambiguous in some respects, in its form it has a certain fixity and security. The reader can consequently not be satisfied "with the purely logical sense of a word"; "indeed countless times one can be not at all satisfied because, in order even to simply grasp the logical meaning it requires more than the logical meaning."[24] A written communication becomes a site of interpretation and misunderstanding. What is clear in writing may be clearer than if spoken, but what is ambiguous is also more ambiguous than if spoken.

So what can the author of *Second Peter* mean by the words, "no prophecy of scripture is a matter of one's own interpretation"? It is not that there is no ambiguity in a text, since a written text discloses and withholds at the same time, but that the interpretation of a text is not purely individual. Texts are identified as authoritative ones from a specific time and place, within a specific perspective—the author of *2 Peter* was aware of that in the course of deleting allusions to non-authoritative texts from what was taken over from the *Letter of Jude*. But texts are also interpreted in an authoritative way from a specific time and place and within a specific perspective. Such complexes of time and place are tantamount to collective identities. This takes us back to the matter of boundary maintenance, which was discussed in the introduction to the *Letter of Jude*.

---

22. Simmel, *Sociology*, 342–45.
23. Ibid., 343.
24. Ibid., 344.

## English Translation

## Second Pseudonymous Letter of Peter

[Textual material dependent on the *Letter of Jude* is <u>underlined</u>.]

1 ¹Simon Peter,²⁵ <u>slave</u> and apostle <u>of Jesus, Messiah</u>, to those receiving, equal to our receiving, the faith in the justice of our God and of our savior Jesus, Messiah: ²Grace <u>and peace to you, for increasing</u> in the knowledge of God and our Lord Jesus.²⁶

³Whereas His divine power has bestowed on us all that contributes to life and piety through the knowledge of the one who called us by his own glory and excellence, ⁴through which the precious and tremendous promises have been given to us, may you become partakers in the divine nature through them, escaping corruption from worldly passions. ⁵And making <u>every effort</u> for this very reason, add virtue to your faith, and knowledge to your virtue, ⁶self-control to your knowledge, fortitude to your self-control, piety to your fortitude, ⁷and affection for others to your piety, and *Christian* love to your affection for others.²⁷ ⁸For these, being yours and abounding, will make you neither useless nor unproductive for the knowledge of our Lord Jesus, Messiah; ⁹for not having these, one who is short-sighted is blind, accepting forgetfulness of the cleansing of one's sins in the past. ¹⁰Therefore, brothers and sisters, be more zealous to make your calling and election firm; for when doing that you will never stumble; ¹¹for thereby the entry into the eternal kingdom of our Lord and savior Jesus, the Messiah, will be generously furnished you.

¹²Therefore I purpose to <u>remind you</u> continually about these matters, even though you know them and have been established in the truth that is present. ¹³And while I am in this tent, I consider it right to arouse you by a reminder, ¹⁴knowing that the shedding of my tent is imminent, as indeed our Lord Jesus, Messiah, made clear to me;²⁸ ¹⁵and after my exodus too I will be eager that you will be remembering these things.

¹⁶For we did not reveal the power and coming of our Lord Jesus, Messiah, to you, following mythical artifice,²⁹ but becoming eyewitnesses of his majesty.

---

25. The ancient manuscript evidence is equally strong for the reading "Simon Peter" and "Symeon Peter"—Metzger, *Textual Commentary*, 699.

26. 2 Pet makes phrases from 1 Pet and Jude more elaborate. "Peter" becomes "Simon Peter." "Apostle" from 1 Pet is supplemented by "slave" from Jude. "May grace and peace increase for you" becomes "Grade and peace to you, for increasing in...."

27. A literal translation of "affection for others" would be "brotherly love"; "*Christian* love" is the Greek *agape*. Palmer, "Second Peter 1:5–7," suggests this translation: "And for this reason use your utmost care to join with your faith virtue, and with virtue knowledge, and with knowledge self-control, and with self-control patience, and patience holiness, and with holiness brotherly affection, and with brotherly affection *Christian* love."

28. This is usually taken to be a reference to John 21:19.

29. In the Greek, "myths" is the noun, and it is modified by a participle from the verb meaning

¹⁷For he was receiving honor and glory from God the Father when a voice was borne to him as from the majesty of glory: "This is my beloved son, in whom I am well pleased."³⁰ ¹⁸And we heard this voice borne from heaven when we were with him on the holy mountain. ¹⁹And we have a most reliable prophetic statement, which you should heed well, as to a lamp shining in a gloomy place, until the day dawns and the morning star³¹ rises in your hearts.³²

²⁰Especially be aware of this: that no prophecy of scripture comes from a private interpretation; ²¹for prophecy was never borne by human will, but humans borne by the Holy Spirit spoke from God.³³ 2 ¹And false prophets too came among the people, just as there will be false teachers among you who will smuggle in destructive heresies, denying the master who redeemed them, bringing themselves to be quickly <u>destroyed</u>.³⁴ ²And many will pursue their passions, for which the way of truth will be reviled; ³and in avarice they will exploit you with contrived sayings; the judgment against them is not long delayed, and their destruction does not lie dormant.

⁴For if God did not spare the sinning <u>angels</u> but handed them over imprisoned in Tartarus³⁵ by the shackles of <u>the dark place</u> , <u>kept</u> for condemnation; ⁵and if He did not spare the archaic world, but protected Noah, the eighth,³⁶ a herald of justice, when bringing a deluge to the world of the ungodly; ⁶and if He condemned the <u>cities</u> of <u>Sodom</u> and <u>Gomorra</u> to ruin,³⁷ reducing them to ashes, making an example of what will happen to the ungodly; ⁷and if He rescued righteous Lot who was troubled by the behavior of people lawless in their sensuality,³⁸ ⁸for when dwelling among them, the just man tortured his

---

both "to deceive" and to devise in a subtle manner.

30. Matt 17:5, the Matthean version of the Transfiguration. Neyrey, "Apocalyptic Use of the Transfiguration," 515, understands the verse as a Parousia-prophecy; he notes that the Ethiopic version of the *Apocalypse of Peter* relates the Transfiguration to the Second Coming—ibid., 512.

31. D. Harrington, "Jude and 2 Peter," 257, points to Rev 22:16, which has Jesus saying he is "the bright star of the morning."

32. Callan, "Note on 2 Peter 1:19–20," proposes that the phrase "in your hearts" modifies the following verbal form, "knowing," in verse 20. Porter and Pitts, "τοῦτο πρῶτον γινώσκοντες ὅτι," point to "I wish you to know that . . . " as a conventional "disclosure formula" that nowhere else has a propositional phrase modifying "know"; hence, they argue that the phrase modifies the previous verb, "spring up."

33. Verses 20 and 21 should not be paragraphed with verses 16–18; they take up a new topic, false prophecy, which the beginning of chapter 2 elaborates.

34. Literally, "bringing themselves to a quick destruction." The translation rephrases it slightly so that the stem taken from Jude 5 could be underlined.

35. "Imprisoned in Tartarus" is a Greek participle, ταρταρώσας, from the verb meaning to keep captive in Tartarus, a subterranean hell lower than Hades where divine punishment was meted out. This parallels Jude 6 and refers to Gen 6:1–4; see D. Harrington, "Jude and 2 Peter," 265.

36. Counting Noah's wife, three sons, and three daughters-in-law, Noah himself was the eighth person saved from the flood in Gen 8.

37. Gen 19:24; Jude 7.

38. Gen 19:1–16. Makujima, "'Trouble' with Lot," observes that others had described Lot as righteous: Wis 10:6; Philo, *De Vita Moses,* 57–59; 1 Clement 11:1; and the midrash Genesis Rabbah

just soul with what he saw and heard day by day, lawless deeds; ⁹then the Lord knows how to rescue the pious from trial but <u>keep</u> the unjust punished at <u>judgment day</u>,³⁹ ¹⁰especially those going <u>after flesh</u> in a passion of corruption and despising <u>authority</u>. Impudent people, arrogant, they do not tremble when <u>reviling the glorious ones</u>,⁴⁰ ¹¹while angels, who are stronger and more powerful, do not bring <u>a reviling judgment</u> from the Lord against them.⁴¹ ¹²<u>But these people</u>, <u>like mindless animals, by nature</u> born for capture and extermination, <u>reviling</u> in matters they do not understand, also to <u>be exterminated</u> in their corruption;⁴² ¹³defrauded of the wages of fraud; led along luxury lane in a day, like <u>stains</u> and blemishes luxuriating in their seductions, <u>feasting together with you</u>;⁴³ ¹⁴having eyes wide open for a paramour and restless for sin; enticing unstable souls; having a heart athleticized in greed; children of a curse; ¹⁵abandoning the straight way they <u>misled</u> themselves, following <u>the way of Balaam</u> son of Bosor, who loved an unjust wage ¹⁶but had a rebuke for his own transgression; a voiceless beast of burden hindered the madness of the prophet by speaking out in a human voice.⁴⁴

¹⁷These people, <u>for</u> whom <u>the black of darkness has been reserved</u>,⁴⁵ are springs without water and mists driven by a cyclone. ¹⁸For while proclaiming puffed worthlessness, with passions, with sensualities of the flesh, they seduce those scarcely escaping the ones who live in error; ¹⁹these people are promising them freedom while existing as slaves of corruption themselves. For to that which one succumbs, to that has one been enslaved. ²⁰For if, by knowledge of our Lord and savior Jesus, Messiah, having escaped the world's contaminations but again, having become entangled in them, being defeated, the end states become worse for them than the first.⁴⁶ ²¹For it would be better for them not to know the way of justice than knowingly turn away from the sacred command that was handed down to them. ²²What is in the true prov-

---

49:13 and Pirqe Rabbi Eliezar 25. He points to the Septuagint version of Gen 19:16, which he punctuates differently from the modern editions; in translation it reads "Getting up, take your wife and two daughters whom you have, and go out lest you be destroyed. And they were troubled by the lawlessness of the city." It is the being troubled by the lawlessness of the city that, Makujima suggests, inspired the author of 2 Pet and the others to describe Lot as righteous.

39. Jude 6.

40. Jude 7–8.

41. Jude 9. Kraus, "Παρὰ κυρίου, παρὰ κυρίῳ oder *omit*," makes a text critical argument for παρὰ κυρίῳ, "before the Lord" (so RSV and *Das neue Testament*), while the majority of the editorial committee of the United Bible Society edition favored παρὰ κυρίου, "from the Lord," as the more difficult meaning. Both fit the sense of Jude 9, where the Archangel Michael did not dare to make a judgment that should be left to God.

42. Jude 10.

43. Jude 12.

44. Num 22:28–30.

45. Jude 13.

46. Matt 12:45b and Luke 11:26b: " . . . and the end states of that person become worse than the first."

erb has come upon them: "A dog returned to its own vomit,"⁴⁷ and "A washed sow wallowing in mud."

3 ¹Beloved, I am writing this second letter to you; in them I am stirring you up a pure conscience with a reminder, ²to recall the words spoken by the holy prophets and the commandment of the Lord and savior spoken by your apostles,⁴⁸ ³knowing this from the outset, that <u>in the last</u> days <u>scoffers</u> will come with their scoffing, <u>going according to their</u> own <u>passions</u>⁴⁹ ⁴and saying, "Where is the promise of his coming? For from when the fathers fell asleep, all things remain the same from the beginning of creation." ⁵For this escapes notice when they want it to: that long ago there were heavens, and land formed from and though water at the word of God; ⁶then through them the world was destroyed by a deluge of water; ⁷but now the heavens and the land have been stored up for fire by that same word, saved for a day of judgment and destruction of ungodly humans.⁵⁰

⁸Now let it not escape your notice, beloved, that one day with the Lord is like a thousand years and a thousand years like one day.⁵¹ ⁹The Lord in the promise is not delaying,⁵² as some regard delay, but He is being patient with you, not wanting to destroy some but to make allowance for all near repentance.⁵³ ¹⁰The day of the Lord will have come like a thief,⁵⁴ when the heavens will be gone with a rush; the elements, burned up, will dissolve; and the earth will be found according to the works upon it.⁵⁵ ¹¹When all these are

---

47. Prov 26:11, not using the wording of the Septuagint.

48. Jude 17. Zmijewski, "Apostolische *paradosis* und Pseudepigraphie," 168, points to believing in the coming of Christ as the commandment in question, and that it comes not from one apostle, as if the author were speaking as Peter alone, but through "your apostles," a collective authority with which the readers are associated—ibid., 166–67. Talbert, "II Peter and the Delay," 139, suggests the commandment in question "does not refer to a single injunction but to the Christian tradition or revelation"; he goes on to say that in particular it was a matter of the "interrelation of the last judgment and ethical living."

49. Jude 18.

50. The author of 2 Pet accepts the statement, "all continues just as it was," but accepts it as a statement of God's consistent action, not a critique. Given God's past acts of punishment, something similar is in store for the future—Meier, "2 Peter 3:3–7."

51. The idea but little of the wording resembles Ps 90:4 (and 89:4 in the Septuagint).

52. The idea but not the wording resembles Hab 2:3.

53. In *De Sera Numinis Vindicta*, Plutarch summarizes and opposes an Epicurean polemic against divine providence, according to Neyrey, "Form and Background," 411; the Epicureans would have God free from trouble (providence), and the wise man who strives for trouble-free calm must reject all that would destroy that calm. The foremost enemy of that calm would be a judging deity, and intricately linked with such a judgment is an afterlife and postmortem retribution. Neyrey sees verse 3:9 as a response to that argument. In a parallel to Wis 12:10, according to Neyrey, ibid., 422, the author sees the denial of providence as a slander against the divine.

54. The reference to the day of the Lord coming like a thief resembles Rev 3:3 more than Rev 16:15, 1 Thess 5:2, Matt 24:43–44, or Luke 12:39–40.

55. Both modern and ancient scholars have taken the verb εὑρεθήσεται, "will be found," to be a scribal error, but Danker, "II Peter 3:10," proposes that five words before it κατά, "according to," had

destroyed in this way, what kind of people is it necessary to be,[56] with holy ways of life and piety [12]that anticipate[57] and hasten the coming of the day of God, on account of which the heavens, burning, will be destroyed and the elements, aflame, will dissolve! [13]So we await, according to His promise, new heavens and a new earth where justice dwells.[58]

[14]Therefore, beloved, awaiting these things, be eager to be found in peace by him, without blemish and blameless, [15]and regard the patience of our Lord as salvation, as our beloved brother Paul also wrote you, according to the wisdom given to him, [16]as speaking in all the letters indeed about these things in them, in which there are some things hard to understand, which the ignorant and unstable twist, as also the other scriptures, to their own destruction. [17]You therefore, beloved, having advance knowledge, guard against being carried away by the error of unprincipled people and losing your grip; [18]but grow in the love and knowledge of our Lord and savior Jesus, Messiah. To him be the glory, both now and up to the day of eternity. Amen.

---

been replaced by καὶ, "and," in a scribal error. His reconstruction would translate "and on earth it will happen according to the works on it." In support of his reconstruction, Danker points to a parallel passage in the non-canonical *Psalm of Solomon* 17:10.

56. Ancient manuscript variations disagree on the reading. The translation presupposes no pronoun as the subject of "to be," following P[72*] and "Vaticanus" (B); other good manuscript witnesses have the pronoun "you," which would make the translation "must you be" (so RSV "ought you be" and *Das neue Testament*). See Metzger, *Textual Commentary*, 707.

57. "Anticipate," προσδοκῶντες, is the participial form of the same verb translated as "await" later in the sentence and in verse 14. In English, one does not speak of a way of life "awaiting."

58. Isa 65:17 and 66:22 refer to new heavens (in the plural, though singular in the Septuagint) and a new earth, and Rev 21:1 refers to a new heaven (in the singular) and a new earth.

# References

## Abbreviations of Selected Periodicals

| | |
|---|---|
| *AJS* | *American Journal of Sociology* |
| *CBQ* | *Catholic Biblical Quarterly* |
| *ExpTim* | *Expository Times* |
| *HTR* | *Harvard Theological Review* |
| *JBL* | *Journal of Biblical Literature* |
| *JSNT* | *Journal for the Study of the New Testament* |
| *JSSR* | *Journal for the Scientific Study of Religion* |
| *JTS* | *Journal of Theological Studies* |
| *NovT* | *Novum Testamentum* |
| *NTS* | *New Testament Studies* |
| *VC* | *Vigiliae Christianae* |
| *ZNW* | *Zeitschrift für die neutestamentliche Wissenschaft* |

*1 Enoch*. Translated by R.H. Charles. http://www.nnu.edu/index.php?id=2126, retrieved March 5, 2015.

Aarde, A.G. van. "The Struggle against Heresy in the Thessalonian Correspondence and the Origin of the Apostolic Tradition." In *The Thessalonian Correspondence*, edited by Raymond F. Collins, 418-25. Leuven: Leuven University Press, 1990.

Achtemeier, Paul J. *1 Peter: A Commentary on First Peter*. Minneapolis: Fortress, 1996.

Albl, Martin C. "'Are Any among You Sick?' The Health Care System in the Letter of James." *JBL* 121 (2002) 131–43.

*Apostolic Constitutions*. www.ccel.org/ccel/schaff/anf07.ix.ii.i.hml. Accessed 12-4-2016.

Aristotle. *The Nicomachean Ethics*. Translated by H. Rackham, 2nd ed. Cambridge, MA: Harvard University Press, 1934.

Arndt, William F., and F. William Gingrich. *A Greek-English Lexicon of the New Testament and other Early Christian Literature*, 2nd edition. Chicago: University of Chicago Press, 1979.

Aus, Roger D. "God's Plan and God's Power: Isaiah 66 and the Restraining Factors of 2 Thess 2:6–7." *JBL* 96 (1977) 537–53.

———. "The Relevance of Isa. 66:7 to Revelation 12 and 2 Thessalonians." *ZNW* 67 (1976) 252–68.

Balch, David L. "Early Christian Criticism of Patriarchal Authority: 1 Peter 2:11—3:12." *Union Seminary Quarterly Review* 39 (1984) 161–73.

Bampfylde, G. "John XIX 28: A Case for a Different Translation." *NovT* 11 (1969) 247–60.

Barnouin, Michel. "Les problèmes de traduction concernent II Thes ii.6-7." *NTS* 23 (1977) 482–98.

Barrett, C.K. *The Gospel according to St. John: An Introduction with Commentary and Notes on the Greek Text*, 2nd ed. Philadelphia: Westminster, 1978.

Bartholomä, Philipp F. "Did Jesus Save the People Out of Egypt? A Re-examination of a Textual Problem in Jude 5." *NovT* 50 (2008) 143–58.

Bassler, Jouette M. "The Enigmatic Sign: 2 Thessalonians 1:5." *CBQ* 46 (1984) 496–510.

Batten, Alicia J. "The Characterization of the Rich in James 5." In *To Set at Liberty: Essays on Early Christianity and its Social World in Honor of John H. Elliott*, edited by Stephen K. Black, 45-61. Sheffield, UK: Sheffield Phoenix.

Bauckham, Richard. *James: Wisdom of James, Disciple of Jesus the Sage*. London: Routledge, 1999.

———. *Jude and the Relatives of Jesus in the Early Church*. London: T. & T. Clark, 2004.

Berger, Peter L., and Thomas Luckmann. *The Social Construction of Reality: A Treatise in the Sociology of Knowledge*. Garden City, NY: Doubleday, 1966.

Best, Ernest. "1 Peter II 4–10: A Reconsideration." *NovT* 11 (1969) 70–93.

Best, Joel. "Social Problems." In *Handbook of Symbolic Interactionism*, edited by Larry T. Reynolds and Nancy J. Herman-Kinney, 981–96. Lanham, MD: Rowman & Littlefield (AltaMira), 2003.

Betz, Otto. "Der Katechon." *NTS* 9 (1962) 276–91.

Bienfait, Agathe. "Zeichen und Wunder. Über die Funktion der Selig- und Heiligsprechenungen in der katholischer Kirche." *Kölner Zeitschrift für Soziologie und Sozialpsychologie* 58 (2008) 1–22.

Black, Alan W. "A Marriage Model of Church Mergers." *Sociological Analysis* 49 (1988) 281–92.

———. "Organizational Imagery and Interdenominational Mergers." *British Journal of Sociology* 41 (1990) 105–27.

Blasi, Anthony J. "Dialecticizing the Types." *Sociological Analysis* 42 (1981) 163–72.

———. *Making Charisma: The Social Construction of Paul's Public Image*. New Brunswick, NJ: Transaction, 1991.

———. *A Sociology of Johannine Christianity*. Lewiston, NY: Edwin Mellen, 1996.

Blass, Friedrich, and Albert Debrunner. *A Greek Grammar of the New Testament and Other Early Christian Literature*. Translated and edited by Robert W. Funk. Chicago: University of Chicago Press, 1961.

Blumer, Herbert. "Social Problems as Collective Behavior." *Social Problems* 18 (1971) 298–306.

Brewer, Raymond R. "Revelation 4:6 and Translations Thereof." *JBL* 71 (1952) 227–31.

Brodie, Thomas C. *The Quest for the Origin of John's Gospel A Source-Oriented Approach*. New York: Oxford University Press, 1993.

Broer, Ingo. "Knowledge of Palestine in the Fourth Gospel?" In *Jesus in Johannine Tradition*, edited by Robert T. Fortna and Tom Thatcher, 83–90. Louisville: Westminster John Knox, 2001.

Brown, Jeannine K. "Just a Busybody? A Look at the Greco-Roman Topos of Meddling for Defining ἀλλοτριεπίσκοπος in 1 Peter 4.15." *JBL* 125 (2006) 549–68.

# References

Brown, Raymond E. *The Community of the Beloved Disciple: The Life, Loves, and Hates of an Individual Church in New Testament Times.* New York: Paulist, 1979.

———. "The Dead Sea Scrolls and the New Testament." In *John and the Dead Sea Scrolls*, edited by James H. Charlesworth, 108. New York: Crossroad, 1991.

———. *The Epistles of John.* New York: Doubleday, 1982.

———. *The Gospel According to John (i–xii).* New York: Doubleday, 1966.

———. *The Gospel According to John (xiii–xxi).* New York: Doubleday, 1970.

———. "Incidents that are Units in the Synoptic Gospels, but Dispersed in St. John." *CBQ* 23 (1963) 143–60.

Brownlee, William H. "Whence the Gospel According to John?" In *John and the Dead Sea Scrolls*, edited by James H. Charlesworth, 166–94. New York: Crossroad, 1991.

Burkett, Delbert. "Two Accounts of Lazarus' Resurrection in John 11." *NovT* 36 (1994) 209–32.

Callan, Terrance. "A Note on 2 Peter 1:19–20." *JBL* 125 (2006) 143–50.

Cao, Nanlai. "The Church as a Surrogate Family for Working Class Immigrant Chinese Youth: An Ethnography of Segmented Assimilation." *Sociology of Religion* 66 (2005) 183–200.

Caragounis, Chrys C. "What Did Jesus Mean by τὴν ἀρχήν in John 8:25?" *NovT* 49 (2007) 129–47.

Carroll, Kenneth L. "The Fourth Gospel and the Exclusion of Christians from the Synagogue." *Bulletin of the John Rylands Library* 40 (1957) 19–32.

Carson, D.A. "Syntactical and Text-critical Observations on John 20:30–31: One More Round on the Purpose of the Fourth Gospel." *JBL* 124 (2005) 693–714.

Charlesworth, James H. *The Beloved Disciple: Whose Witness Validates the Gospel of John?* Valley Forge, PA: Trinity, 1995.

Chaves, Mark, and John R. Sutton. "Organizational Consolidation in American Protestant Denominations, 1890–1990." *JSSR* 43 (2004) 51–66.

Chilton, Bruce. "John XII 34 and Targum Isaiah LII 13." *NovT* 22 (1980) 176–78.

Christiano, Kevin J., et al. *Sociology of Religion: Contemporary Developments,* 2nd ed. Lanham, MD: Rowman & Littlefield, 2008.

Collins, Adela Yarbro. "Dating the Apocalypse of John." *Biblical Research* 26 (1981) 33–45.

———. "Vilification and Self-definition in the Book of Revelation." *HTR* 79 (1986) 308–20.

Collins, J.J. *The Apocalyptic Imagination.* New York: Crossroad, 1987.

Collins, Raymond F. *Letters That Paul Did Not Write: The Epistle to the Hebrews and the Pauline Pseudepigrapha.* Wilmington, DE: Michael Glazier, 1988.

———. "Proverbial Sayings in John's Gospel." In *These Things Have Been Written: Studies on the Fourth Gospel*, edited by Raymond F. Collins, 128–50. Leuven: Peeters/Grand Rapids: Eerdmans, 1990.

———. "Representative Figures." In *These Things Have Been Written: Studies on the Fourth Gospel*, edited by Raymond F. Collins, 1–45. Leuven: Peeters/Grand Rapids: Eerdmans, 1990.

Connor, Phillip. "Increase or Decrease? The Impact of the International Migratory Event on Immigrant Religious Participation." *JSSR* 47 (2008) 243–57.

———. "International Migration and Religious Participation. The Mediating Impact of Individual and Contextual Effects. *Sociological Forum* 24 (2009) 779–803.

Cook, David. "1 Peter iii.20: An Unnecessary Problem." *JTS* 31 (1980) 72–78.

Danker, Frederick W. "II Peter 3:10 and Psalm of Solomon 17:10." *ZNW* 53 (1962) 82–86.

Derrett, J. Duncan M. "Law in the New Testament: The Story of the Woman Taken in Adultery." *NTS* (1963–64) 1–26.

## References

deSilva, David A. "The Revelation to John: A Case Study in Apocalyptic Propaganda and the Maintenance of Sectarian Identity." *Sociological Analysis* 53 (1992) 375–95.

Desjardins, Michel. "The Portrayal of the Dissidents in 2 Peter and Jude: Does it Tell Us More about the 'Godly' than the 'Ungodly'?" *JSNT* 30 (1987) 89–102.

Dewailly, Louis-Marie. "Course et gloire de la parole (II Thess., III,1)." *Revue Biblique* 71 (1964) 25–41.

Dhooghe, Jos. "Le protestantisme en Belgique." *Recherches sociologique* 16 (1985) 311–32.

Diel, Claudia, and Matthias Koenig. "Religiosität türkischer Migranten im Generationenverlauf: Ein Befund und einige Erklärungsversuche." *Zeitschrift für Soziologie* 38 (2009) 300–19.

Dimaggio, Paul J., and Walter W. Powell. "The Iron Cage Revisited: Institutional Isomorphism and Collective Rationality in Organizational Fields." *American Sociological Review* 48 (1983) 147–60.

Donelson, Lewis R. "Gathering Apostolic Voices: Who Wrote 1 and 2 Peter and Jude?" In *Reading 1–2 Peter and Jude: A Resource for Students*, edited by Eric F. Mason and Troy W. Martin, 11–26. Atlanta: Society of Biblical Literature, 2014.

Dornbusch, Sanford M., and Roger Irle. "The Failure of Presbyterian Union." *AJS* 64 (1959) 352–56.

Douglas, Mary. *Natural Symbols: Explorations in Cosmology*. London: Barrie & Rockliff, 1970.

Durkheim, Émile. *The Rules of Sociological Method*. Translated by W.D. Halls. New York: Free Press/Macmillan, 1982.

Ebaugh, Helen Rose, and Janet Saltzman Chafetz. "Introduction." In *Religion and the New Immigrants: Continuities and Adaptations in Immigrant Congregations*, edited by Helen Rose Ebaugh and Janet Saltzman Chafetz, 13–28. Walnut Creek, CA: AltaMira, 2000.

Eberts, Harry W. Jr., and Paul R. Eberts. *The Early Jesus Movement and Its Parties: A New Way to Look at the New Testament*. New York, YBK, 2009.

Ehrman, Bart D. "Heracleon, Origen, and the Text of the Fourth Gospel." *VC* 47 (1991) 105–18.

Elliott, John H. *Conflict, Community, and Honor: 1 Peter in Social-Scientific Perspective*. Eugene, OR: Cascade, 2007.

———. "The Epistle of James in Rhetorical and Social Scientific Perspective: Holiness-wholeness and Patterns of Replication." *Biblical Theology Bulletin* 23 (1993) 71–81.

———. *A Home for the Homeless: A Sociological Exegesis of 1 Peter, Its Situation and Strategy*. Philadelphia: Fortress, 1981.

Eubank, Nathan. "Almsgiving as 'the Commandment': A Note on 1 Timothy 6.6–19." *NTS* 58 (2011) 144–50.

Eusebius of Caesarea. *Ecclesiastical History*. Translated by Kirsop Lake. Cambridge, MA: Harvard University Press, 1998.

Fee, Gordon D. "Once More—John 7:37–39." *ExpTim* 89 (1978) 116–18.

Fekkes III, Jan. "'His Bride Has Prepared Herself': Revelation 19–21 and Isaian Mystical Imagery." *JBL* 109 (1990) 269–87.

Felton, Tom, and Tom Thatcher. "Stylometry and the Signs Gospel." In *Jesus in Johannine Tradition*, edited by Robert T. Fortna and Tom Thatcher, 209–18. Louisville: Westminster John Knox, 2001.

Fiore, Benjamin. *The Pastoral Epistles: First Timothy. Second Timothy. Titus*. Collegeville, MN: Liturgical (Michael Glazier), 2007.

Ford, Josephine Massyngberde. "'Mingled blood' from the Side of Christ (John XIX.34)." *NTS* 15 (1969) 337–38.

———. "A Note on Proto-montanism in the Pastoral Epistles." *NTS* 17 (1971) 338–46.

———. *Revelation: Introduction, Translation and Commentary*. Garden City, NY: Doubleday, 1975.

Förster, Hans. "Die syntaktische Funktion von ὅτι in Joh 8.47." *NTS* 62 (2016) 157–66.

———. "Überlegungen zur Grammatik von Joh 8.25 in Lichte der handschriftlichen Überlieferung." *ZNW* 107 (2016) 1–29.

Fortna, Robert T. *The Fourth Gospel and Its Predecessor*. Edinburgh: T. & T. Clark, 1988.

Freed, Edwin D. *Old Testament Quotations in the Gospel of John*. Leiden: Brill, 1965.

Friesen, Steven J. "Myth and Symbolic Resistance in Revelation 13." *JBL* 123 (2004) 281–313.

———. "Satan's Throne, Imperial Cults and the Social Settings of Revelation." *JSNT* 27 (2005) 351–73.

Fry, C. Luther. *The New and Old Immigrant on the Land: A Study of Americanization and the Church*. New York: Doran, 1922.

Funk, Robert W. "Papyrus Bodmer II (P66) and John 8.25." *HTR* 51 (1958) 95–100.

Furfey, Paul Hanly. "The Mystery of Lawlessness (2 Thess 2,7)." *CBQ* 8 (1946) 179–91.

Gaborieau, Marc. "Le cult des saints chez les Musulmans au Népal et en Inde du Nord." *Social Compass* 25 (1978) 477–94.

Garfinkel, Harold. "Conditions of Successful Degradation Ceremonies." *AJS* 61 (1956) 420–24.

Garrow, Alan J.P. *Revelation*. London: Routledge, 1997.

*The Gospel of Peter*. Translated by Raymond E. Brown. http://www.earlychristianwritings.com/text/gospelpeter-brown.html, retrieved 2-28-2015.

Gray, Patrick. "Athenian Curiosity (Acts 17:21)." *NovT* 47 (2005) 109–16.

*Greek New Testament, Third Edition*. Edited by Kurt Aland et al. New York: United Bible Societies 1975.

Green, Michael. *The Second Epistle General of Peter and the General Epistle of Jude: An Introduction and Commentary*. Grand Rapids: Eerdmans, 1968.

Gundry, Robert H., and Russell W. Howell. "The Sense and Syntax of John 3:14–17 With Special Reference to the Use of οὕτως . . . ὥστε in John 3.16." *NovT* 41 (1999) 24–39.

Gunther, John J. "The Alexandrian Epistle of Jude." *NTS* 30 (1984) 549–62.

Gurvitch, Georges. "Sociologie en profondeur." In *Traité de Sociologie, Tome premier*, edited by Georges Gurvitch, 157–71. Paris: Presses Universitaires de France, 1958.

———. *Sociology of Law*. London: Routledge & Kegan Paul, 1947.

Haenchen, Ernst. *John 1: A Commentary on the Gospel of John Chapters 1–6*. Philadelphia: Fortress, 1984.

Hagan, Jacqueline Maria, and Helen Rose Ebaugh. "Calling Upon the Sacred: Migrants' Use of Religion in the Migration Process." *International Migration Review* 37 (2003) 1145–53.

Hanson, Anthony T. "John's Citation of Psalm lxxxii. John x.33–6." *NTS* 11 (1965) 158–62.

———. "John's Citation of Psalm lxxxii Reconsidered." *NTS* 13 (1967) 363–67.

Harrill, J Albert. "The Vice of Slave Dealers in Greco-Roman Society: The Use of a Topos in 1 Timothy 1:10." *JBL* 118 (1999) 97–122.

Harrington, Daniel J. "Jude and 2 Peter." In *1 Peter: Jude and 2 Peter*, edited by Donald P. Senior and Daniel J. Harrington, 161–299. Collegeville, MN: Liturgical (Michael Glazier), 2003.

Harrington, Wilfrid J. *Revelation*. Collegeville, MN: Liturgical (Michael Glazier), 1993.

Hartin, Patrick J. *James*. Collegeville, MN: Liturgical (Michael Glazier), 2003.

Hartmann, Gert. "Die Vorlage der Osterberichte in Joh 20." *ZNW* 55 (1964) 197–220.

Hawley, Amos. "Human Ecology." In *International Encyclopedia of the Social Sciences,* vol. 4, edited by David L. Sills, 328–37. New York: Macmillan, 1968.

# References

Hedrick, Charles W. "Vestigial Scenes in John: Settings without Dramatization." *NovT* 47 (2005) 354–66.

Hemer, Colin J. *The Letters to the Seven Churches of Asia in their Local Setting*. Grand Rapids: Eerdmans, 2001.

Hengel, Martin. *The Johannine Question*. London: SCM/Philadelphia: Trinity, 1989.

Hervieu-Léger, Danièle. *Religion as a Chain of Memory*. New Brunswick, NJ: Rutgers University Press, 2000.

———. "Secularization and Religious Modernity in Western Europe." In *Religion, Mobilization, and Social Action*, edited by Anson Shupe and Bronislaw Misztal, 15–31. Westport, CT: Praeger, 1998.

Hill, John Spencer. "τὰ βαΐα τῶν φοινίκων (John 12.:13): Pleonasm or Prolepsis?" *JBL* 101 (1982) 133–35.

Hirschman, Charles. "The Role of Religion in the Origins and Adaptation of Immigrant Groups in the United States." *International Migration Review* 38 (2004) 1206–34.

Horrell, David G. "'Honour Everyone . . .' (1 Peter 2.17): The Social Strategy of 1 Peter and its Significance for Early Christianity." In *To Set at Liberty: Essays on Early Christianity and its Social World in Honor of John H. Elliott*, edited by Stephen K. Black. Sheffield, UK: Sheffield Phoenix, 192–210.

———. "The Label Χριστιανός: 1 Peter 4:16 and the Formation of Christian Identity." *JBL* 126 (2007) 361–81.

———. "The Product of a Petrine Circle? A Reassessment of the Origin and Character of 1 Peter." *JSNT* 86 (2002) 29–60.

Horvath, Tibor. "3 Jn 11b: An Early Ecumenical Creed?" *ExpTim* 85 (1974) 339–40.

Houlden, J.L. *The Pastoral Epistles: 1 and 2 Timothy, Titus*. Harmondsworth, UK: Penguin, 1976.

Hulster, Izaak J. de. "The Two Angels in John 20.12: An Egyptian Icon of Resurrection." *NTS* 59 (2013) 20–49.

Hultin, Jeremy F. "The Literary Relationship among 1 Peter, 2 Peter, and Jude." In *Reading 1–2 Peter and Jude: A Resource for Students*, edited by Eric F. Mason and Troy W. Martin, 27–45. Atlanta: Society of Biblical Literature, 2014.

Irenaeus of Lyons. "Against Heresies." In *Ante-Nicene Fathers, Vol. I: The Apostolic Fathers with Justin Martyr and Irenaeus*. Edited by Alexander Roberts and James Donaldson. Peabody, MA: Hendricksen, 1994.

Jackson-McCabe, Matt. "The Messiah Jesus in the Mythic World of James." *JBL* 122 (2003) 701–30.

Jaubert, Annie. "The Calendar of Qumran and the Passion Narrative in John." In *John and the Dead Sea Scrolls*, edited by James H. Charlesworth, 62–75. New York: Crossroad, 1991.

Jensen, Matthew D. *Affirming the Resurrection of the Incarnate Christ: A Reading of 1 John*. Cambridge: Cambridge University Press, 2012.

Johnson, Benton. "Church and Sect Revisited." *JSSR* 10 (1971) 124–37.

———. "On Church and Sect." *American Sociological Review* 28 (1963) 539–49.

Johnson, Luke Timothy. "James 3:12–4.10 and the Topos περὶ φθὸνου." *NovT* 25 (1983) 327–47.

———. *The Letter of James*. New York: Doubleday, 1995.

Josephus, Flavius. *The Antiquities of the Jews*. Translated by William Whiston. Start (online), 2013.

———. *The Jewish War*. Edited by Gaalya Cornfeld. Grand Rapids: Zondervan, 1982.

# References

Joubert, Stephan J. "Facing the Past: Transtextual Relationships and Historical Understanding in the Letter of Jude." *Biblische Zeitschrift* 42 (1998) 56–70.

———. "Language, Ideology and the Social Context of the Letter of Jude." *Neotestamentlica* 24 (1990) 335–49.

Justin Martyr. "Dialogue with Trypho." In *Ante-Nicene Fathers, Vol: I. The Apostolic Fathers with Justin Martyr and Irenaeus*. Edited by Alexander Roberts and James Donaldson. Peabody, MA: Hendricksen, 1994.

Keener, Craig S. *The Gospel of John: A Commentary, Vol. I*. Peabody, MA: Hendricksen, 2003.

Kiley, Mark. "Like Sara: The Tale of Terror behind 1 Peter 3:6." *JBL* 106 (1987) 689–92.

Kilpatrick, G.D. "1 Peter 1:11 TINA 'H POION KAIRON." *NovT* 28 (1986) 91–92.

Kim, Hong Bom. "The Interpretation of μάλιστα in 1 Timothy 5:17." *NovT* 46 (2004) 360–68.

Kim, Sharon. "Replanting Sacred Spaces: The Emergence of Second-generation Korean-American Churches." In *Religion and Spirituality in Korean America*, edited by David K. Yoo and Ruth H. Chung, 151–70. Urbana: University of Illinois Press, 2008.

Kloppenborg, John S. "James 1:2–15 and Hellenistic Psychagogy." *NovT* 52 (2010) 37–71.

Kmec, Vladimir. "Religion as a Response to the Crisis of Modernity: Perspectives of Immigrants in Ireland." In *Religion in Times of Crisis*, edited by Gladys Ganiel, et al., 33–53. Leiden: Brill, 2014.

Kooten, George H. van. "The Year of the Four Emperors and the Revelation of John: The 'Pro-Neronian' Emperors Otho and Vitellius, and the Image and Colossus of Nero in Rome." *JSNT* 30 (2007) 205–48.

Kraftchick, Steven J. *Jude, 2 Peter*. Nashville: Abingdon, 2002.

Kraus, Thomas J. "Παρὰ κυρίου, παρὰ κυρίῳ oder *omit* in 2 Peter 2,11. Textkritik und Interpretation vor dem Hintergrund juristischer Diktion und der Verwendung von παρά." *ZNW* 91 (2000) 265–73.

Lagrange, M.J. "Évangile selon Saint Jean." 5th ed. Paris: Gabalda, 1936.

Laughlin, John C.H. *Fifty Major Cities of the Bible*. London: Routledge, 2006.

Lindars, Barnabas. "Traditions Behind the Fourth Gospel." In *L'Évangile de Jean. Sources, Rédaction, Théologie*, edited by M. de Jonge, 107–24. Leuven: Leuven University Press/Uitgeverij Peeters Leuven, 1987.

Lukács, Georg. *History and Class Consciousness: Studies in Marxist Dialectics*. Cambridge, MA: MIT Press, 1971.

Makujima, John. "The 'Trouble' with Lot in 2 Peter: Locating Peter's Source for Lot's Torment." *Westminster Theological Journal* 60 (1998) 255–69.

Malherbe, Abraham J. "'In Season and out of Season': 2 Timothy 4:2." *JBL* 193 (1984) 235–43.

———. "The Inhospitality of Diotrephes." In *God's Christ and His People: Studies in Honour of Nils Alstrup Dahl*, edited by Jacob Jervell and Wayne A. Meeks, 222–32. Oslo: Universitetsforlaget, 1977.

Maloney, Francis J. *The Gospel of John*. Collegeville. MN: Liturgical (Michael Glazier), 1998.

Mann, William E. "The Canadian Church Union, 1929." In *Institutionalism and Church Unity*, edited by Nils Ehrenstrum and Walter Muelder, 171–93. New York: Association, 1963.

Mannheim, Karl. "Conservative Thought." In *From Karl Mannheim*, edited by Kurt H. Wolff, 132–222. New York: Oxford University Press, 1971.

Manns, Fréderic. *John and Jamnia: How the Break Occurred Between Jews and Christians c.80–100 A.D.* Translated by Mildred Duel and Marina Riadi. Jerusalem: Franciscan, 1988.

Manson, T.W. "The Periscope *De Aldultera* (Joh 753–811)." *ZNW* 44 (1952–53) 255–56.

Marcus, Joel. "Rivers of Living Water from Jesus' Belly (John 7:38)." *JBL* 117 (1998) 328–30.

Martin, Troy. "Emotional Physiology and Consolatory Etiquette: Reading the Present Indicative with Future Reference in the Eschatological Statement in 1 Peter 1:6." *JBL* 135 (2016) 649–60.

———. "The Present Indicative in the Eschatological Statements of 1 Peter 1:6–8." *JBL* 111 (1992) 307–12.

Massey, Douglas S., and Monica Espinoza Higgins. "The Effect of Immigration on Religious Belief and Practice: A Theologizing or Alienating Experience?" *Social Science Research* 40 (2010) 1371–89.

Mayer, John W., and Brian Rowan. "Institutional Organizations: Formal Structure as Myth and Ceremony." *AJS* 83 (1977) 340–63.

McGinn, Sheila E. *The Jesus Movement and the World of the Early Church*. Winona, MN: Anselm Academic, 2014.

McGinn, Sheila E., and Megan T. Wilson-Reitz. "Welfare Wastrels or Swanky Socialites: 2 Thess 3:6–15 and the Problem of the *Ataktoi*: A Pauline Critique of 'White-collar Welfare.'" In *By Bread Alone: Approaching the Bible Through a Hermeneutic of Hunger*, edited by Sheila E. McGinn, et al., 185–208. Minneapolis: Fortress, 2014.

McGuire, Meredith B. *Pentecostal Catholics. Power, Charisma, and Order in a Religious Movement*. Philadelphia: Temple University Press, 1982.

McGuire, Meredith B., with the assistance of Debra Kantor. *Ritual Healing in Suburban America*. New Brunswick, NJ: Rutgers University Press, 1988.

McNeil, Brian. "The Quotation at John xii 34." *NovT* 19 (1977) 22–33.

Meier, Sam. "2 Peter 3:3–7: An Early Jewish and Christian Response to Eschatological Skepticism." *Biblische Zeitschrift* 32 (1988) 255–57.

Menken, Maarten J.J. "The Origin of the Old Testament Quotation in John 7:38." *NovT* 38 (1996) 160–75.

Merton, Robert K. *Social Theory and Social Structure* (Enlarged Edition). New York: Free Press, 1968.

Metzger, Bruce M. *A Textual Commentary on the Greek New Testament*. London, New York: United Bible Societies, 1971, 1975.

Miller, Robert J. "Is There Independent Attestation for the Transfiguration in 2 Peter?" *NTS* 42 (1996) 620–25.

Min, Pyong Gap. "The Structure and Social Functions of Korean Immigrant Churches in the United States." *International Migration Review* 26 (1992) 1370–94.

Minear, Paul S. "Far as the Curse is Found: The Point of Revelation 12:15–16." *NovT* 33 (1991) 71–77.

———. "Writing on the Ground: The Puzzle in John 8:1–11." *Horizons in Biblical Theology* 13 (1991) 23–37.

Mitchell, Margaret M. "'Diotrephes Does Not Receive Us': The Lexicographical and Social Context of 3 John 9–10." *JBL* 117 (1998) 303–20.

Moore, Robert K. "Commemorating 500 Years of the Greek New Testament in Print: Erasmus and his Legacy." *Expository Times* 127 (2016) 488–93.

Morris, Leon. *The Gospel according to John, Revised Ed*. Grand Rapids: Eerdmans, 1995.

Neyrey, Jerome H. "The Apocalyptic Use of the Transfiguration in 2 Peter 1:16–21." *CBQ* 42 (1980) 504–19.

———. "The Form and Background of the Polemic in 2 Peter." *JBL* 99 (1980) 407–31.

———. "'I Said: You Are Gods': Psalm 82:6 and John 10." *JBL* 108 (1989) 647–63.

# References

Nicholson, Godfrey C. *Death as Departure: The Johannine Descent-Ascent Scheme*. Chico, CA: Scholars, 1983.

Niebuhr, H. Richard. *The Social Sources of Denominationalism*. New York: Holt, Rinehart & Winston, 1929.

Nongbri, Brent. "Reconsidering the Place of Papyrus Bodmer XIV–XV (P75) in the Textual Criticism of the New Testament." *JBL* 135 (2016) 405–37.

———. "The Use and Abuse of P52: Papyrological Pitfalls in the Dating of the Fourth Gospel." *HTR* 98 (2005) 23–48.

*Novum Testamentum Graece*. Edited by Kurt Aland et al. Stuttgart: Deutsche Bibelstiftung, 1979.

O'Connell, Jake H. "A Note on Papias's Knowledge of the Fourth Gospel." *JBL* 129 (2010) 793–94.

O'Day, Gail R. "John 7:53—8:11: A Study in Misreading." *JBL* 111 (1992) 631–40.

O'Dea, Thomas F. "Five Dilemmas in the Institutionalization of Religion." *JSSR* 1 (1961) 30–39.

O'Neill, J.C. "Son of Man, Stone of Blood (John 1:51)." *NovT* 45 (2003) 374–81.

Odgers, Olga. "Construcción del espacio y religion en la experiencia de la movilidad: Los santos patronos como vinculos espaciales en la migración México/Estados Unidos." *Migraciones Internacionales* 4 (2005) 5–26.

Olssen, Birger. "The History of the Johannine Movement." In *Aspects on the Johannine Literature*, edited by Lars Hartman and Birger Olsson, 27–43. Uppsala: Almquist & Wiksell International, 1987.

Painter, John. *1, 2, and 3 John*. Collegeville, Minnesota: Liturgical (Michael Glazier), 2002.

Palmer, Francis L. "Second Peter 1:5–7: A Study in Translation." *The Biblical World* 35 (1910) 93–96.

Park, Jerry Z., and Elaine Howard Ecklund. "Negotiating Continuity: Family and Religious Socialization for Second Generation Asian Americans." *Sociological Quarterly* 38 (2007) 93–118.

Parsons, Talcott. *The Social System*. New York: Free, 1951.

Perkins, Pheme. "Koinonia in 1 John 1:3–7: The Social Context of Division in the Johannine Letters." *CBQ* 45 (1983) 631–41.

Philo of Alexandria. "On the Life of Moses." In *The Works of Philo, Complete and Unabridged*. Edited and translated by C.D. Yonge. Peabody, MA: Hendrickson, 1993.

———. *Questions and Answers on Exodus* (Supplement II). Translated by Ralph Marcus. Cambridge, MA: Harvard University Press, 1953.

Pierce, Madison N., and Benjamin E. Reynolds. "The Perfect Tense-form and the Son of Man in John 3.13: Developments in Greek Grammar as a Viable Solution to the Timing of the Ascent and Descent." *NTS* 60 (2014) 149–55.

Pietersen, Lloyd. "Despicable Deviants: Labelling Theory and the Polemics of the Pastorals." *Sociology of Religion* 58 (1997) 343–52.

Pobee, John. "Aspects of African Traditional Religion." *Sociological Analysis* 37 (1976) 1–18.

Porter, Stanley E., and Andrew W. Pitts. "τοῦτο πρῶτον γινώσκοντες ὅτι in 2 Peter 1:20 and Hellenistic Epistolary Convention." *JBL* 127 (2008) 165–71.

Rainbow, Jesse. "Male μαστοί in Revelation 1.13." *JSNT* 30 (2007) 249–53.

Ramelli, Ilaria L.E. "'Simon Son of John, Do You Love Me?' Some Reflections on John 21:15." *NovT* 50 (2008) 332–50.

Reader, William W. "The Twelve Jewels of Revelation 21:19–20: Tradition History and Modern Interpretations." *JBL* 100 (1981) 433–57.

## References

Reicke, Bo. *The Epistles of James, Peter, and Jude: Introduction, Translation, and Notes.* Garden City, NY: Doubleday, 1964.

Richard, Earl J. *First and Second Thessalonians.* Collegeville, MN: Liturgical (Michael Glazier), 1995.

Richards, E. Randolph. "Silvanus Was Not Peter's Secretary: Theological Bias in Interpreting διὰ Σιλουανοῦ . . . ἔγραψα in 1 Peter 5:12." *Journal of the Evangelical Theological Society* 43 (2000) 417–32.

Robinson, John A.T. "The 'Other' of John 4.38." In *Twelve New Testament Studies*, John A.T. Robinson, 61–66. London: SCM, 1962.

Root, Bradley W. *First Century Galilee: A Fresh Examination of the Sources.* Tübingen: Mohr Siebeck, 2014.

Ross, Edward Alsworth. *Social Control: A Survey of the Foundations of Order.* New York: Macmillan, 1929.

Ruckstuhl, Eugen. "Johannine Language and Style. The Question of Their Unity." In *L'Évangile de Jean: Sources, Rédaction, Théologie*, edited by M. de Jonge., 125–47. Leuven: Leuven University Press/Uitgeverij Peeters Leuven, 1987.

Russell, Ronald. "The Idle in 2 Thess 3:6–12: An Eschatological or a Social Problem?" *NTS* 38 (1988) 105–19.

Scheler, Max. *Ressentiment.* Translated by William W. Holdheim. New York: Free Press of Glencoe, 1961.

Schmidt, Daryl D. "The Syntactical Style of 2 Thessalonians: How Pauline Is It?" In *The Thessalonian Correspondence*, edited by Raymond F. Collins, 385–93. Leuven: Leuven University Press, 1990.

Schmitt, John J. "You Adulteresses! The Image in James 4.4." *NovT* 28 (1986) 327–37.

Schutz, Alfred. "Edmund Husserl's Ideas Volume II." In *Alfred Schutz, Collected Papers III: Studies in Pheomenological Philosophy*, edited by I. Schutz, 15–39. The Hague: Martinus Nijhoff, 1975.

Schutz, Alfred, and Thomas Luckmann. *The Structures of the Life-World.* Translated by Richard M. Zaner and H. Tristram Englehardt Jr. Evanston, IL: Northwestern University Press, 1973.

Sellin, Gerhard. "Die Häeretiker des Judasbrief." *ZNW* 77 (1986) 206–25.

Senior, Donald P. "1 Peter." In *1 Peter, Jude and 2 Peter*, Donald P. Senior and Daniel Harrington, 3–158. Collegeville, MN: Liturgical (Michael Glazier), 2003.

———. *1 & 2 Peter.* Wilmington, DE: Michael Glazier, 1980.

*Septuaginta. Id est Vetus Testamentum graece iuxta LXX interpretes, 9th ed.* 2 vols. Edited by Alfred Rahlfs. Stuttgart: Deutsche Bibelstiftung, 1935.

Sharma, Ursula M. "The Immortal Cowherd and the Saintly Carrier: An Essay in the Study of Cults." *Sociological Bulletin* 19 (1970) 137–52.

Shils, Edward. *Tradition.* Chicago: University of Chicago Press, 1981.

Silcox, Claris Edwin. *Church Union in Canada: Its Causes and Consequences.* New York: Institute of Social and Religious Research, 1933.

Simmel, Georg. *Sociology: Inquiries into the Construction of Social Forms*, Vols 1 and 2. Translated and edited by Anthony J. Blasi, et al. Leiden: Brill, 2009.

Sly, Dorothy I. "1 Peter 3:66b in the Light of Philo and Josephus." *JBL* 110 (1991) 126–29.

Smith, D. Moody. *John among the Gospels: The Relationship in Twentieth-Century Research.* Minneapolis: Fortress, 1992.

# References

———. *Johannine Christianity: Essays on Its Setting, Sources, and Theology*. Columbia: University of South Carolina Press, 1984.

Soards, Marion L. "1 Peter, 2 Peter, and Jude as Evidence for a Petrine School." *Aufstieg und Niedergang der römischen Welt* II (1988) 3827–49.

Stark, Werner. *The Sociology of Religion: A Study of Christendom. Volumes One, Two, and Three*. New York: Fordham University Press, 1966–67.

Stegemann, Ekkehard W., and Wolfgang Stegemann. *The Jesus Movement: A Social History of Its First Century*. Translated by O.C. Dean Jr. Minneapolis: Fortress, 1999.

Strabo. *The Geography of Strabo*. Translated by Horace Leonard Jones. Cambridge, MA: Harvard University Press, 20th century dates vary by volume.

Swatos, William H. Jr. "Monopolism, Pluralism, Acceptance, and Rejection: An Integrated Model for Church-sect Theory." *Review of Religious Research* 16 (1975) 174–85.

Talbert, Charles H. "II Peter and the Delay of the Parousia." *VC* 20 (1966) 137–45.

Templeton, Mark N., and Nicholas Jay Demerath III. "The Presbyterian Re-formation: Pushes and Pulls in an American Mainline Schism." In *Sacred Companies: Organizational Aspects of Religion and Religious Aspects of Organizations*, edited by N.J. Demerath III, et al., 195–207. New York: Oxford University Press, 1998.

Tenney, Merrill C. "The Footnotes of John's Gospel." *Bibliotheca Sacra* 117 (1960) 350–64.

Thatcher, Tom. "Introduction." In *Jesus in Johannine Tradition*, edited by Robert T. Fortna and Tom Thatcher, 1–9. Louisville: Westminster John Knox, 2001.

Thurén, Lauri. "Risky Rhetoric in James?" *NovT* 37 (1995) 262–84.

Tuberville, Gus. "Religious Schism in the Methodist Church: A Sociological Analysis of the Pine Grove Case." *Rural Sociology* 14 (1949) 29–51.

Ulrichsen, Jarl Henning. "Die sieben Häupter und die zen Hörner: Zur Datierung der Offenbarung des Johannes." *Studia Theological/Scandinavian Journal of Theology* 39 (1985) 1–20.

Van Unnik, W.C. "The Quotation from the Old Testament in John 12:34." *NovT* 3 (1959) 174–79.

Vanni, U. "Il terzo 'sigillo' dell' Apocalisse (AP 6:5-6): Simbolo dell'ingiustizia sociale?" *Gregorianum* 59 (1978) 691–719.

Varga, Ivan. "La sécularisation de la jeunesse hongroise." *Archives de sociologie des religions* 12/23 (1967) 45–63.

Verseput, Donald J. "James 1:17 and the Jewish Morning Prayer." *NovT* 39 (1997) 177–91.

Von Wahlde, Urban C. *The Earliest Versions of John's Gospel: Recovering the Gospel of Signs*. Wilmington, DE: Michael Glazier, 1989.

Wallace, Daniel B. "John 5:2 and the Date of the Fourth Gospel." *Biblica* 71 (1990) 177–205.

Ward, Roy Bowen. "Partiality in the Assembly: James 2:2–4." *HTR* 62 (1969) 87–97.

Waters, Kenneth L. "Saved through Childbearing: Virtues as Children in 1 Timothy 2:11–15." *JBL* 123 (2004) 703–35.

Watson, Duane F. *Invention, Arrangement, and Style: Rhetorical Criticism of Jude and 2 Peter*. Atlanta: Scholars, 1988.

Weber, Max. *Economy and Society: An Outline of Interpretive Sociology* (2 vols). Translated and edited by Guenther Roth and Claus Wittich. Berkeley, CA: University of California Press, 1978.

———. "The Protestant Sects and the Spirit of Capitalism." In *From Max Weber: Essays in Sociology*. Translated and edited by Hans H. Gerth and C. Wright Mills, 302–22. New York: Oxford University Press, 1946.

## References

Weiss, Harold. "Foot Washing in the Johannine Community." *NovT* 21 (1979) 298–325.

Whitacre, Rodney A. *Johannine Polemic: The Role of Tradition and Theology*. Chico, CA: Scholars, 1982.

Wilkinson, Richard H. "The ΣΤΥΛΟΣ of Revelation 3:12 and Ancient Coronation Rites." *JBL* 107 (1988) 498–501.

Young, Pauline V. *The Pilgrims of Russian-town: The Community of Spiritual Christian Jumpers in America. The Struggle of a Primitive Religious Society to Maintain Itself in an Urban Environment*. Chicago: University of Chicago Press, 1932.

Zeman, Josefa Humpal. "The Bohemian People in Chicago." In *Hull-House Maps and Papers*, Residents of Hull-House, 115–28. New York: Thomas Y. Crowell, 1895.

Zeublin, Charles. "The Chicago Ghetto." In *Hull-House Maps and Papers*, Residents of Hull-House, 91–114. New York: Thomas Y. Crowell, 1895.

Zmijewski, Josef. "Apostolische *paradosis* und Pseudepigraphie im Neuen Testament. 'Durch Erinnerung wachhalten' (2 Petr 1,13; 3,1)." *Biblische Zeitschrift* 23 (1979) 161–71.

www.ingramcontent.com/pod-product-compliance
Lightning Source LLC
Chambersburg PA
CBHW080549230426
43663CB00015B/2762